Library Wars

Love & War

15

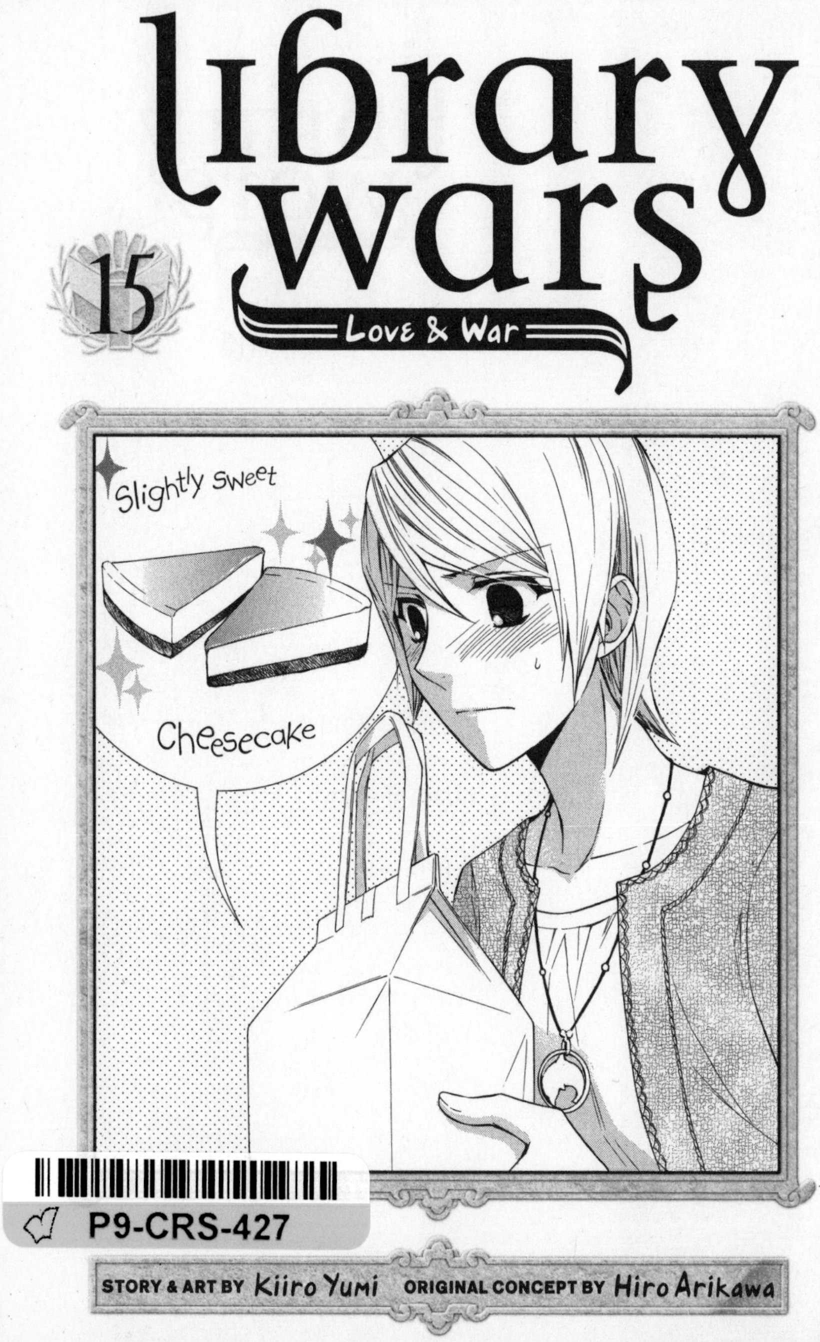
Slightly sweet
Cheesecake

STORY & ART BY Kiiro Yumi ORIGINAL CONCEPT BY Hiro Arikawa

Library Wars
Love & War

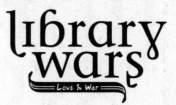

Contents

The Library Freedom Act

Libraries have the freedom to acquire their collections.

Libraries have the freedom to circulate
materials in their collections.

Libraries guarantee the privacy of their patrons.

Libraries oppose any type of censorship.

When libraries are imperiled,
librarians will join together
to secure their freedom.

library wars
Love & War

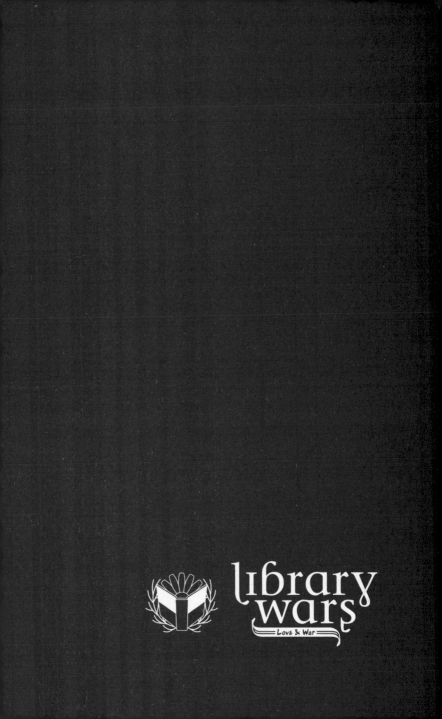

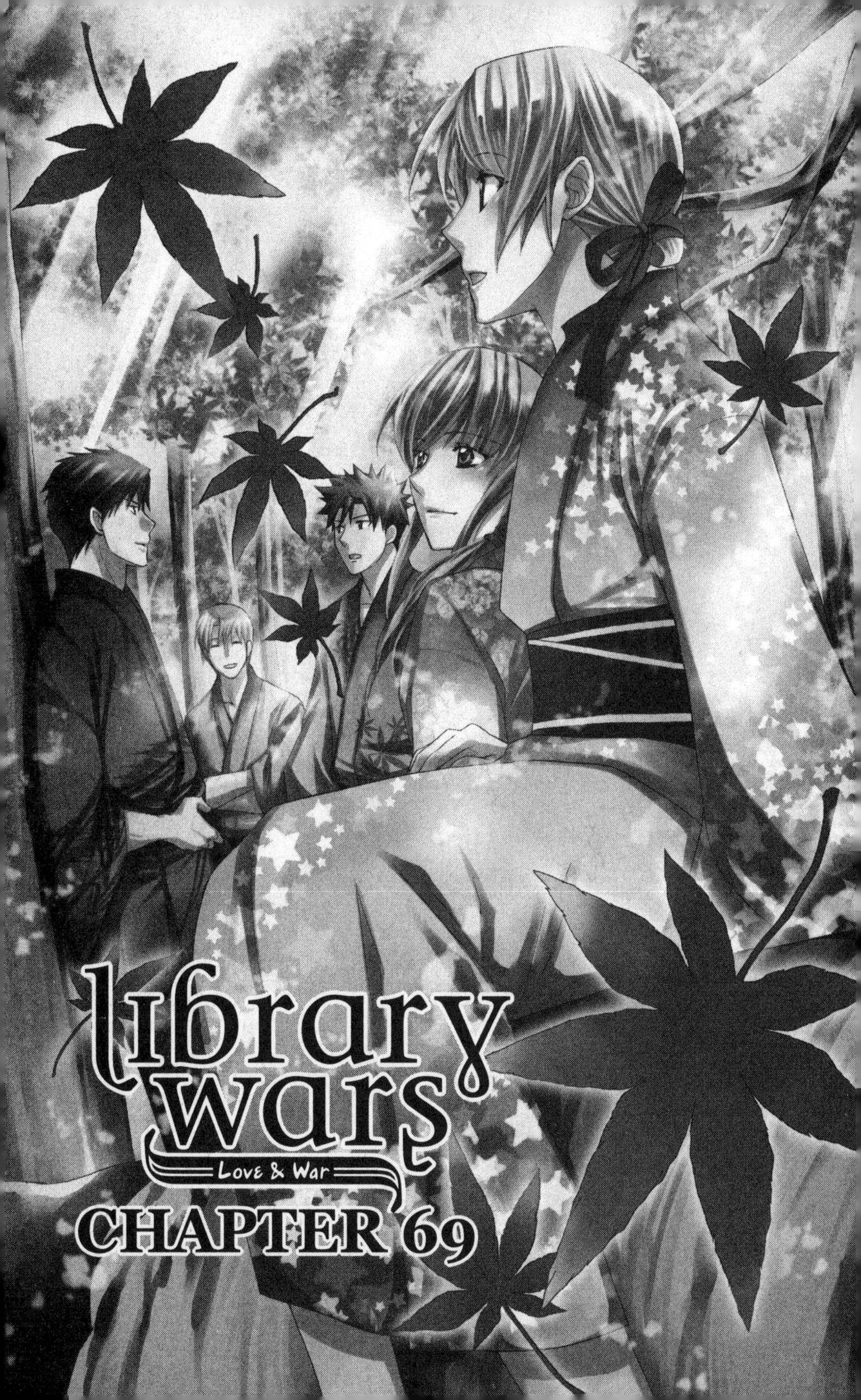
library wars
Love & War
CHAPTER 69

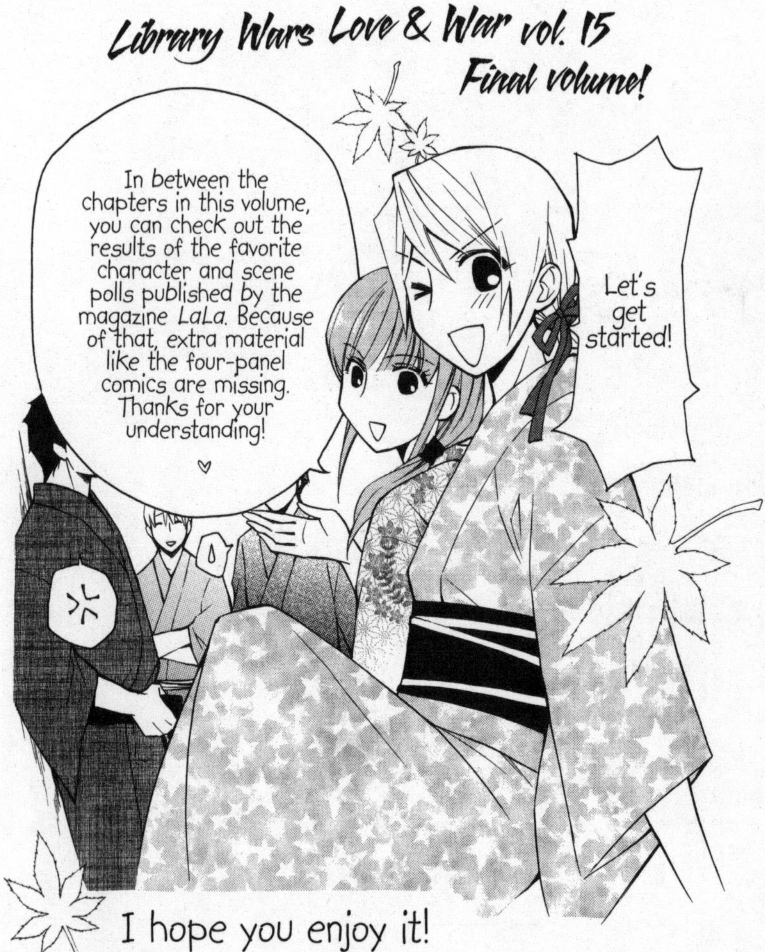
Library Wars Love & War vol. 15
Final volume!
Let's get started!
In between the chapters in this volume, you can check out the results of the favorite character and scene polls published by the magazine *LaLa*. Because of that, extra material like the four-panel comics are missing. Thanks for your understanding! ♡
I hope you enjoy it!

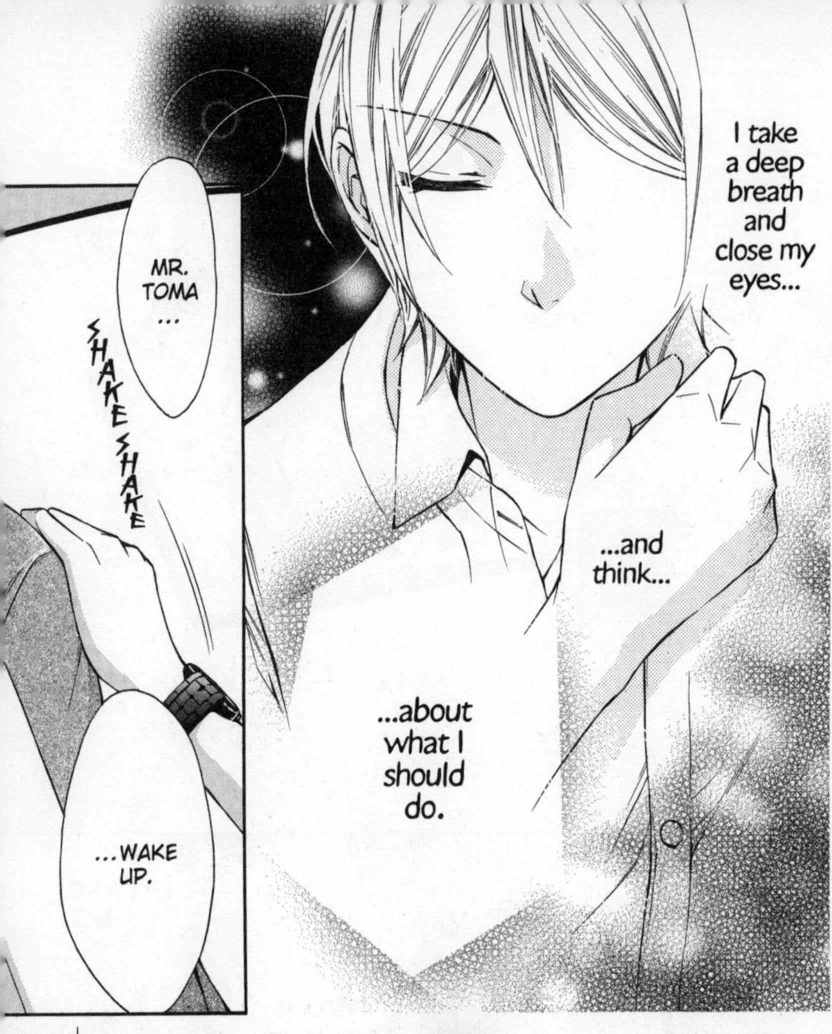
I take a deep breath and close my eyes...
...and think...
...about what I should do.
MR. TOMA...
SHAKE SHAKE
...WAKE UP.

CHAPTER 1

1. "The history of the battle"

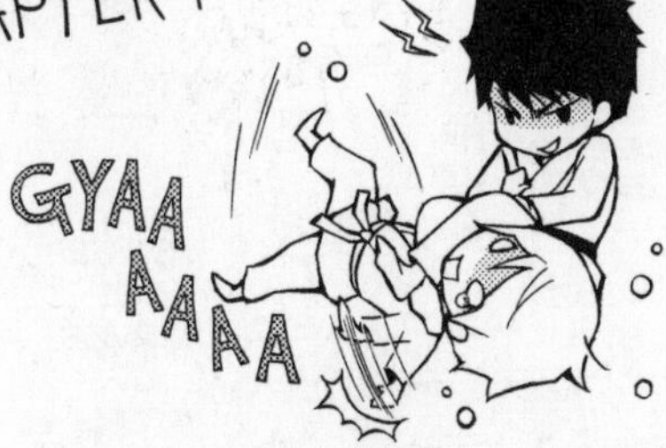
GYAAAAAAA

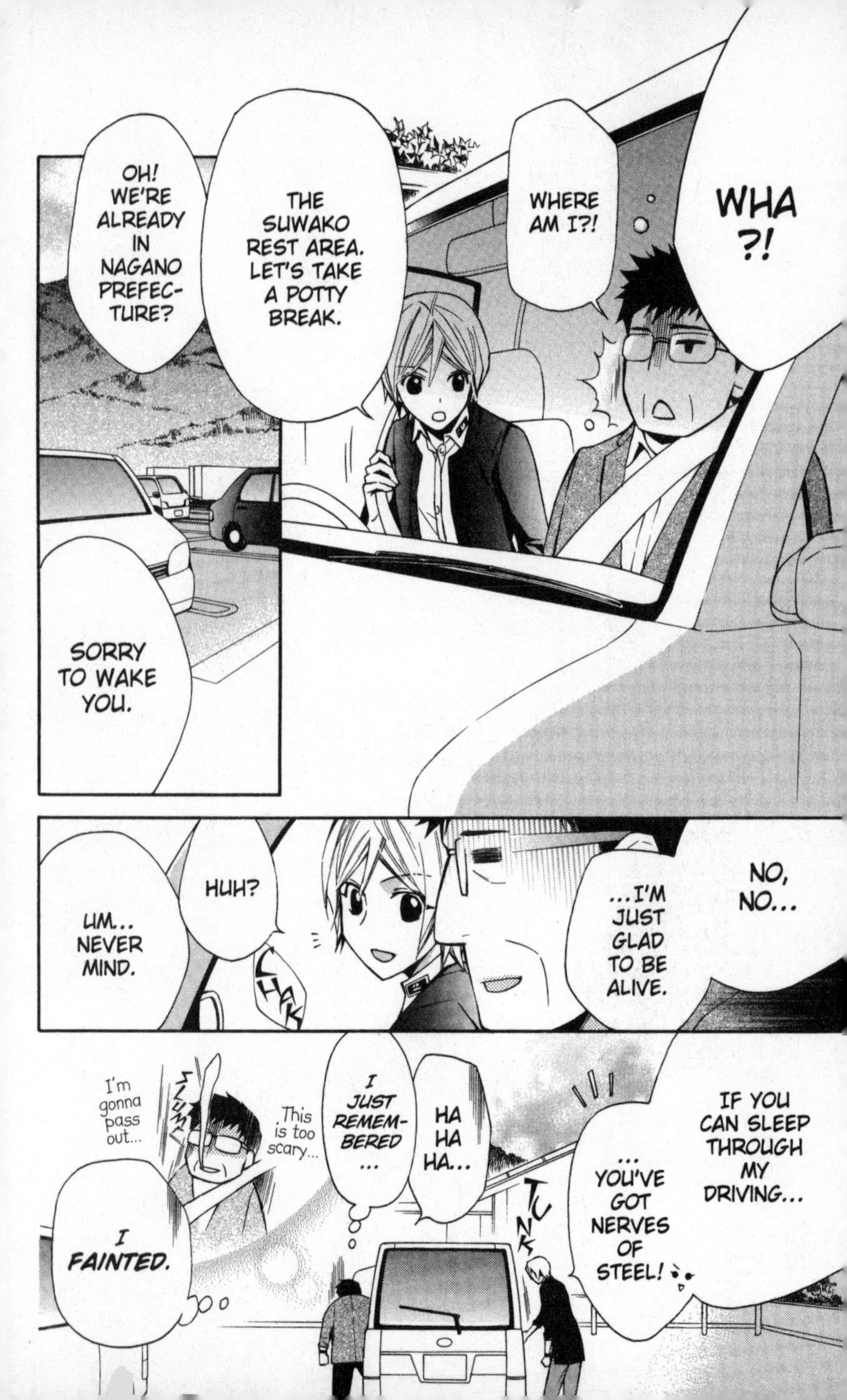
WHA ?!
WHERE AM I?!
THE SUWAKO REST AREA. LET'S TAKE A POTTY BREAK.
OH! WE'RE ALREADY IN NAGANO PREFEC-TURE?
SORRY TO WAKE YOU.
NO, NO...
...I'M JUST GLAD TO BE ALIVE.
HUH?
CHAK
UM... NEVER MIND.
IF YOU CAN SLEEP THROUGH MY DRIVING...
...YOU'VE GOT NERVES OF STEEL!
TUNK
HA HA HA...
I JUST REMEM-BERED...
This is too scary...
I'm gonna pass out...
SLUMP
I FAINTED.

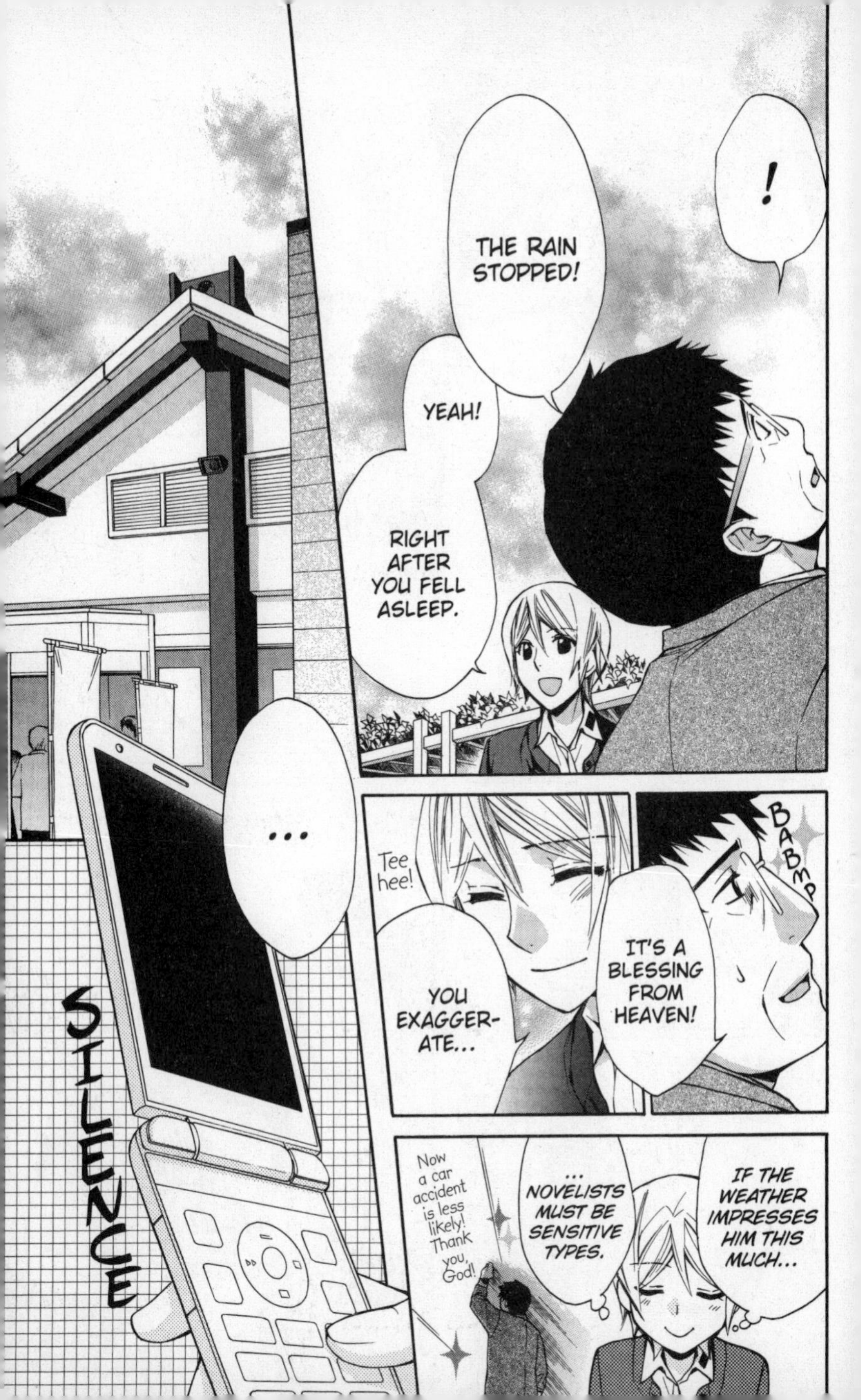
!
THE RAIN STOPPED!
YEAH!
RIGHT AFTER YOU FELL ASLEEP.
BABMP
IT'S A BLESSING FROM HEAVEN!
Tee hee!
YOU EXAGGERATE...
IF THE WEATHER IMPRESSES HIM THIS MUCH...
... NOVELISTS MUST BE SENSITIVE TYPES.
Now a car accident is less likely! Thank you, God!
...
SILENCE

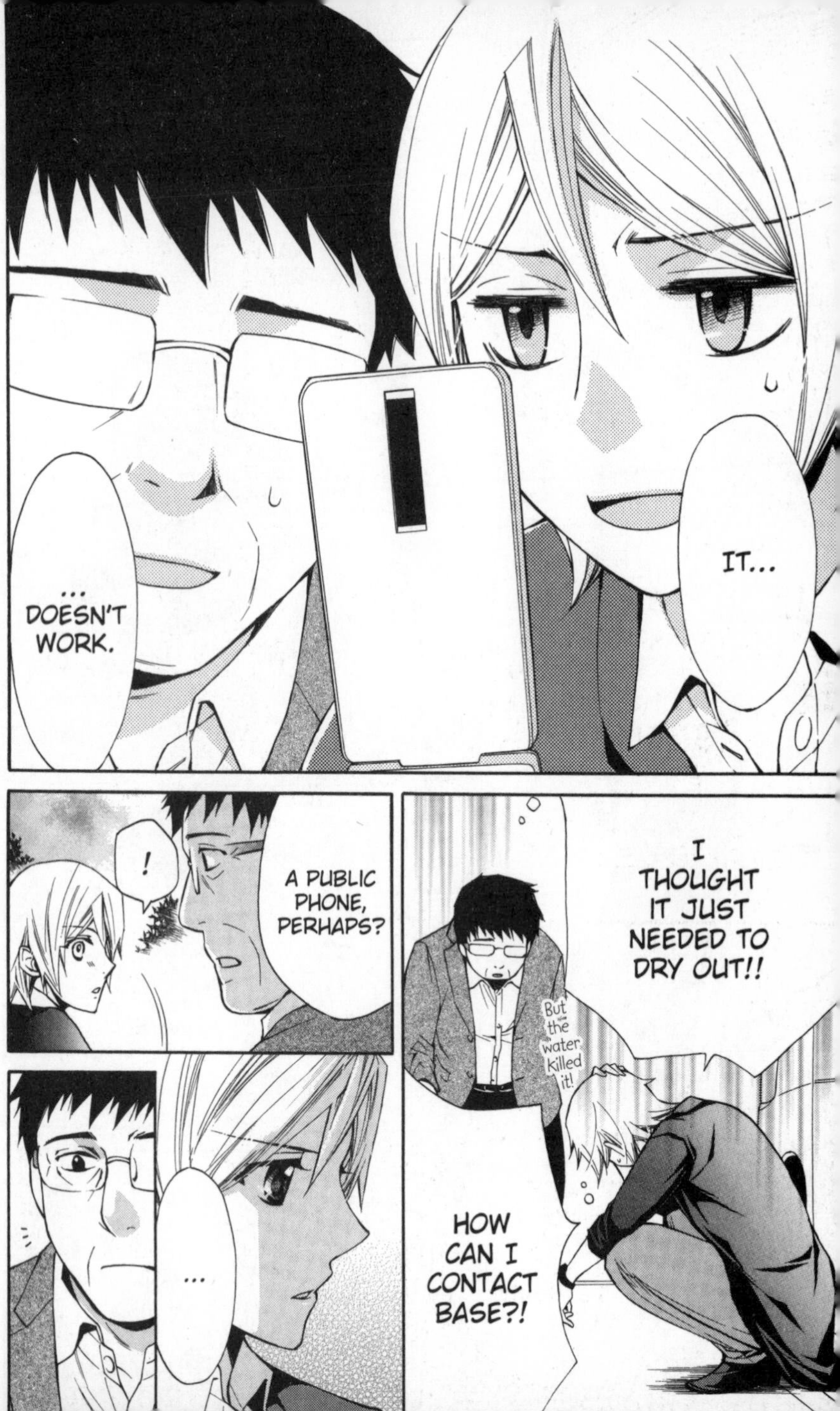
IT...
... DOESN'T WORK.
I THOUGHT IT JUST NEEDED TO DRY OUT!!
But the water killed it!
HOW CAN I CONTACT BASE?!
A PUBLIC PHONE, PERHAPS?
!
...

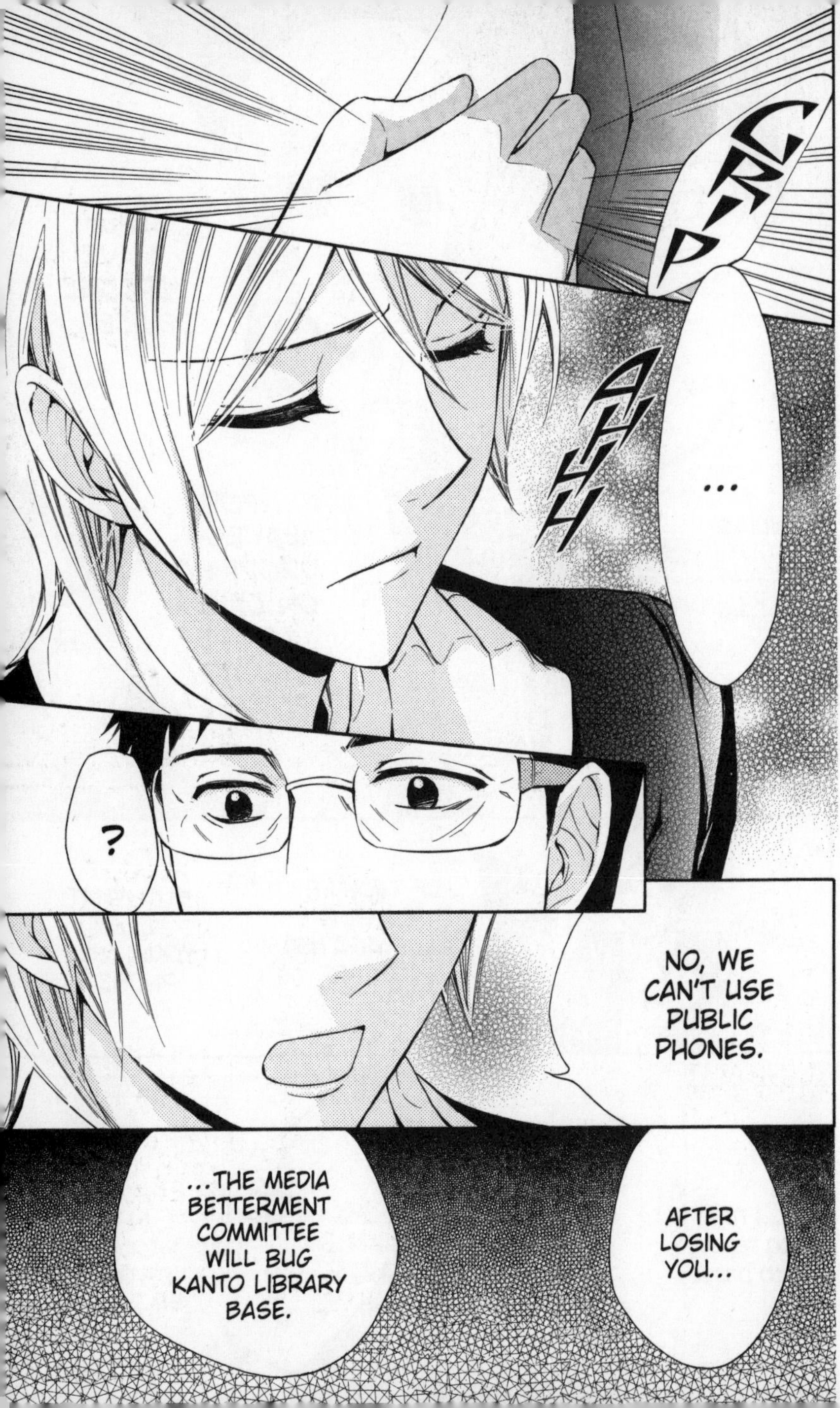
GRIP
...
AHH
?
NO, WE CAN'T USE PUBLIC PHONES.
AFTER LOSING YOU...
...THE MEDIA BETTERMENT COMMITTEE WILL BUG KANTO LIBRARY BASE.

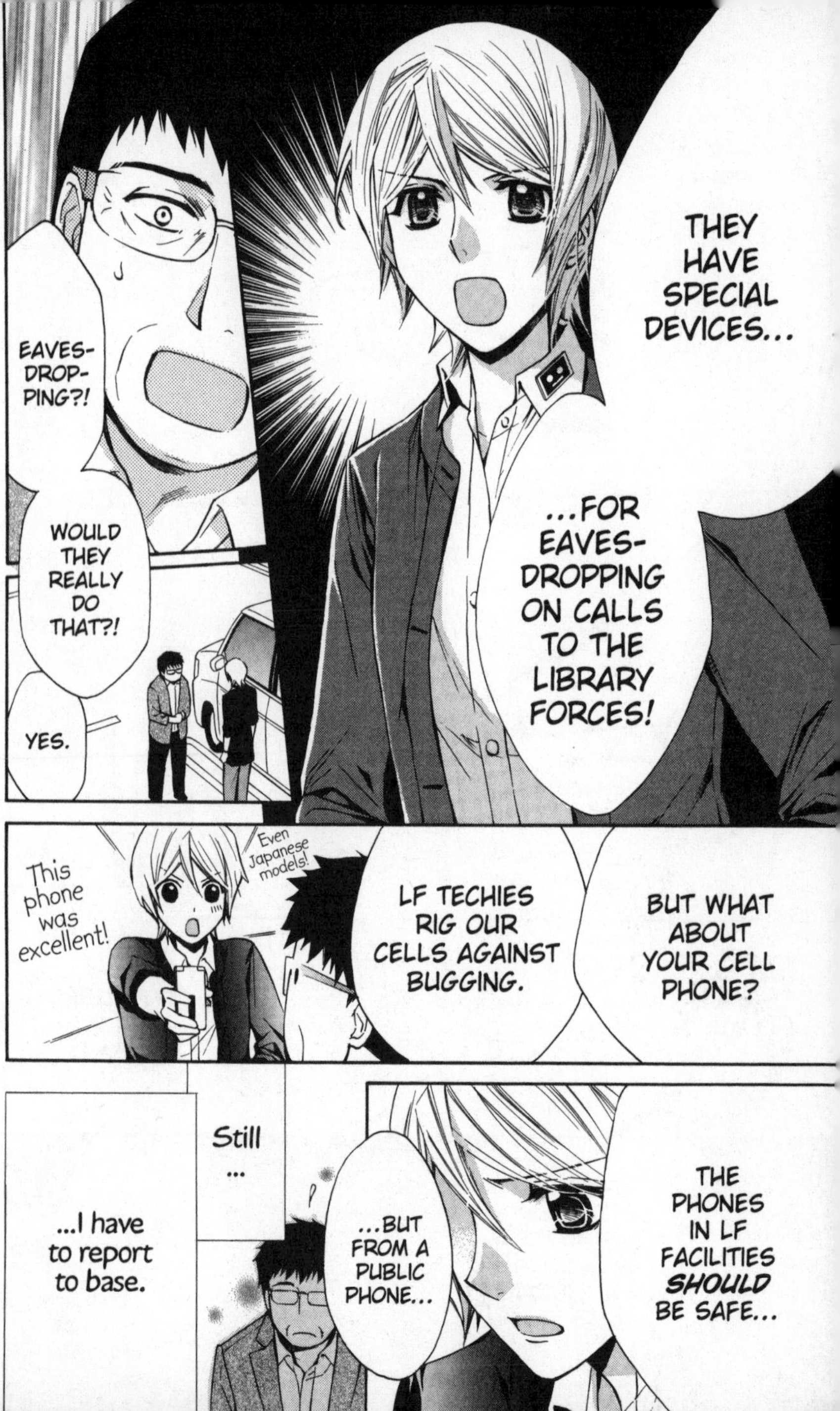
THEY HAVE SPECIAL DEVICES...
...FOR EAVES-DROPPING ON CALLS TO THE LIBRARY FORCES!
EAVES-DROP-PING?!
WOULD THEY REALLY DO THAT?!
YES.
BUT WHAT ABOUT YOUR CELL PHONE?
LF TECHIES RIG OUR CELLS AGAINST BUGGING.
Even Japanese models!
This phone was excellent!
THE PHONES IN LF FACILITIES *SHOULD* BE SAFE...
...BUT FROM A PUBLIC PHONE...
Still ...
...I have to report to base.

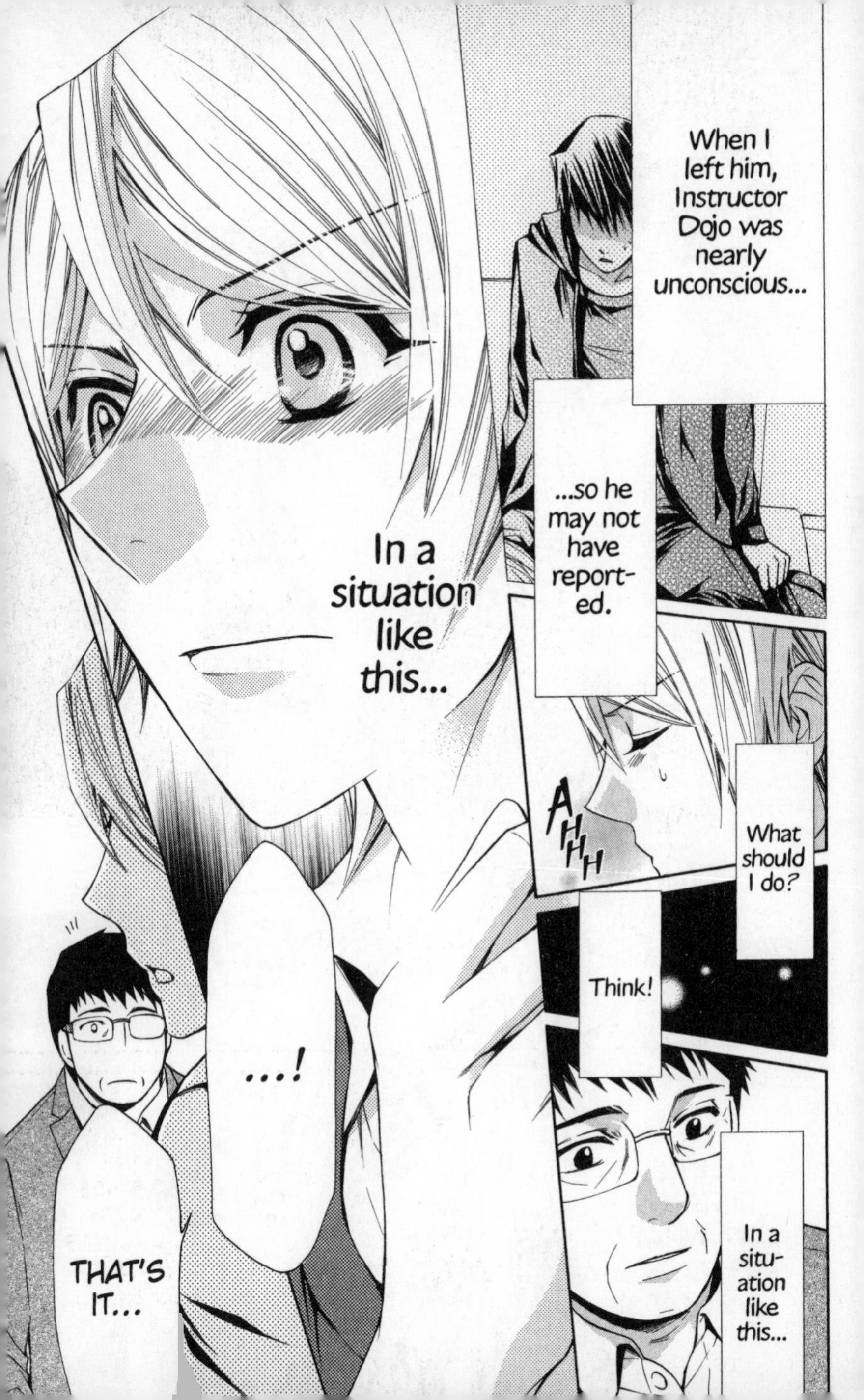
When I left him, Instructor Dojo was nearly unconscious...
...so he may not have reported.
AHHH
What should I do?
Think!
In a situation like this...
In a situation like this...
...!
THAT'S IT...

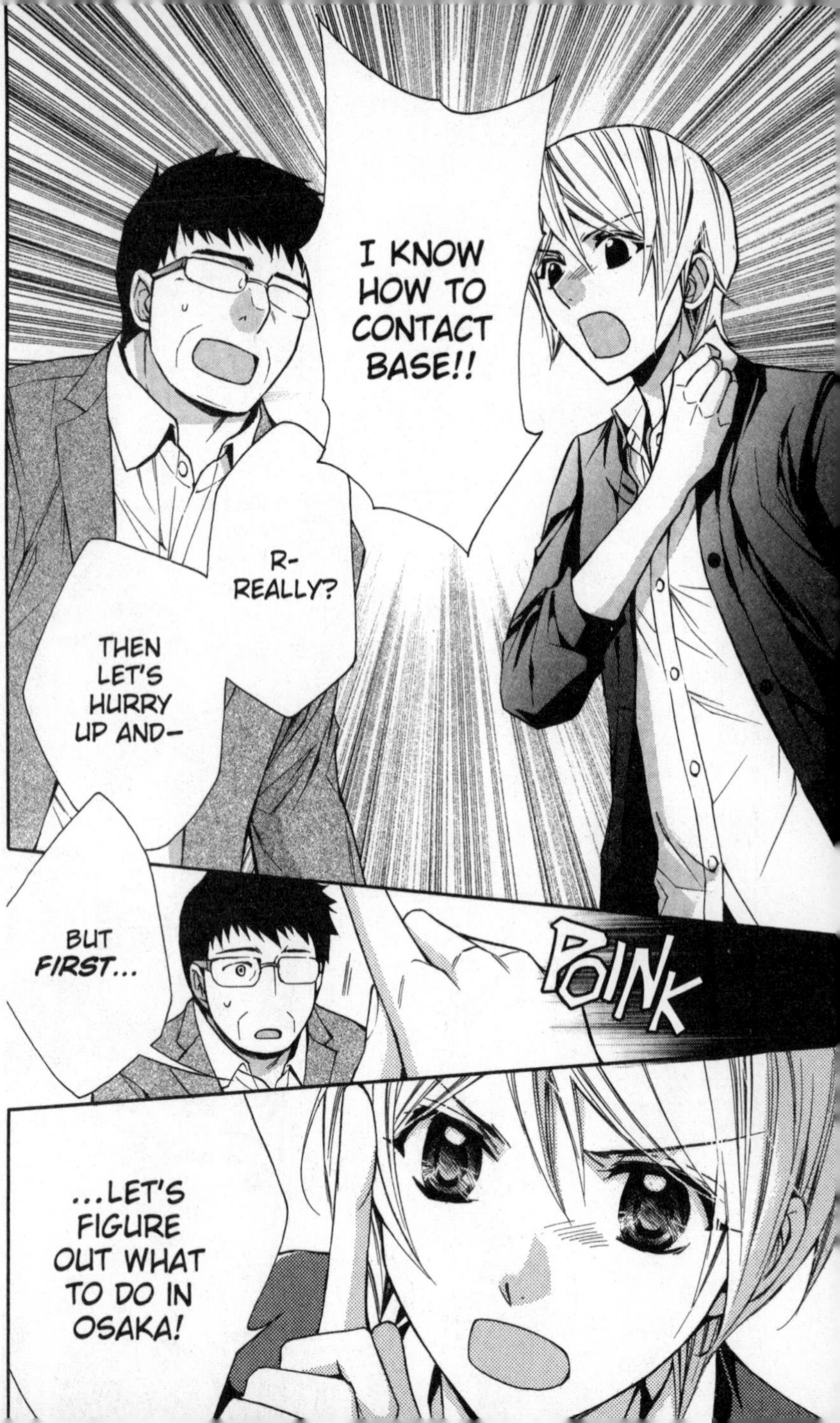
I KNOW HOW TO CONTACT BASE!!
R-REALLY?
THEN LET'S HURRY UP AND—
POINK
BUT *FIRST*...
...LET'S FIGURE OUT WHAT TO DO IN OSAKA!

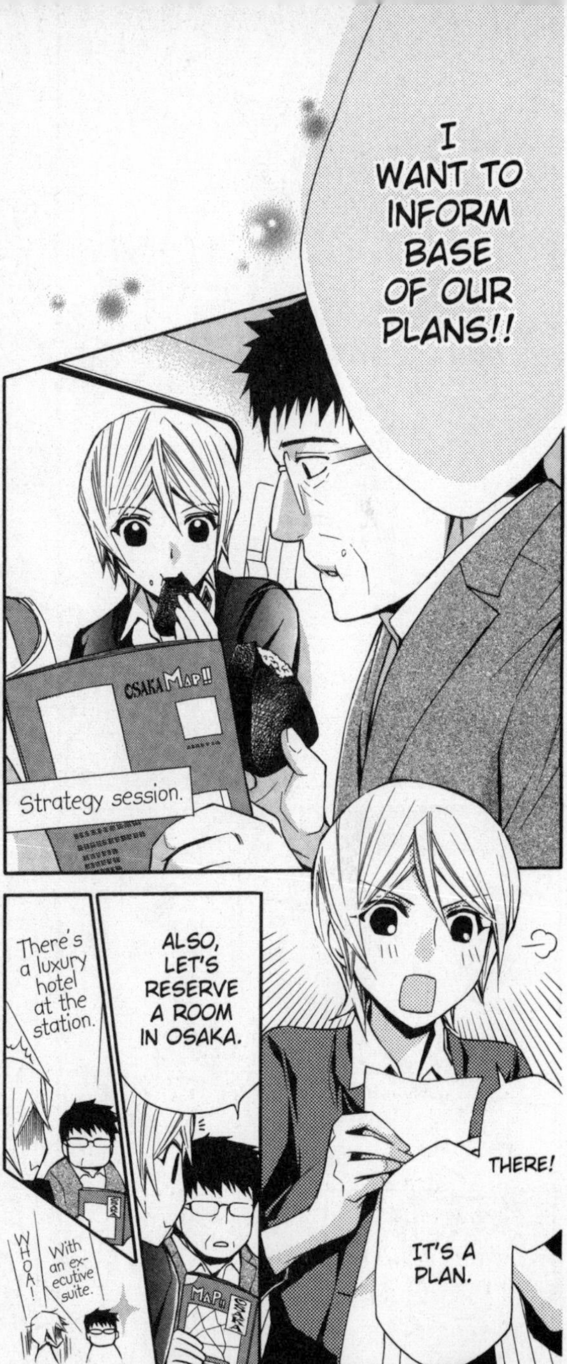
I WANT TO INFORM BASE OF OUR PLANS!!
OSAKA MAP!!
Strategy session.
THERE!
IT'S A PLAN.
ALSO, LET'S RESERVE A ROOM IN OSAKA.
There's a luxury hotel at the station.
With an executive suite.
WHOA!
MAP!!
OSAKA

1

*

Hi, I'm Kiiro Yumi and this is *Library Wars*, volume 15!

The original series of *Library Wars* novels consists of four novels telling the main story and two extra volumes for a total of six volumes. With this volume, I finished the volume of the main story, titled *Revolution*. In other words, this is the final volume of the main story. I'm so glad I made it this far!

I'm deeply thankful to everyone who was involved with this manga and to everyone who read it. Thank you! The manga may not be the most skillful, but I hope you enjoyed it.

*

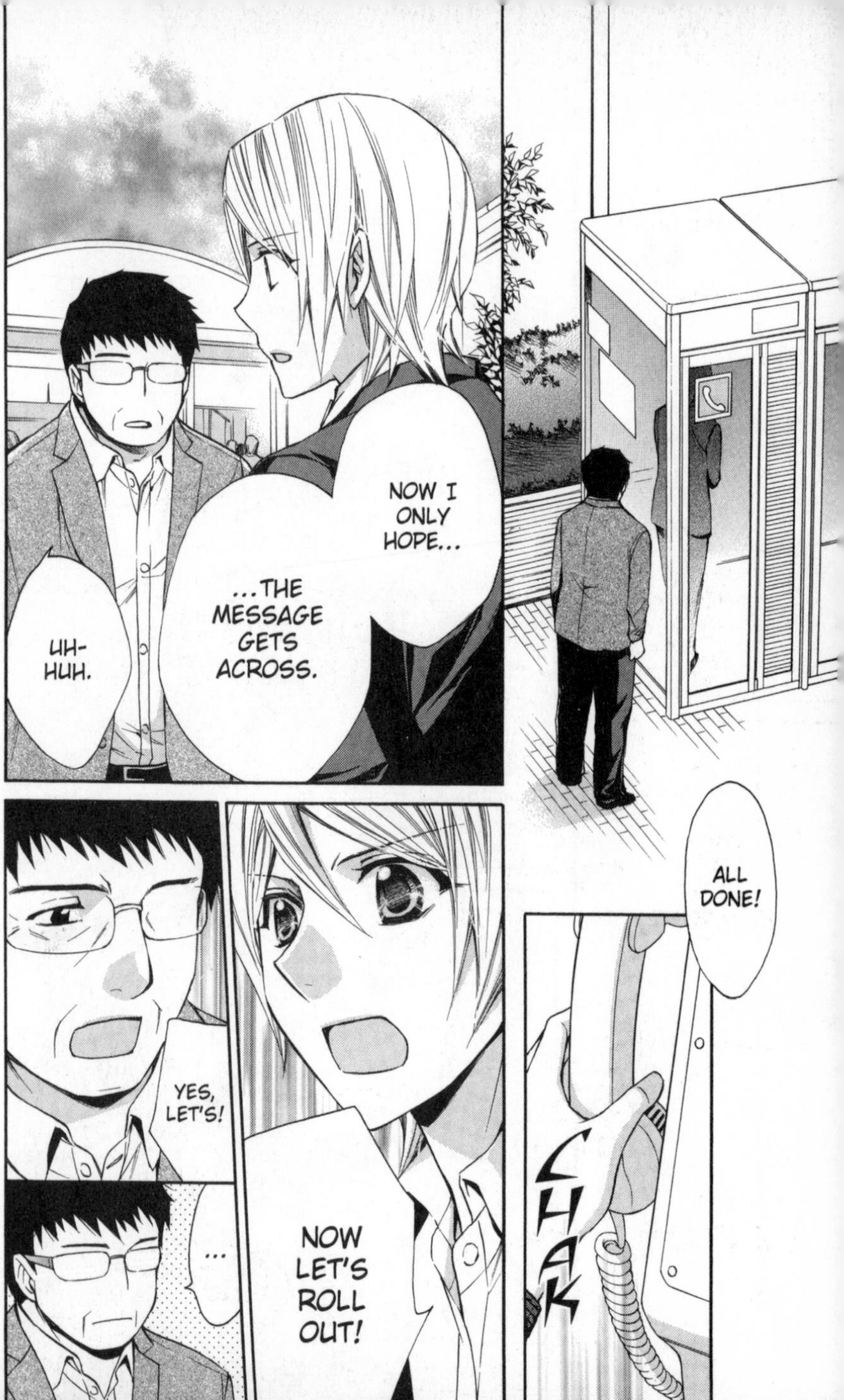
NOW I ONLY HOPE...
...THE MESSAGE GETS ACROSS.
UH-HUH.
ALL DONE!
CHAK
NOW LET'S ROLL OUT!
YES, LET'S!
...

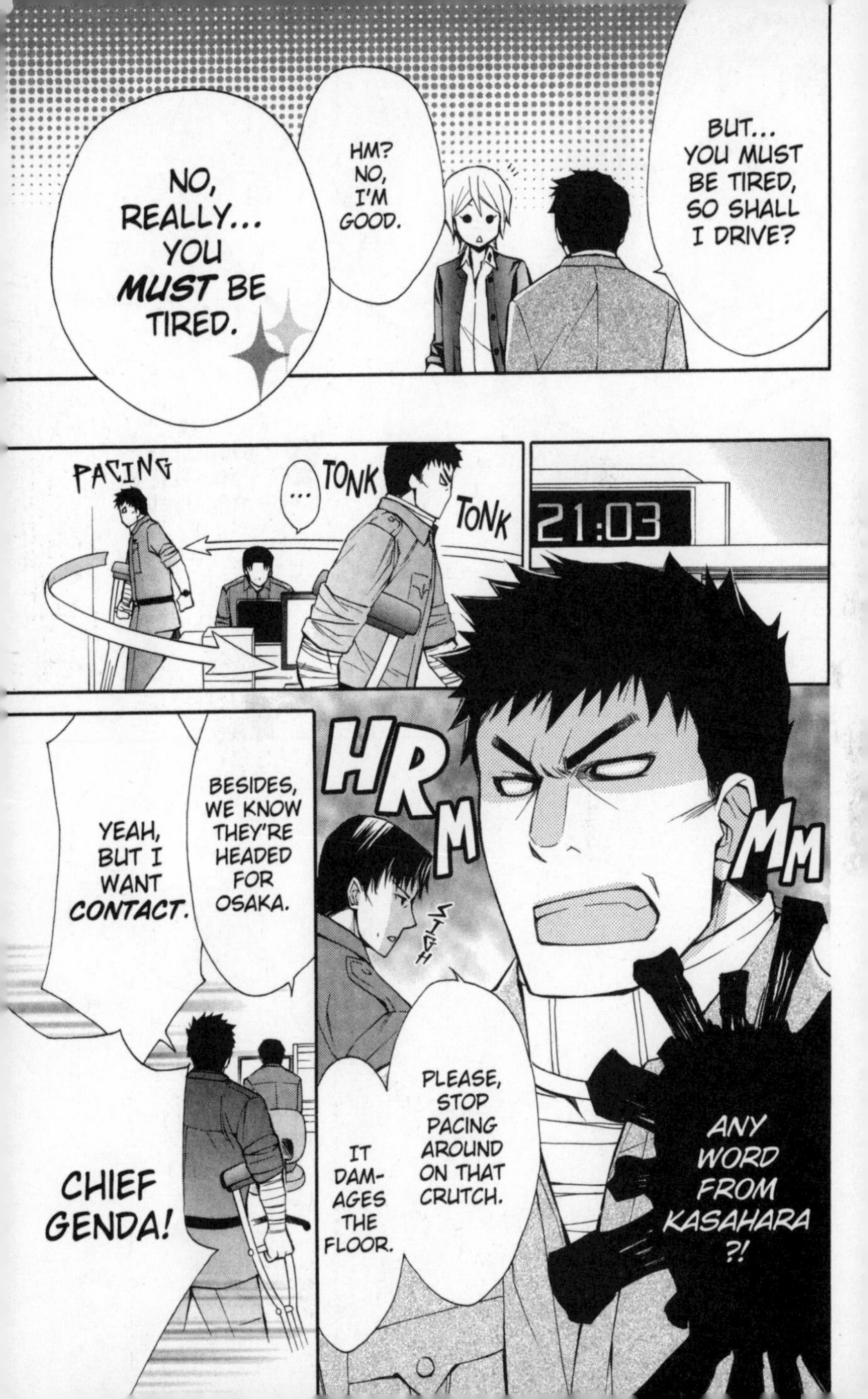
BUT... YOU MUST BE TIRED, SO SHALL I DRIVE?
HM? NO, I'M GOOD.
NO, REALLY... YOU *MUST* BE TIRED.
21:03
TONK
TONK
...
PACING
HRMMM
ANY WORD FROM KASAHARA?!
PLEASE, STOP PACING AROUND ON THAT CRUTCH.
SIGH
IT DAMAGES THE FLOOR.
BESIDES, WE KNOW THEY'RE HEADED FOR OSAKA.
YEAH, BUT I WANT **CONTACT**.
CHIEF GENDA!

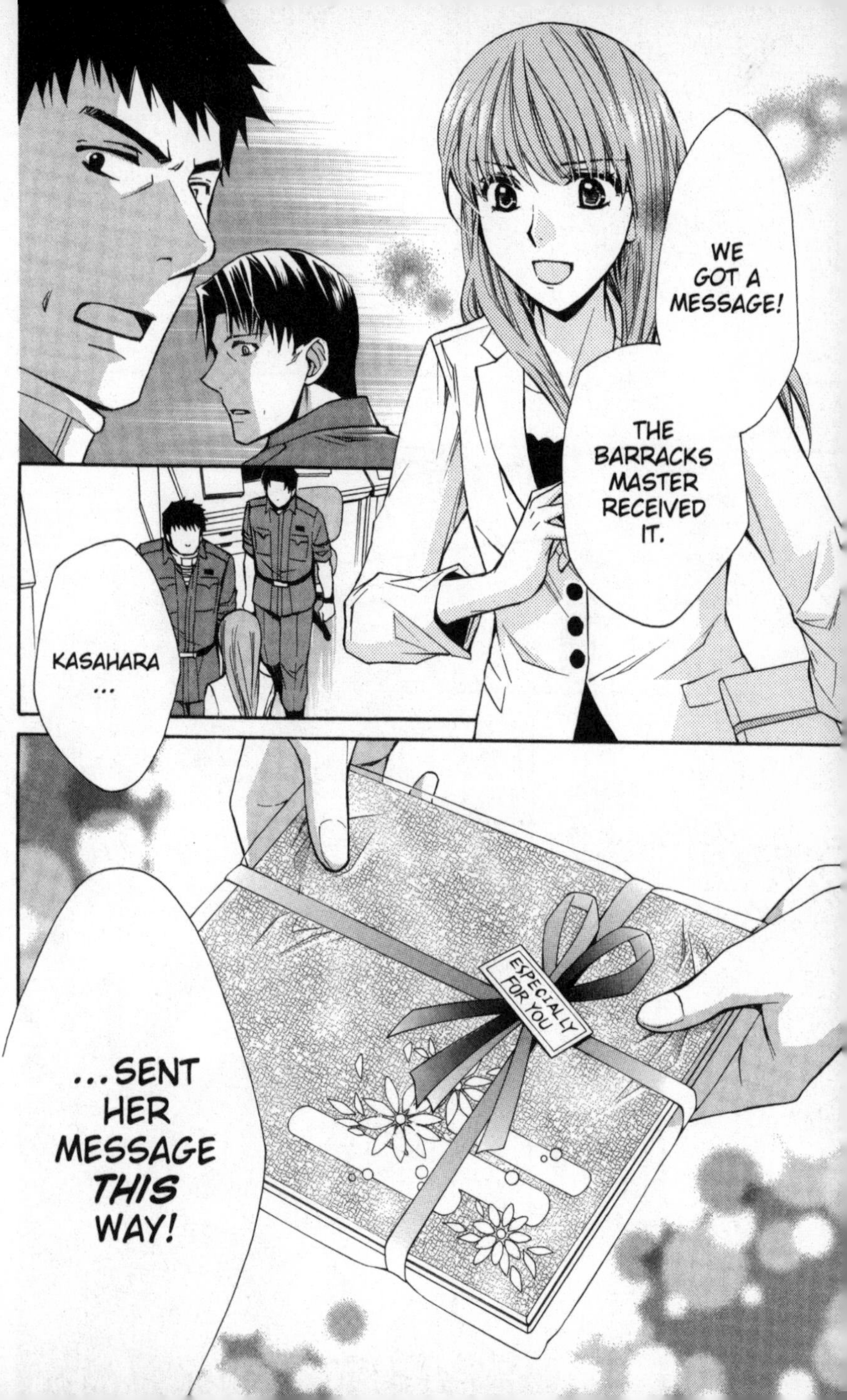
WE GOT A MESSAGE!
THE BARRACKS MASTER RECEIVED IT.
KASAHARA ...
...SENT HER MESSAGE *THIS* WAY!
ESPECIALLY FOR YOU

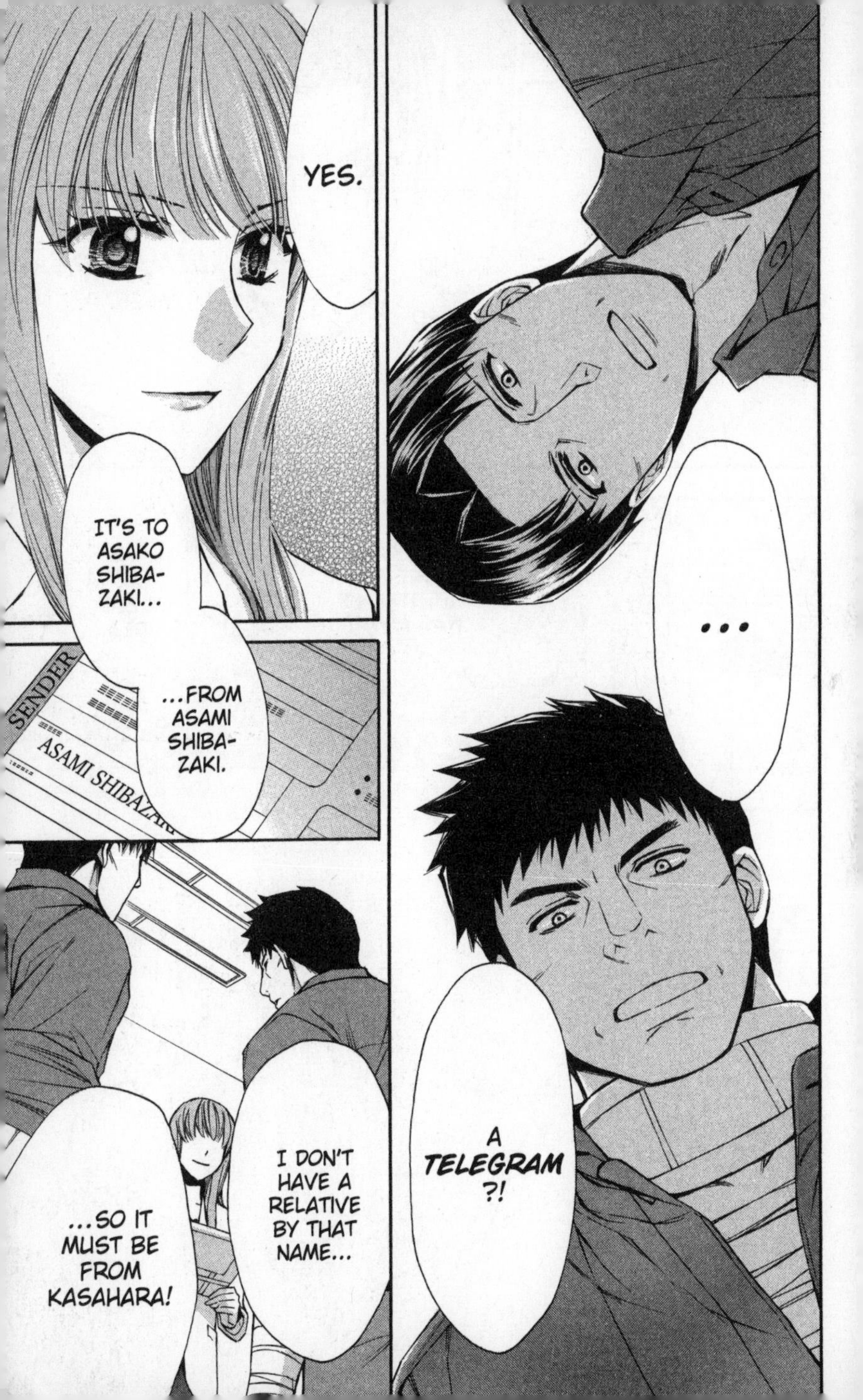
...
A TELEGRAM?!
YES.
IT'S TO ASAKO SHIBAZAKI...
...FROM ASAMI SHIBAZAKI.
SENDER
ASAMI SHIBAZAKI
I DON'T HAVE A RELATIVE BY THAT NAME...
...SO IT MUST BE FROM KASAHARA!

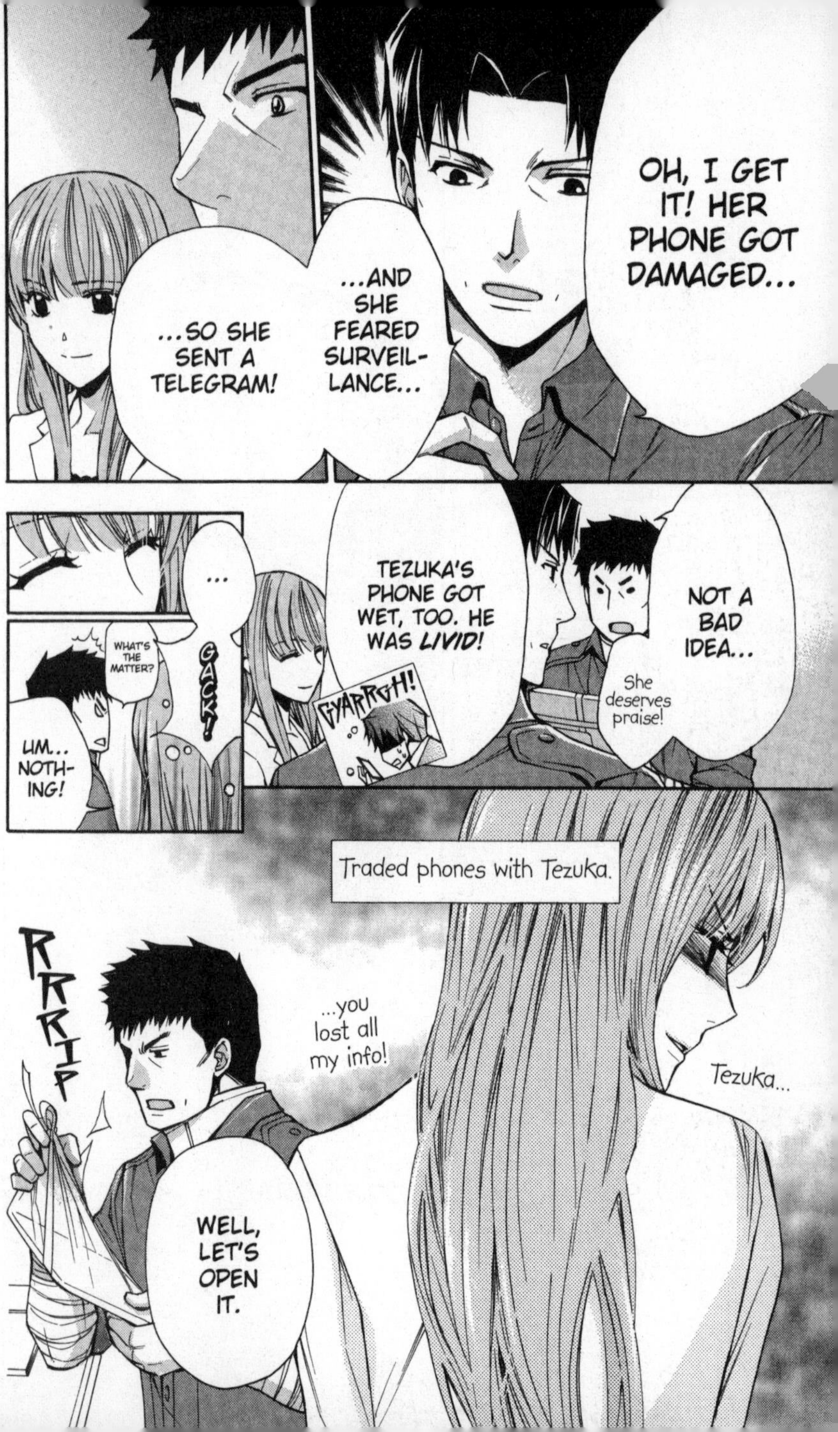
OH, I GET IT! HER PHONE GOT DAMAGED...
...AND SHE FEARED SURVEIL-LANCE...
...SO SHE SENT A TELEGRAM!
NOT A BAD IDEA...
She deserves praise!
TEZUKA'S PHONE GOT WET, TOO. HE WAS *LIVID!*
GYARRGH!
...
WHAT'S THE MATTER?
GACK!
UM... NOTH-ING!
Traded phones with Tezuka.
Tezuka...
...you lost all my info!
RRRIP
WELL, LET'S OPEN IT.

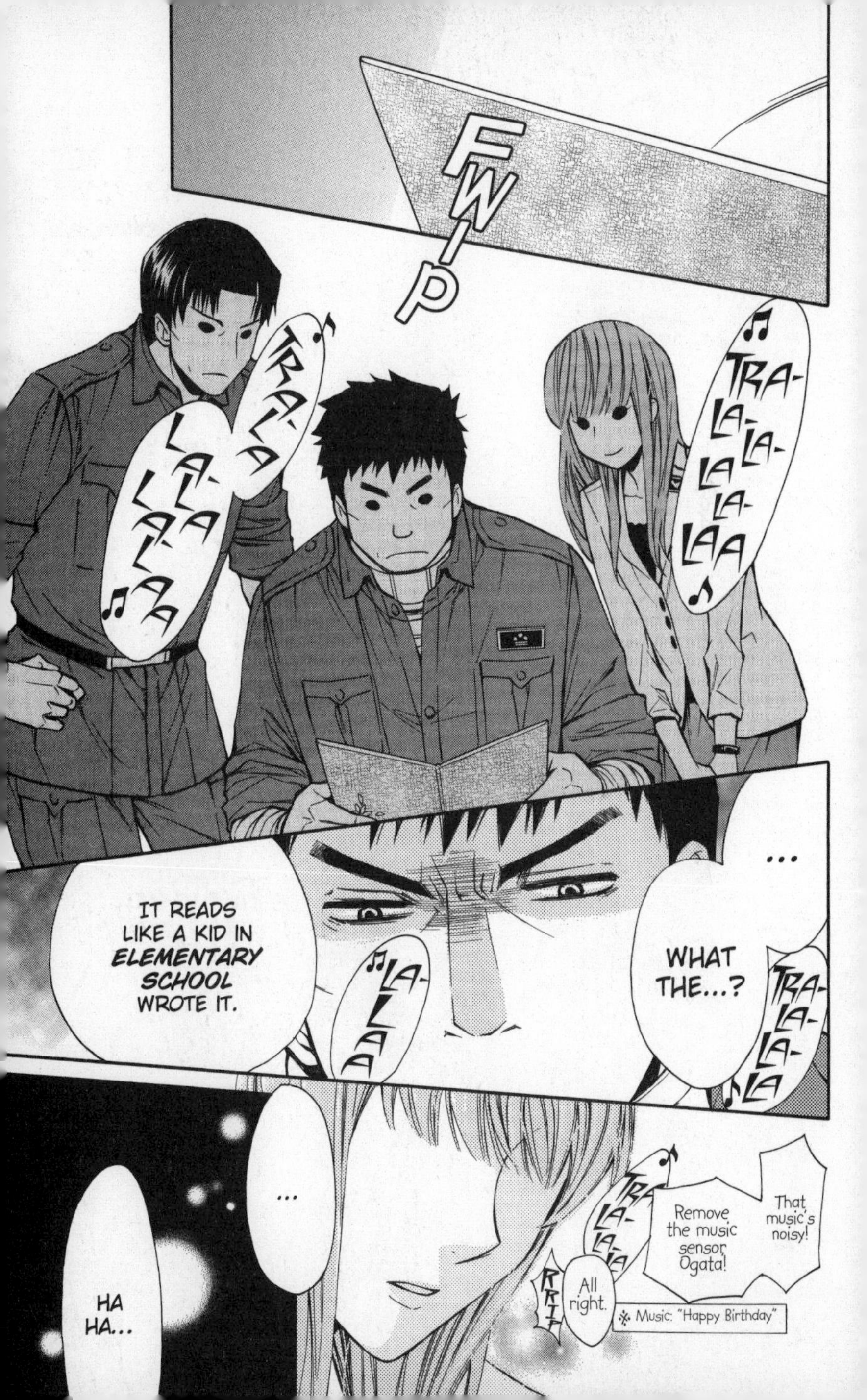
FWIP
♪TRA-LA-LA-LA-LA-LAA♪
♪TRA-LA LA-LA-LA-LAA♪
...
WHAT THE...?
TRA-LA-LA-LA♪
IT READS LIKE A KID IN ELEMENTARY SCHOOL WROTE IT.
♪LA-LAA
That music's noisy!
Remove the music sensor, Ogata!
TRA-LA-LA-LA♪
All right.
RRIP
※ Music: "Happy Birthday"
...
HA HA...

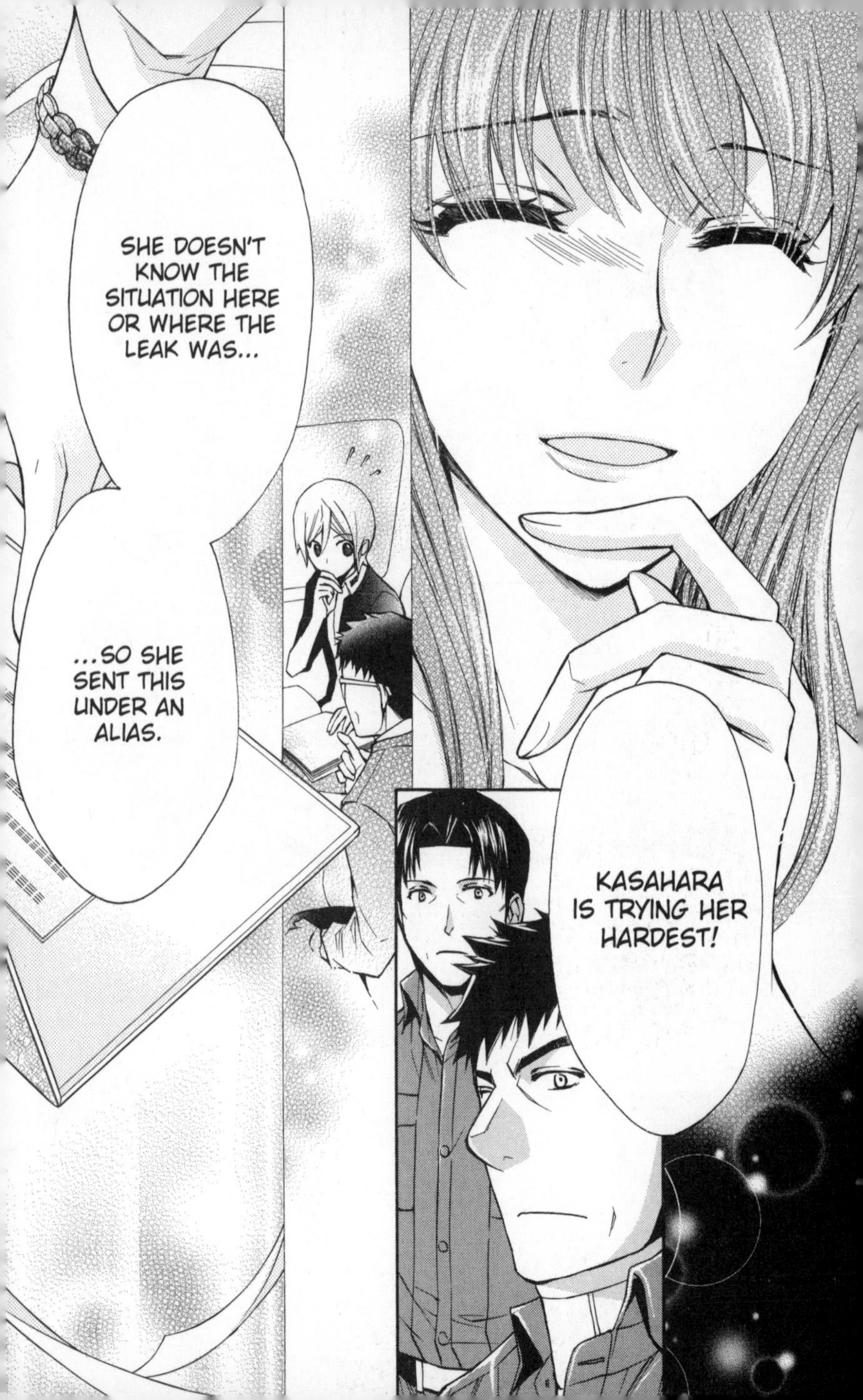
KASAHARA IS TRYING HER HARDEST!
SHE DOESN'T KNOW THE SITUATION HERE OR WHERE THE LEAK WAS...
...SO SHE SENT THIS UNDER AN ALIAS.

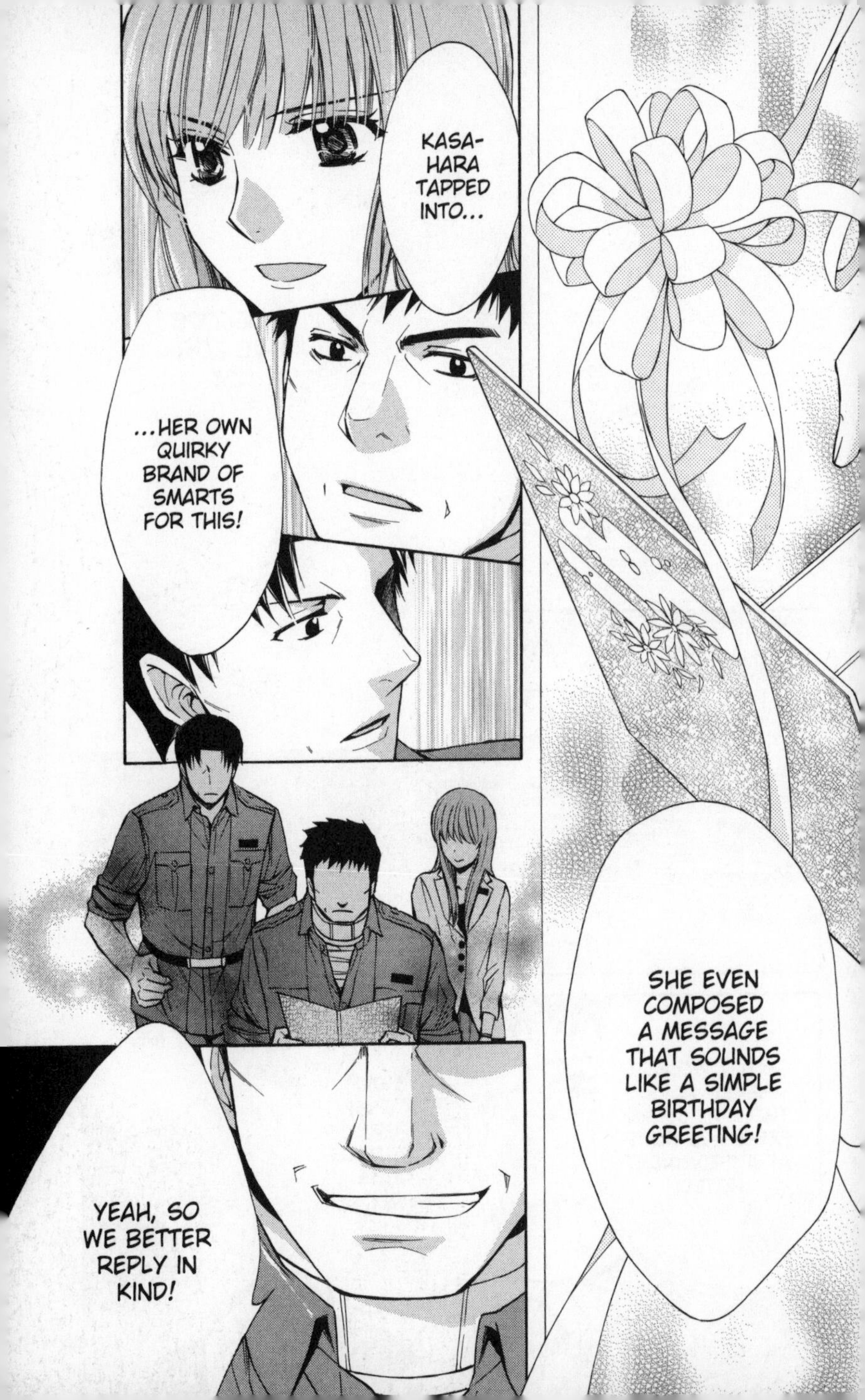
SHE EVEN COMPOSED A MESSAGE THAT SOUNDS LIKE A SIMPLE BIRTHDAY GREETING!
KASA-HARA TAPPED INTO...
...HER OWN QUIRKY BRAND OF SMARTS FOR THIS!
YEAH, SO WE BETTER REPLY IN KIND!

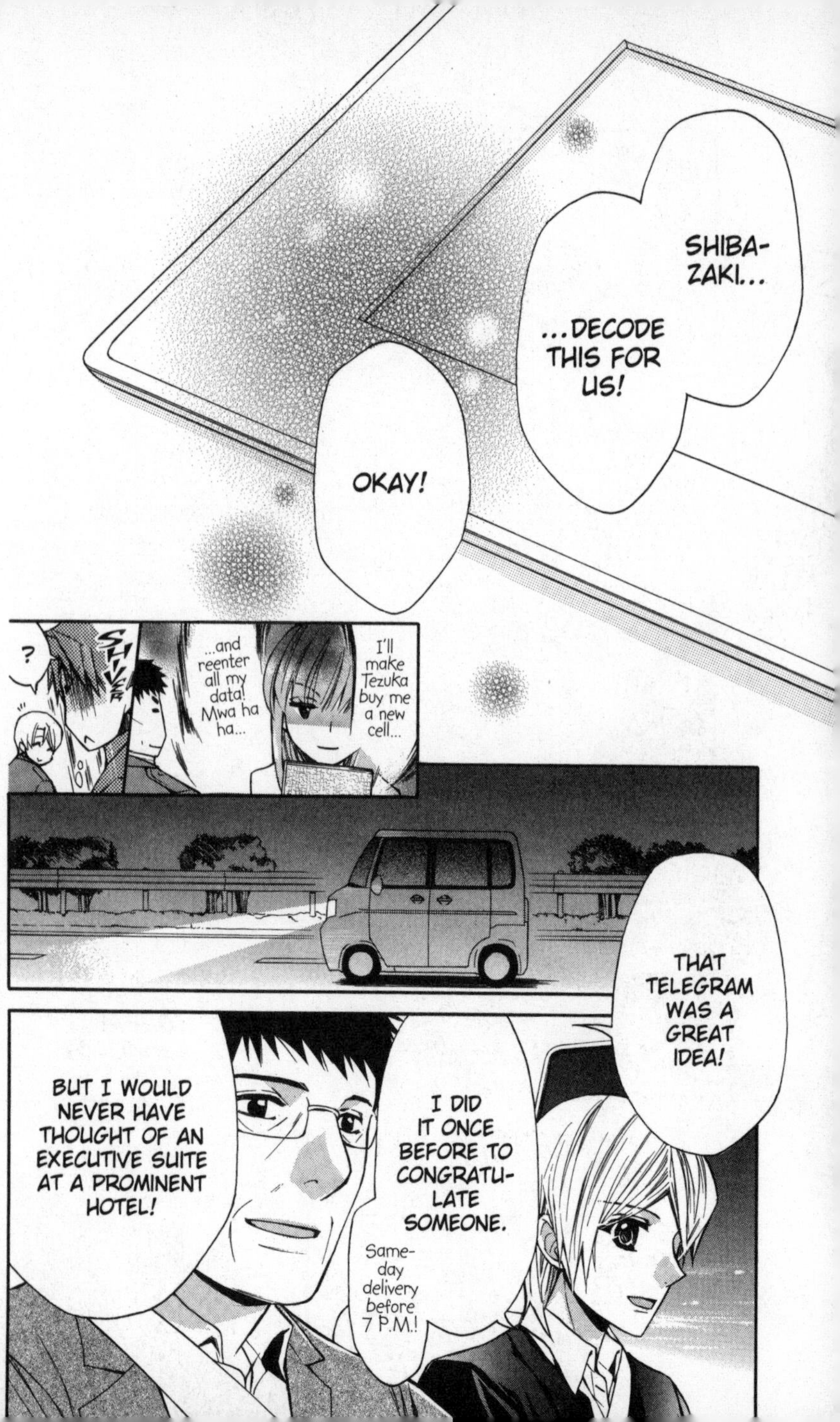
SHIBA-ZAKI...
...DECODE THIS FOR US!
OKAY!
I'll make Tezuka buy me a new cell...
...and reenter all my data! Mwa ha ha...
SHIVER
?
THAT TELEGRAM WAS A GREAT IDEA!
I DID IT ONCE BEFORE TO CONGRATU-LATE SOMEONE.
Same-day delivery before 7 P.M.!
BUT I WOULD NEVER HAVE THOUGHT OF AN EXECUTIVE SUITE AT A PROMINENT HOTEL!

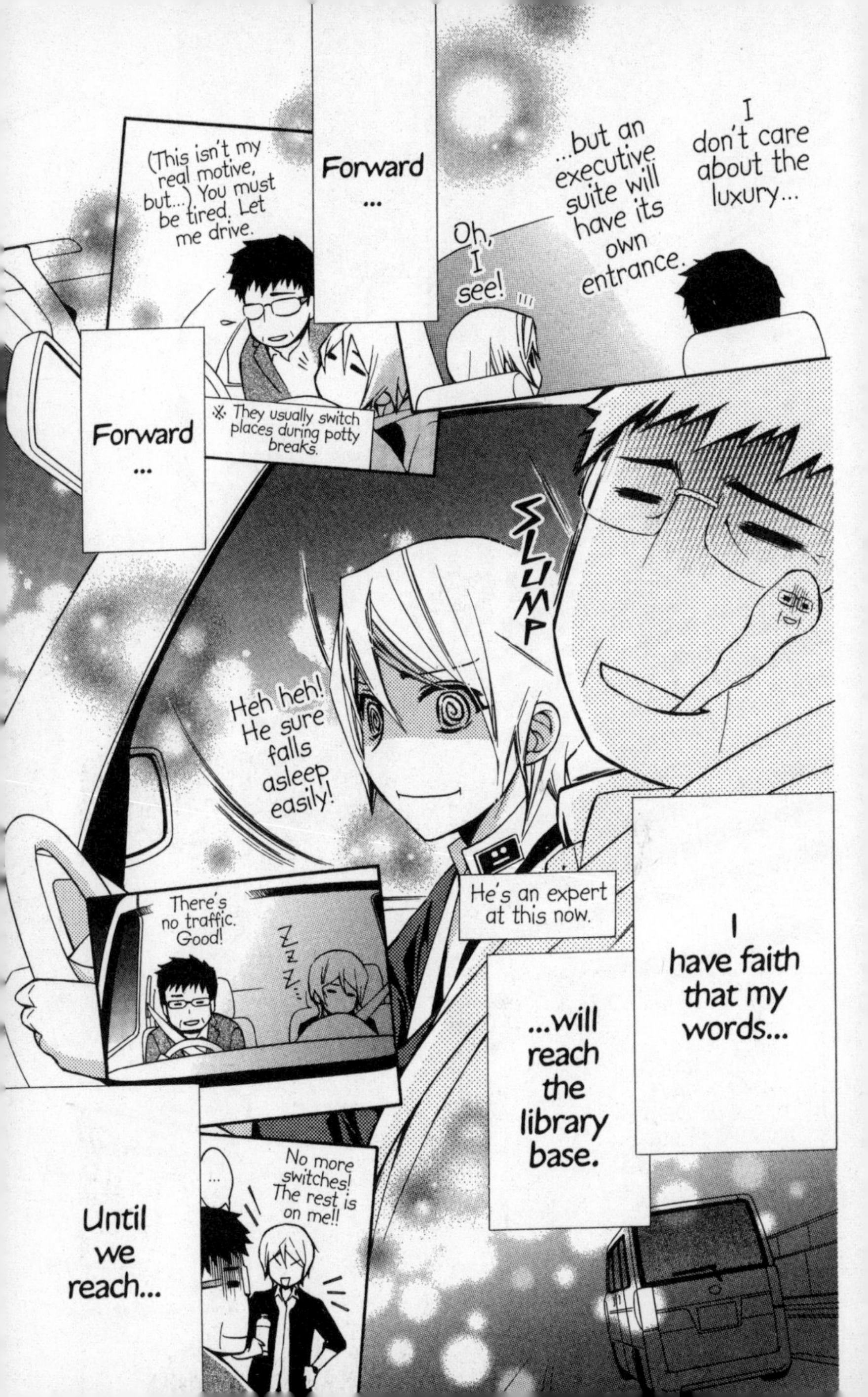

I don't care about the luxury...
...but an executive suite will have its own entrance.
Oh, I see!
Forward...
(This isn't my real motive, but...) You must be tired. Let me drive.
Forward...
※ They usually switch places during potty breaks.
SLUMP
Heh heh! He sure falls asleep easily!
He's an expert at this now.
I have faith that my words...
...will reach the library base.
There's no traffic. Good!
ZZZ...
No more switches! The rest is on me!!
...
Until we reach...

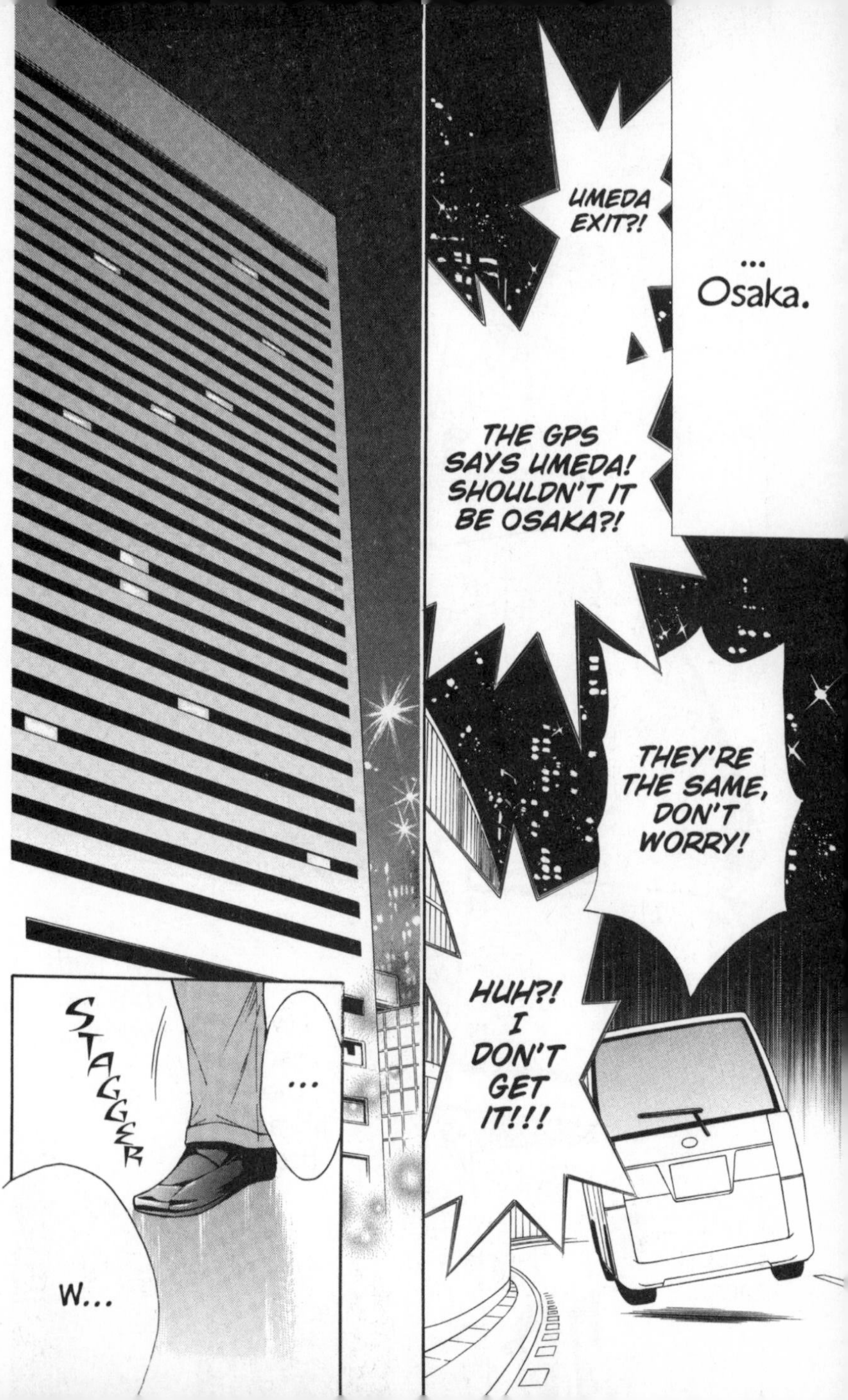
... Osaka.
UMEDA EXIT?!
THE GPS SAYS UMEDA! SHOULDN'T IT BE OSAKA?!
THEY'RE THE SAME, DON'T WORRY!
HUH?! I DON'T GET IT!!!
...
STAGGER
W...

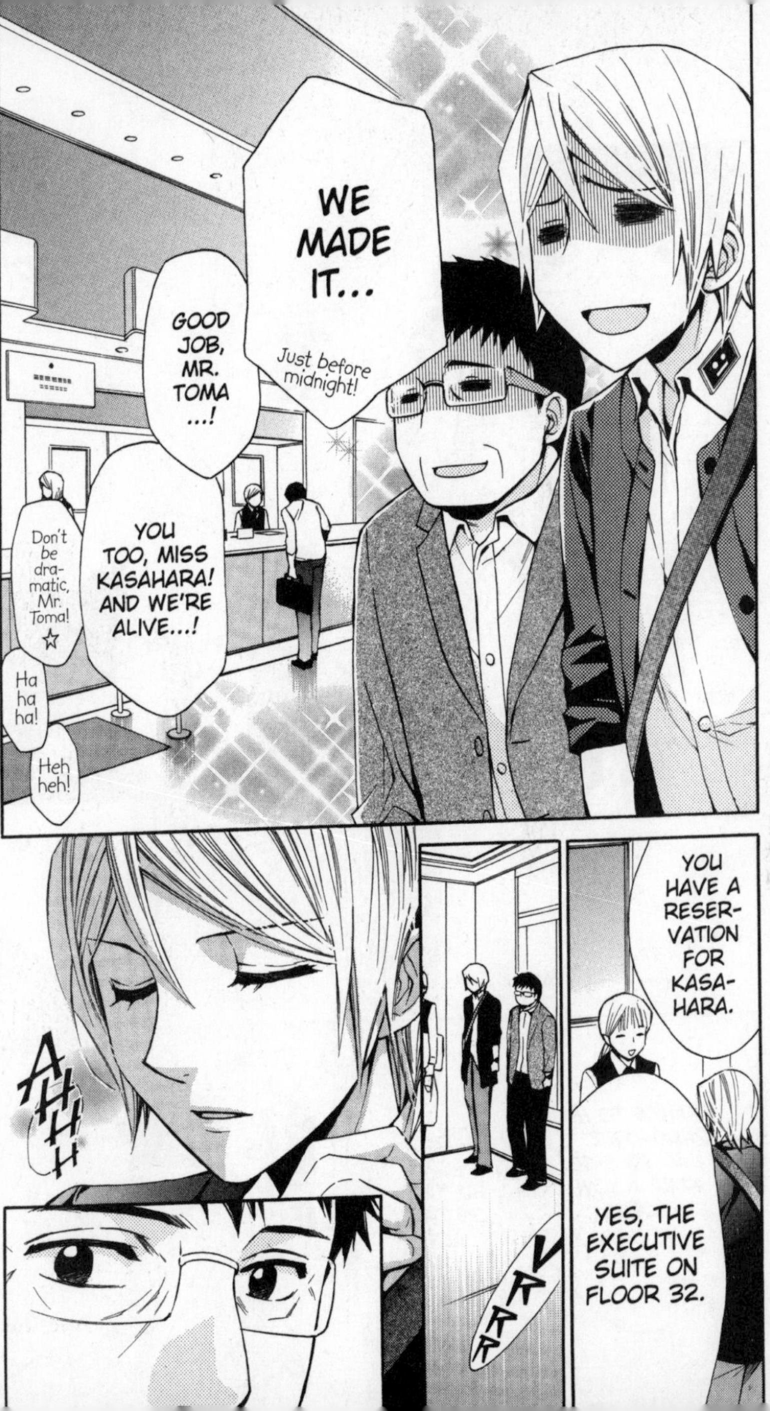
WE MADE IT...
Just before midnight!
GOOD JOB, MR. TOMA...!
YOU TOO, MISS KASAHARA! AND WE'RE ALIVE...!
Don't be dramatic, Mr. Toma! ☆
Ha ha ha!
Heh heh!
YOU HAVE A RESERVATION FOR KASAHARA.
YES, THE EXECUTIVE SUITE ON FLOOR 32.
VRRR
AHHH

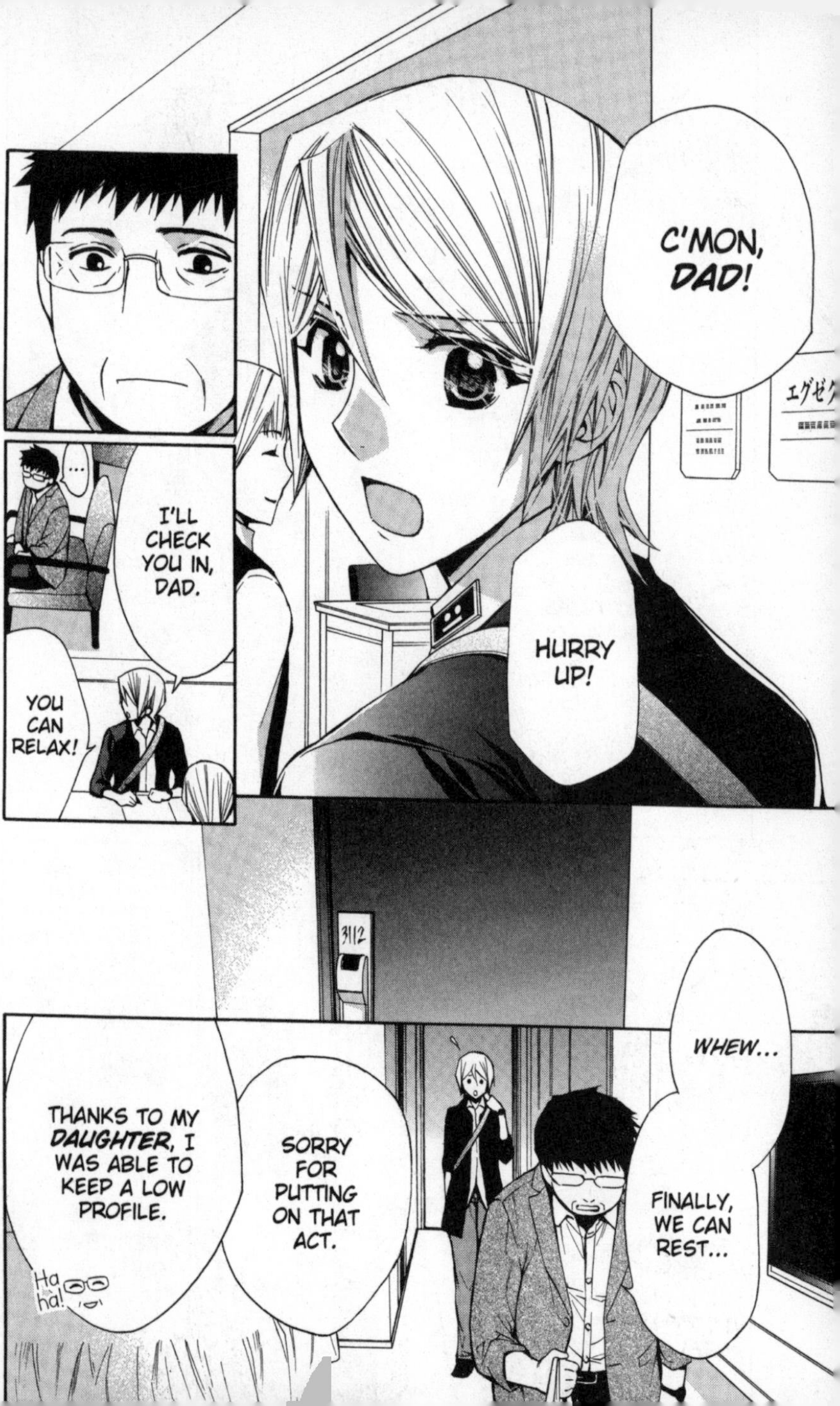
C'MON, DAD!
HURRY UP!
...
I'LL CHECK YOU IN, DAD.
YOU CAN RELAX!
3112
WHEW...
FINALLY, WE CAN REST...
SORRY FOR PUTTING ON THAT ACT.
THANKS TO MY *DAUGHTER*, I WAS ABLE TO KEEP A LOW PROFILE.
Ha ha!

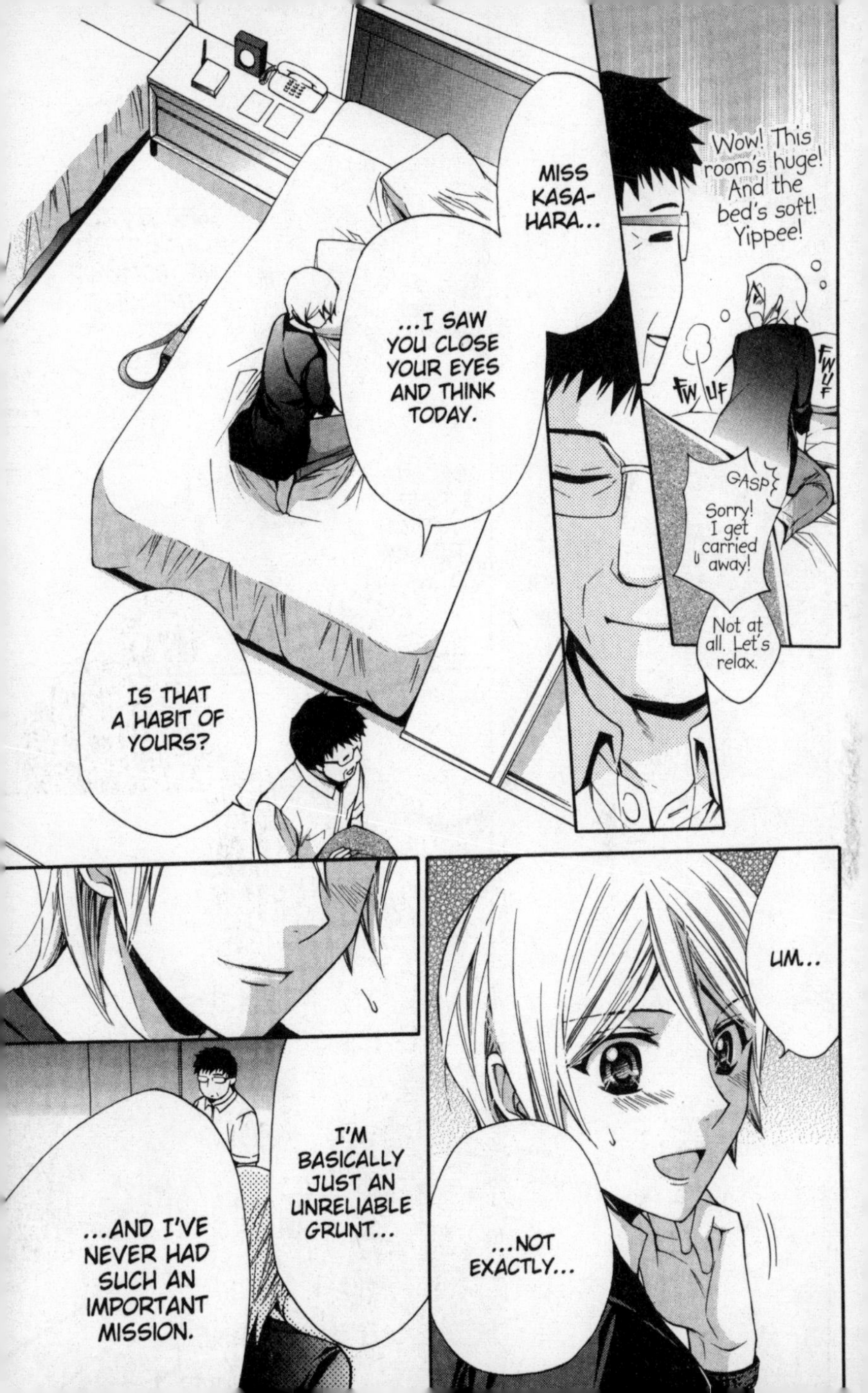

Wow! This room's huge! And the bed's soft! Yippee!
FWUF
FWUF
GASP
Sorry! I get carried away!
Not at all. Let's relax.
MISS KASA-HARA...
...I SAW YOU CLOSE YOUR EYES AND THINK TODAY.
IS THAT A HABIT OF YOURS?
UM...
...NOT EXACTLY...
I'M BASICALLY JUST AN UNRELIABLE GRUNT...
...AND I'VE NEVER HAD SUCH AN IMPORTANT MISSION.

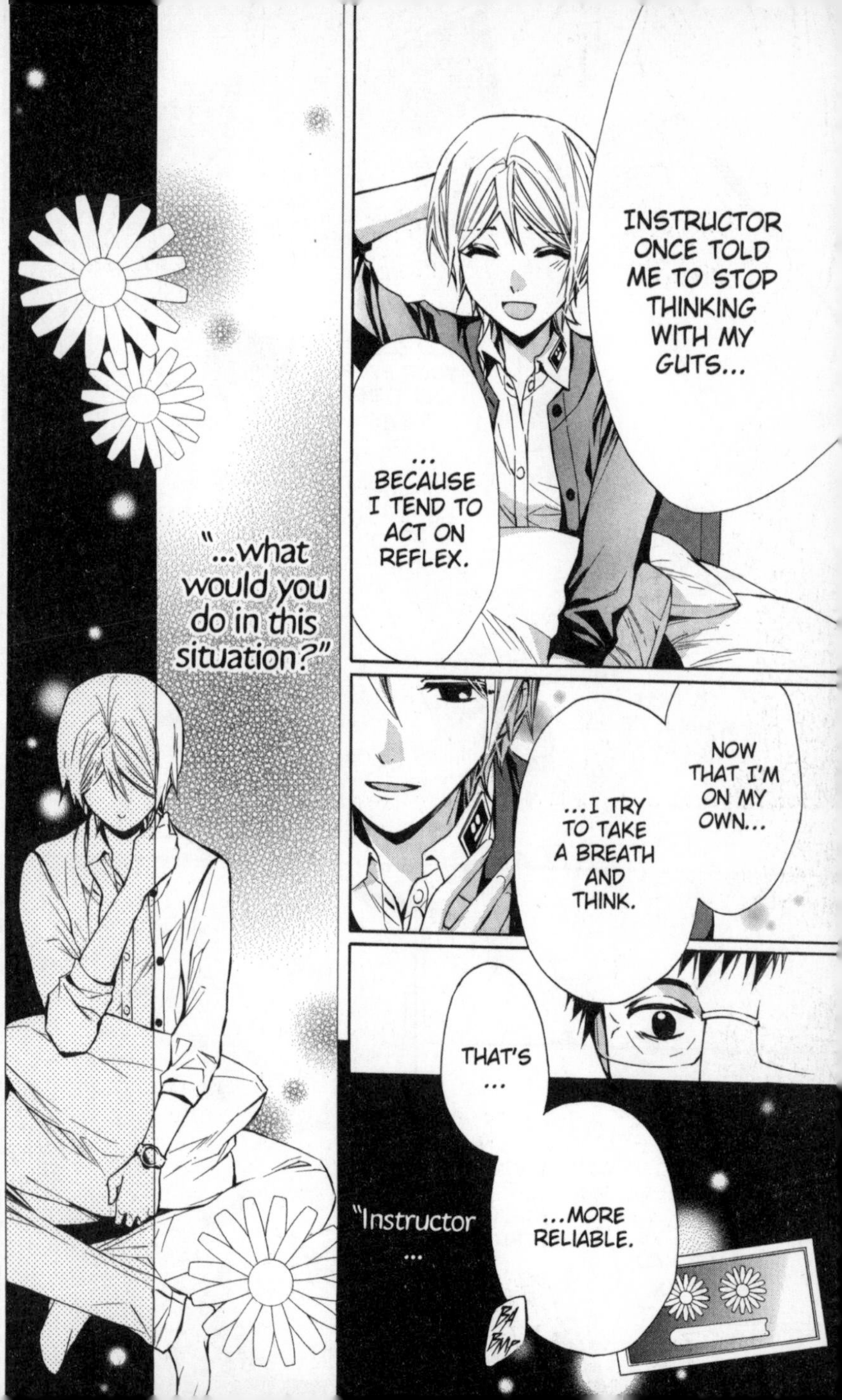
INSTRUCTOR ONCE TOLD ME TO STOP THINKING WITH MY GUTS...
...BECAUSE I TEND TO ACT ON REFLEX.
NOW THAT I'M ON MY OWN...
...I TRY TO TAKE A BREATH AND THINK.
THAT'S ...
...MORE RELIABLE.
BA BMP
"Instructor ...
"...what would you do in this situation?"

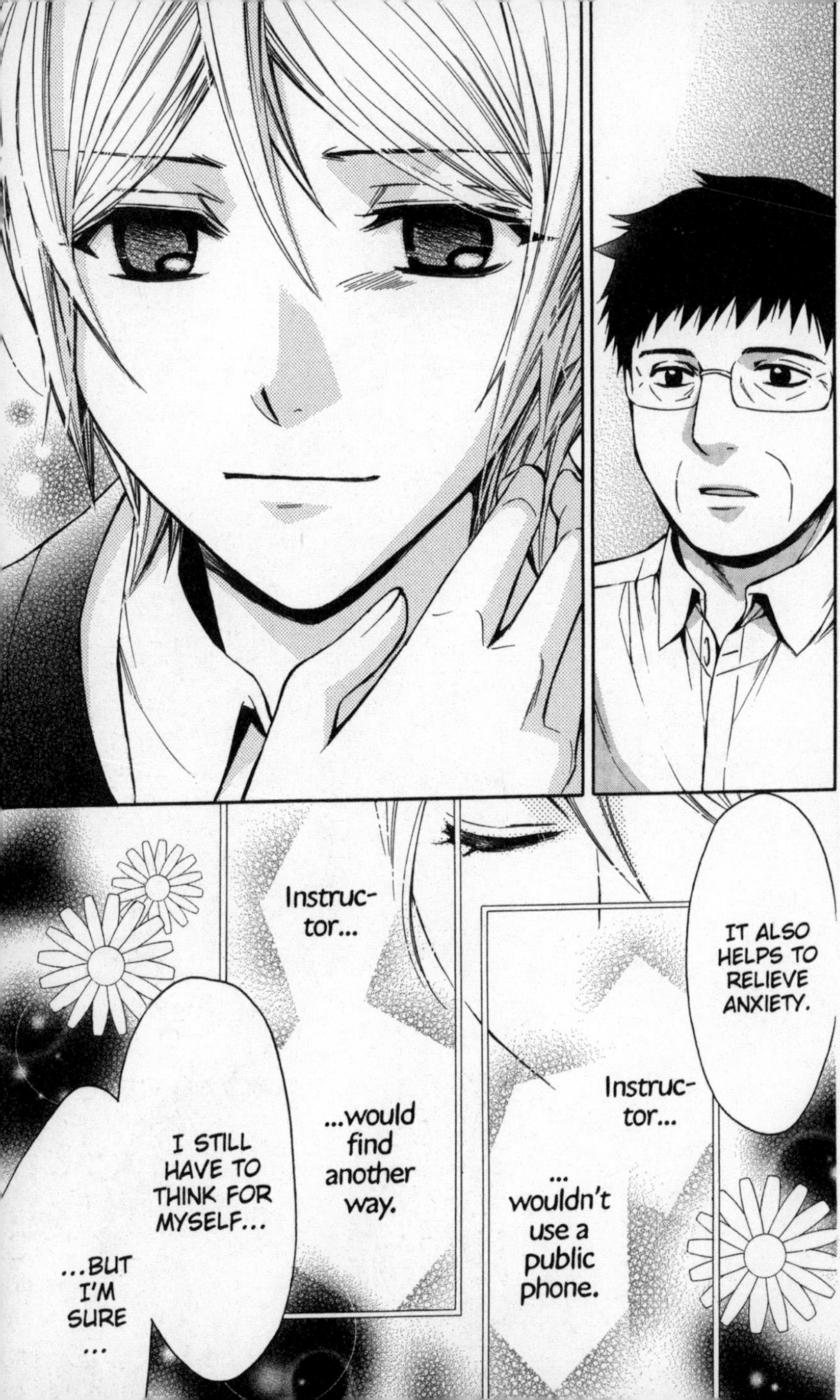
IT ALSO HELPS TO RELIEVE ANXIETY.
Instruc-tor...
...wouldn't use a public phone.
Instruc-tor...
...would find another way.
I STILL HAVE TO THINK FOR MYSELF...
...BUT I'M SURE ...

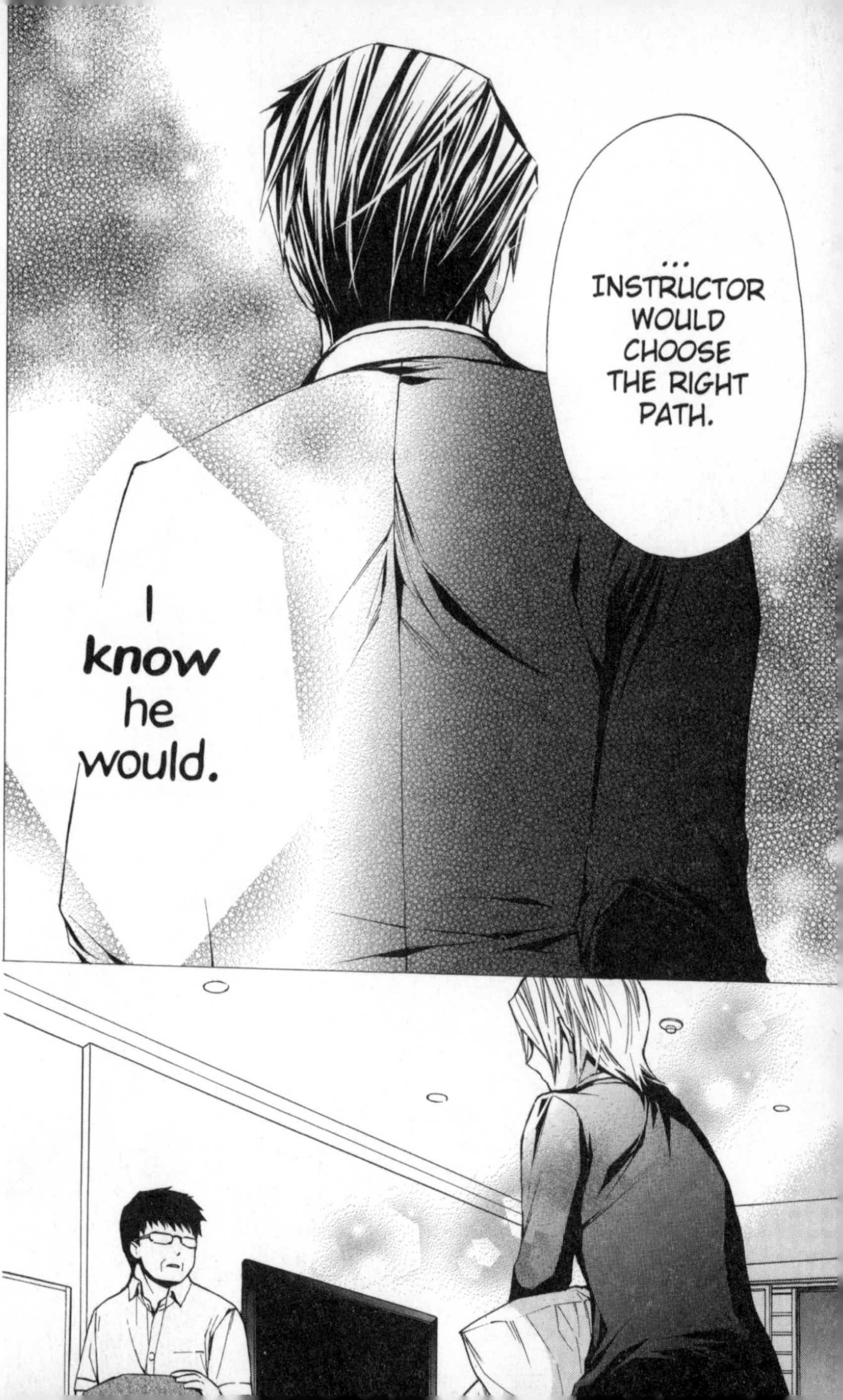
...
INSTRUCTOR WOULD CHOOSE THE RIGHT PATH.
I know he would.

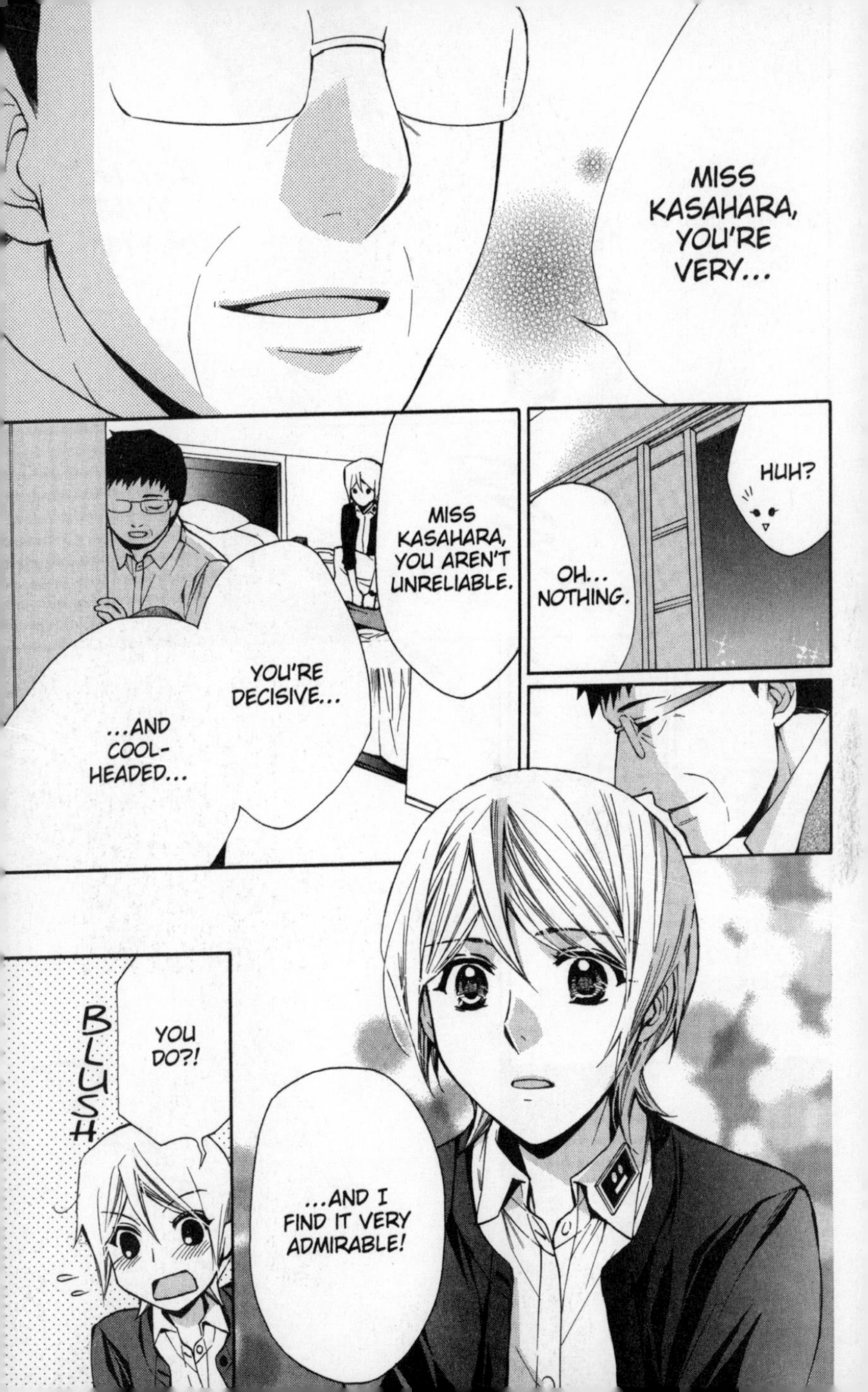
MISS KASAHARA, YOU'RE VERY...
HUH?
OH... NOTHING.
MISS KASAHARA, YOU AREN'T UNRELIABLE.
YOU'RE DECISIVE...
...AND COOL-HEADED...
...AND I FIND IT VERY ADMIRABLE!
YOU DO?!
BLUSH

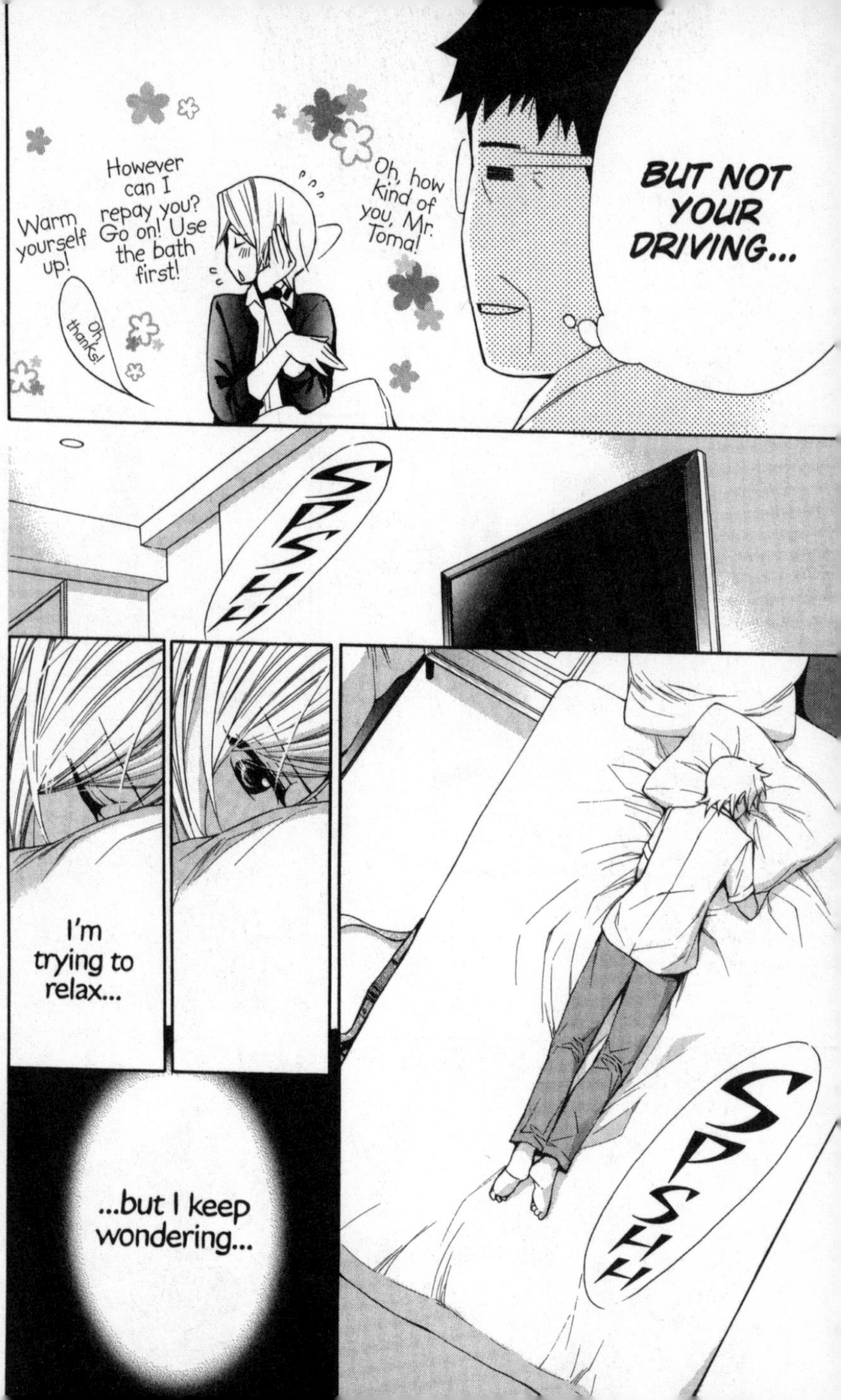
BUT NOT YOUR DRIVING...
Oh, how kind of you, Mr. Toma!
However can I repay you? Go on! Use the bath first!
Warm yourself up!
Oh, thanks!
SPSHH
SPSHH
I'm trying to relax...
...but I keep wondering...

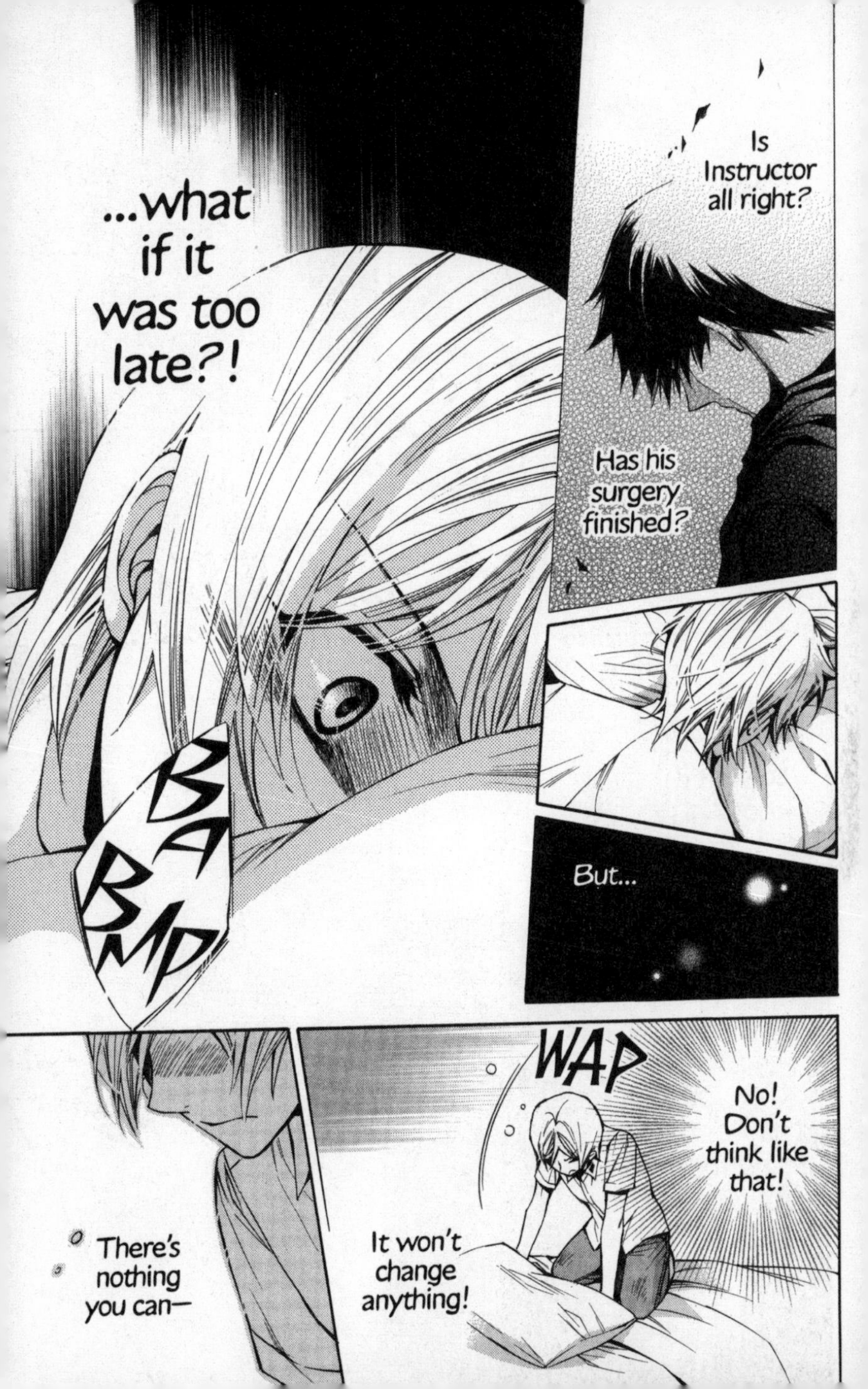
Is Instructor all right?
Has his surgery finished?
But...
...what if it was too late?!
BA BMP
WAP
No! Don't think like that!
It won't change anything!
There's nothing you can—

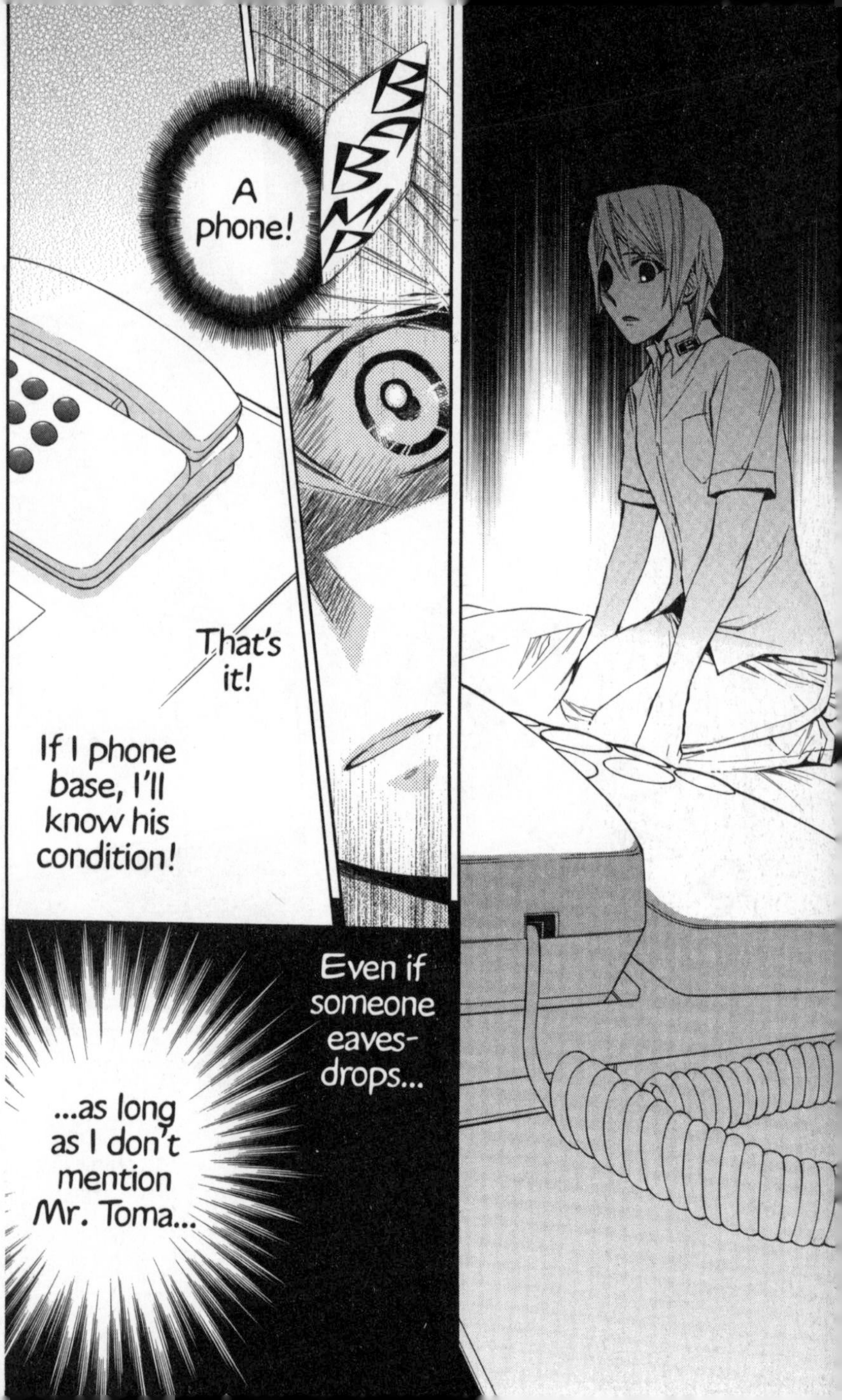
BABMP
A phone!
That's it!
If I phone base, I'll know his condition!
Even if someone eaves-drops...
...as long as I don't mention Mr. Toma...

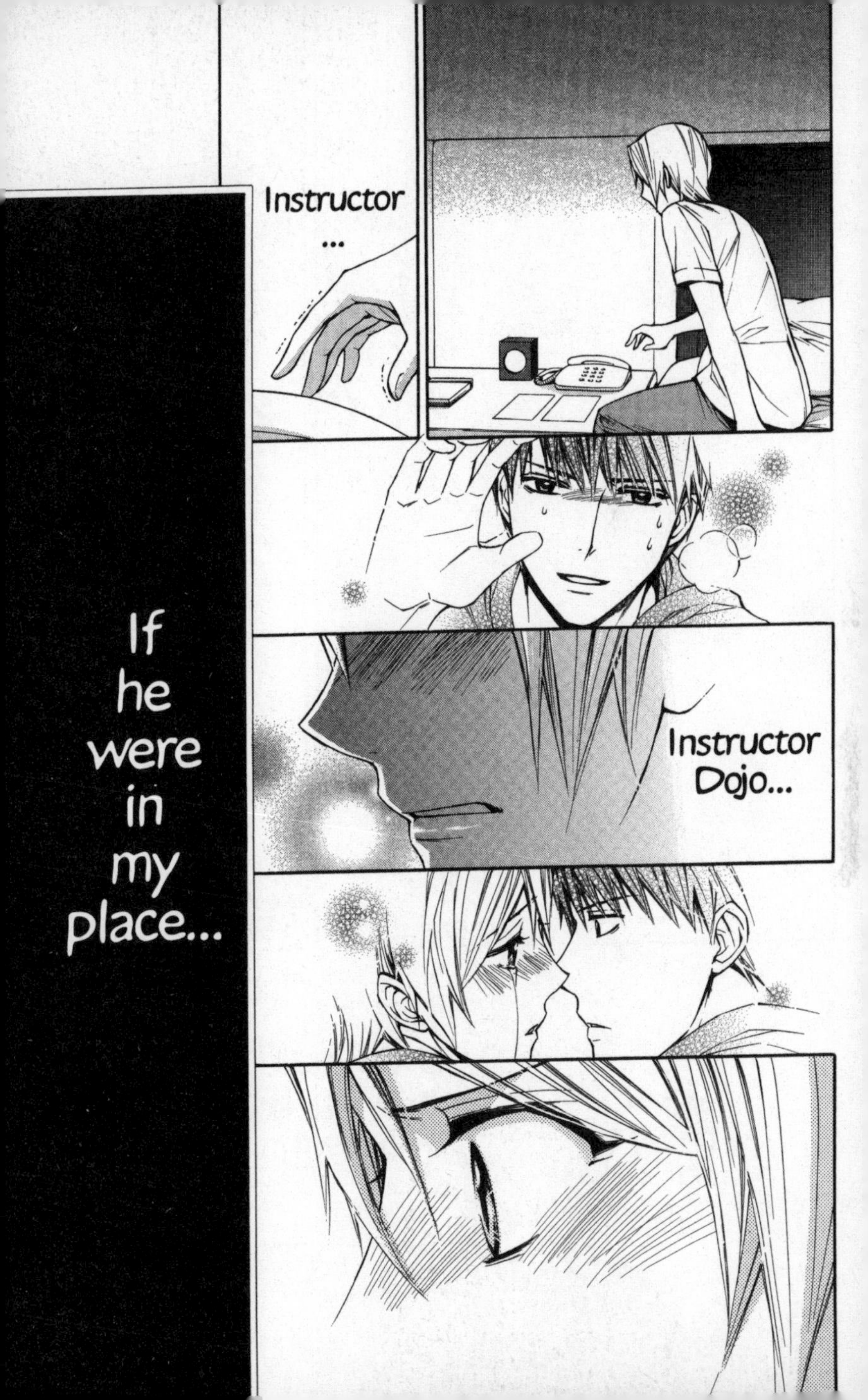
Instructor ...
Instructor Dojo...
If he were in my place...

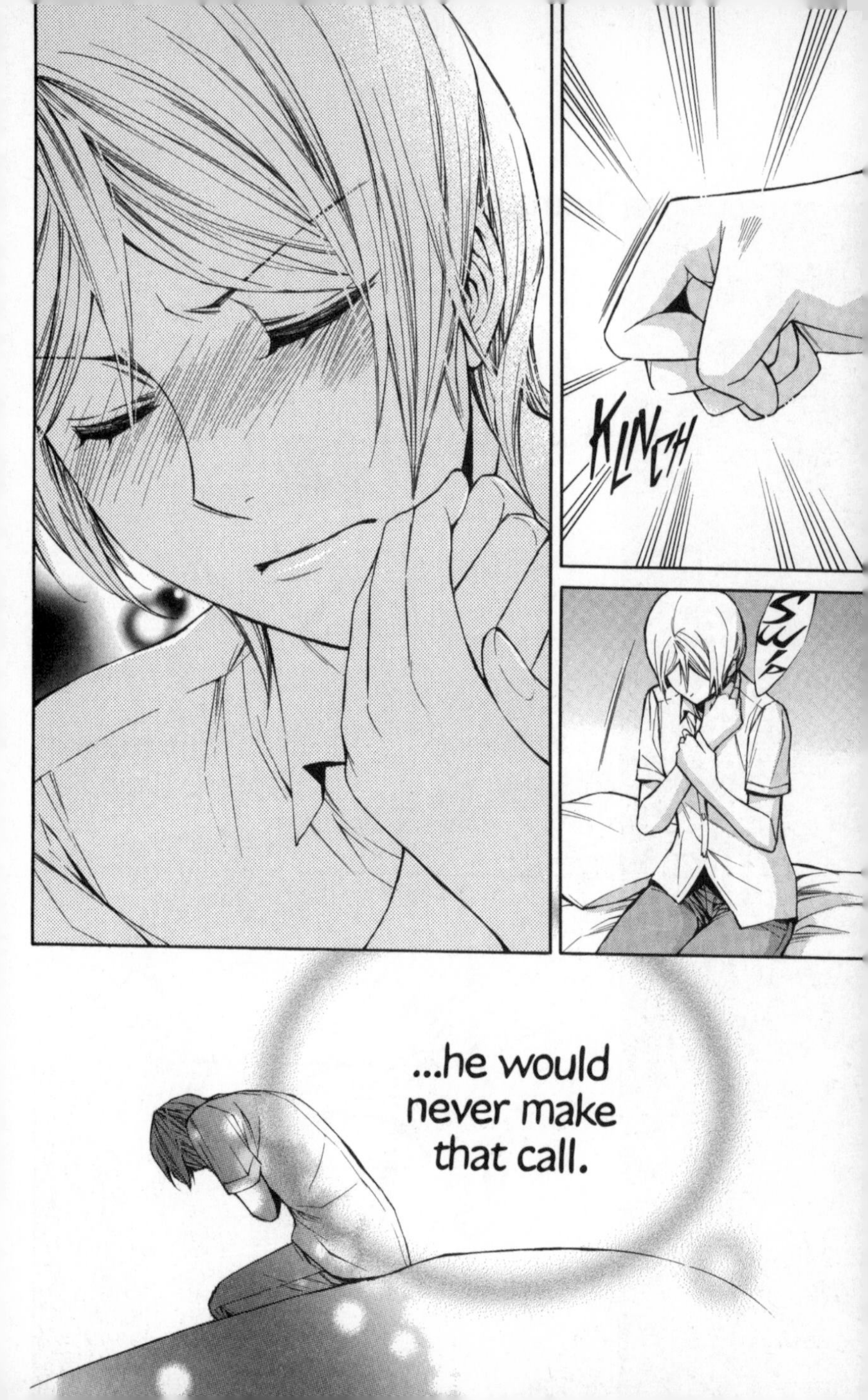
KLINCH
SWIP
...he would never make that call.

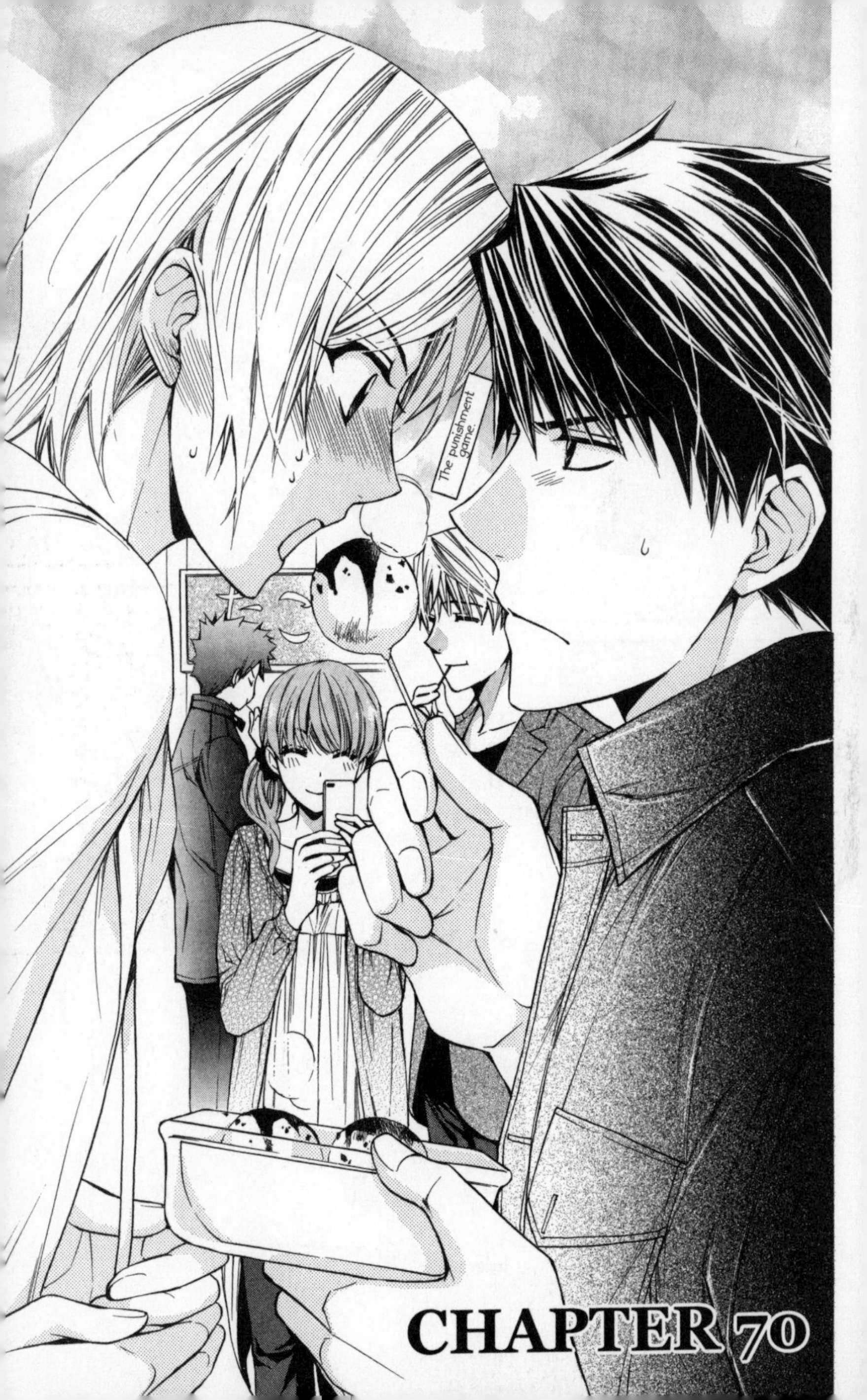
The punishment game.
CHAPTER 70

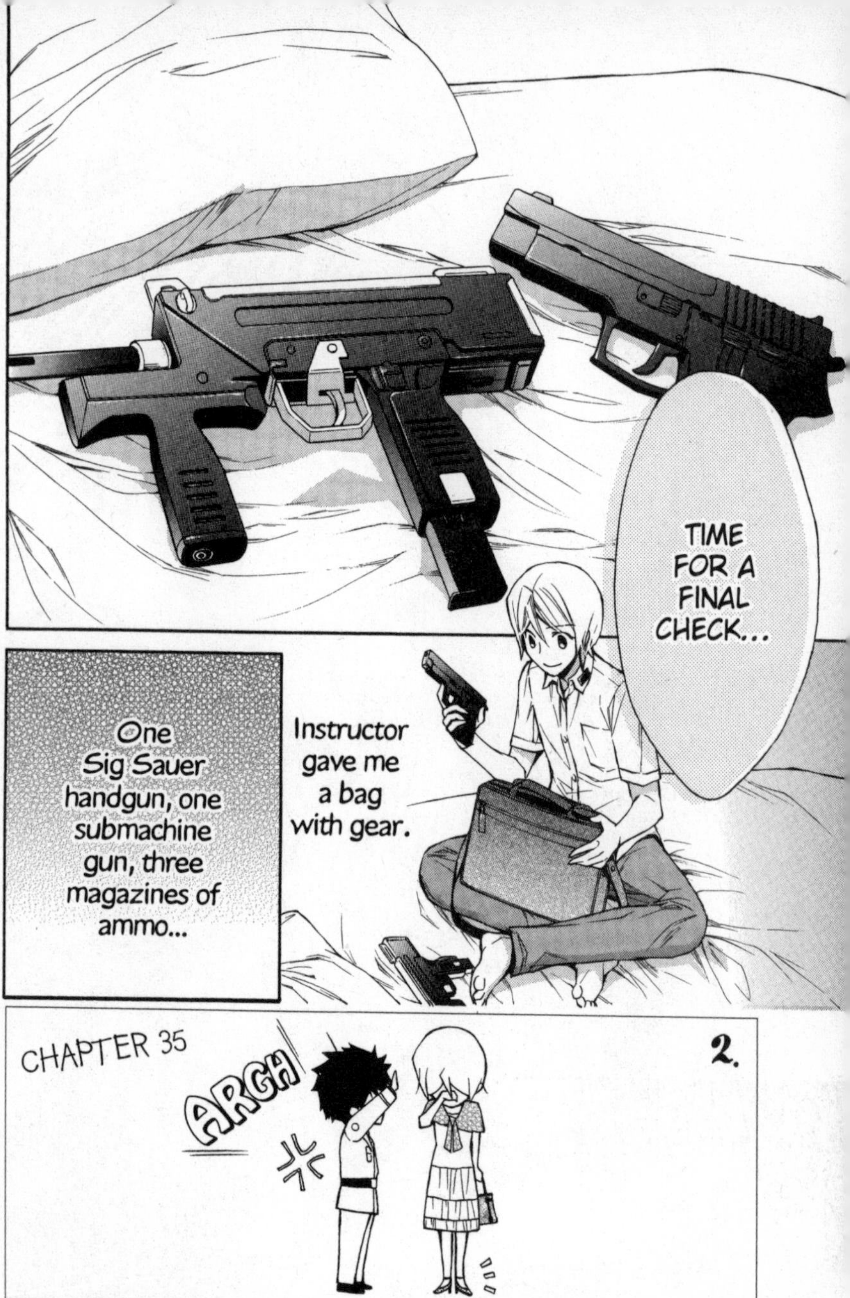
TIME FOR A FINAL CHECK...
Instructor gave me a bag with gear.
One Sig Sauer handgun, one submachine gun, three magazines of ammo...
CHAPTER 35
2.
ARGH

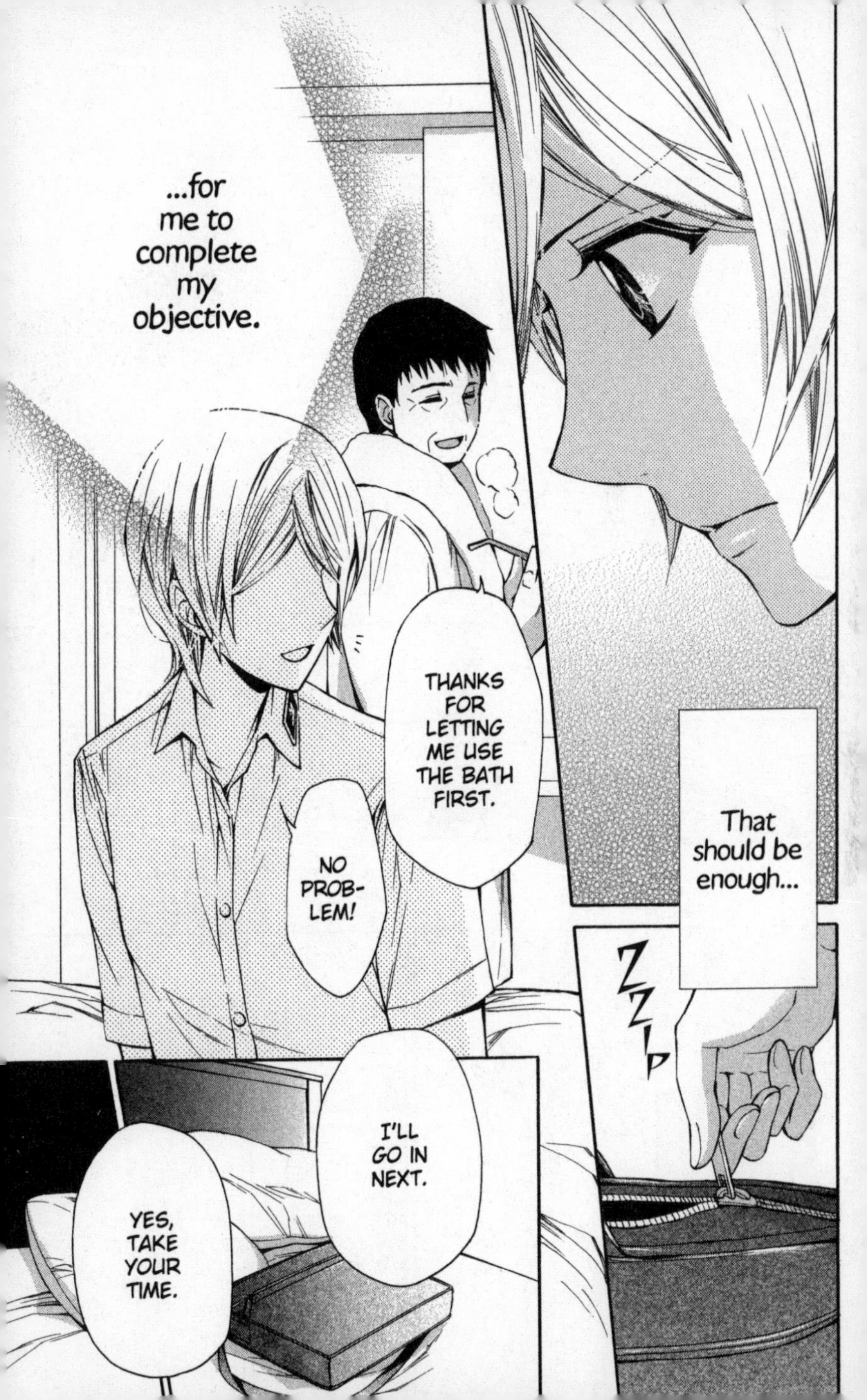
That should be enough...
ZZZIP
...for me to complete my objective.
THANKS FOR LETTING ME USE THE BATH FIRST.
NO PROB-LEM!
I'LL GO IN NEXT.
YES, TAKE YOUR TIME.

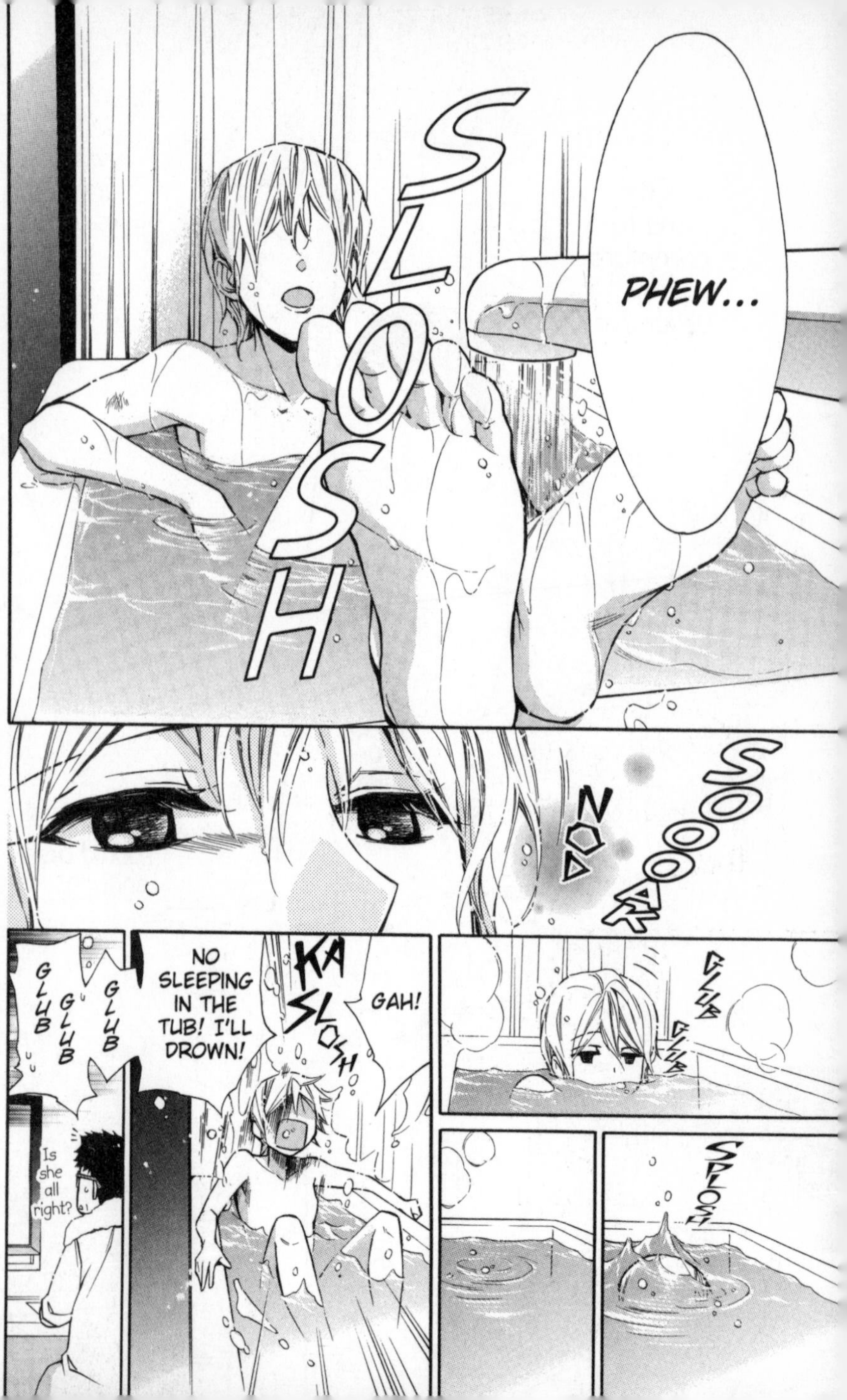
PHEW...
SLOSH
SOOOAR
NOD
GLUB GLUB
SPLOSH
GAH!
KA SLOSH
NO SLEEPING IN THE TUB! I'LL DROWN!
GLUB GLUB GLUB
Is she all right?

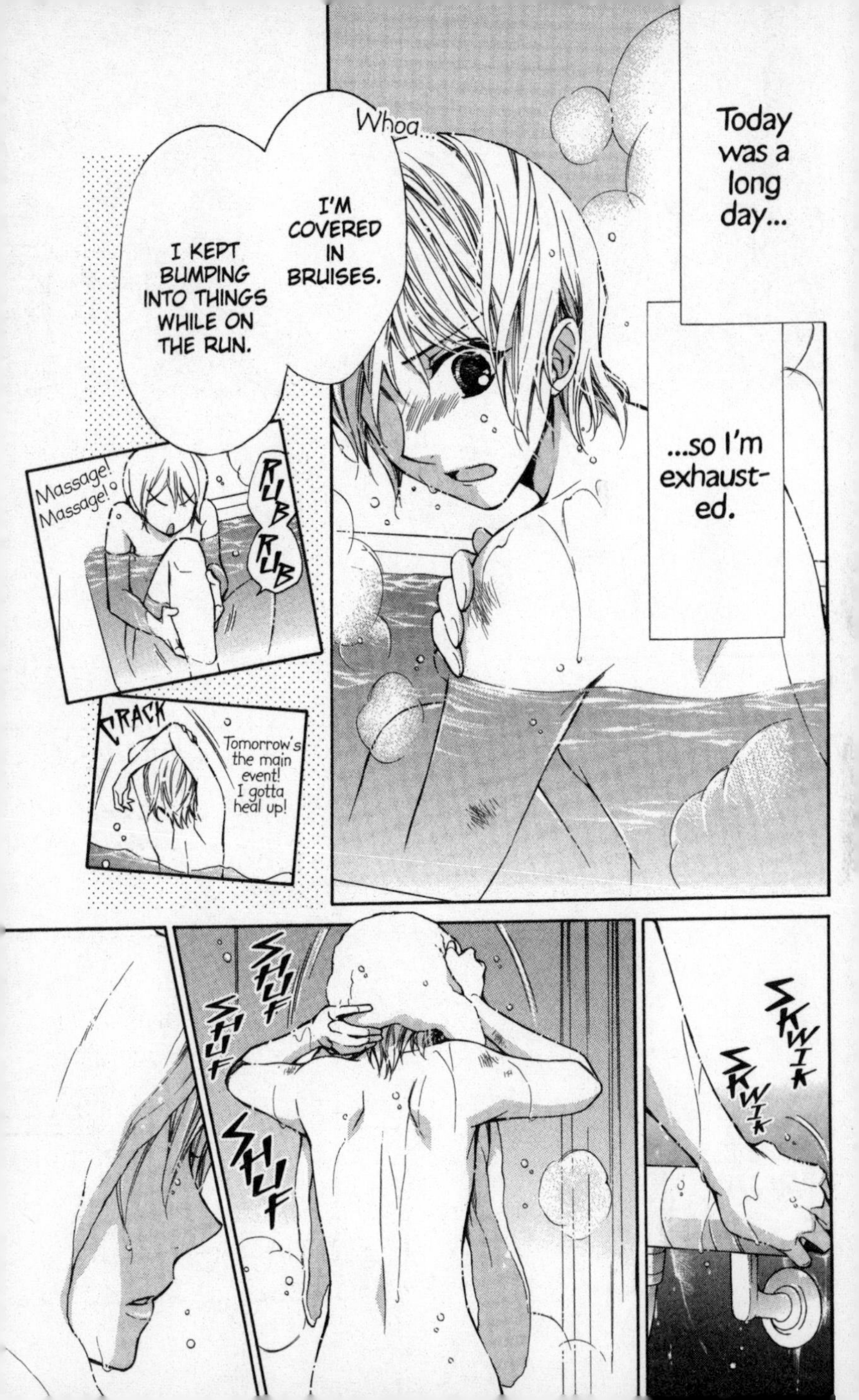
Today was a long day...
...so I'm exhausted.
Whoa...
I'M COVERED IN BRUISES.
I KEPT BUMPING INTO THINGS WHILE ON THE RUN.
Massage! Massage!
RUB RUB
CRACK
Tomorrow's the main event! I gotta heal up!
SKWIK SKWIK
SHUF SHUF
SHUF

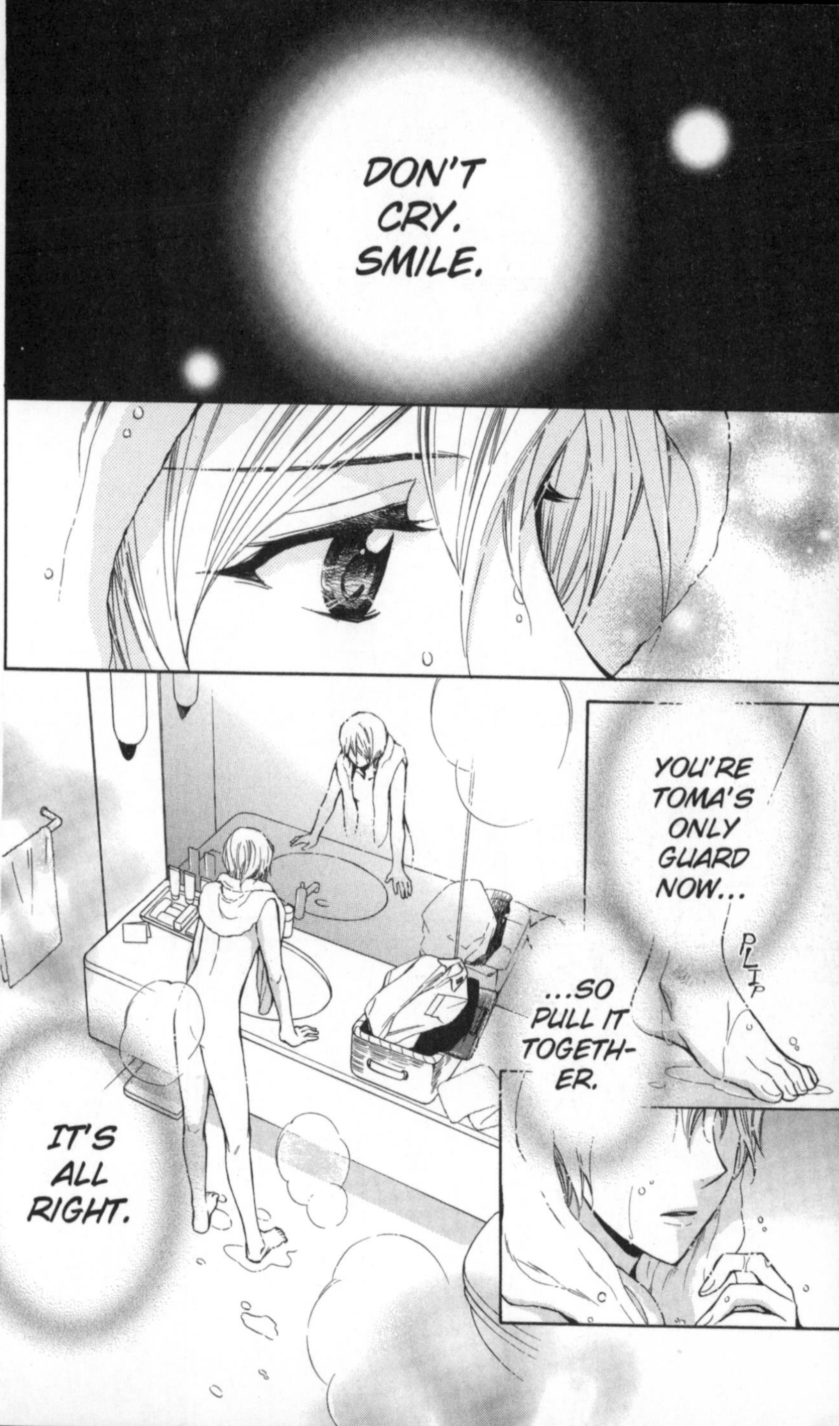
DON'T CRY. SMILE.
YOU'RE TOMA'S ONLY GUARD NOW...
PLIP
...SO PULL IT TOGETH-ER.
IT'S ALL RIGHT.

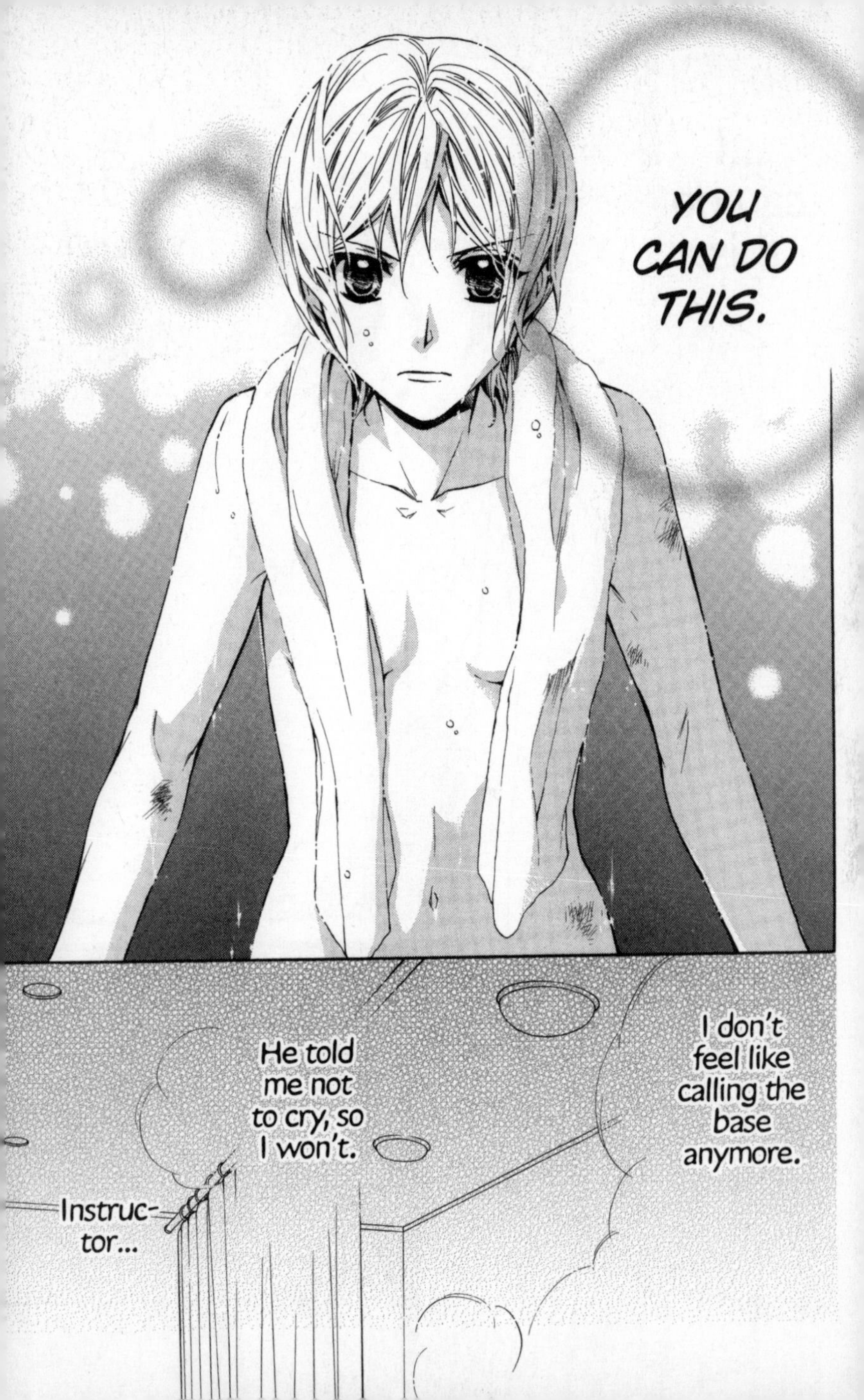
YOU CAN DO THIS.
I don't feel like calling the base anymore.
He told me not to cry, so I won't.
Instructor...

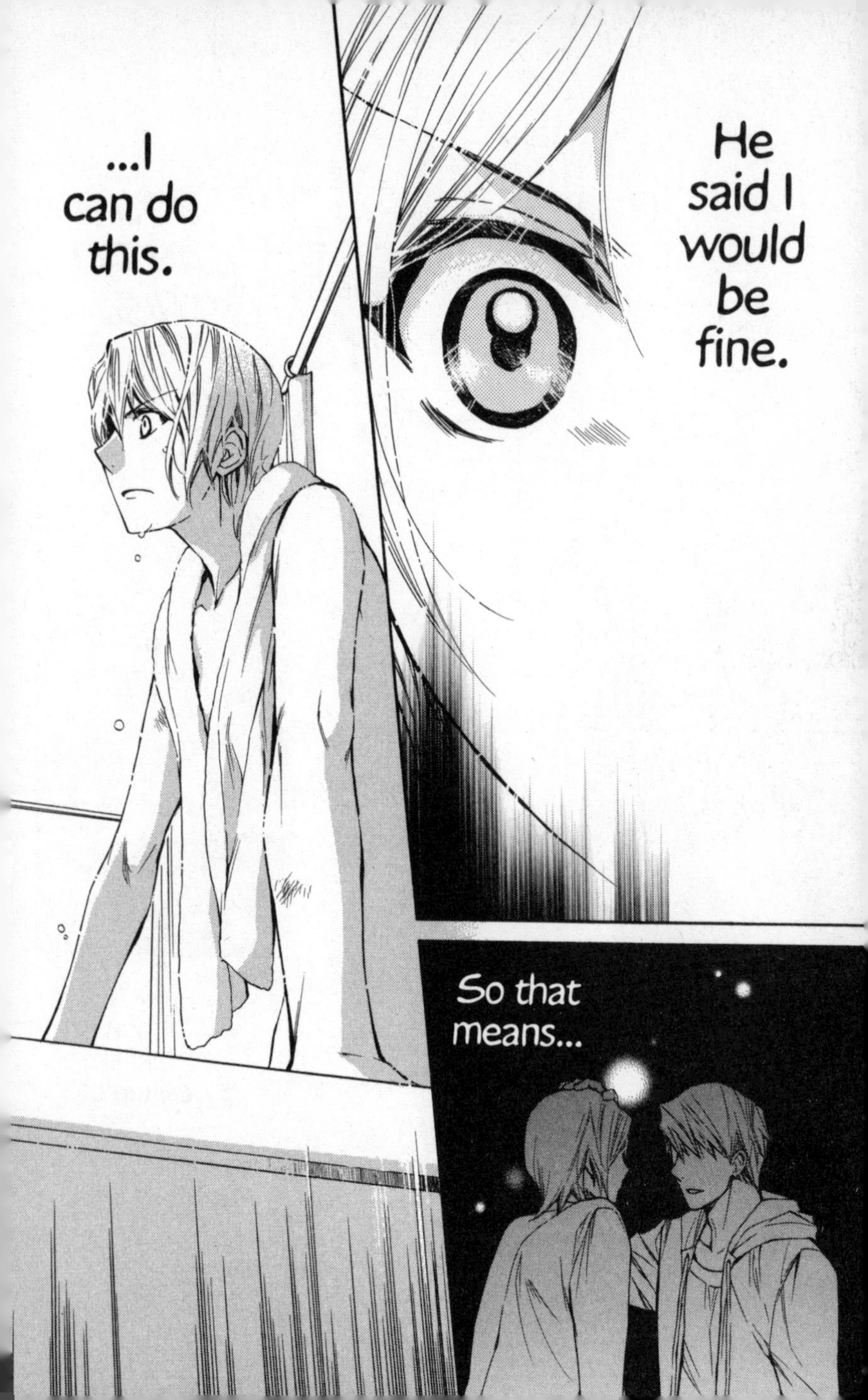
He said I would be fine.
So that means...
...I can do this.

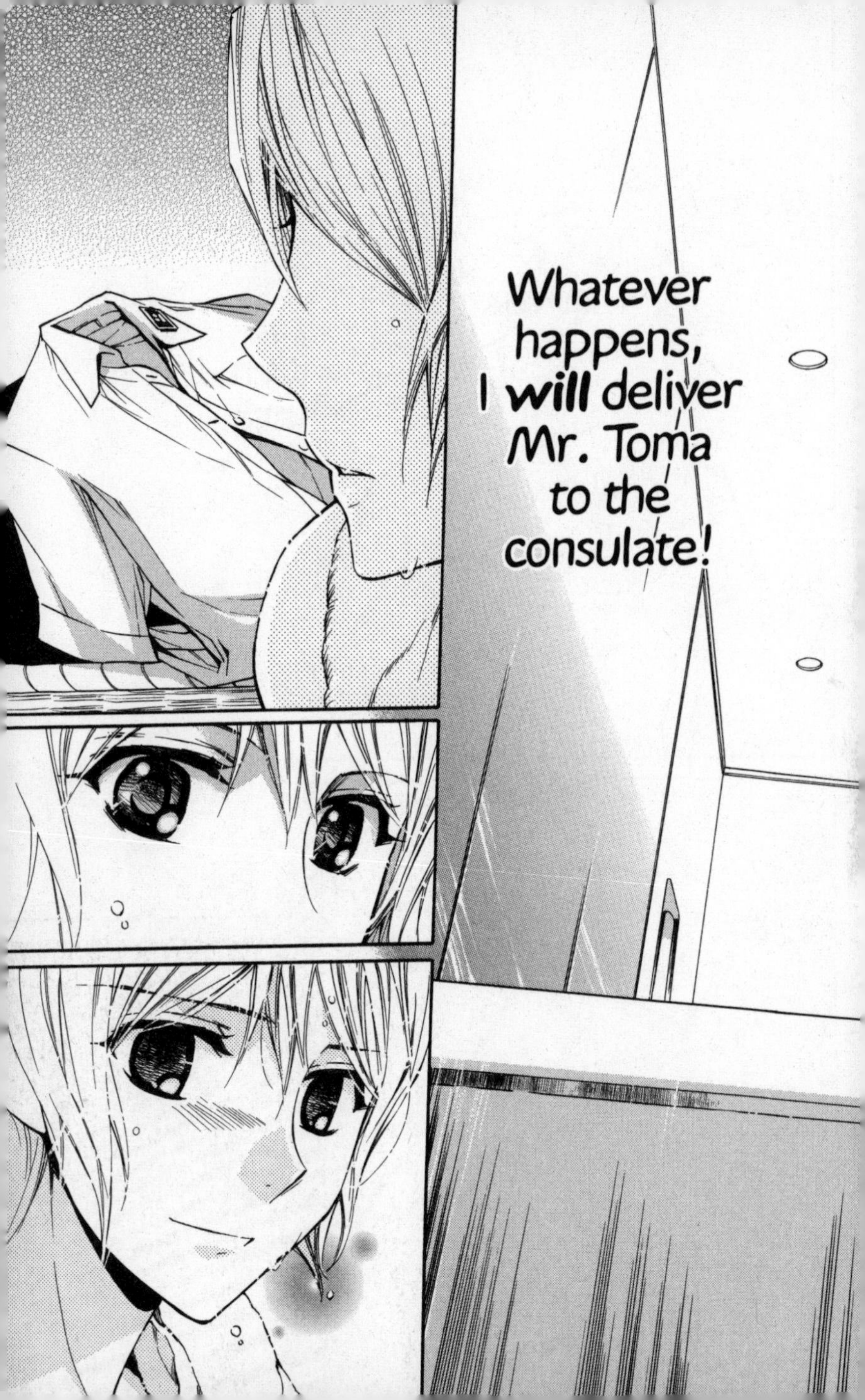
Whatever happens, I **will** deliver Mr. Toma to the consulate!

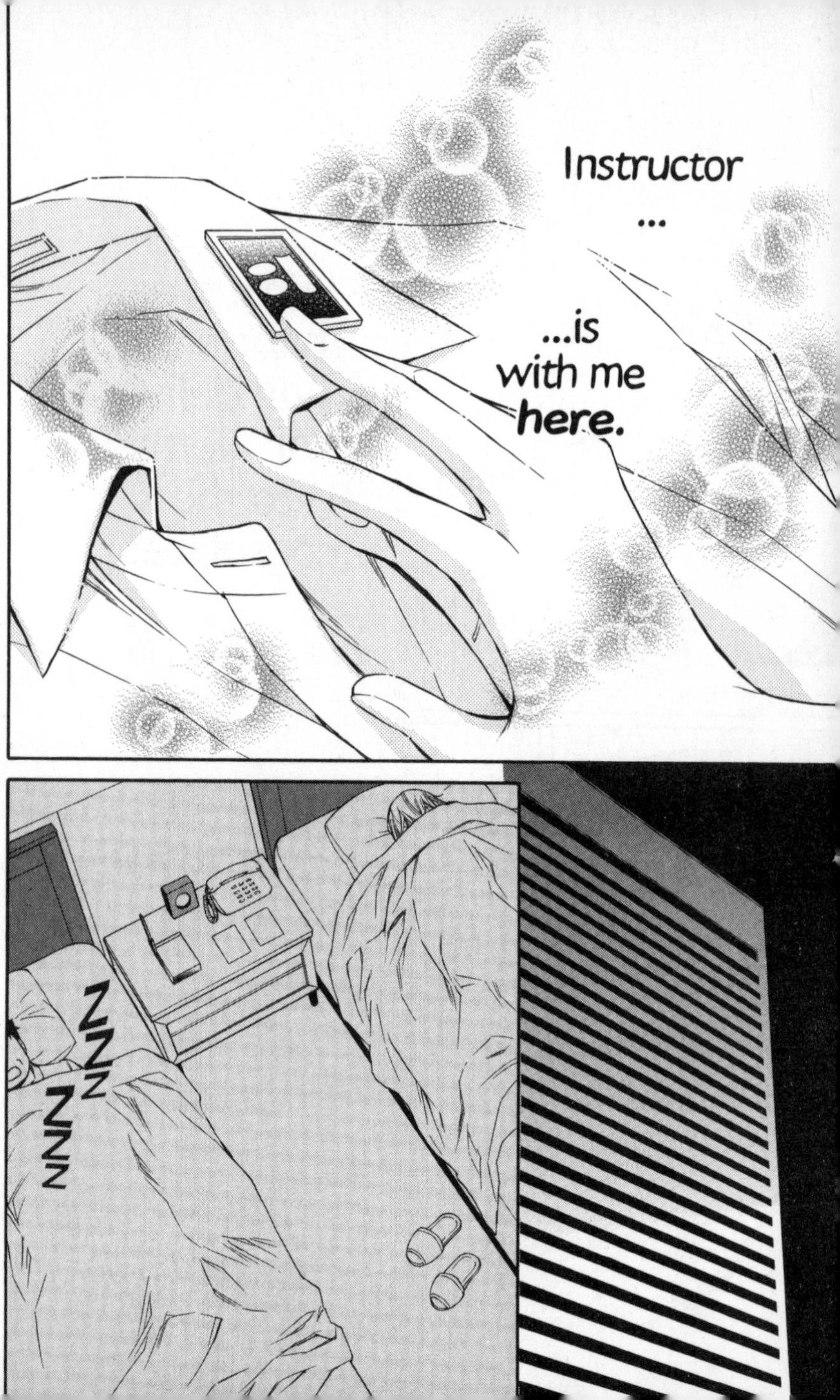
Instructor
...
...is
with me
here.
ZZZ
ZZZ

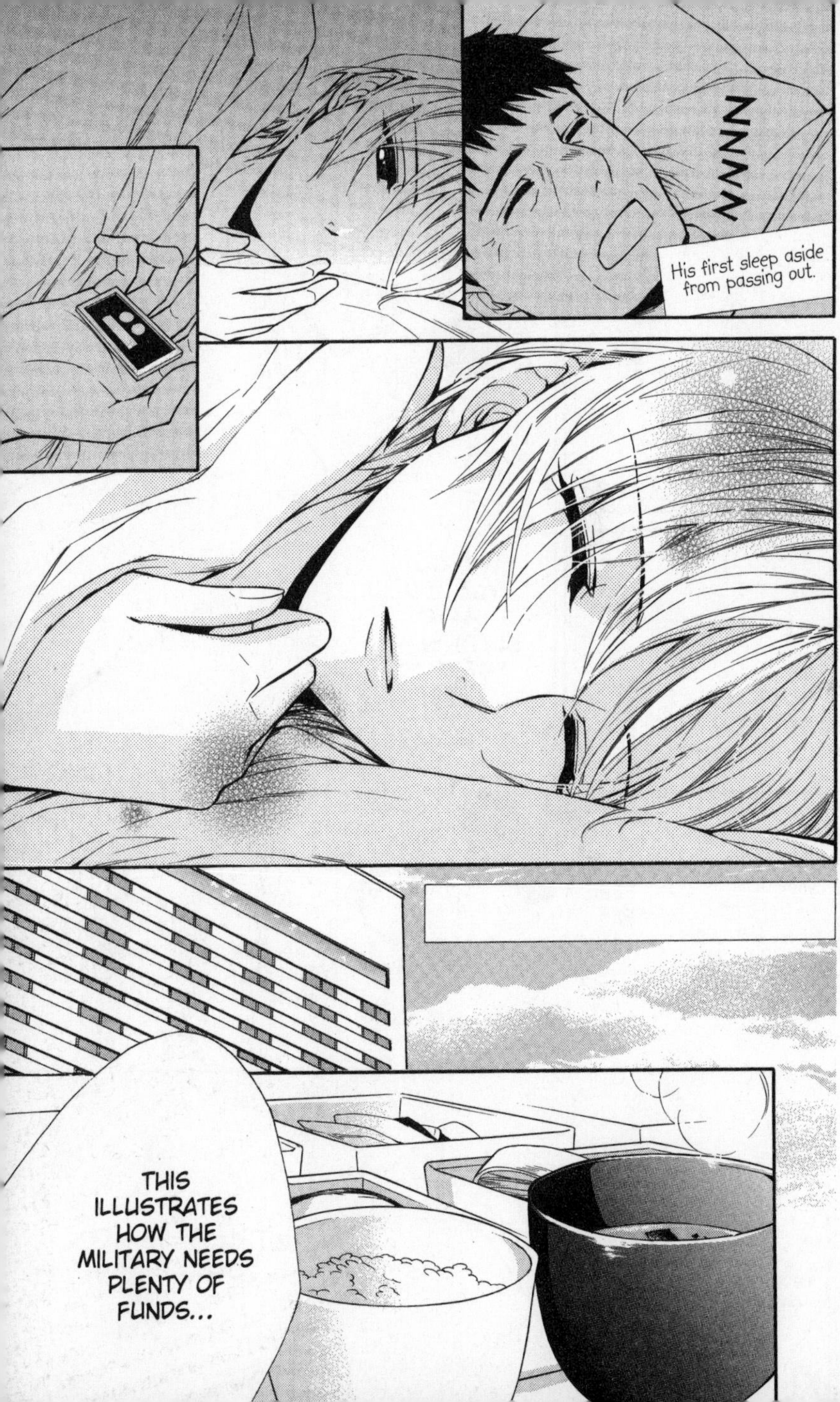
NNNN
His first sleep aside from passing out.
THIS ILLUSTRATES HOW THE MILITARY NEEDS PLENTY OF FUNDS...

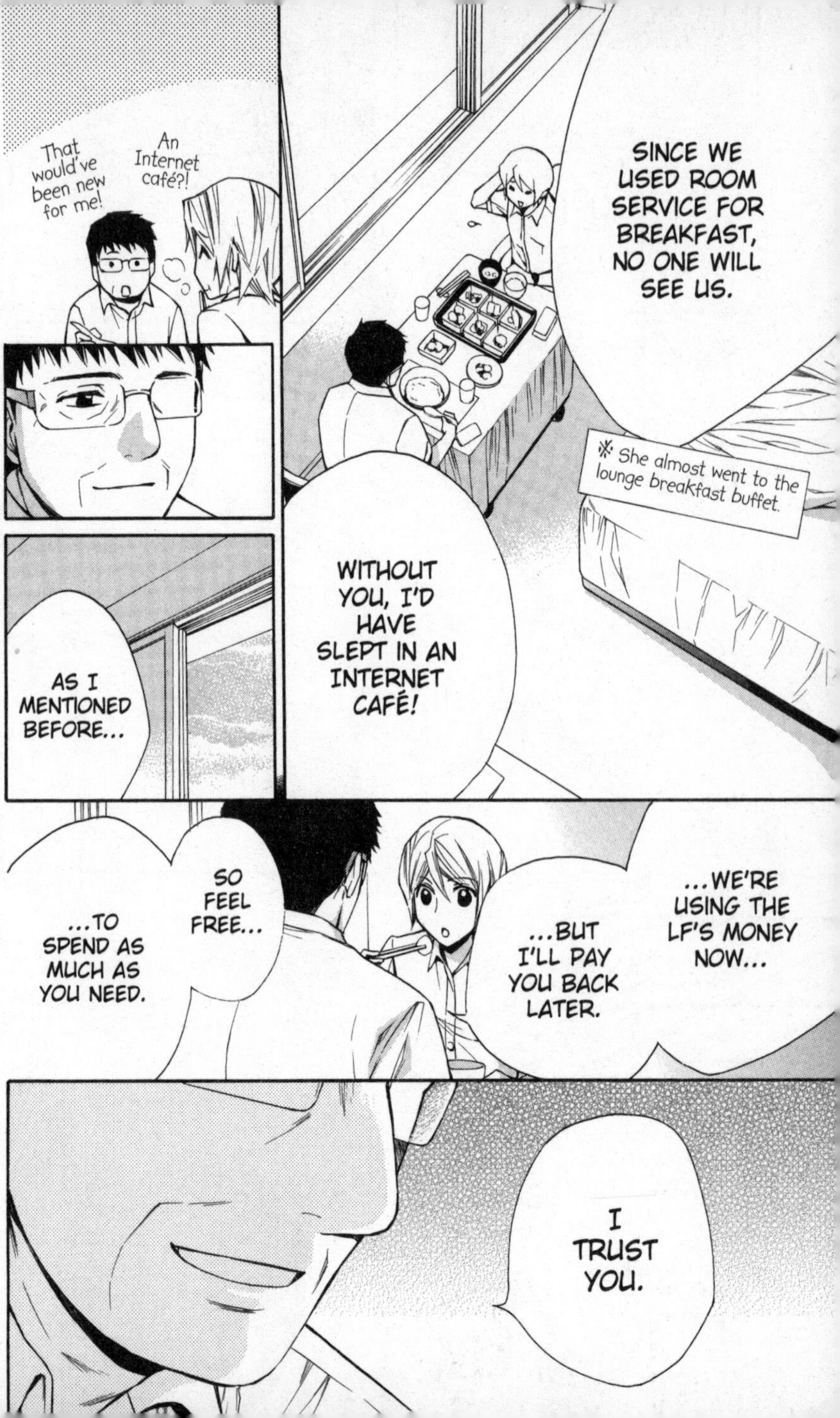
SINCE WE USED ROOM SERVICE FOR BREAKFAST, NO ONE WILL SEE US.
※ She almost went to the lounge breakfast buffet.
WITHOUT YOU, I'D HAVE SLEPT IN AN INTERNET CAFÉ!
An Internet café?!
That would've been new for me!
AS I MENTIONED BEFORE...
...WE'RE USING THE LF'S MONEY NOW...
...BUT I'LL PAY YOU BACK LATER.
SO FEEL FREE...
...TO SPEND AS MUCH AS YOU NEED.
I TRUST YOU.

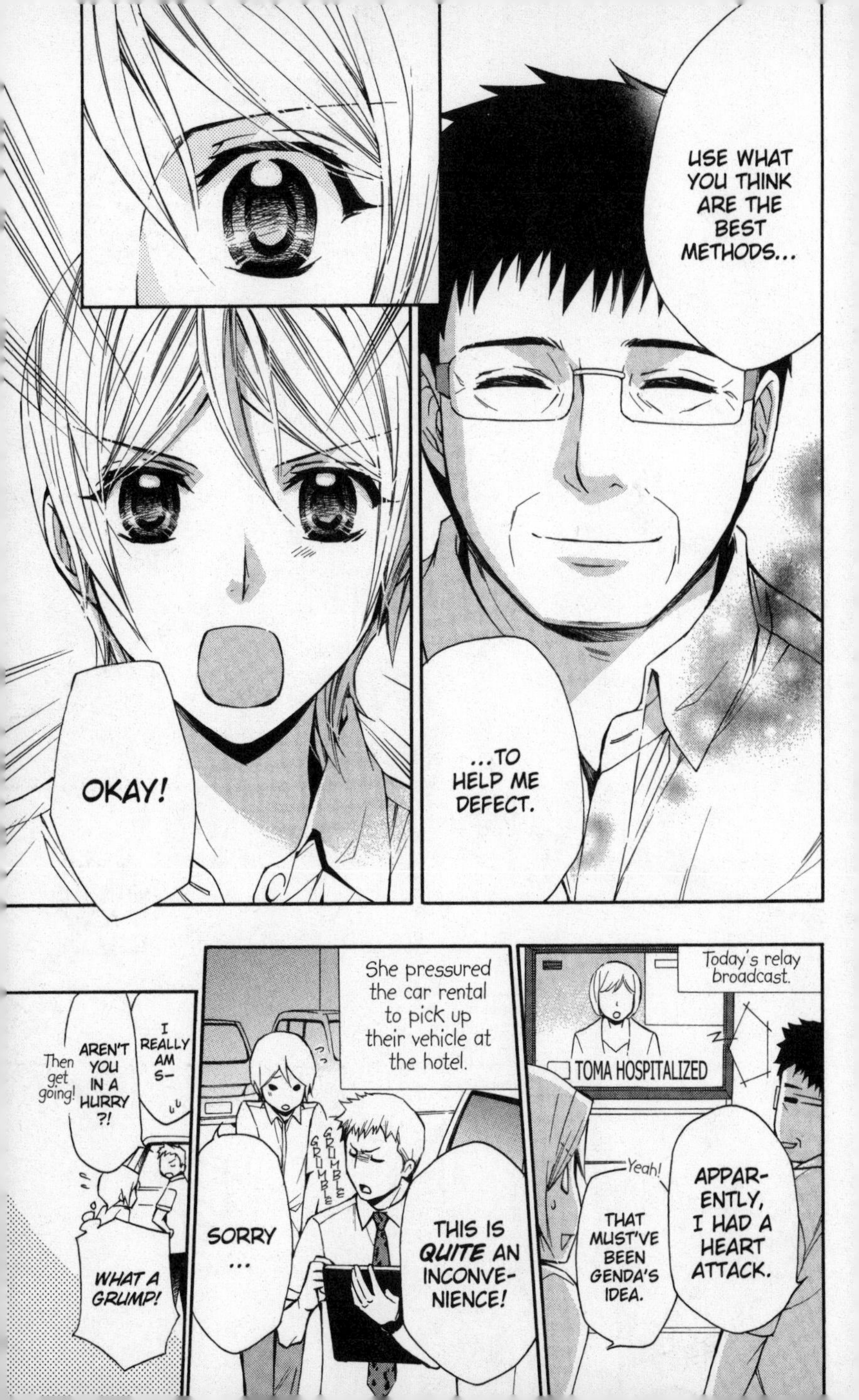
USE WHAT YOU THINK ARE THE BEST METHODS...
...TO HELP ME DEFECT.
OKAY!
Today's relay broadcast.
TOMA HOSPITALIZED
APPAR-ENTLY, I HAD A HEART ATTACK.
Yeah!
THAT MUST'VE BEEN GENDA'S IDEA.
She pressured the car rental to pick up their vehicle at the hotel.
GRUMBLE GRUMBLE
THIS IS QUITE AN INCONVE-NIENCE!
SORRY...
I REALLY AM S-
AREN'T YOU IN A HURRY?!
Then get going!
WHAT A GRUMP!

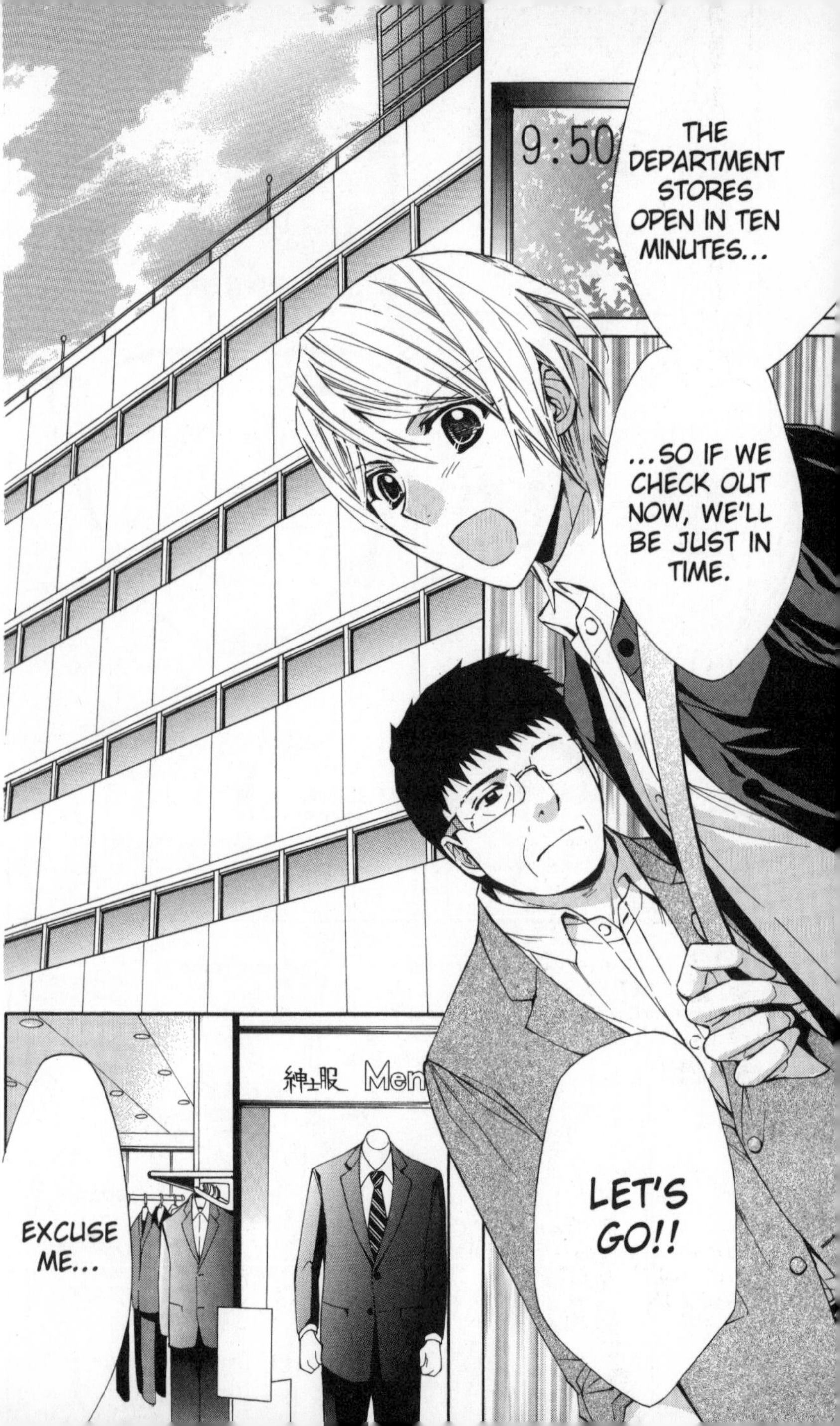
9:50
THE DEPARTMENT STORES OPEN IN TEN MINUTES...
...SO IF WE CHECK OUT NOW, WE'LL BE JUST IN TIME.
LET'S GO!!
紳士服 Men
EXCUSE ME...

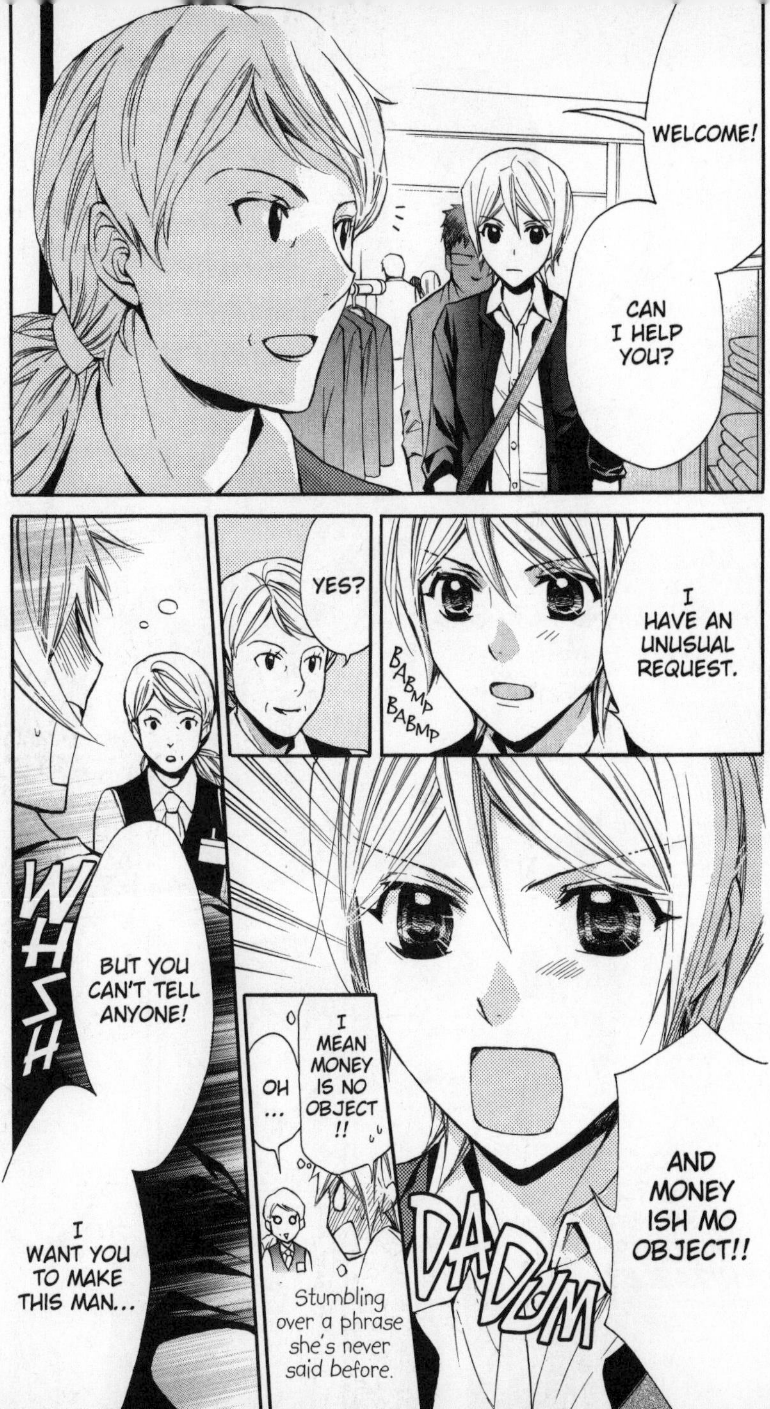
WELCOME!
CAN I HELP YOU?
I HAVE AN UNUSUAL REQUEST.
BABMP BABMP
YES?
AND MONEY ISH MO OBJECT!!
DADUM
I MEAN MONEY IS NO OBJECT!!
OH...
Stumbling over a phrase she's never said before.
WHSH
BUT YOU CAN'T TELL ANYONE!
I WANT YOU TO MAKE THIS MAN...

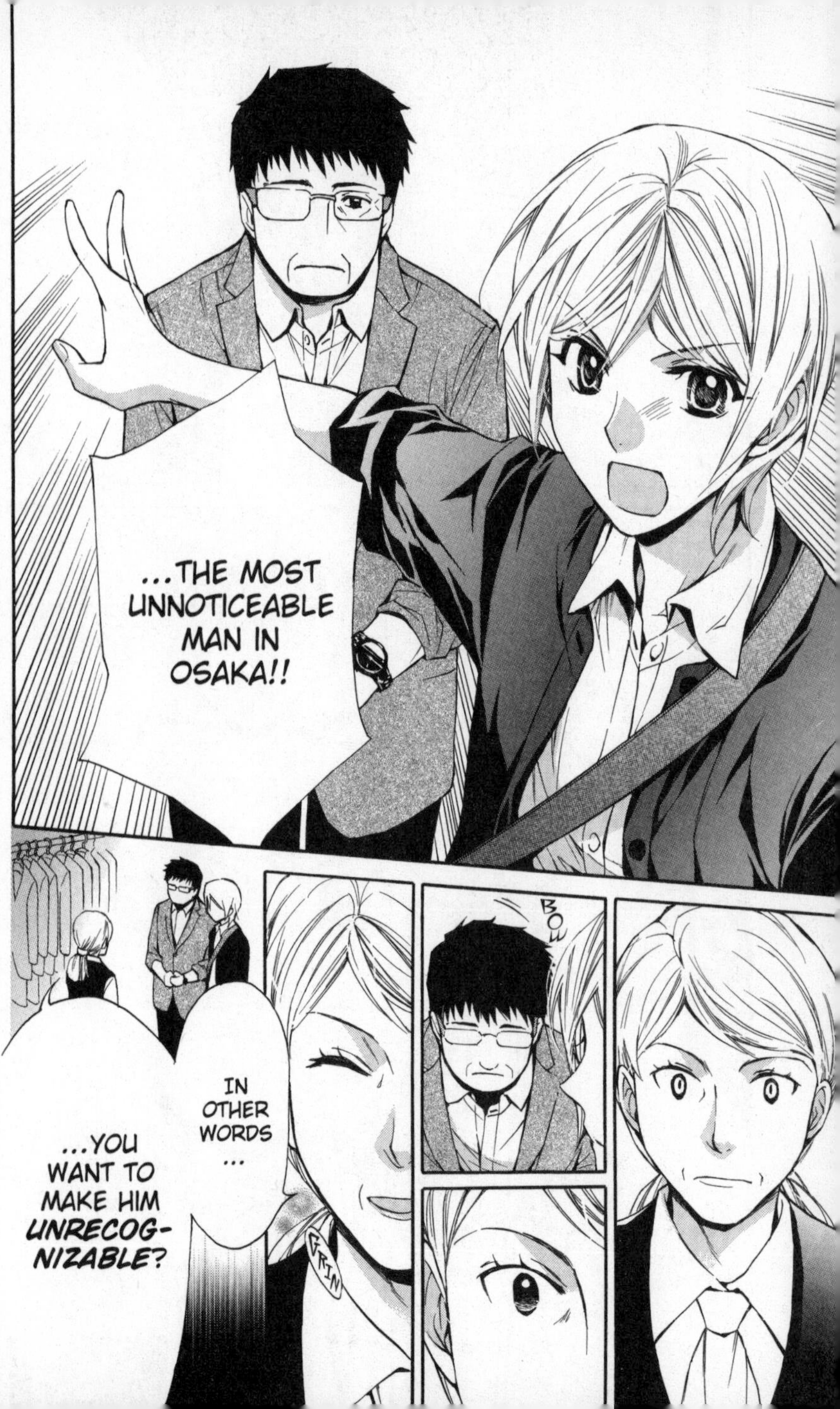
...THE MOST UNNOTICEABLE MAN IN OSAKA!!
BOW
IN OTHER WORDS...
...YOU WANT TO MAKE HIM UNRECOG-NIZABLE?
GRIN

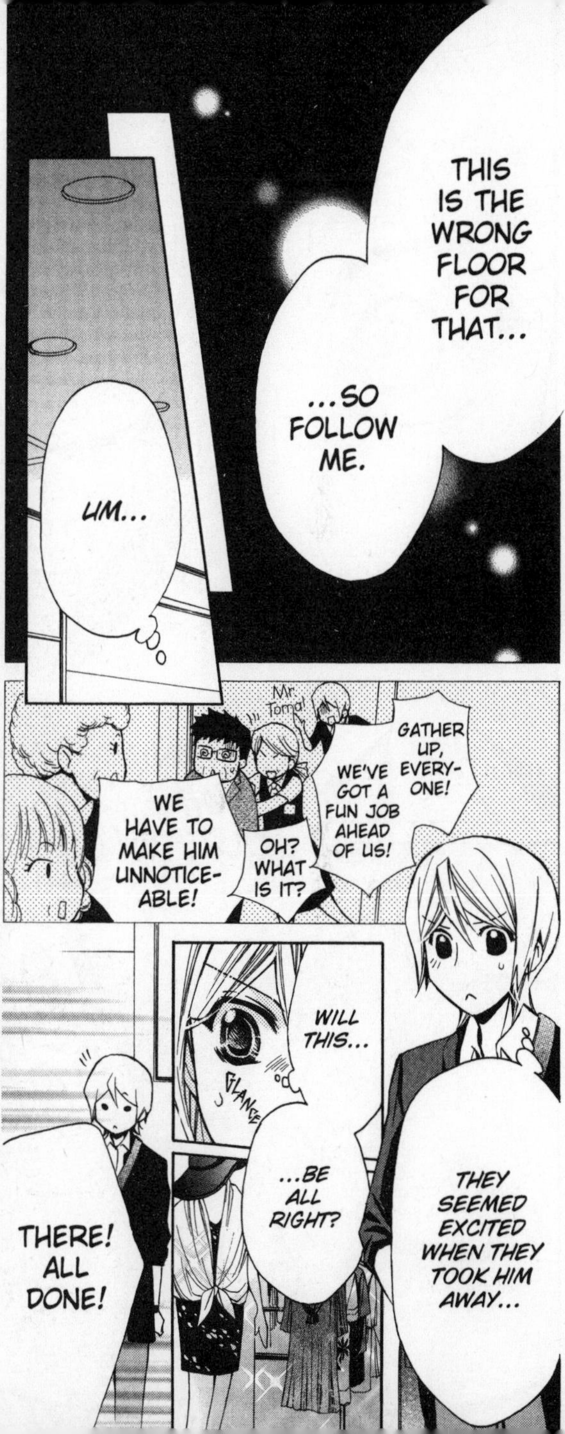
THIS IS THE WRONG FLOOR FOR THAT...
...SO FOLLOW ME.
UM...
Mr. Toma!
GATHER UP, EVERYONE!
WE'VE GOT A FUN JOB AHEAD OF US!
OH? WHAT IS IT?
WE HAVE TO MAKE HIM UNNOTICE-ABLE!
THEY SEEMED EXCITED WHEN THEY TOOK HIM AWAY...
WILL THIS...
GLANCE
...BE ALL RIGHT?
THERE! ALL DONE!

2

This manga began serialization in the November 2007 issue of *LaLa*, which went on sale in September. Back then, the novel called *Revolution* hadn't been published yet. Seven years and three months later, I've finally reached the end of it!

To be honest, I didn't think I would be able to continue to the end because I don't have the compositional ability, drawing skill or a big enough name to turn such wonderful novels into manga. I'm really grateful for the opportunity to keep going so long!

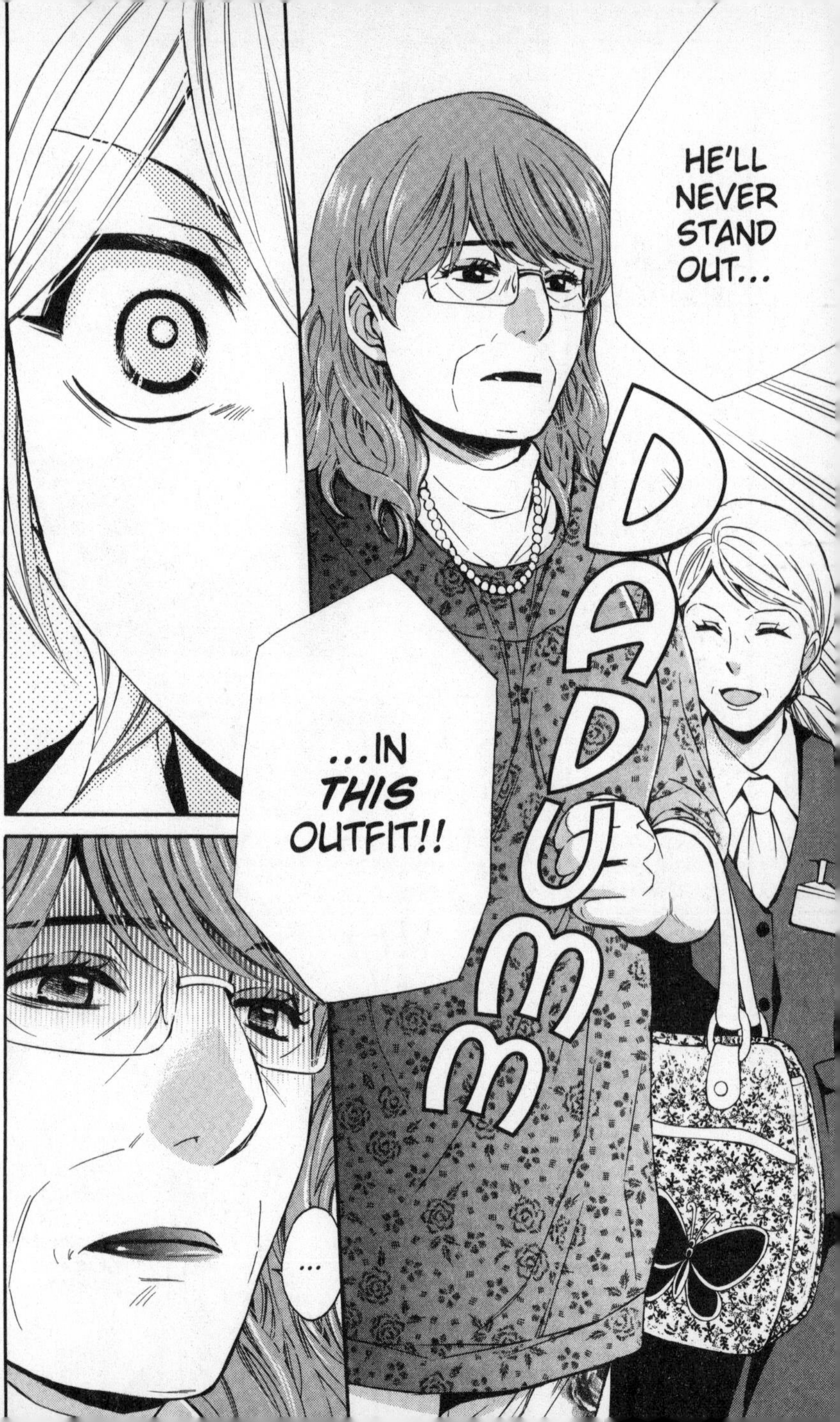
HE'LL NEVER STAND OUT...
...IN THIS OUTFIT!!
DADUMMM
...

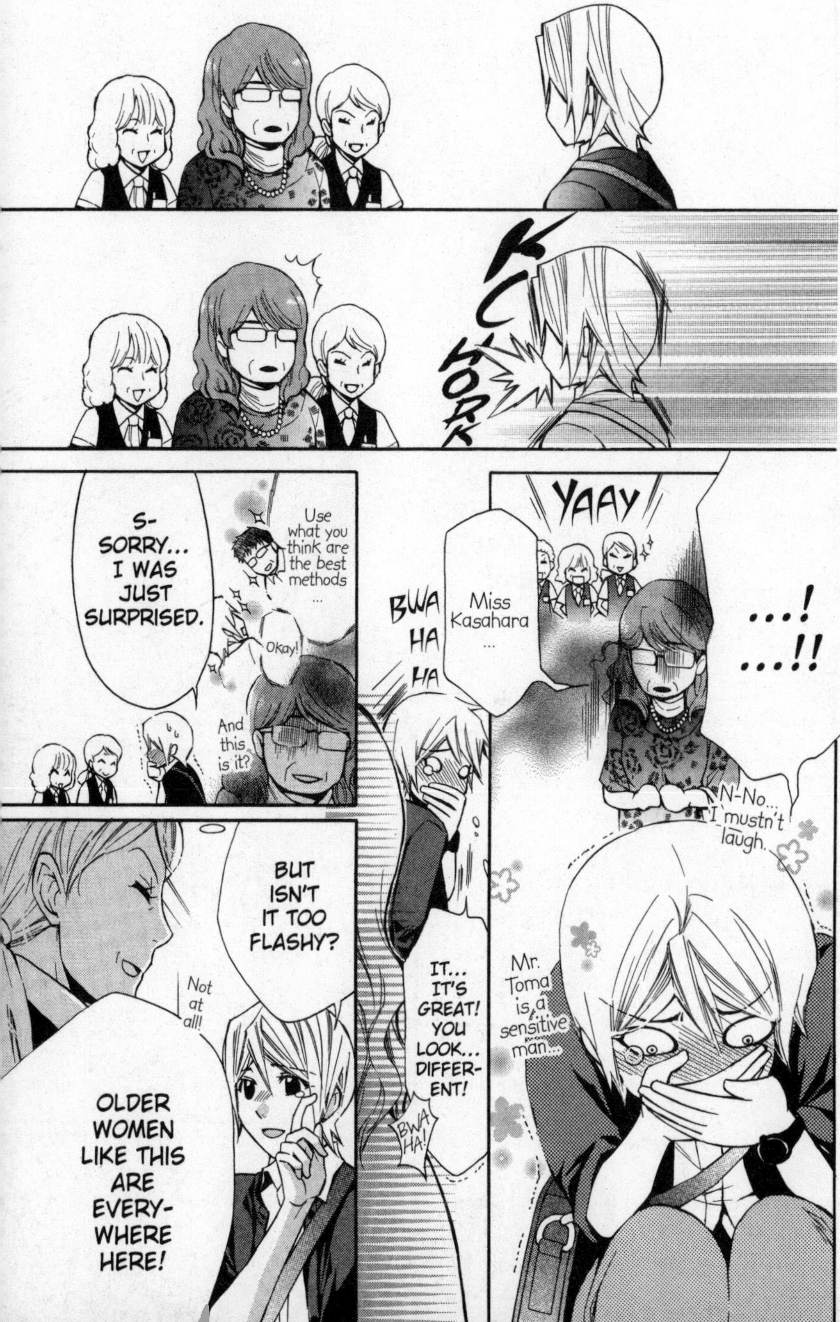
KCHORK
YAAY
...!
...!!
N-No... I mustn't laugh.
Mr. Toma is a sensitive man...
Miss Kasahara ...
BWA HA HA
IT... IT'S GREAT! YOU LOOK... DIFFERENT!
BWA HA!
S- SORRY... I WAS JUST SURPRISED.
Use what you think are the best methods ...
Okay!
And this is it?
BUT ISN'T IT TOO FLASHY?
Not at all!
OLDER WOMEN LIKE THIS ARE EVERYWHERE HERE!

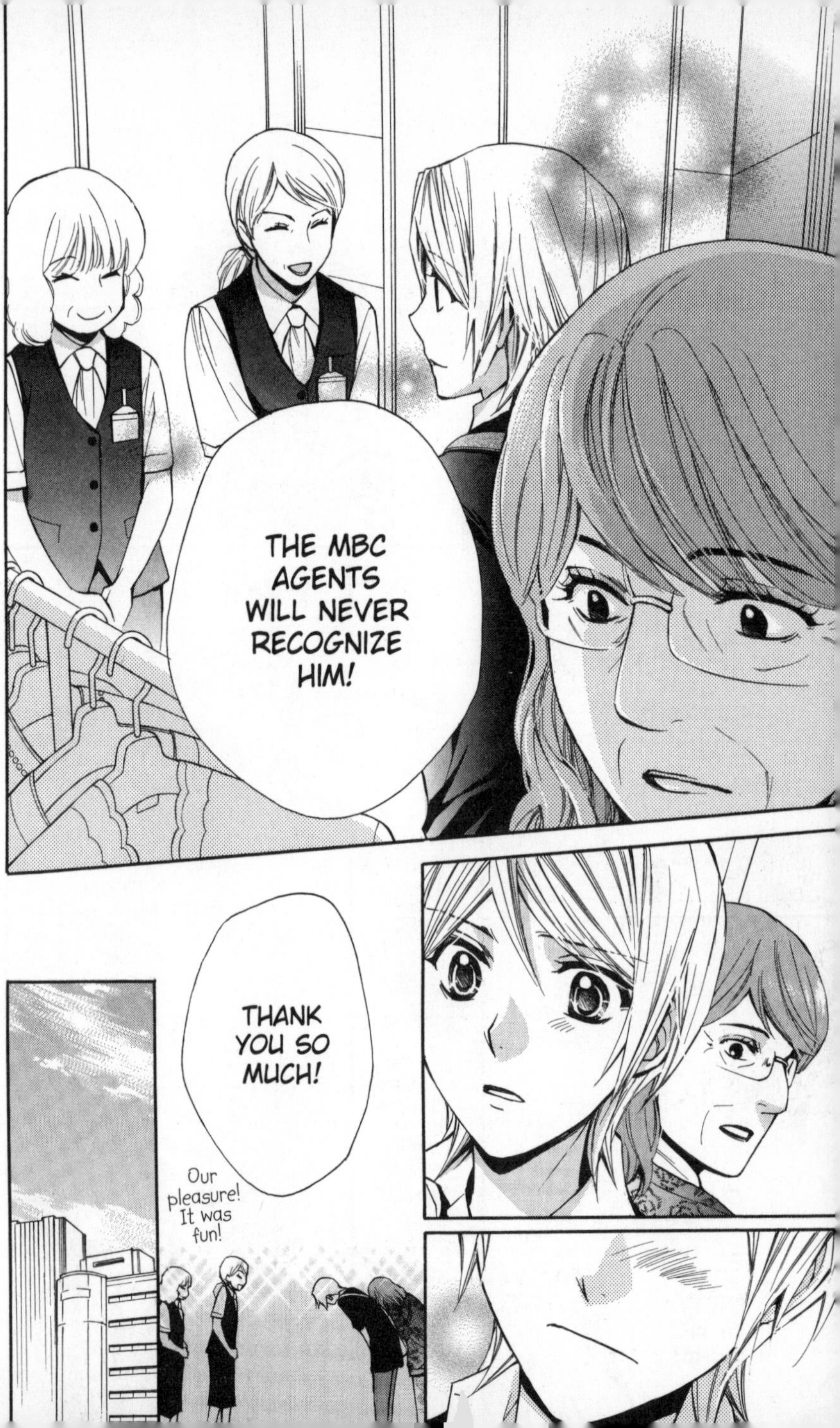
THE MBC AGENTS WILL NEVER RECOGNIZE HIM!
THANK YOU SO MUCH!
Our pleasure! It was fun!

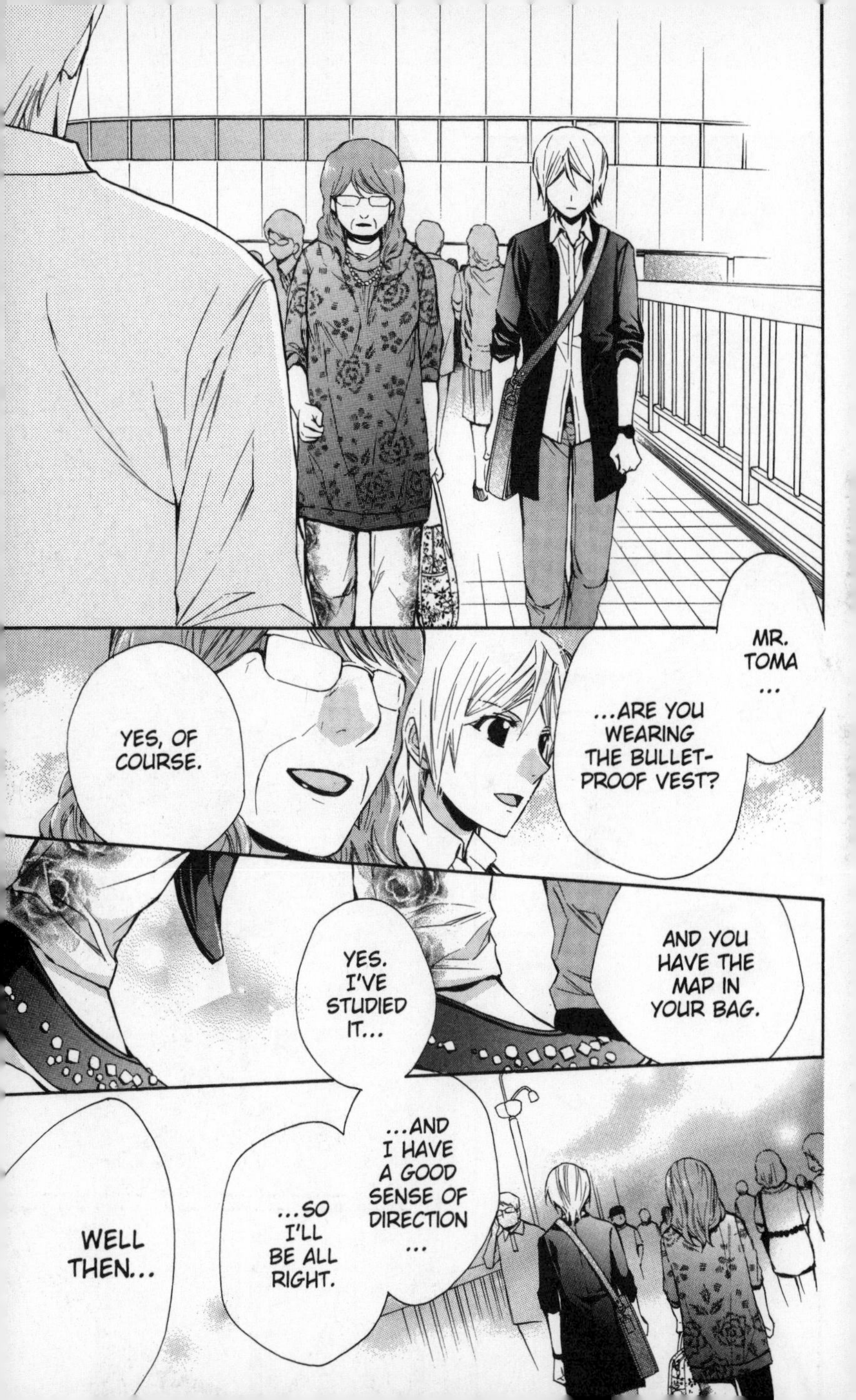
MR. TOMA...
...ARE YOU WEARING THE BULLET-PROOF VEST?
YES, OF COURSE.
AND YOU HAVE THE MAP IN YOUR BAG.
YES. I'VE STUDIED IT...
...AND I HAVE A GOOD SENSE OF DIRECTION...
...SO I'LL BE ALL RIGHT.
WELL THEN...

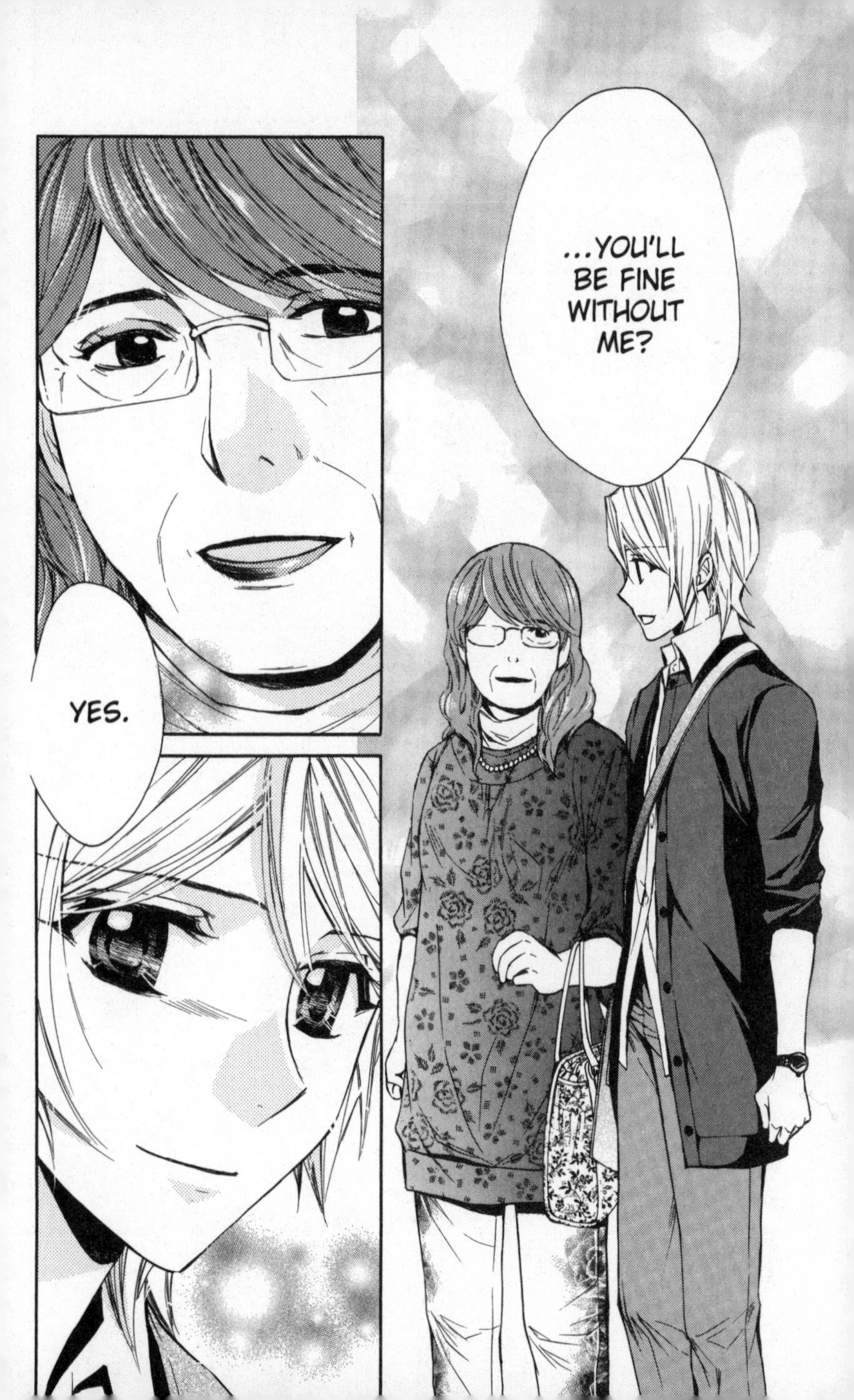
...YOU'LL BE FINE WITHOUT ME?
YES.

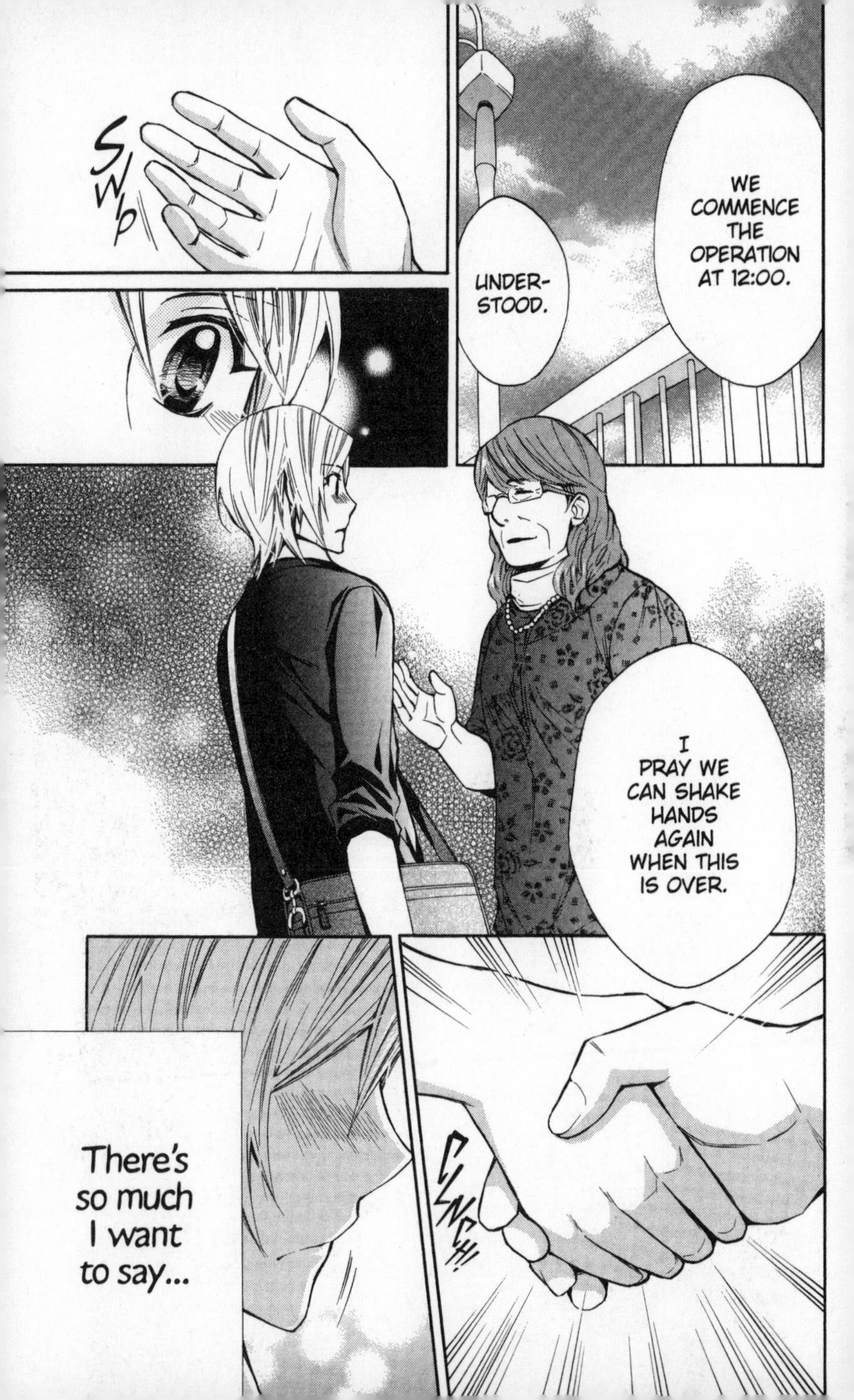
WE COMMENCE THE OPERATION AT 12:00.
UNDER-STOOD.
SWIP
I PRAY WE CAN SHAKE HANDS AGAIN WHEN THIS IS OVER.
CLINCH!!
There's so much I want to say...

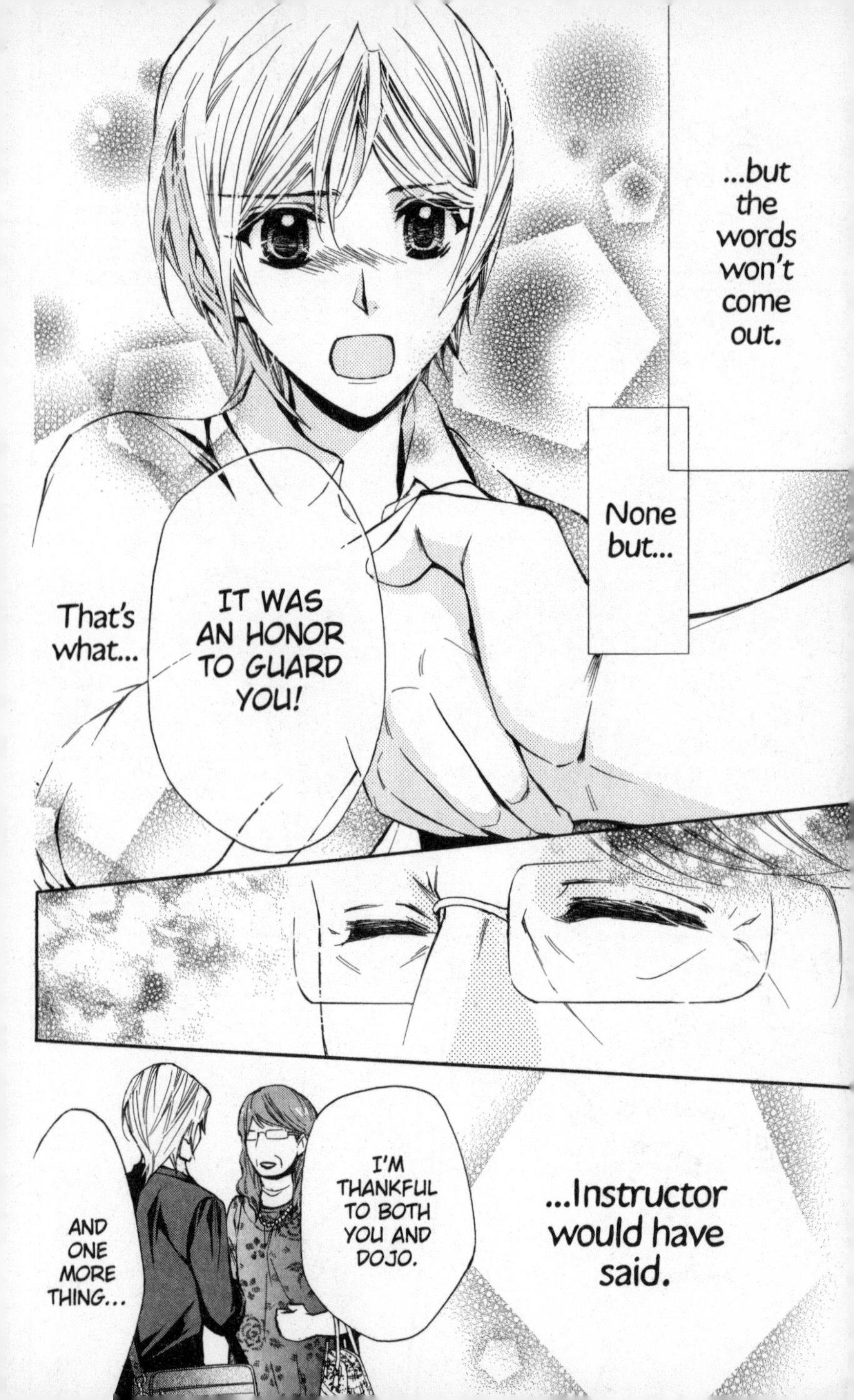
...but the words won't come out.
None but...
IT WAS AN HONOR TO GUARD YOU!
That's what...
...Instructor would have said.
I'M THANKFUL TO BOTH YOU AND DOJO.
AND ONE MORE THING...

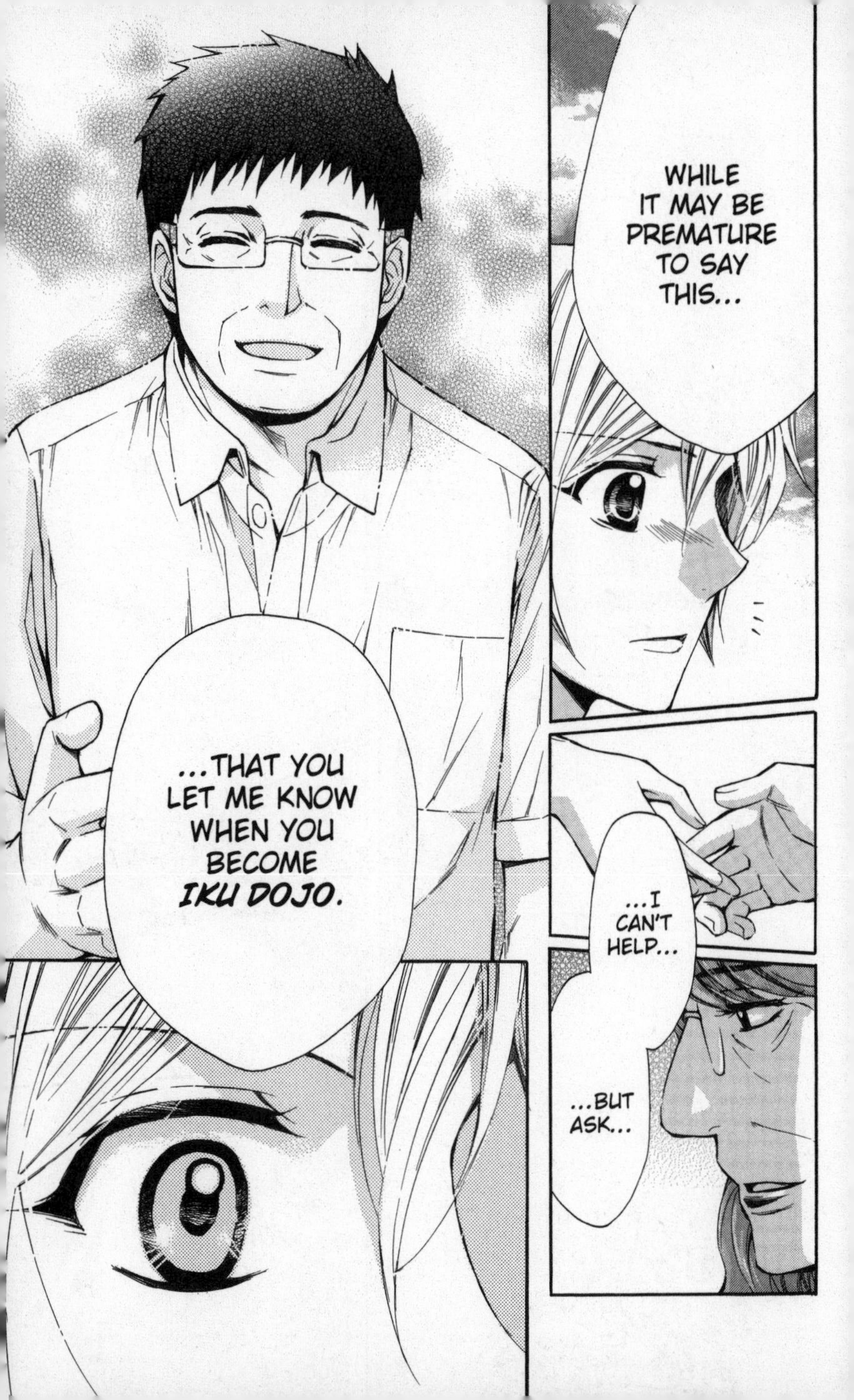
WHILE IT MAY BE PREMATURE TO SAY THIS...
...I CAN'T HELP...
...BUT ASK...
...THAT YOU LET ME KNOW WHEN YOU BECOME *IKU DOJO*.

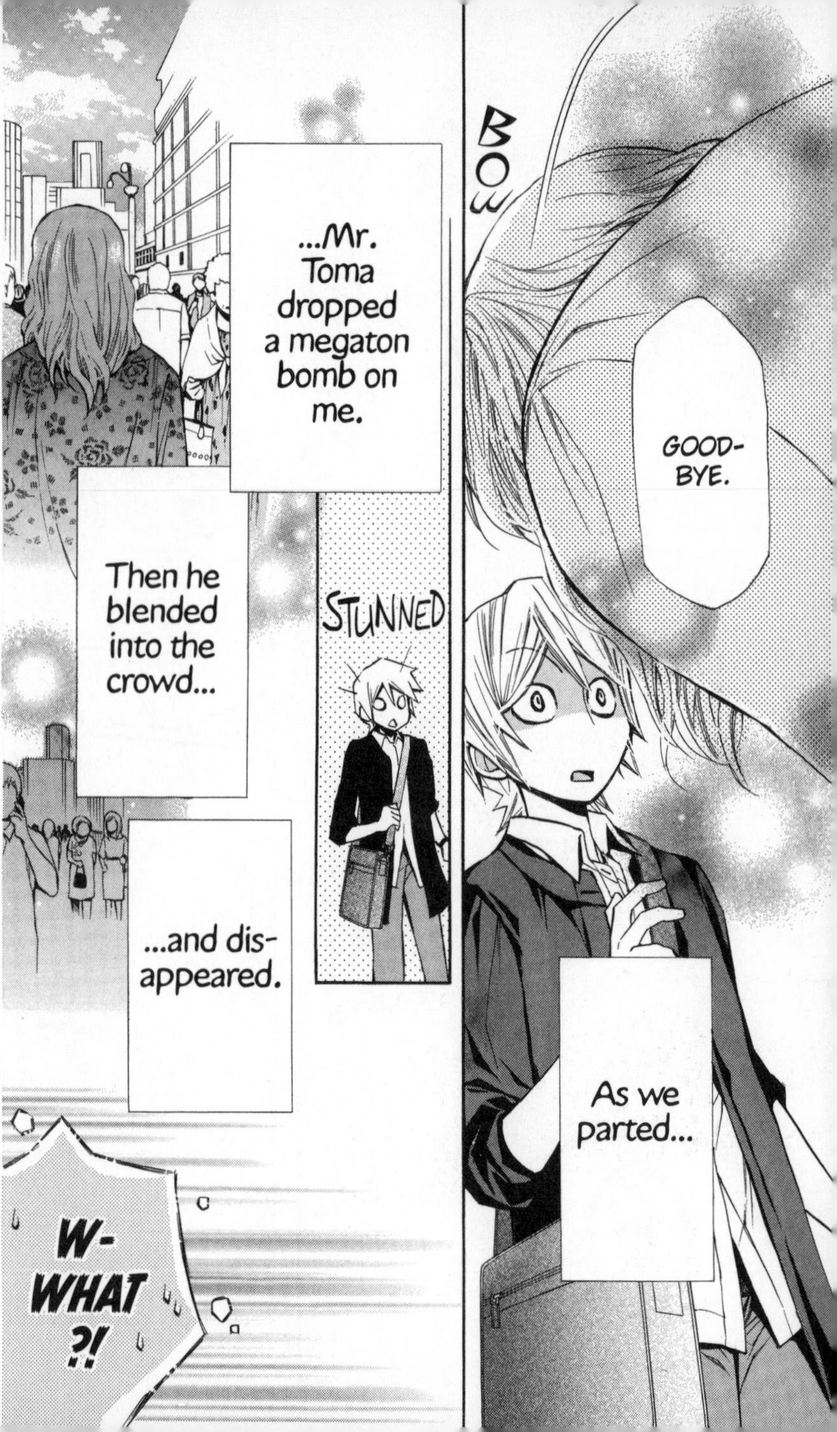
GOOD-BYE.
BOW
As we parted...
...Mr. Toma dropped a megaton bomb on me.
STUNNED
Then he blended into the crowd...
...and dis-appeared.
W-WHAT?!

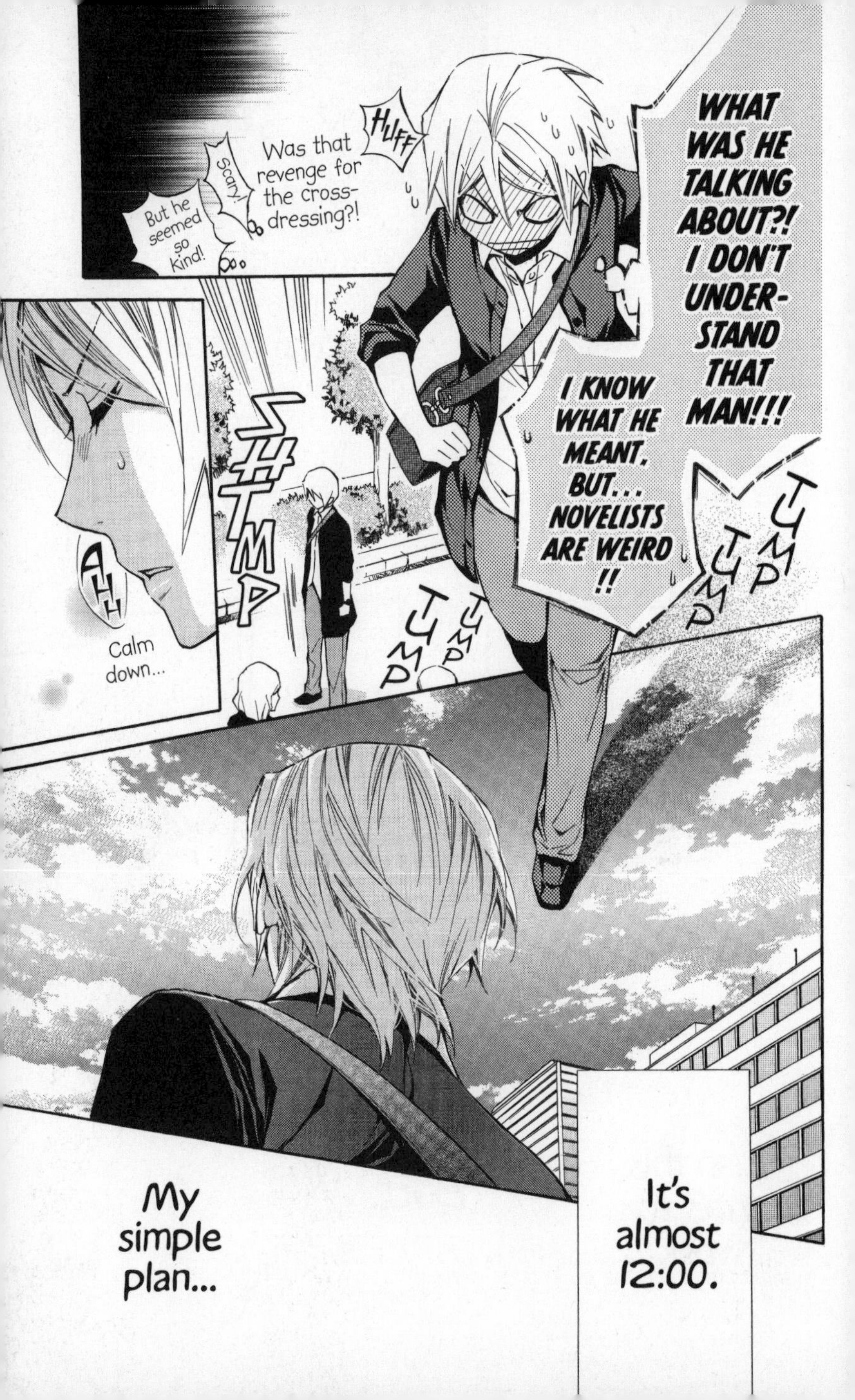
WHAT WAS HE TALKING ABOUT?! I DON'T UNDER-STAND THAT MAN!!!
I KNOW WHAT HE MEANT, BUT... NOVELISTS ARE WEIRD!!
TUMP TUMP TUMP
HUFF
Was that revenge for the cross-dressing?!
Scary!
But he seemed so kind!
TUMP TUMP
SHTMP
AHH
Calm down...
It's almost 12:00.
My simple plan...

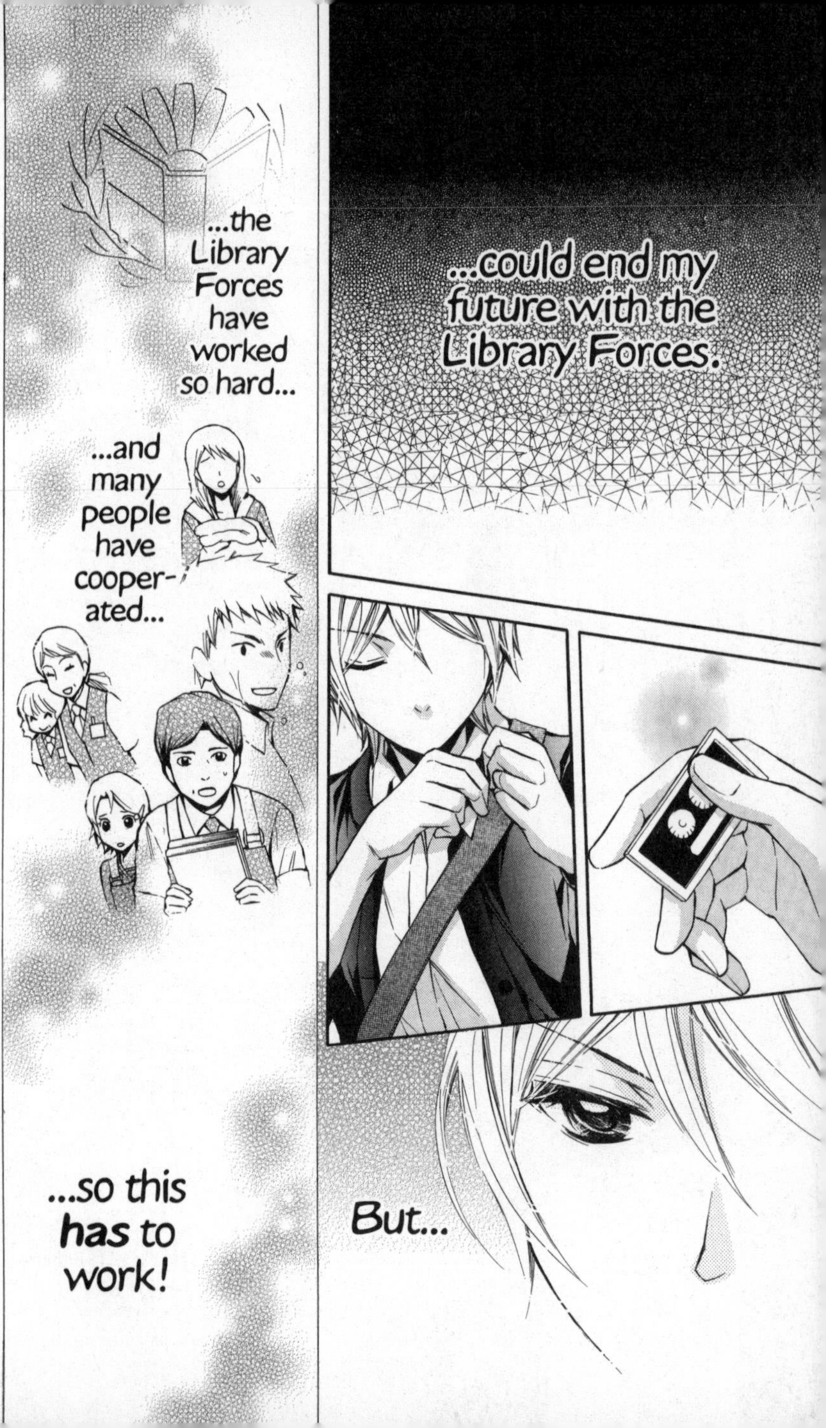
...could end my future with the Library Forces.
But...
...the Library Forces have worked so hard...
...and many people have cooperated...
...so this has to work!

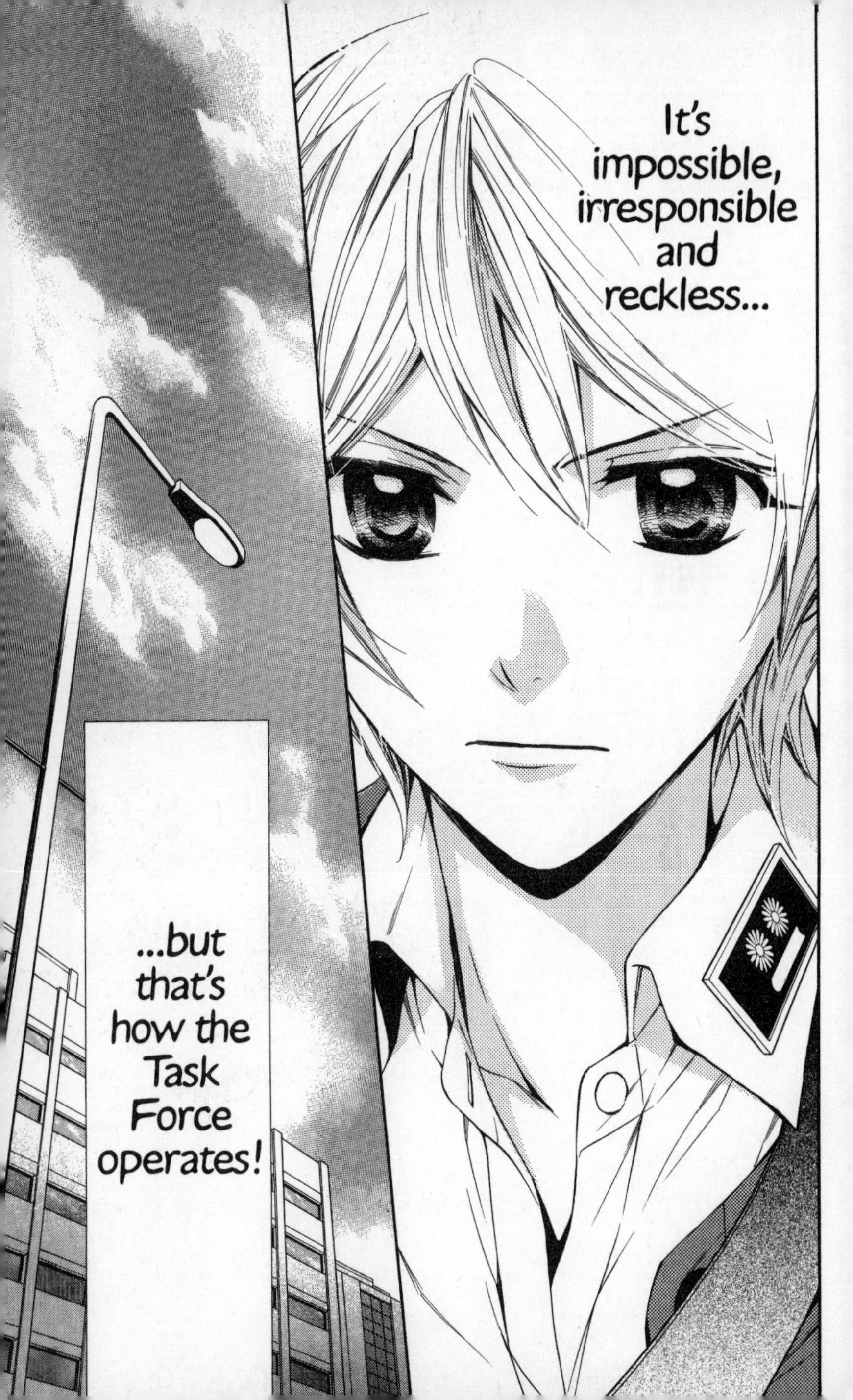
It's impossible, irresponsible and reckless...
...but that's how the Task Force operates!

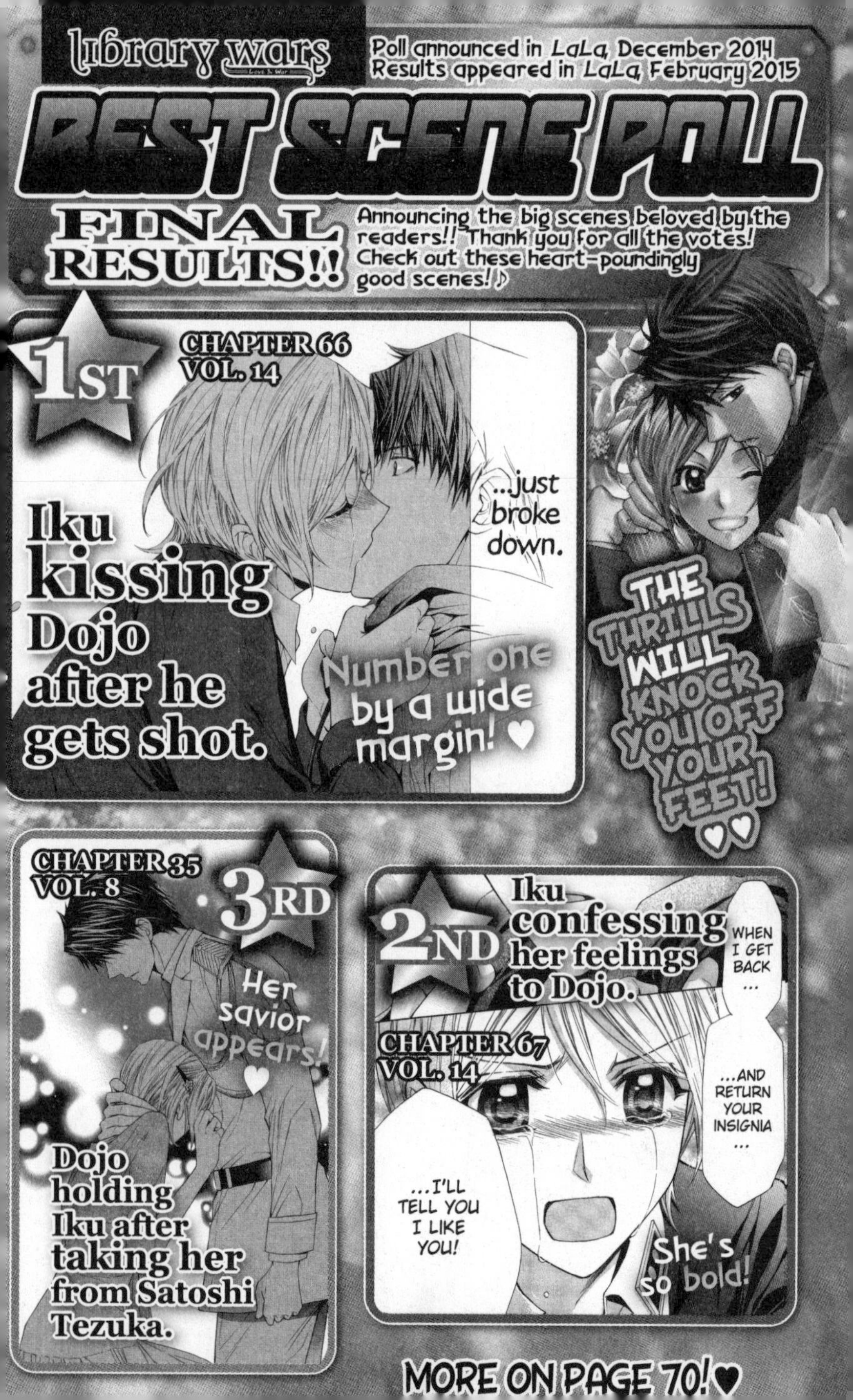
library wars
Love & War
Poll announced in LaLa, December 2014
Results appeared in LaLa, February 2015
BEST SCENE POLL
FINAL RESULTS!!
Announcing the big scenes beloved by the readers!! Thank you for all the votes! Check out these heart-poundingly good scenes! ♪
1ST
CHAPTER 66
VOL. 14
Iku kissing Dojo after he gets shot.
...just broke down.
Number one by a wide margin! ♥
THE THRILLS WILL KNOCK YOU OFF YOUR FEET! ♥♥
2ND
Iku confessing her feelings to Dojo.
CHAPTER 67
VOL. 14
WHEN I GET BACK...
...AND RETURN YOUR INSIGNIA...
...I'LL TELL YOU I LIKE YOU!
She's so bold!
3RD
CHAPTER 35
VOL. 8
Her savior appears! ♥
Dojo holding Iku after taking her from Satoshi Tezuka.
MORE ON PAGE 70! ♥

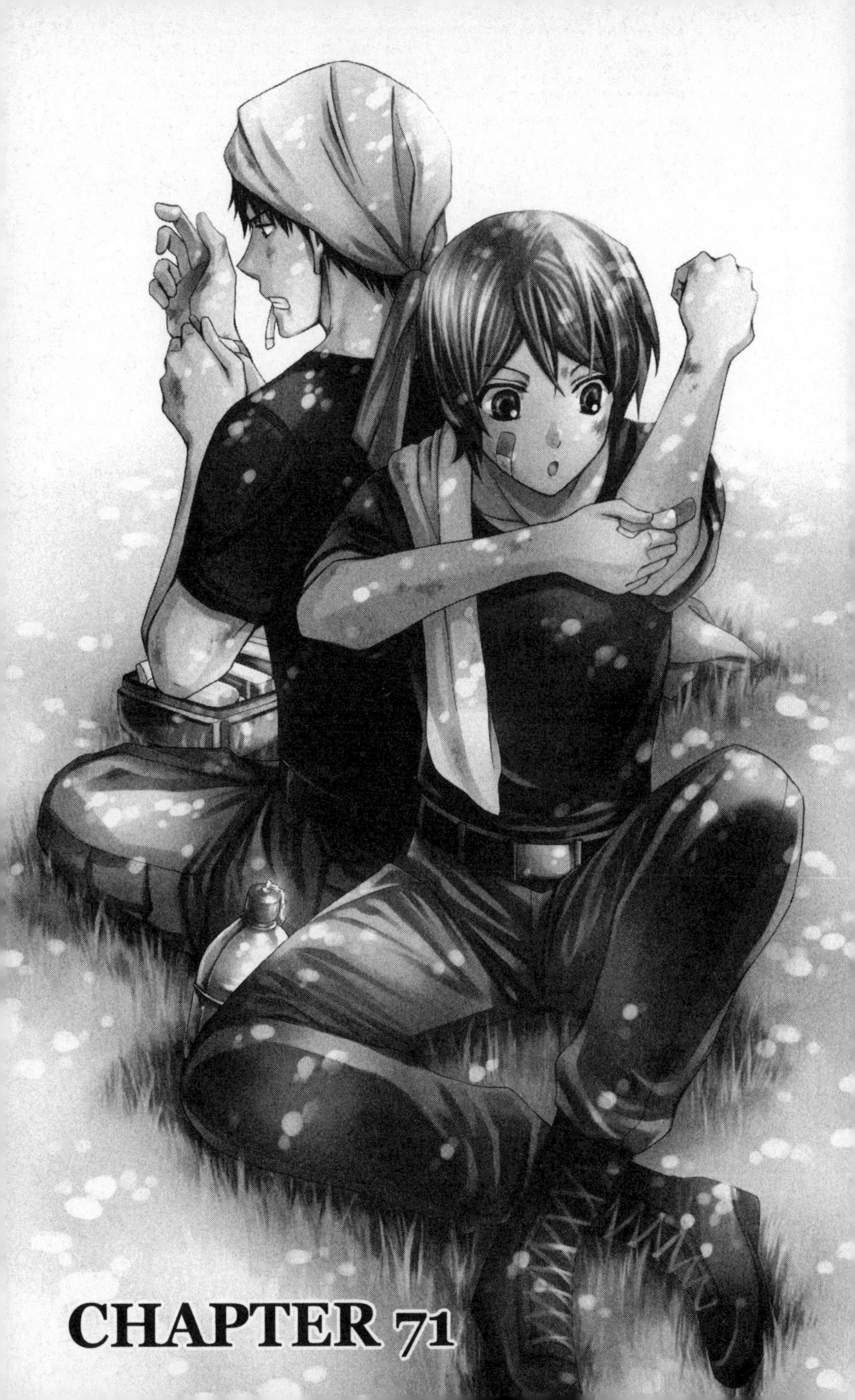

CHAPTER 71

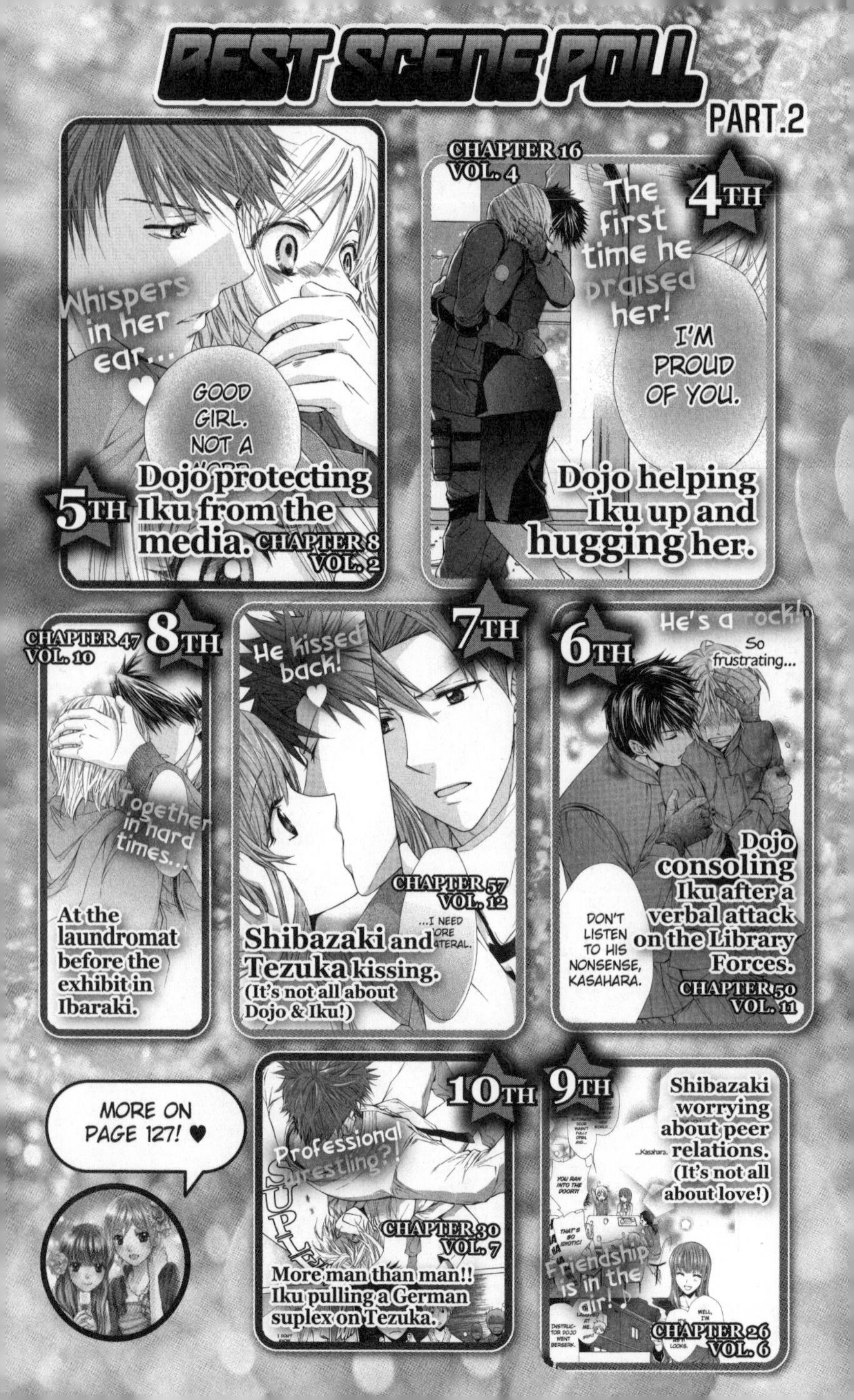
BEST SCENE POLL
PART.2
CHAPTER 16
VOL. 4
4TH
The first time he praised her!
I'M PROUD OF YOU.
Dojo helping Iku up and hugging her.
Whispers in her ear...
GOOD GIRL. NOT A
5TH
Dojo protecting Iku from the media.
CHAPTER 8
VOL. 2
6TH
He's a rock!
So frustrating...
Dojo consoling Iku after a verbal attack on the Library Forces.
DON'T LISTEN TO HIS NONSENSE, KASAHARA.
CHAPTER 50
VOL. 11
7TH
He kissed back!
CHAPTER 57
VOL. 12
Shibazaki and Tezuka kissing.
(It's not all about Dojo & Iku!)
CHAPTER 47
VOL. 10
8TH
Together in hard times...
At the laundromat before the exhibit in Ibaraki.
9TH
Shibazaki worrying about peer relations.
(It's not all about love!)
...Kasahara.
YOU RAN INTO THE DOOR!?
THAT'S SO IDIOTIC!
Friendship is in the air!
INSTRUCTOR DOJO WENT BERSERK.
CHAPTER 26
VOL. 6
10TH
Professional wrestling?!
SUPLEX
CHAPTER 30
VOL. 7
More man than man!! Iku pulling a German suplex on Tezuka.
MORE ON PAGE 127! ♥

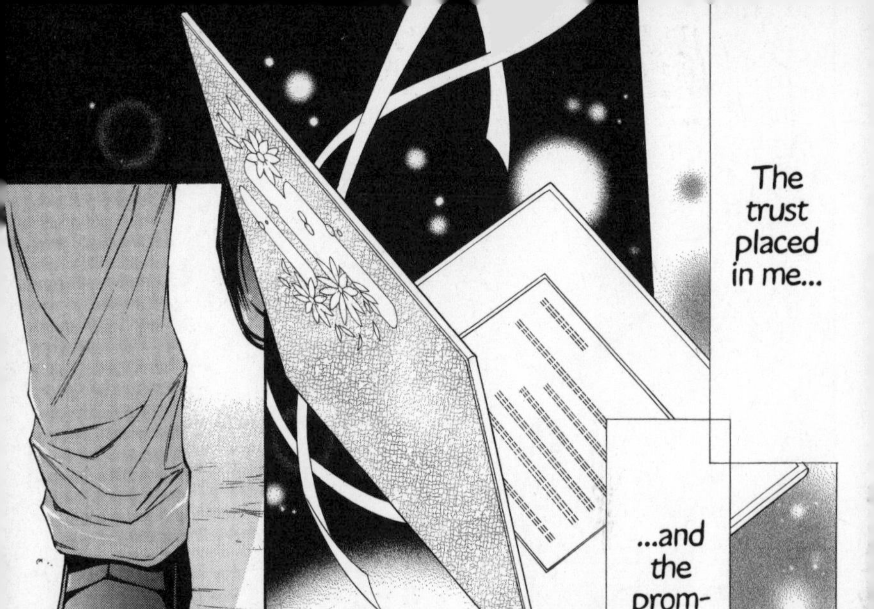
The trust placed in me...
...and the prom-ises I've made...
They all culminate in this moment.
TUMP
TUMP

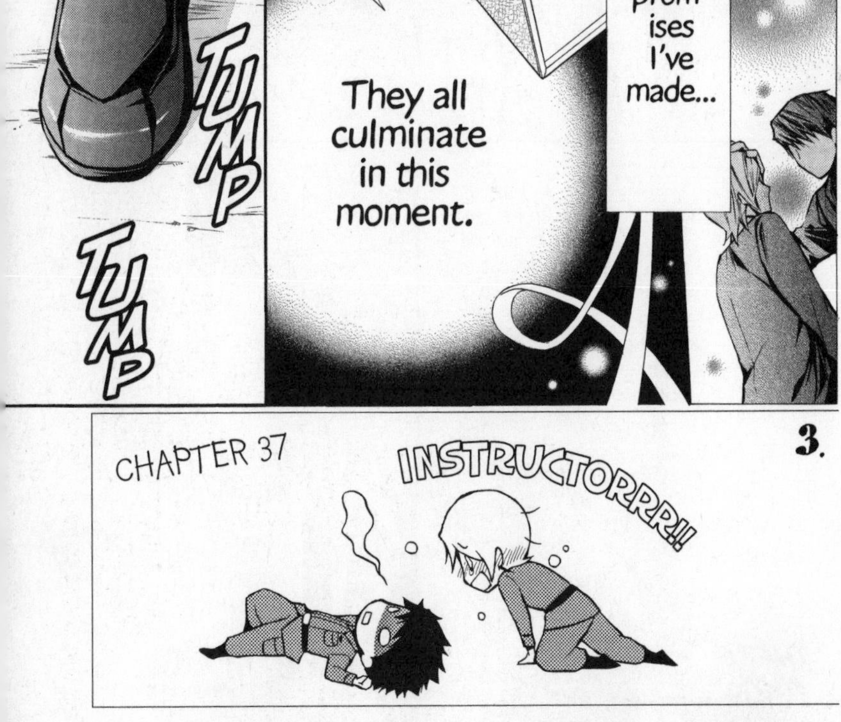
3.
CHAPTER 37
INSTRUCTORRRR!!

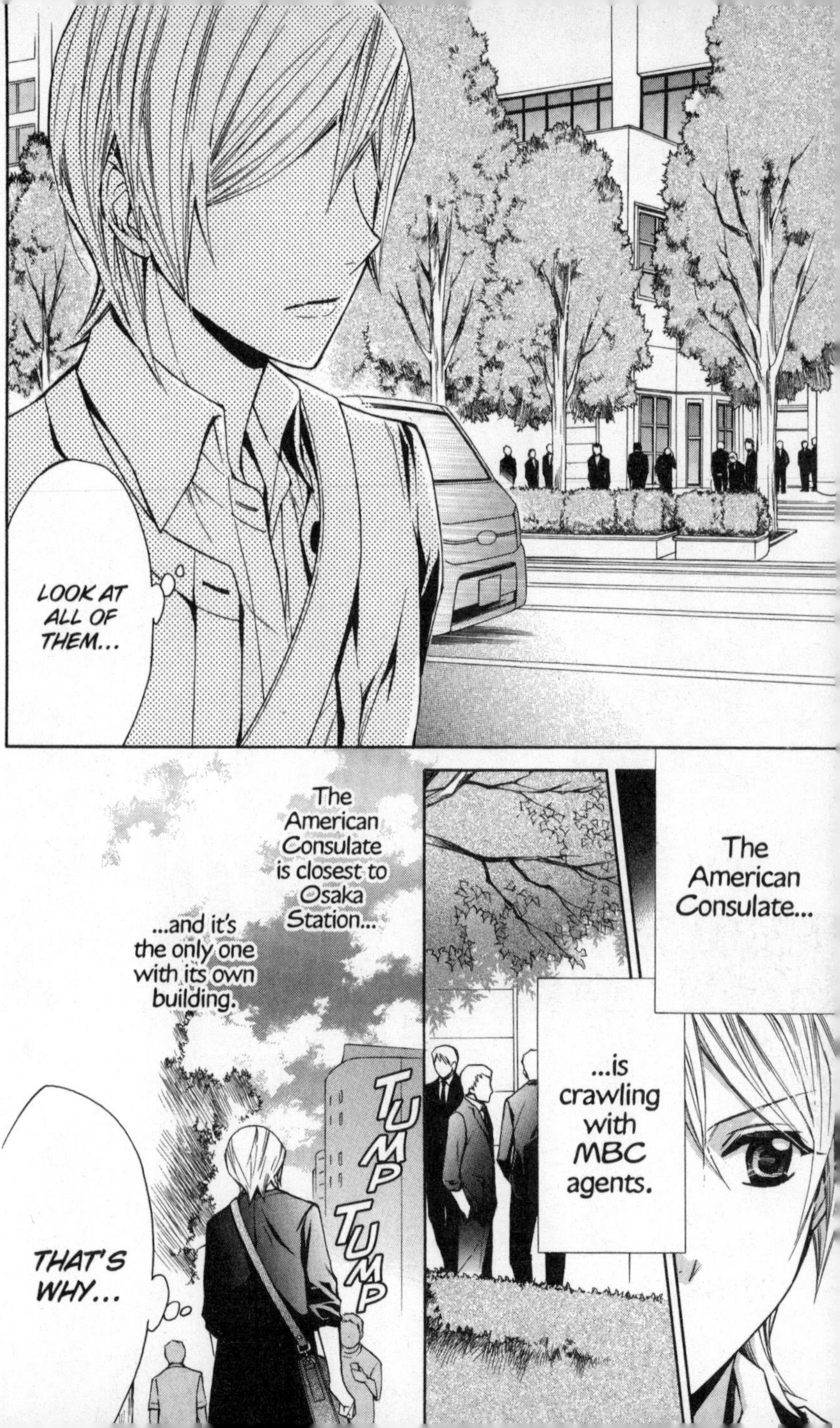
LOOK AT ALL OF THEM...
The American Consulate...
...is crawling with MBC agents.
The American Consulate is closest to Osaka Station...
...and it's the only one with its own building.
TUMP TUMP
THAT'S WHY...

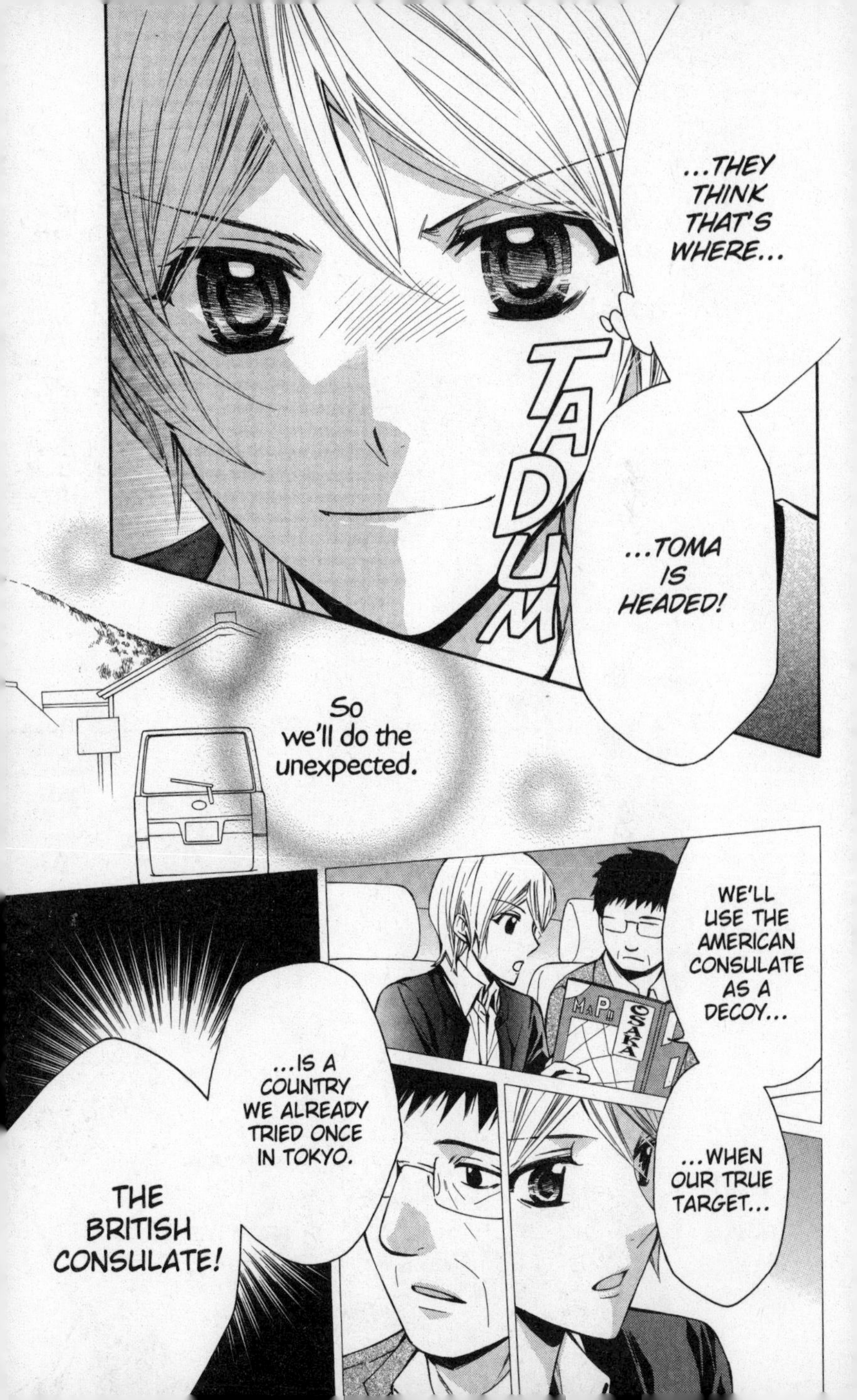
...THEY THINK THAT'S WHERE...
...TOMA IS HEADED!
TADUM
So we'll do the unexpected.
WE'LL USE THE AMERICAN CONSULATE AS A DECOY...
...WHEN OUR TRUE TARGET...
...IS A COUNTRY WE ALREADY TRIED ONCE IN TOKYO.
THE BRITISH CONSULATE!

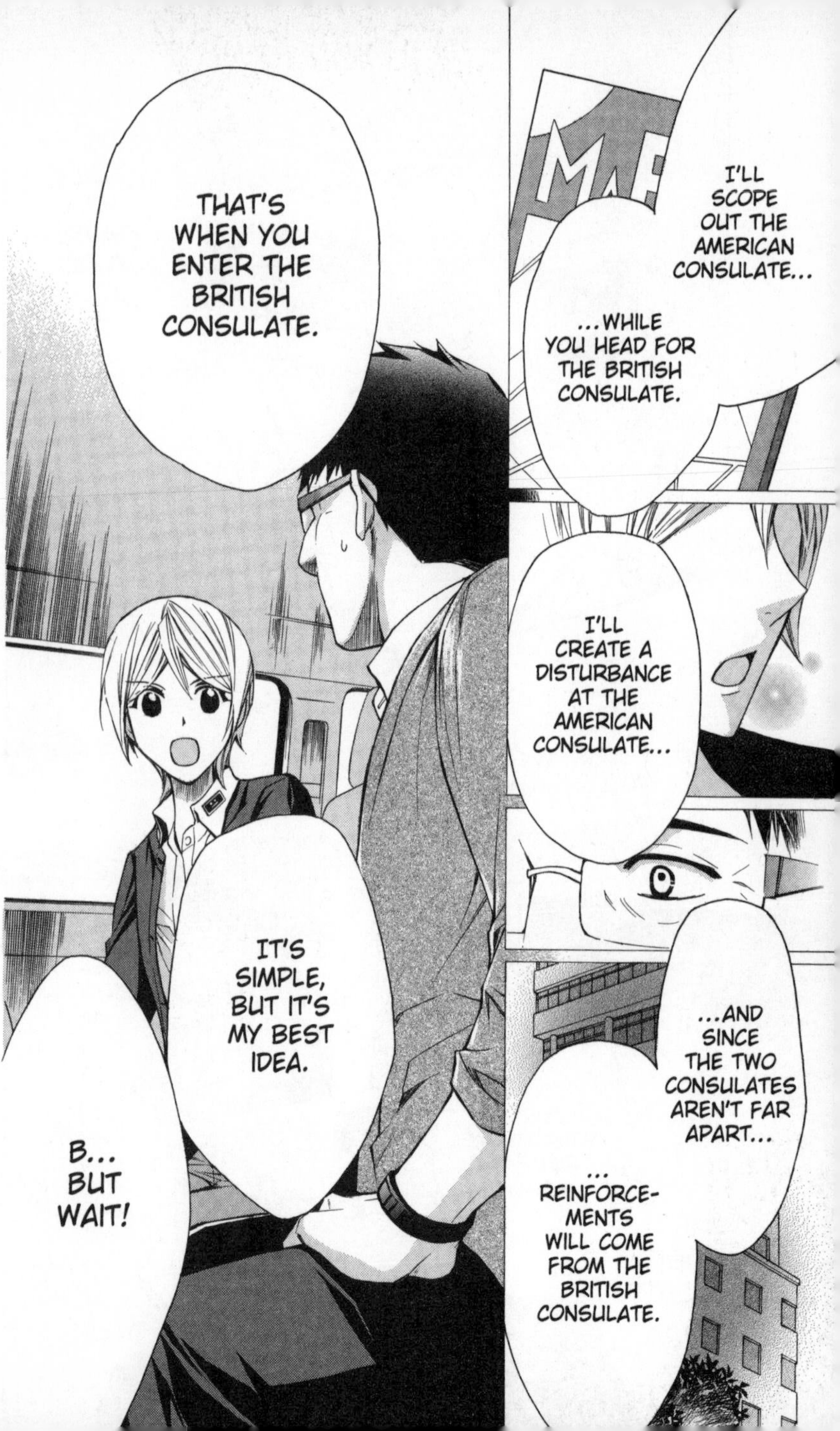
I'LL SCOPE OUT THE AMERICAN CONSULATE...
...WHILE YOU HEAD FOR THE BRITISH CONSULATE.
I'LL CREATE A DISTURBANCE AT THE AMERICAN CONSULATE...
...AND SINCE THE TWO CONSULATES AREN'T FAR APART...
...REINFORCEMENTS WILL COME FROM THE BRITISH CONSULATE.
THAT'S WHEN YOU ENTER THE BRITISH CONSULATE.
IT'S SIMPLE, BUT IT'S MY BEST IDEA.
B... BUT WAIT!

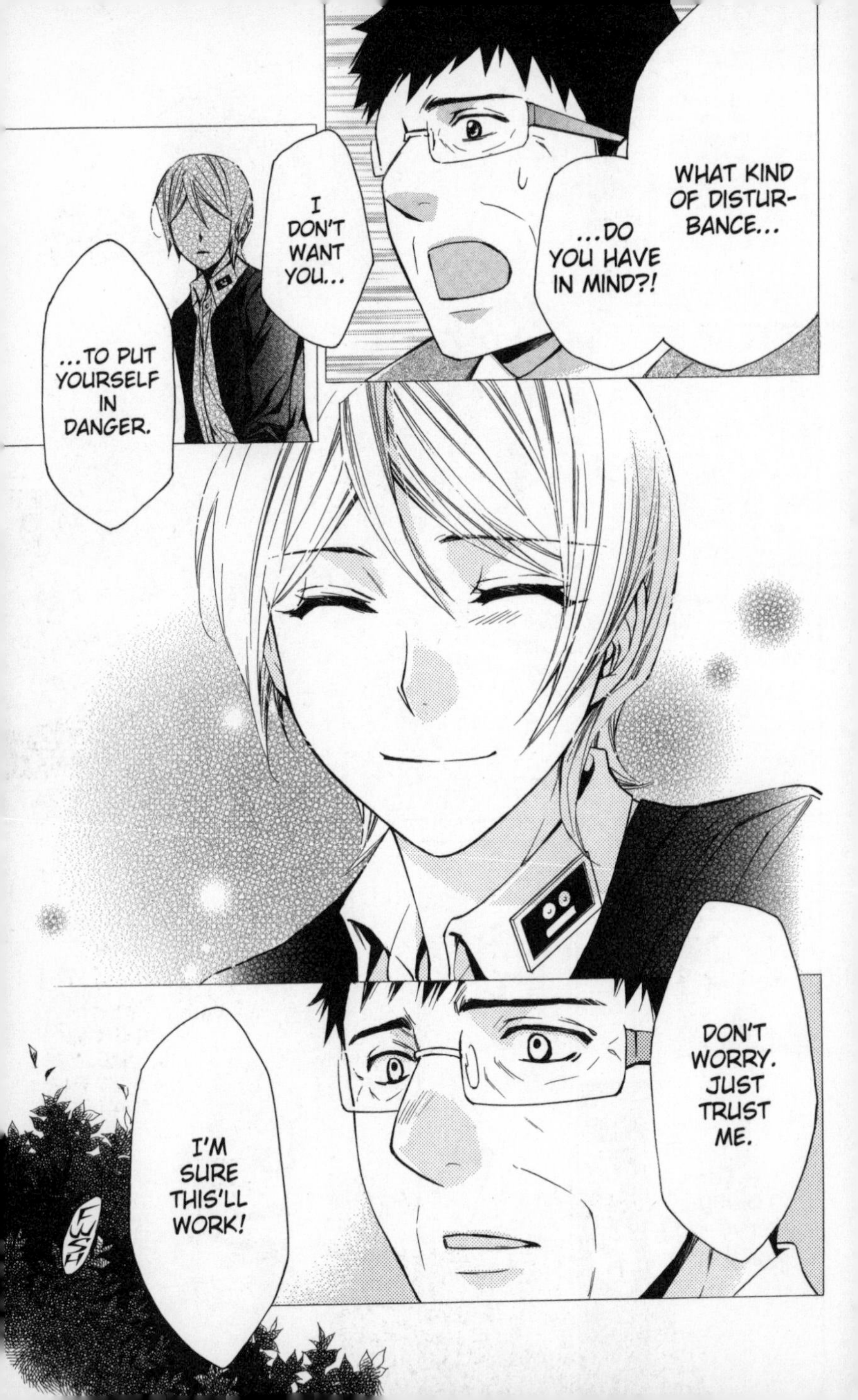
WHAT KIND OF DISTURBANCE...
...DO YOU HAVE IN MIND?!
I DON'T WANT YOU...
...TO PUT YOURSELF IN DANGER.
DON'T WORRY. JUST TRUST ME.
I'M SURE THIS'LL WORK!
FWSH

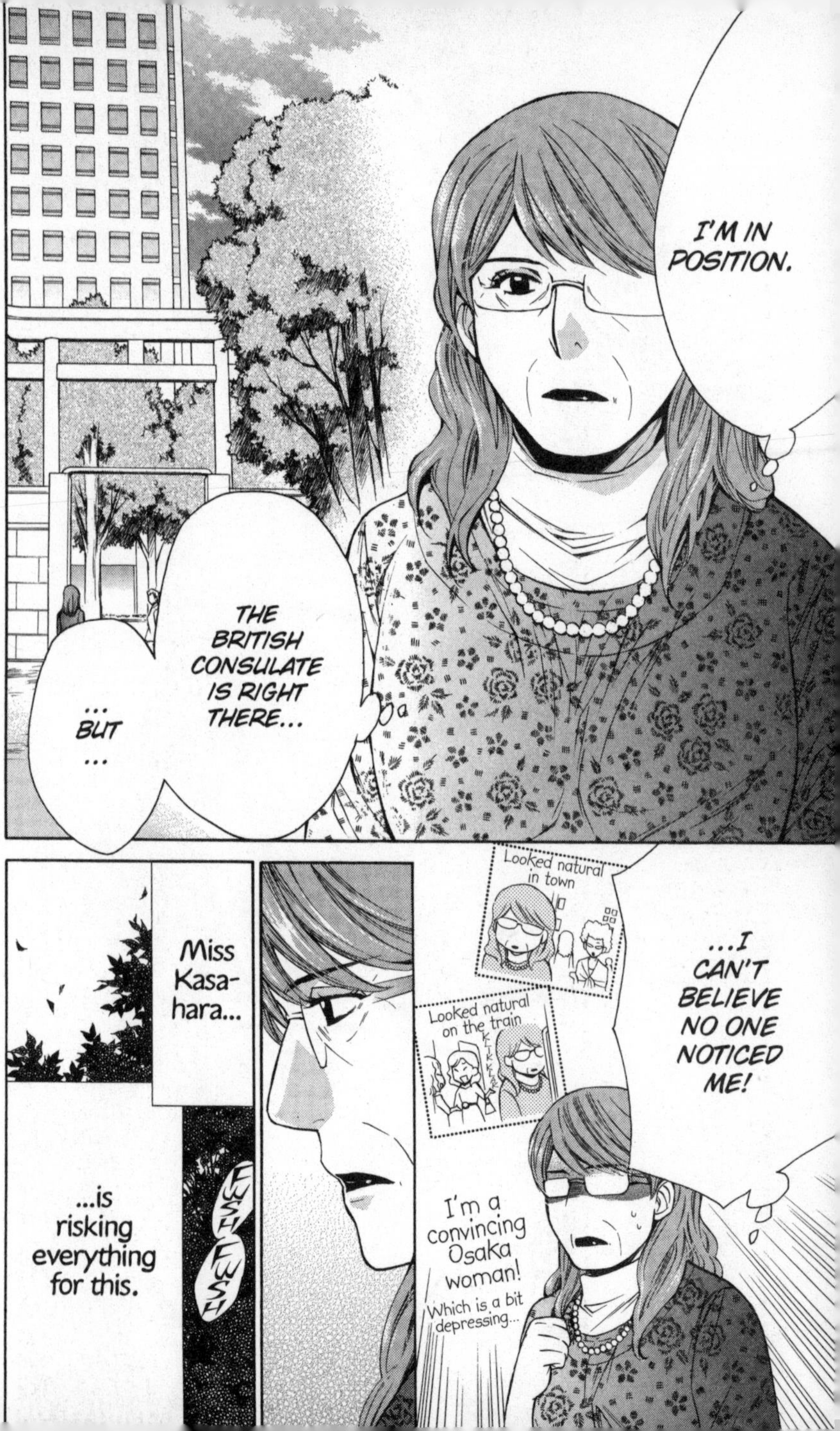
I'M IN POSITION.
THE BRITISH CONSULATE IS RIGHT THERE...
...BUT...
...I CAN'T BELIEVE NO ONE NOTICED ME!
Looked natural in town
Looked natural on the train
I'm a convincing Osaka woman!
Which is a bit depressing...
Miss Kasa-hara...
FWSH FWSH
...is risking everything for this.

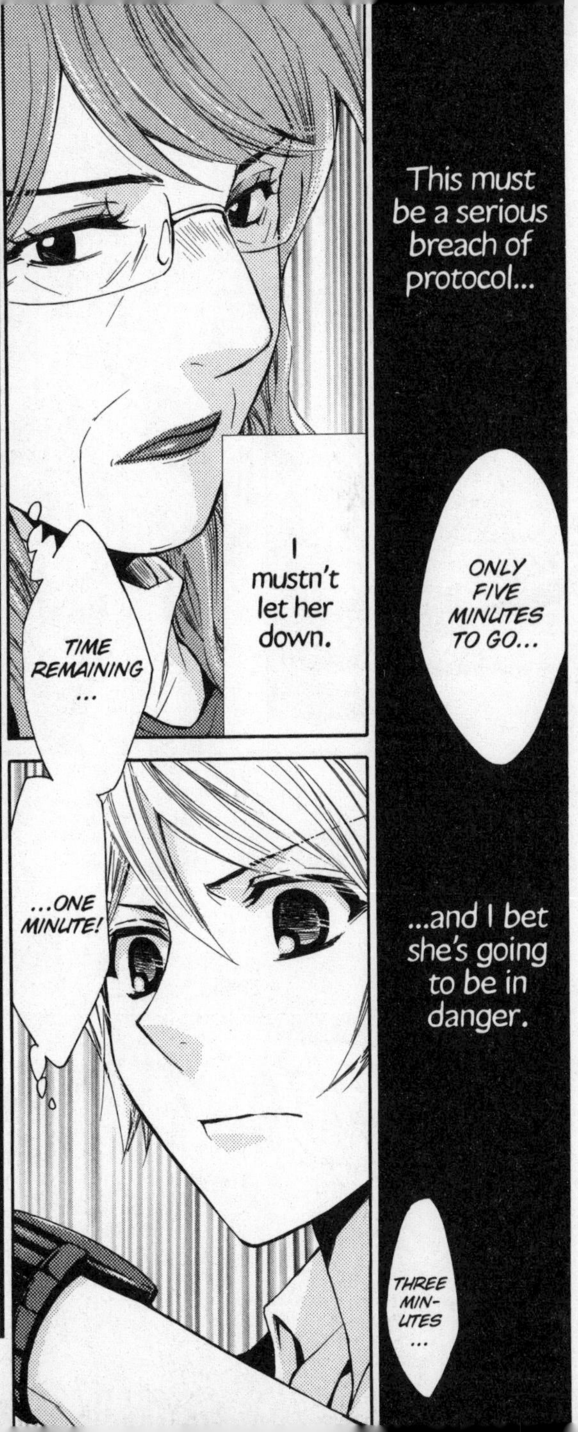
This must be a serious breach of protocol...
ONLY FIVE MINUTES TO GO...
...and I bet she's going to be in danger.
THREE MIN-UTES ...
I mustn't let her down.
TIME REMAINING ...
...ONE MINUTE!

3

The *Library Wars* novel became an animated TV series, animated movie and live-action film. It's amazing what a great story it is!

This manga was the first to appear in the media mix. I wonder if the manga would have turned out differently if it had appeared later. If the anime had appeared first, the Library Forces in the manga may have had uniforms for clerical workers and Shibazaki may have had black hair, etc. Or maybe I wouldn't have done the manga! Now that I've imagined it differently, I'm glad it all turned out the way it did!

*In the original novel, there weren't any uniforms for clerical workers.

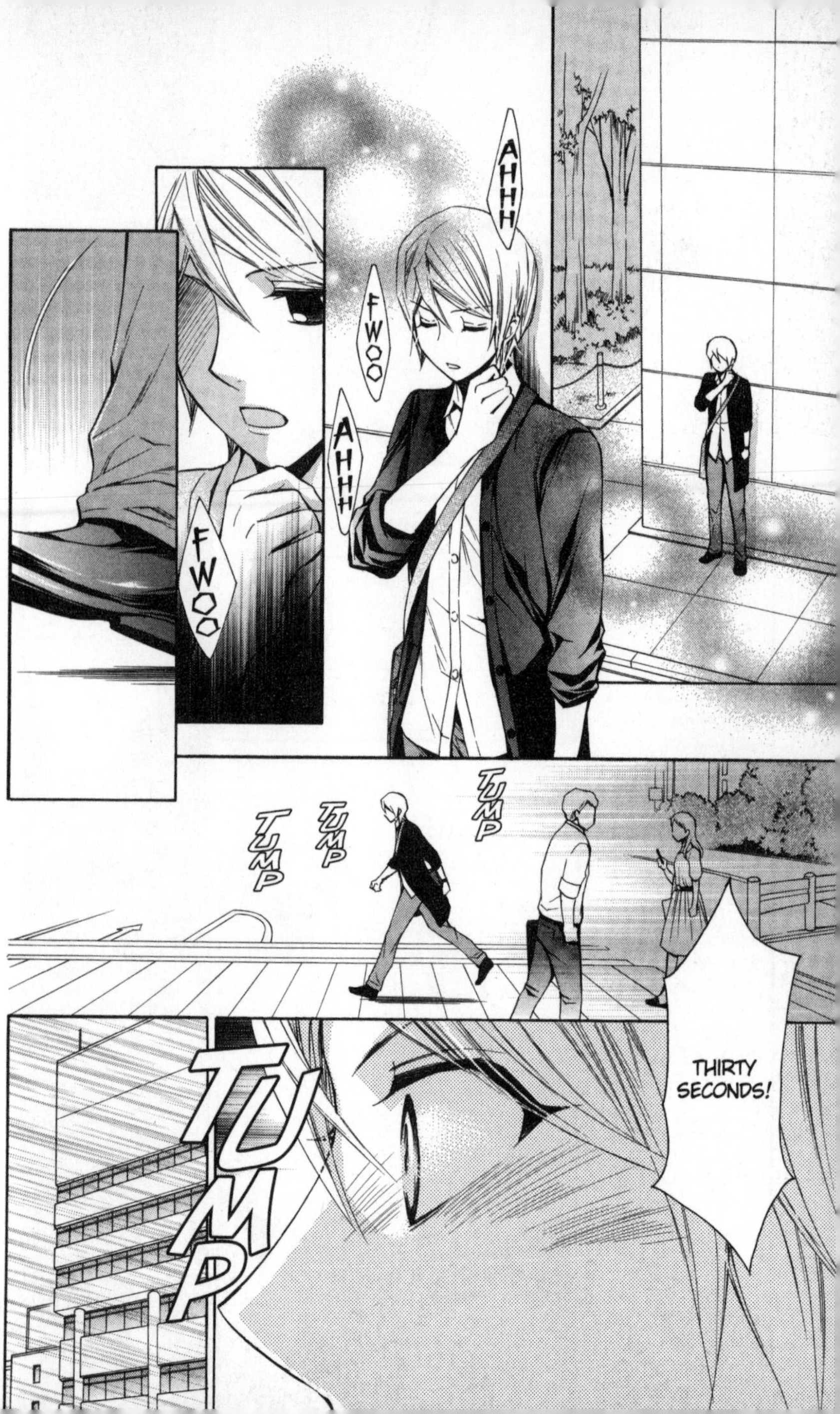
AHHH
FWOO
AHHH
FWOO
TUMP
TUMP
TUMP
THIRTY SECONDS!
TUMP

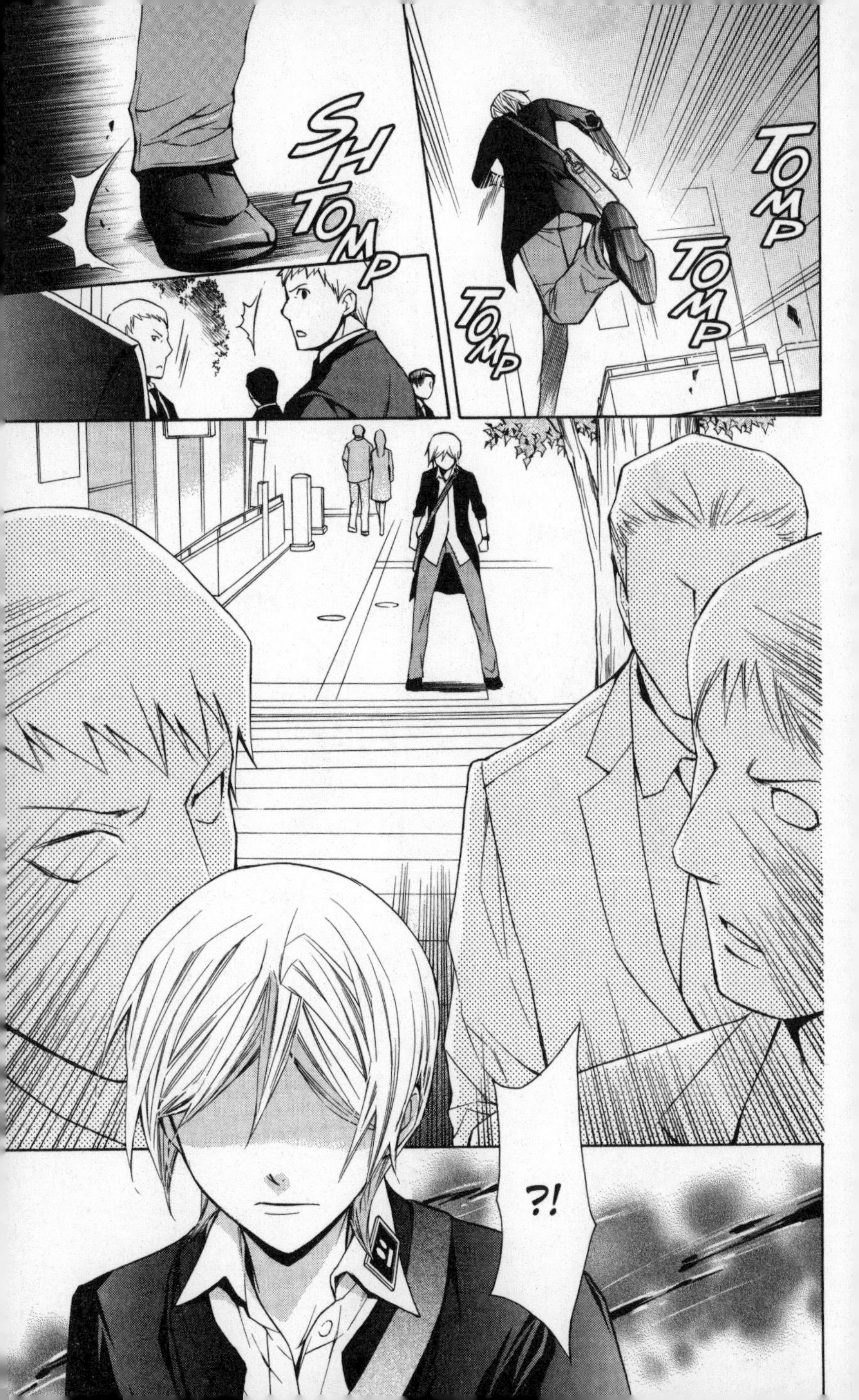
TOMP
TOMP
TOMP
SHTOMP
?!

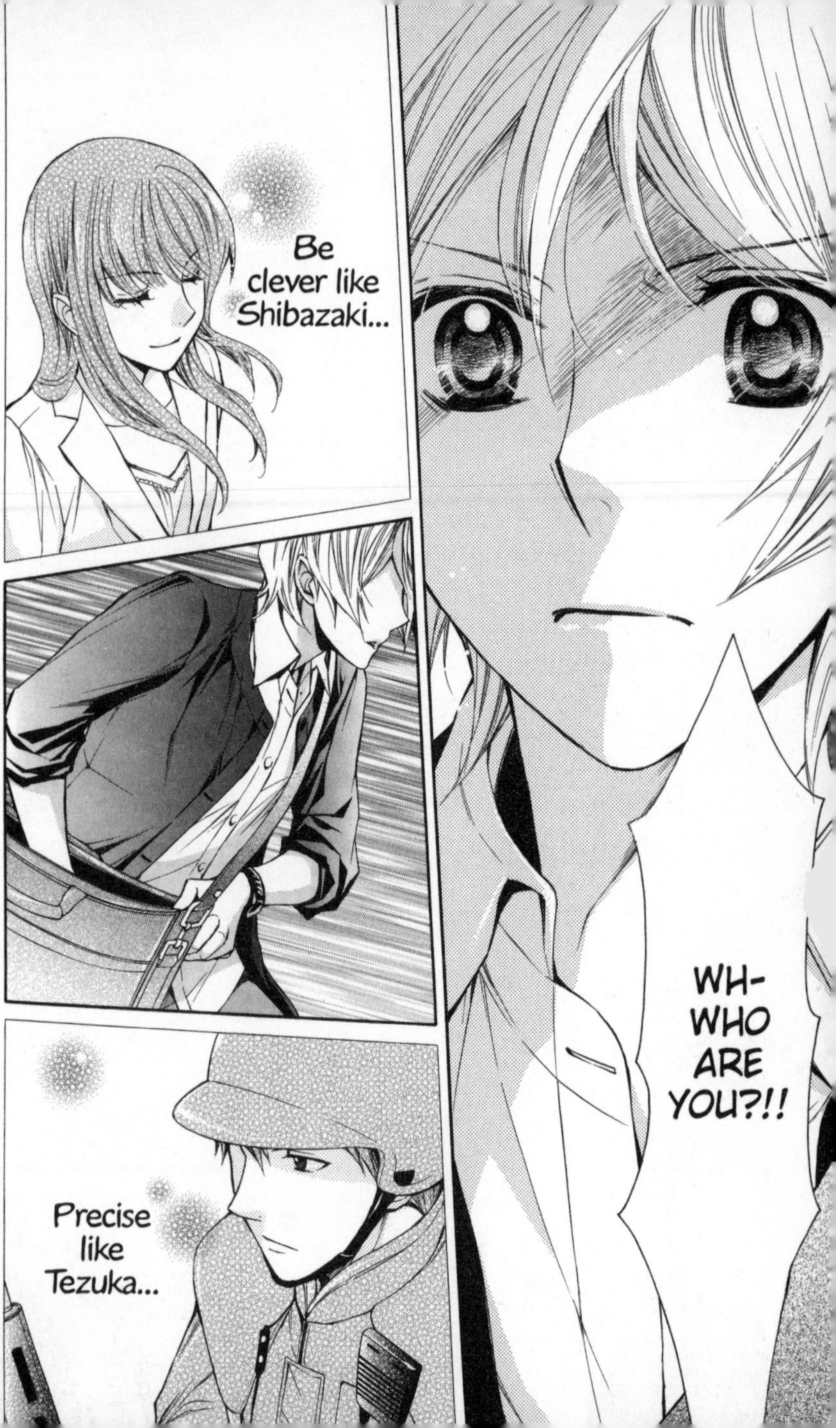
WH- WHO ARE YOU?!!
Be clever like Shibazaki...
Precise like Tezuka...

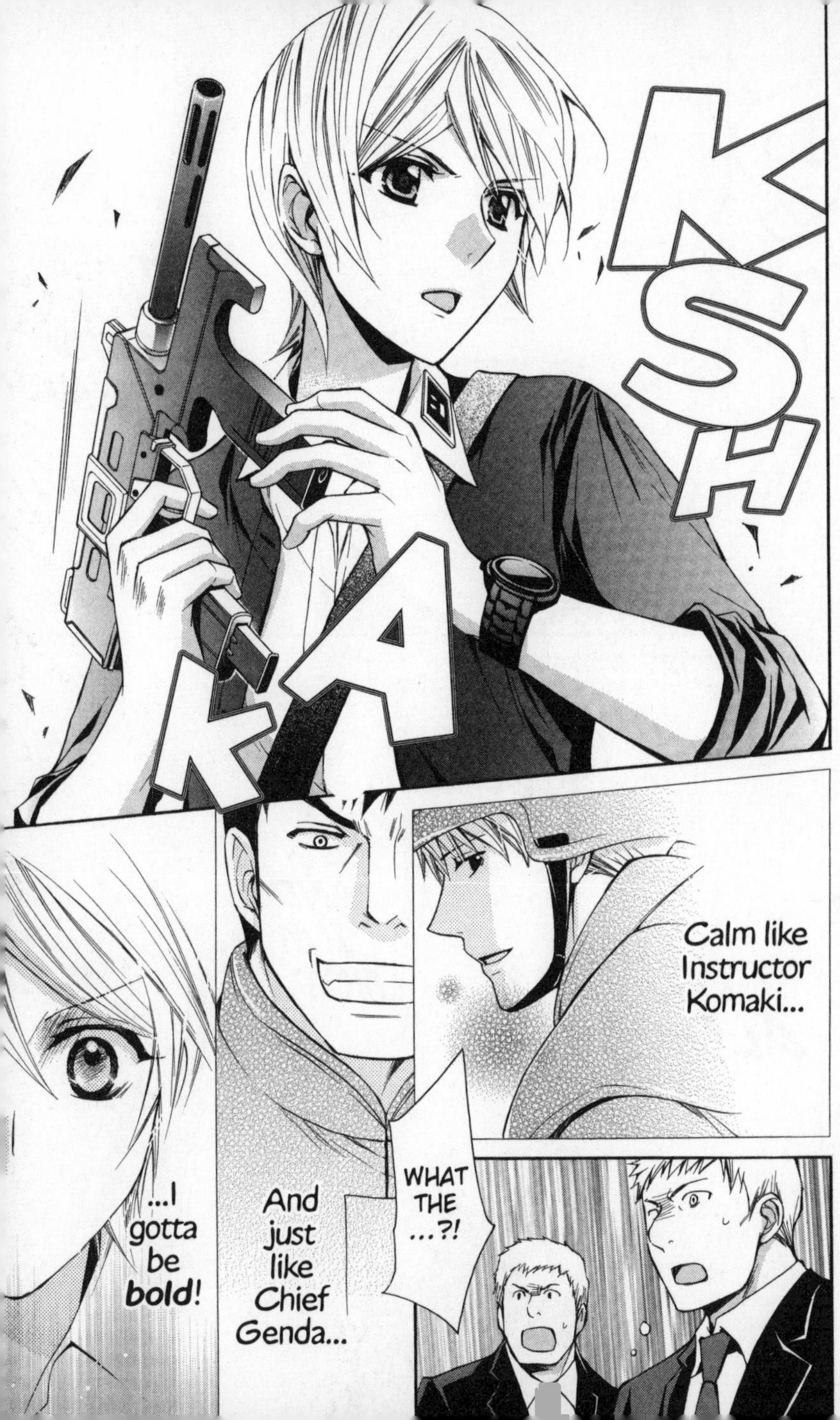
KASH
KA
Calm like Instructor Komaki...
WHAT THE ...?!
And just like Chief Genda...
...I gotta be **bold**!

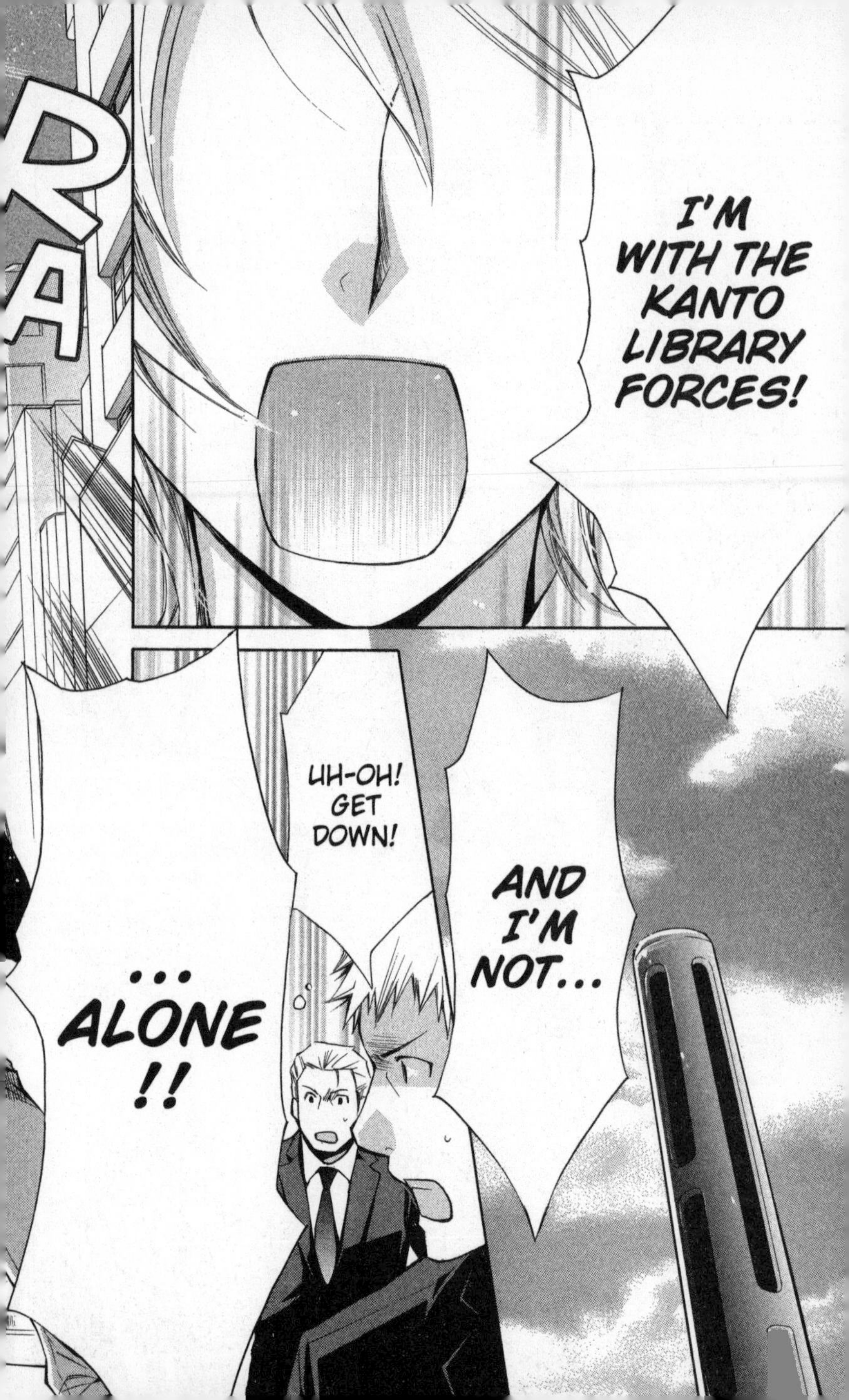
I'M WITH THE KANTO LIBRARY FORCES!
AND I'M NOT...
UH-OH! GET DOWN!
...ALONE!!

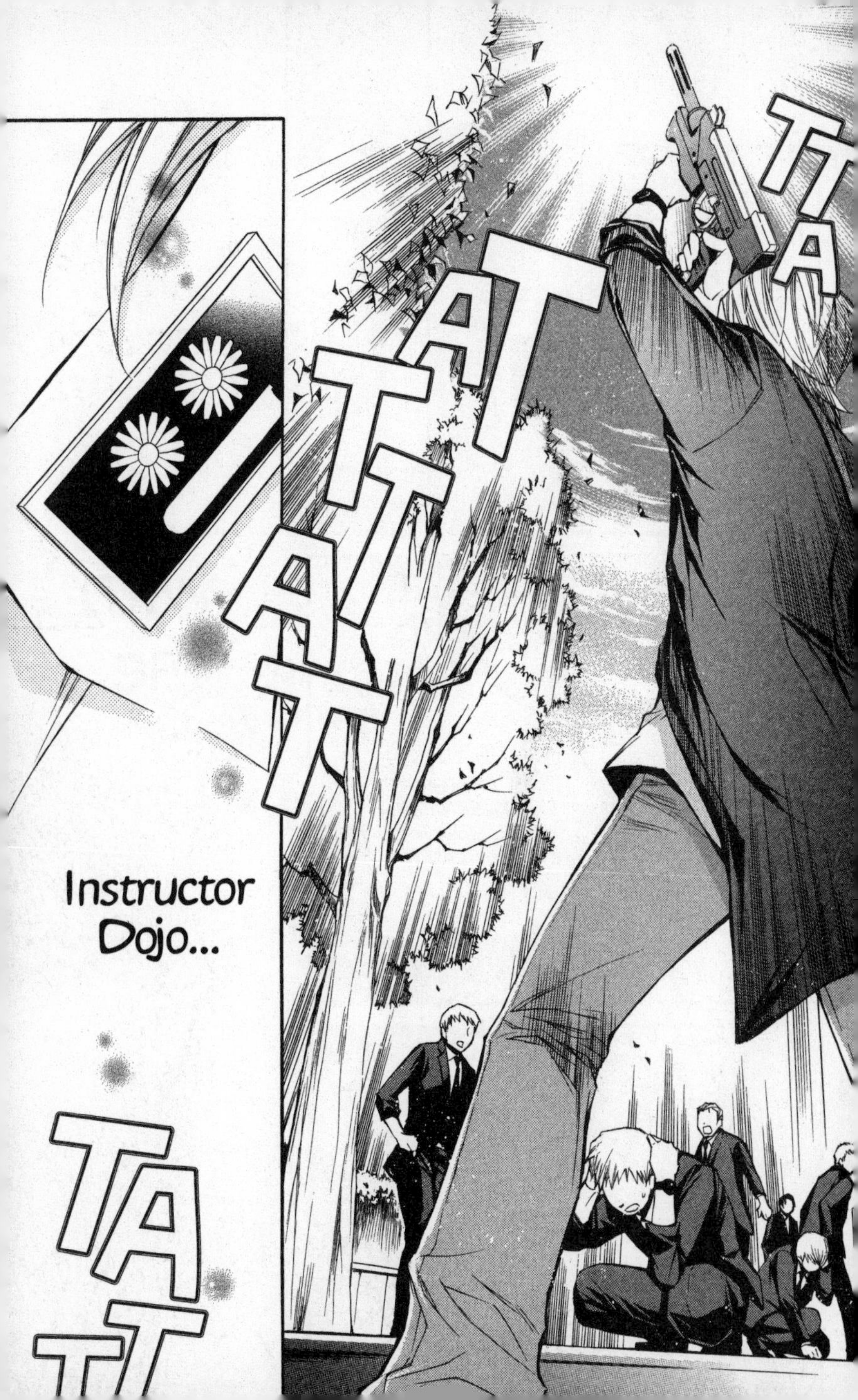
TTA
Instructor Dojo...
TA
TT

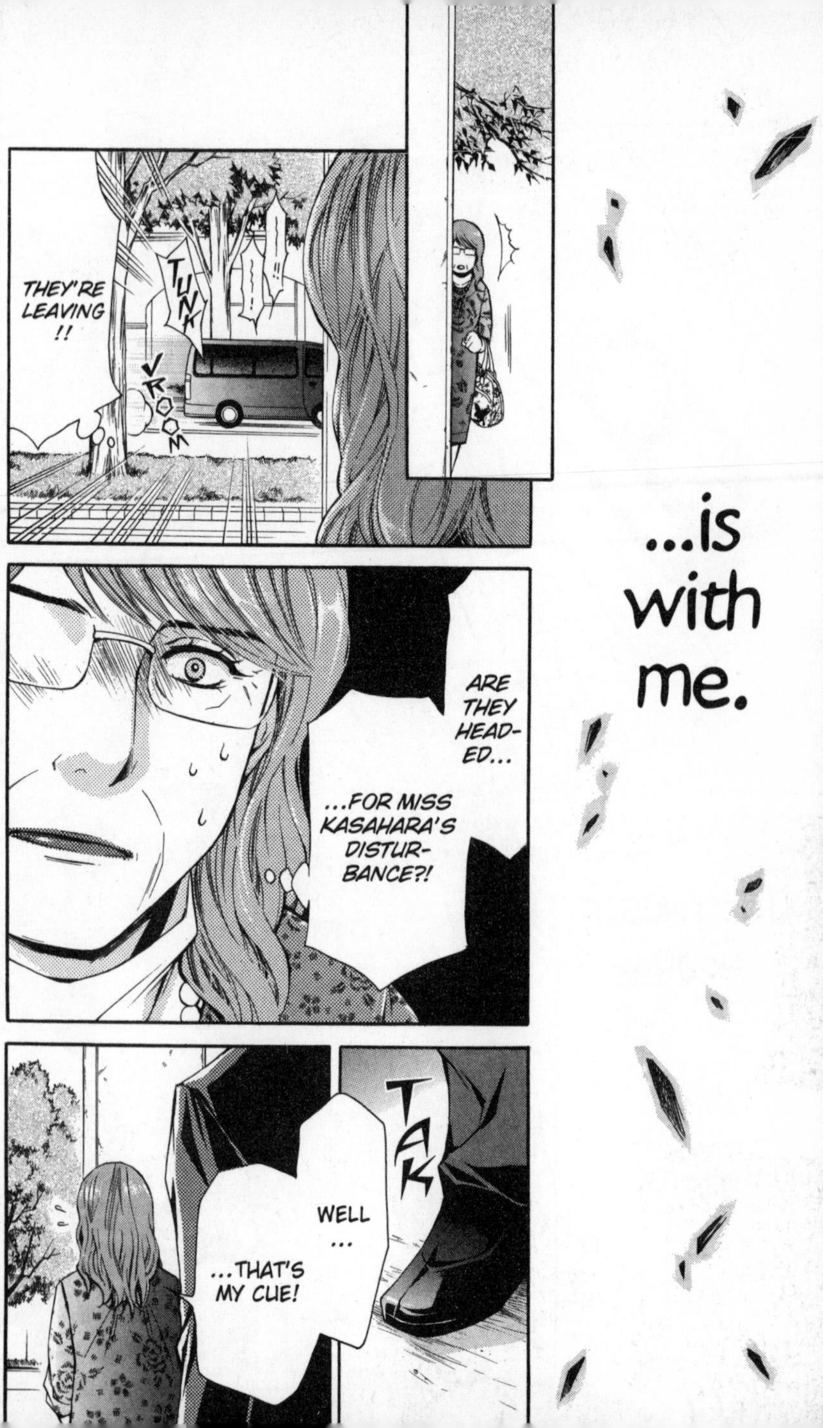
...is with me.
TUNK
VROOM
THEY'RE LEAVING!!
ARE THEY HEADED...
...FOR MISS KASAHARA'S DISTURBANCE?!
TAK
WELL...
...THAT'S MY CUE!

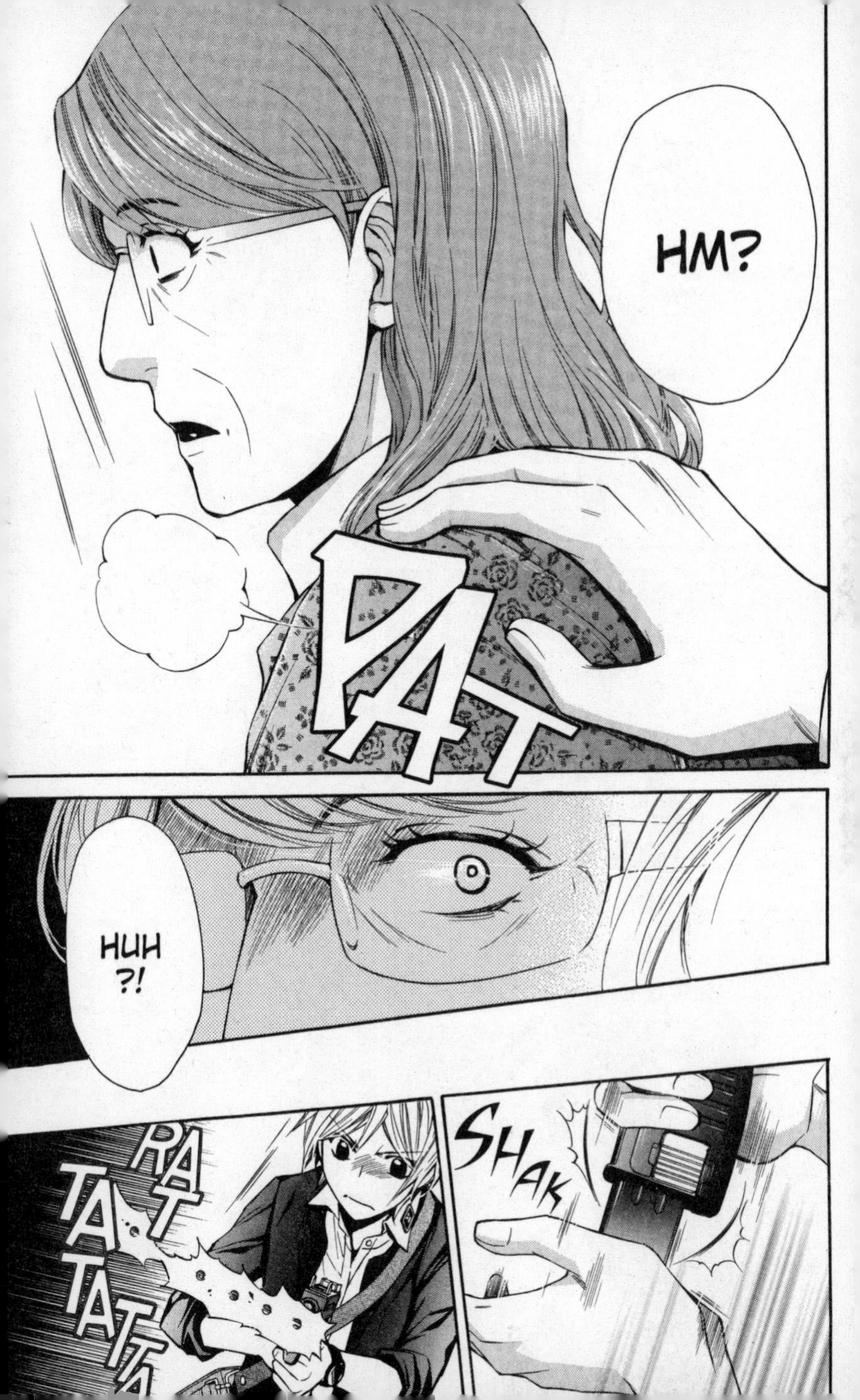
HM?
PAT
HUH ?!
SHAK
RATATTATTA

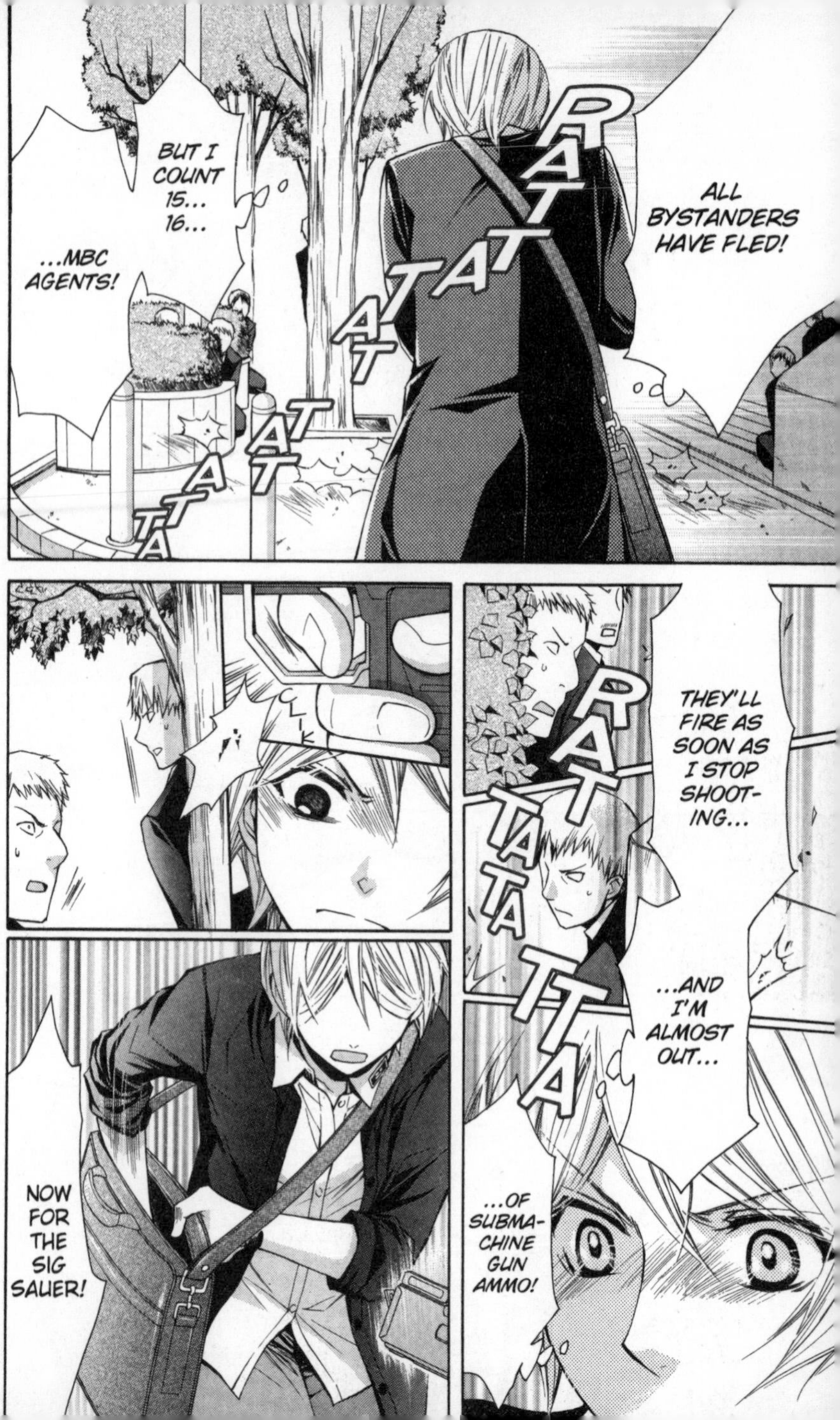
ALL BYSTANDERS HAVE FLED!
RATTATATTATATTA
BUT I COUNT 15... 16...
...MBC AGENTS!
THEY'LL FIRE AS SOON AS I STOP SHOOTING...
RATTATATATTA
CLIK
...AND I'M ALMOST OUT...
...OF SUBMACHINE GUN AMMO!
NOW FOR THE SIG SAUER!

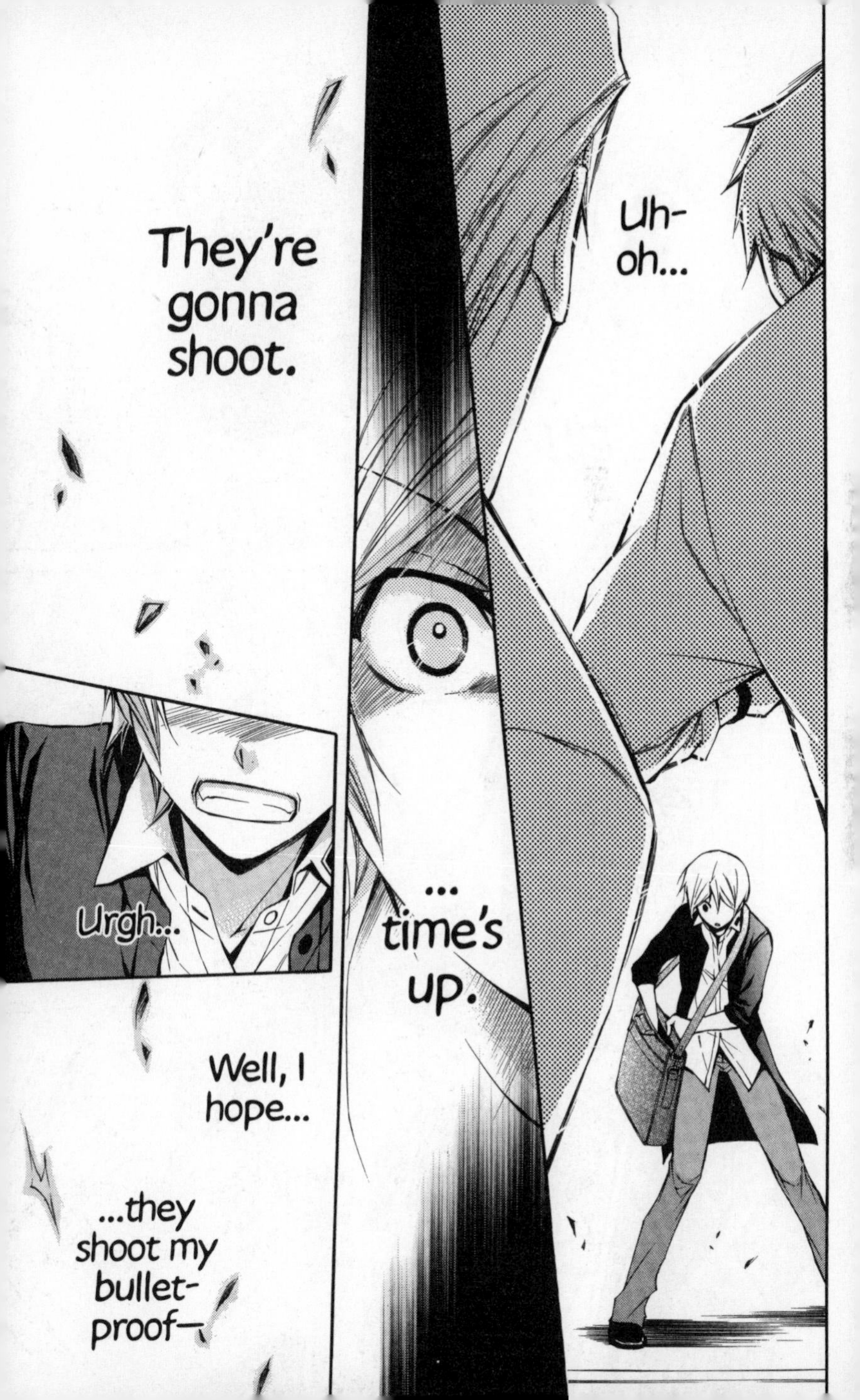
Uh-oh...
...time's up.
They're gonna shoot.
Urgh...
Well, I hope...
...they shoot my bulletproof—

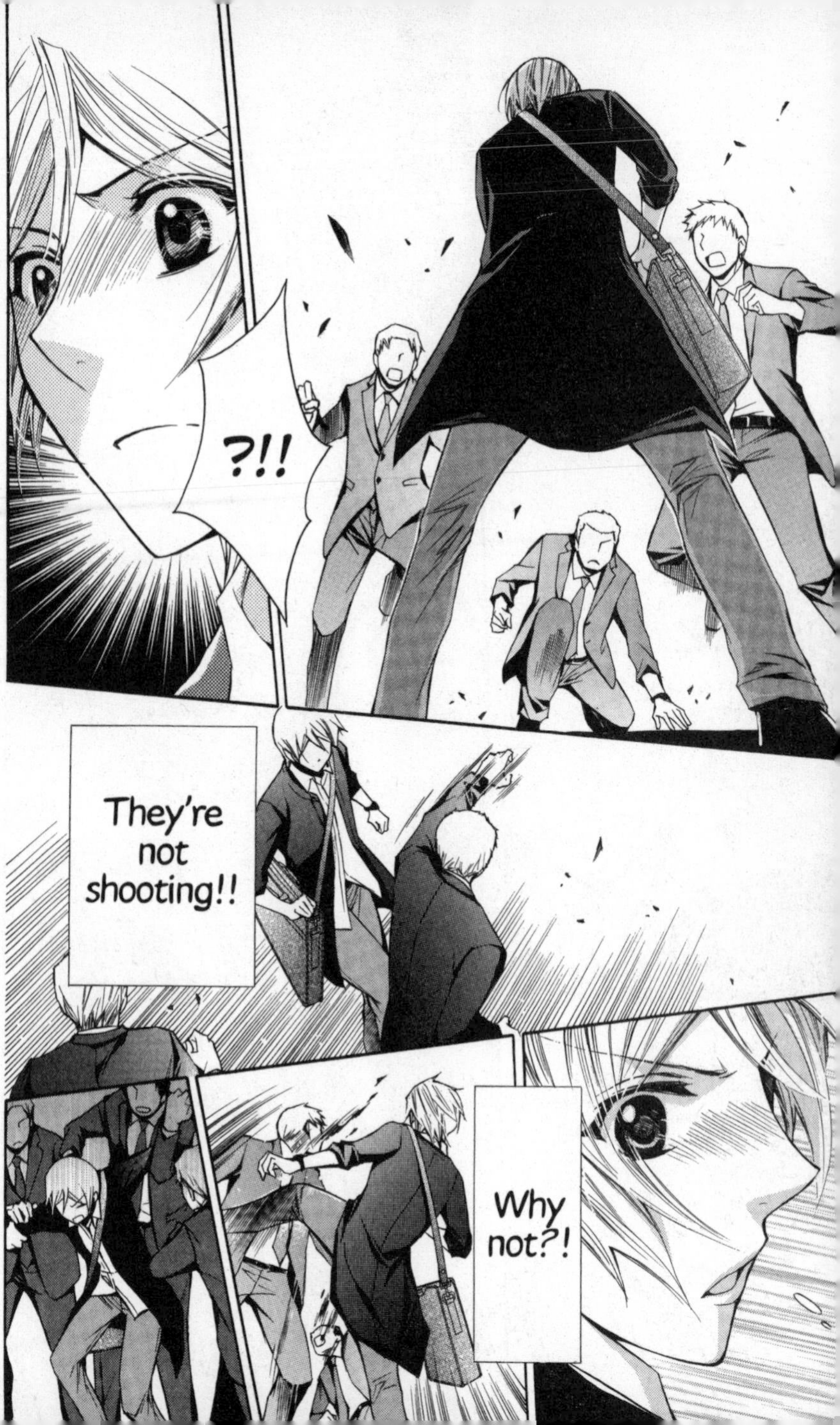
?!!
They're not shooting!!
Why not?!

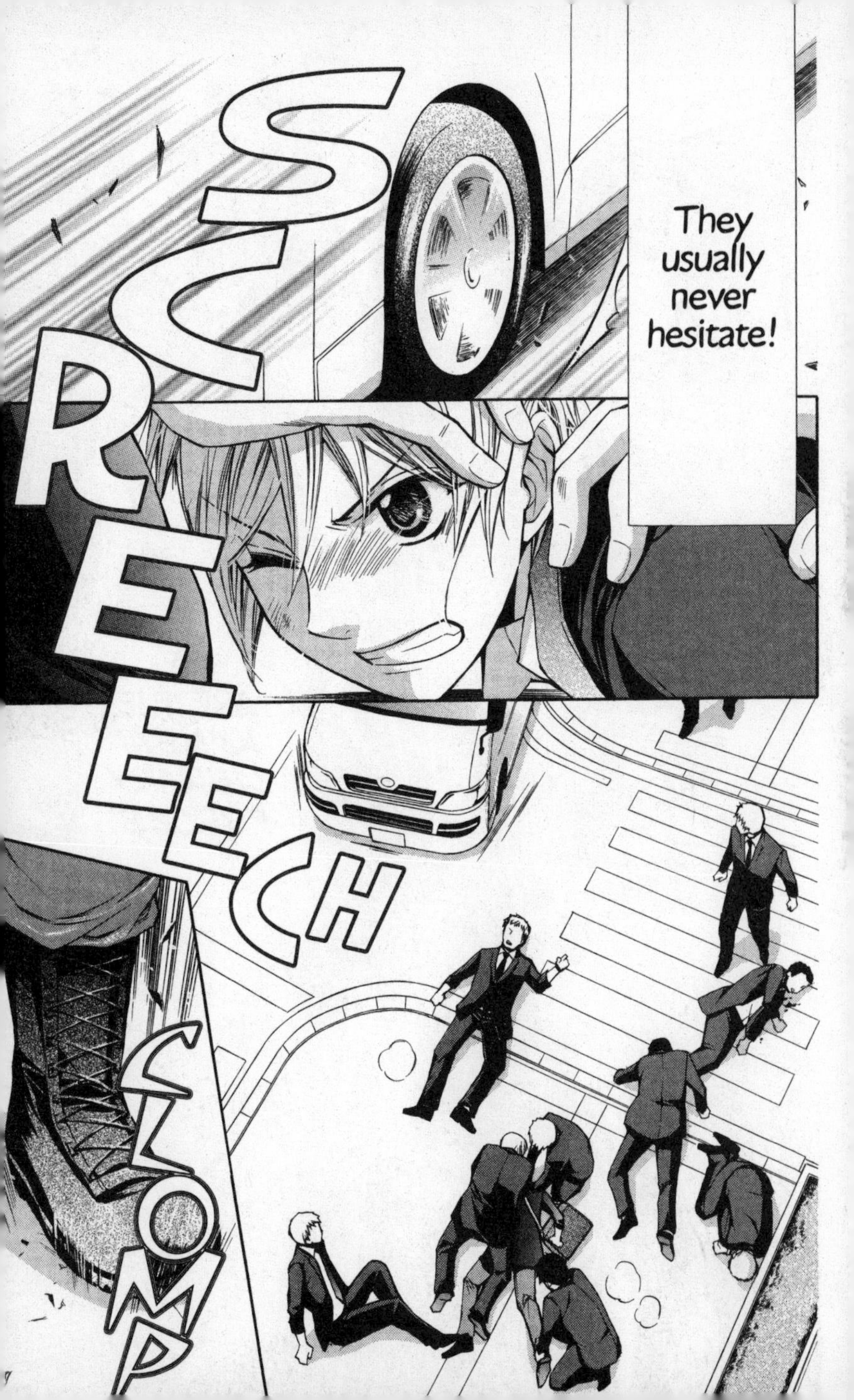
They usually never hesitate!
SCREEEECH
CLOMP

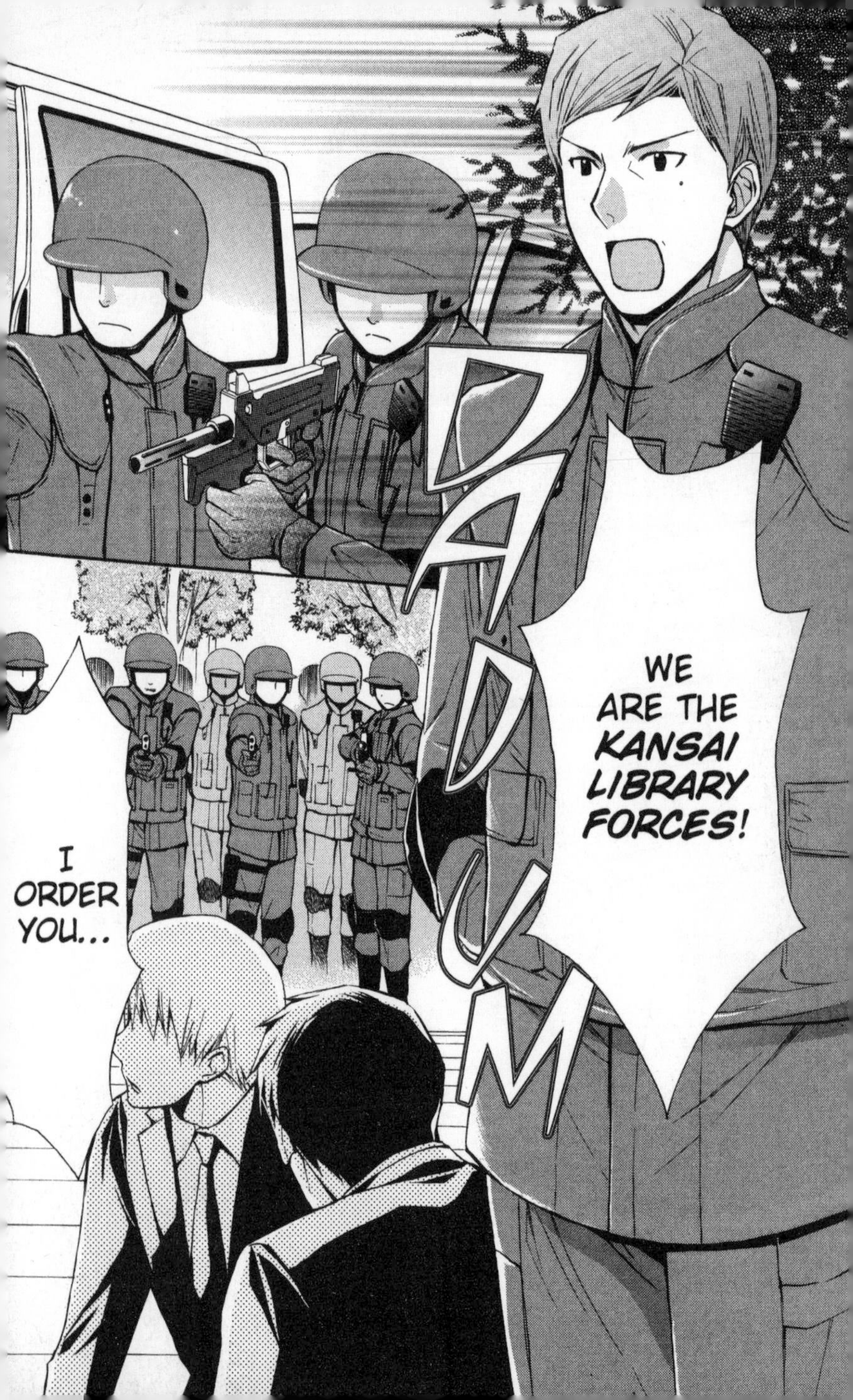
WE ARE THE KANSAI LIBRARY FORCES!
DADUM
I ORDER YOU...

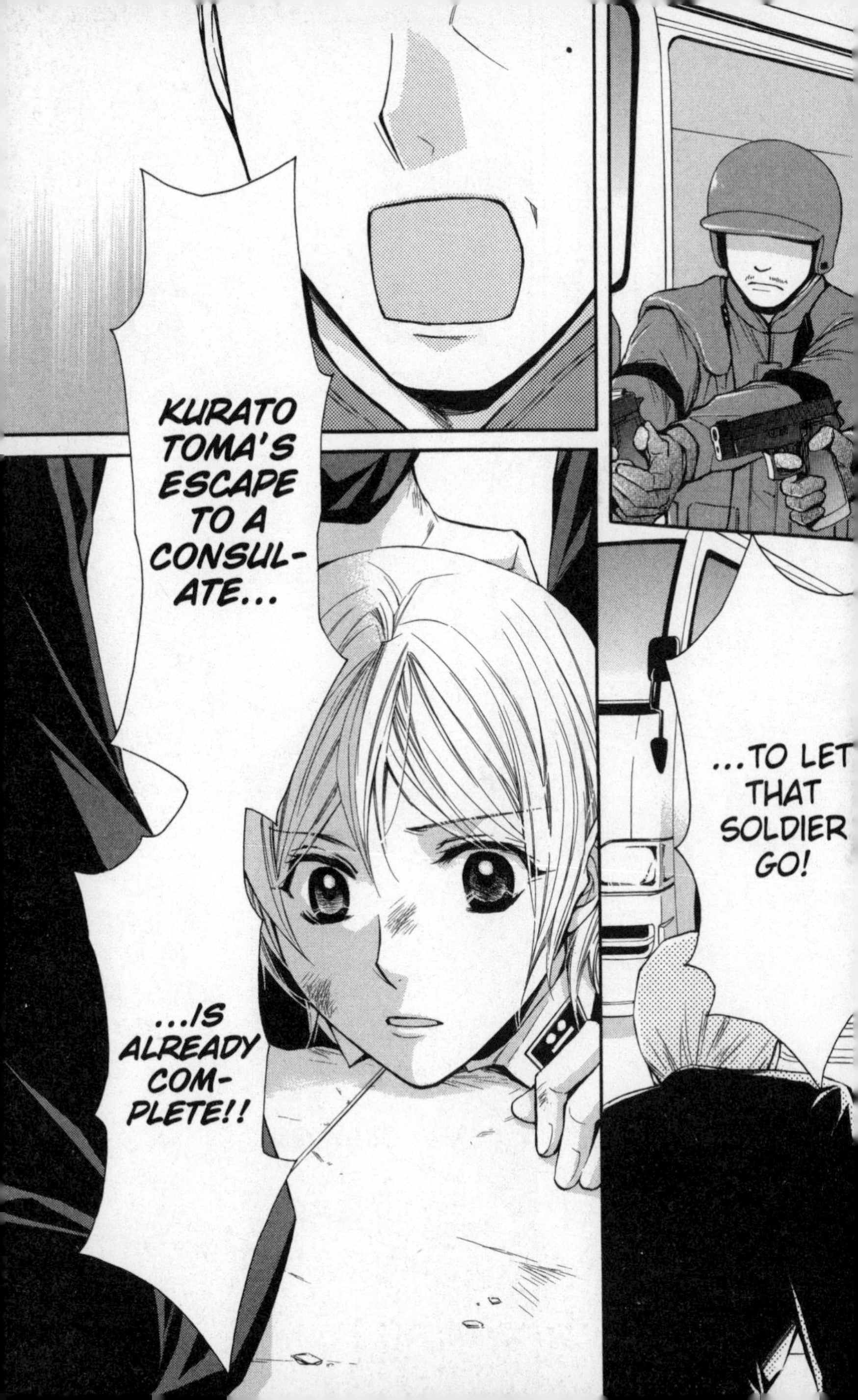
KURATO TOMA'S ESCAPE TO A CONSUL-ATE...
...TO LET THAT SOLDIER GO!
...IS ALREADY COM-PLETE!!

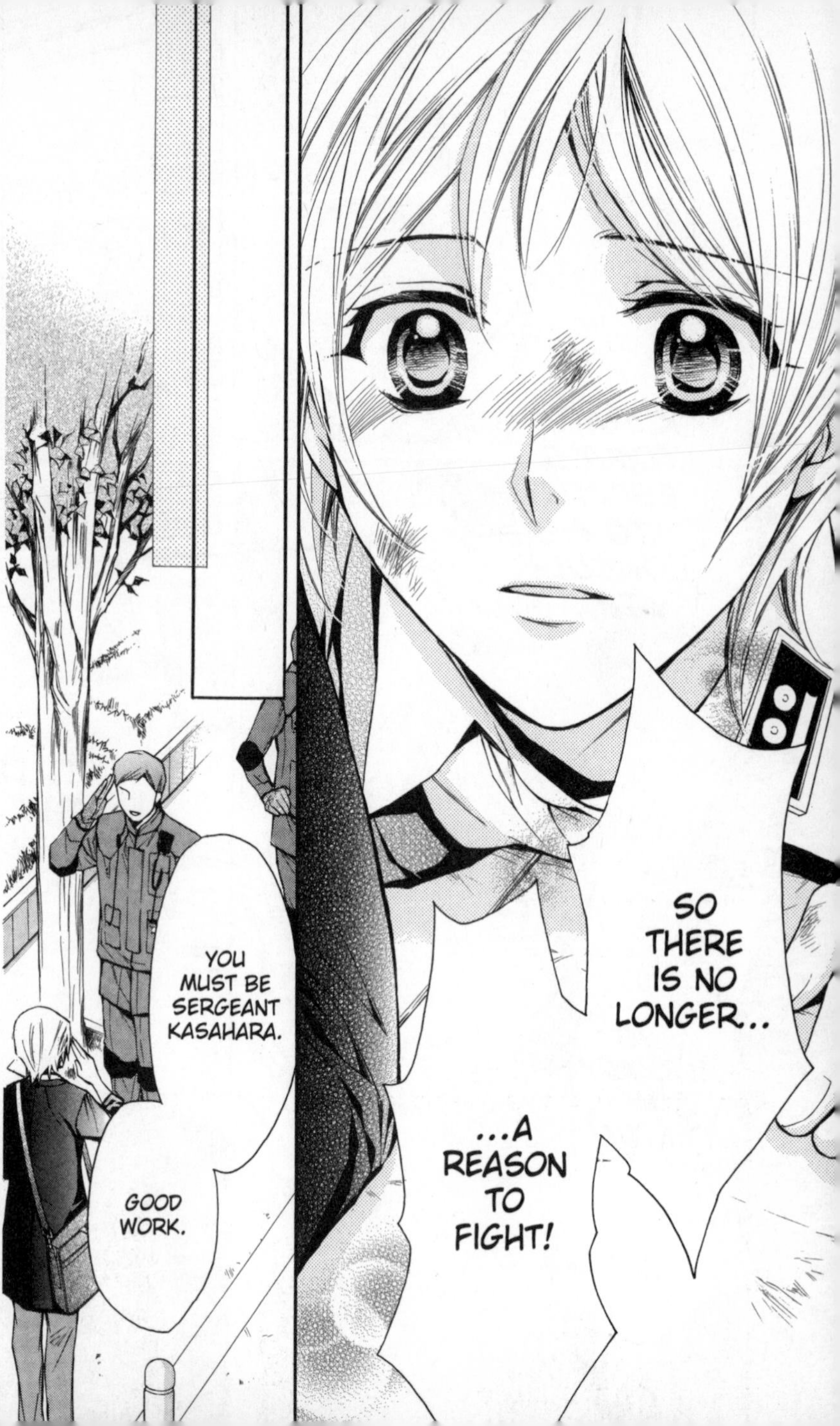
SO THERE IS NO LONGER..
...A REASON TO FIGHT!
YOU MUST BE SERGEANT KASAHARA.
GOOD WORK.

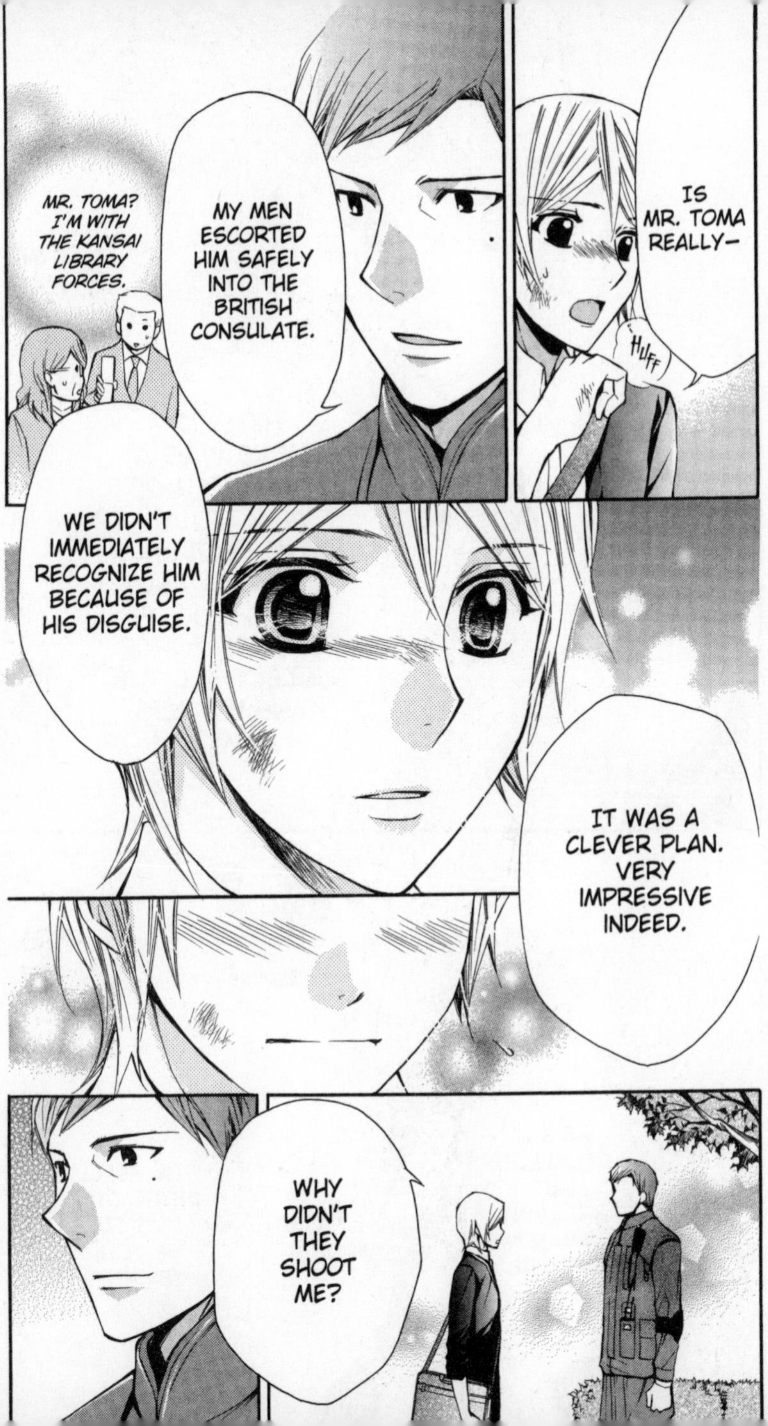
IS MR. TOMA REALLY—
HUFF
MY MEN ESCORTED HIM SAFELY INTO THE BRITISH CONSULATE.
MR. TOMA? I'M WITH THE KANSAI LIBRARY FORCES.
WE DIDN'T IMMEDIATELY RECOGNIZE HIM BECAUSE OF HIS DISGUISE.
IT WAS A CLEVER PLAN. VERY IMPRESSIVE INDEED.
WHY DIDN'T THEY SHOOT ME?

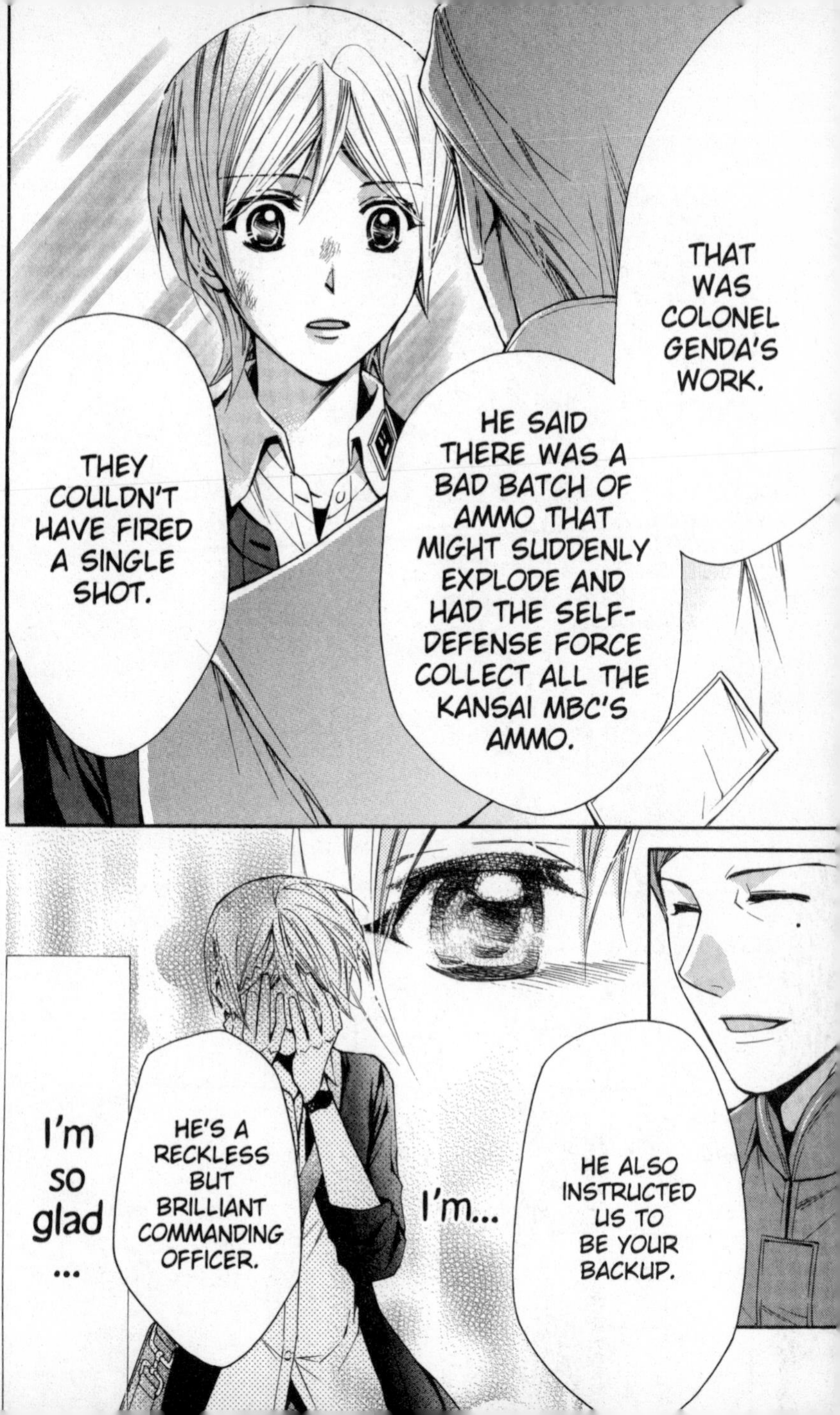
THAT WAS COLONEL GENDA'S WORK.
HE SAID THERE WAS A BAD BATCH OF AMMO THAT MIGHT SUDDENLY EXPLODE AND HAD THE SELF-DEFENSE FORCE COLLECT ALL THE KANSAI MBC'S AMMO.
THEY COULDN'T HAVE FIRED A SINGLE SHOT.
HE ALSO INSTRUCTED US TO BE YOUR BACKUP.
I'm...
HE'S A RECKLESS BUT BRILLIANT COMMANDING OFFICER.
I'm so glad ...

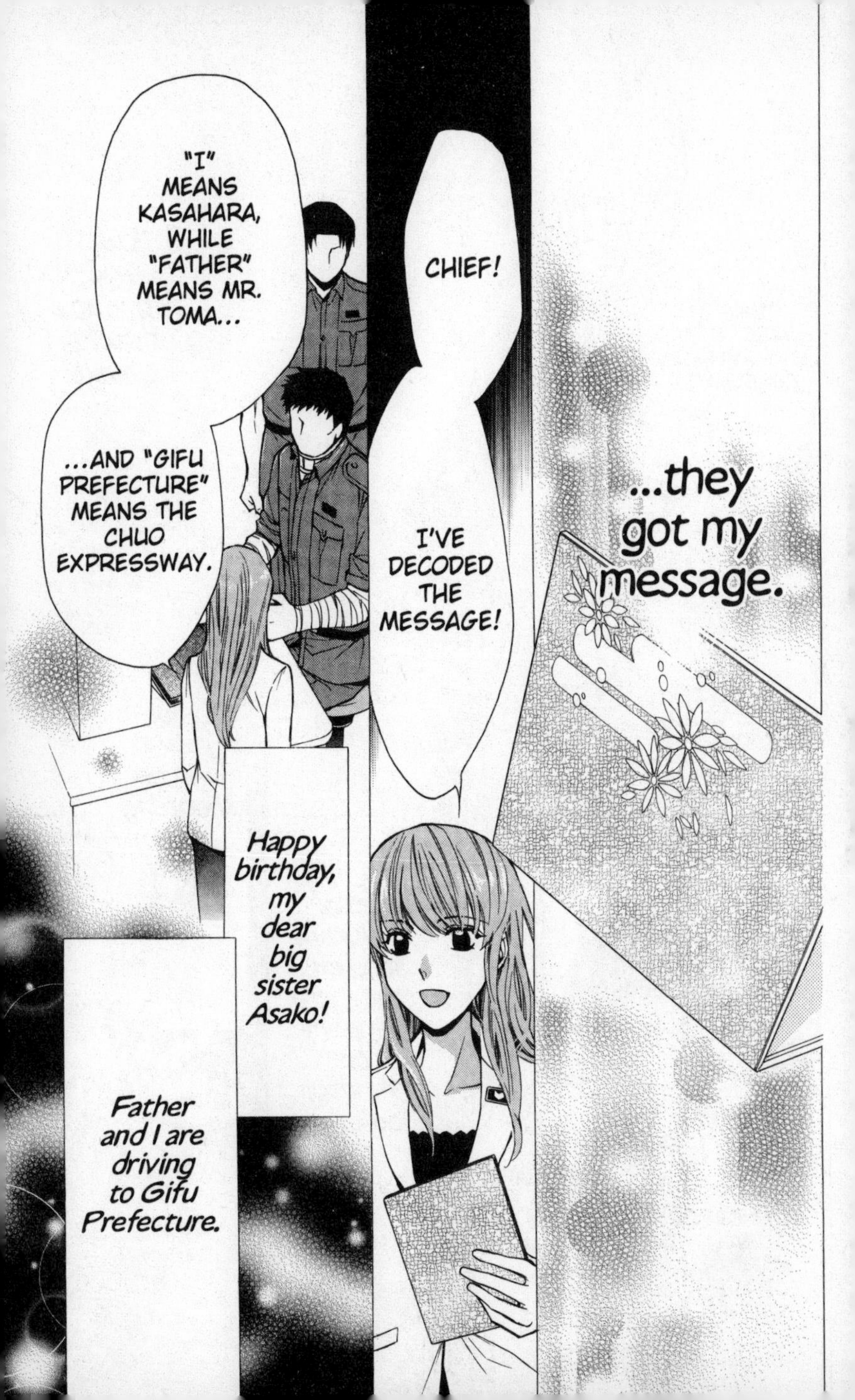
...they got my message.
CHIEF!
I'VE DECODED THE MESSAGE!
"I" MEANS KASAHARA, WHILE "FATHER" MEANS MR. TOMA...
...AND "GIFU PREFECTURE" MEANS THE CHUO EXPRESSWAY.
Happy birthday, my dear big sister Asako!
Father and I are driving to Gifu Prefecture.

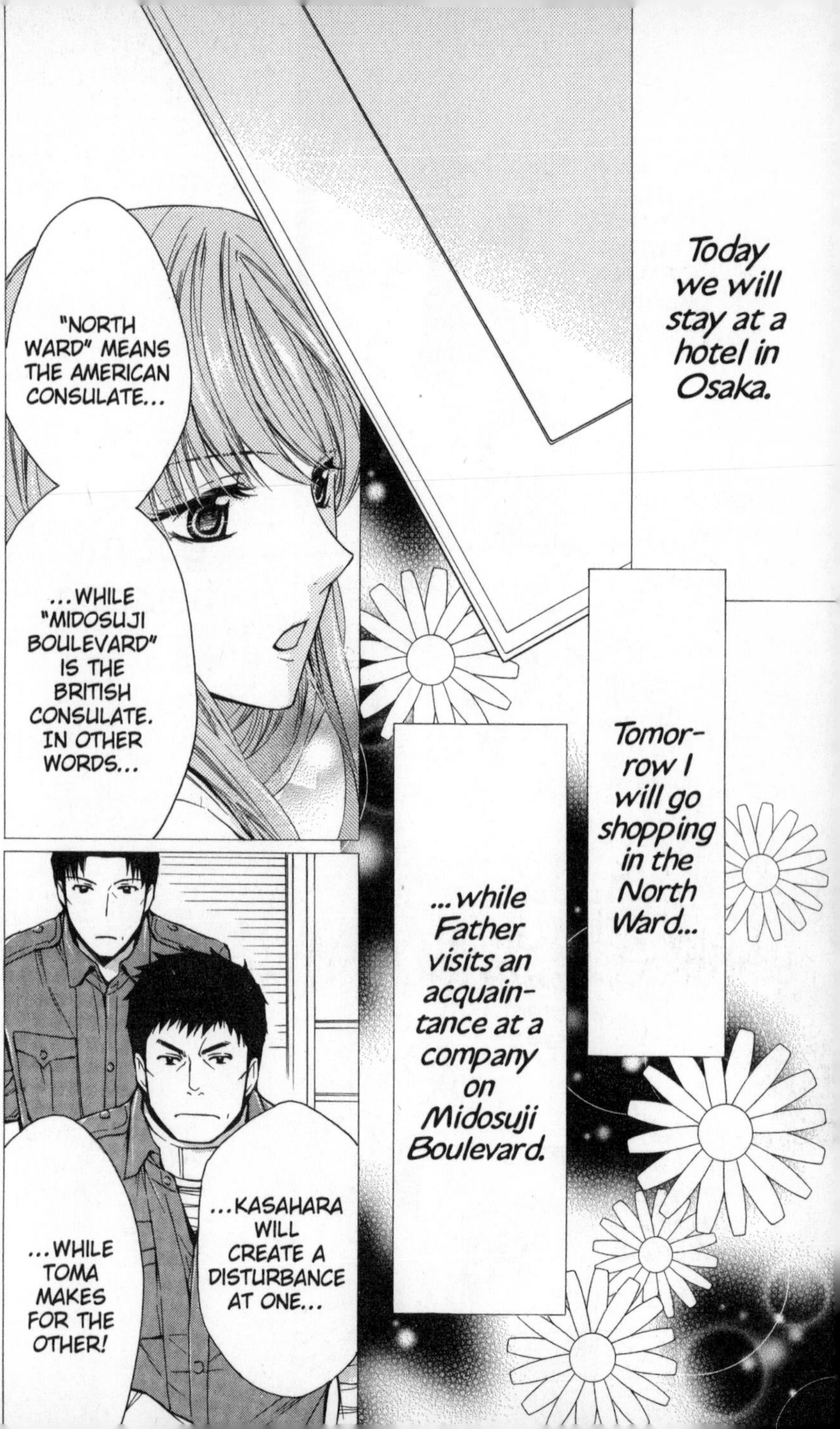
Today we will stay at a hotel in Osaka.
Tomorrow I will go shopping in the North Ward...
...while Father visits an acquaintance at a company on Midosuji Boulevard.
"NORTH WARD" MEANS THE AMERICAN CONSULATE...
...WHILE "MIDOSUJI BOULEVARD" IS THE BRITISH CONSULATE. IN OTHER WORDS...
...KASAHARA WILL CREATE A DISTURBANCE AT ONE...
...WHILE TOMA MAKES FOR THE OTHER!

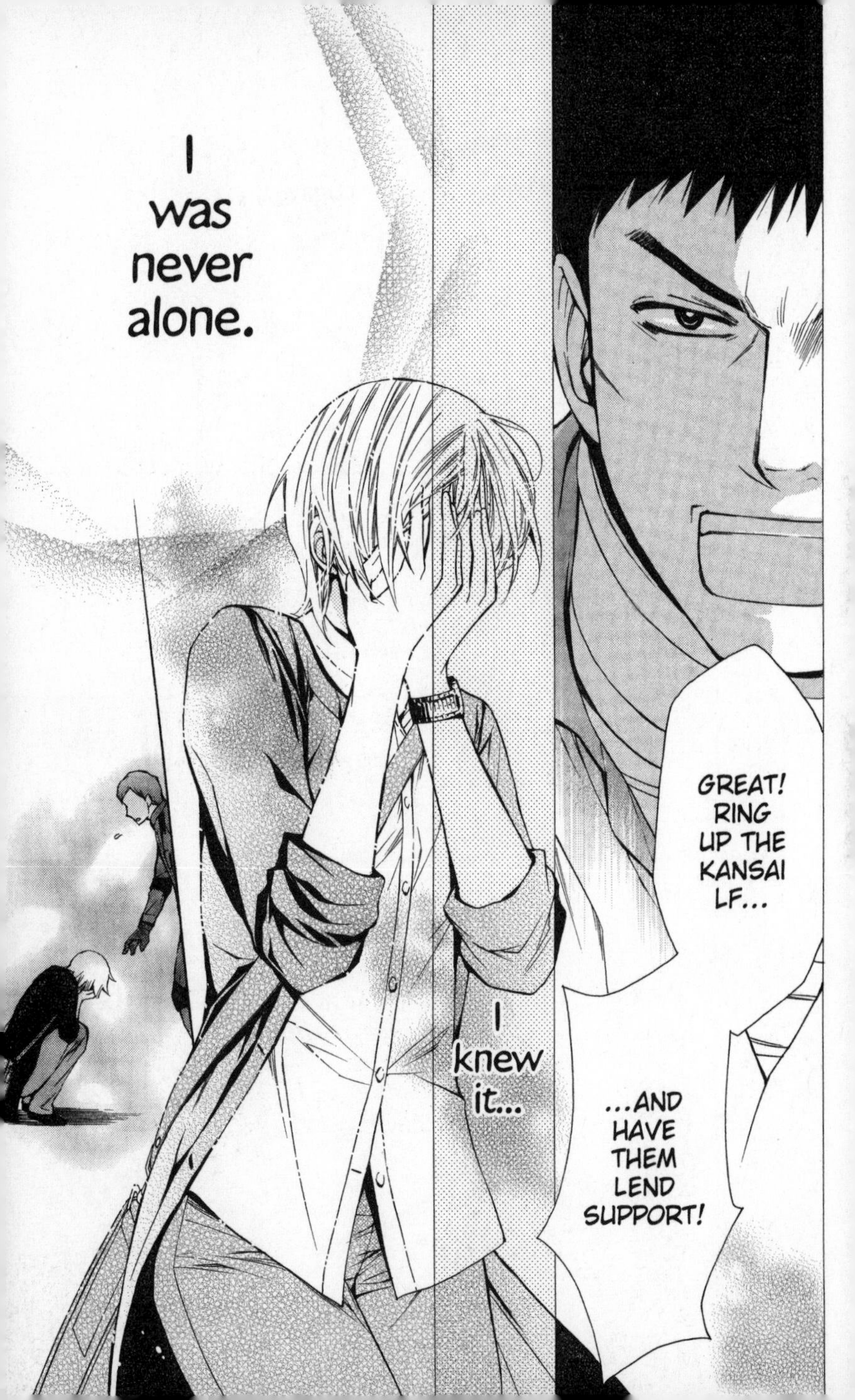
GREAT! RING UP THE KANSAI LF...
...AND HAVE THEM LEND SUPPORT!
I knew it...
I was never alone.

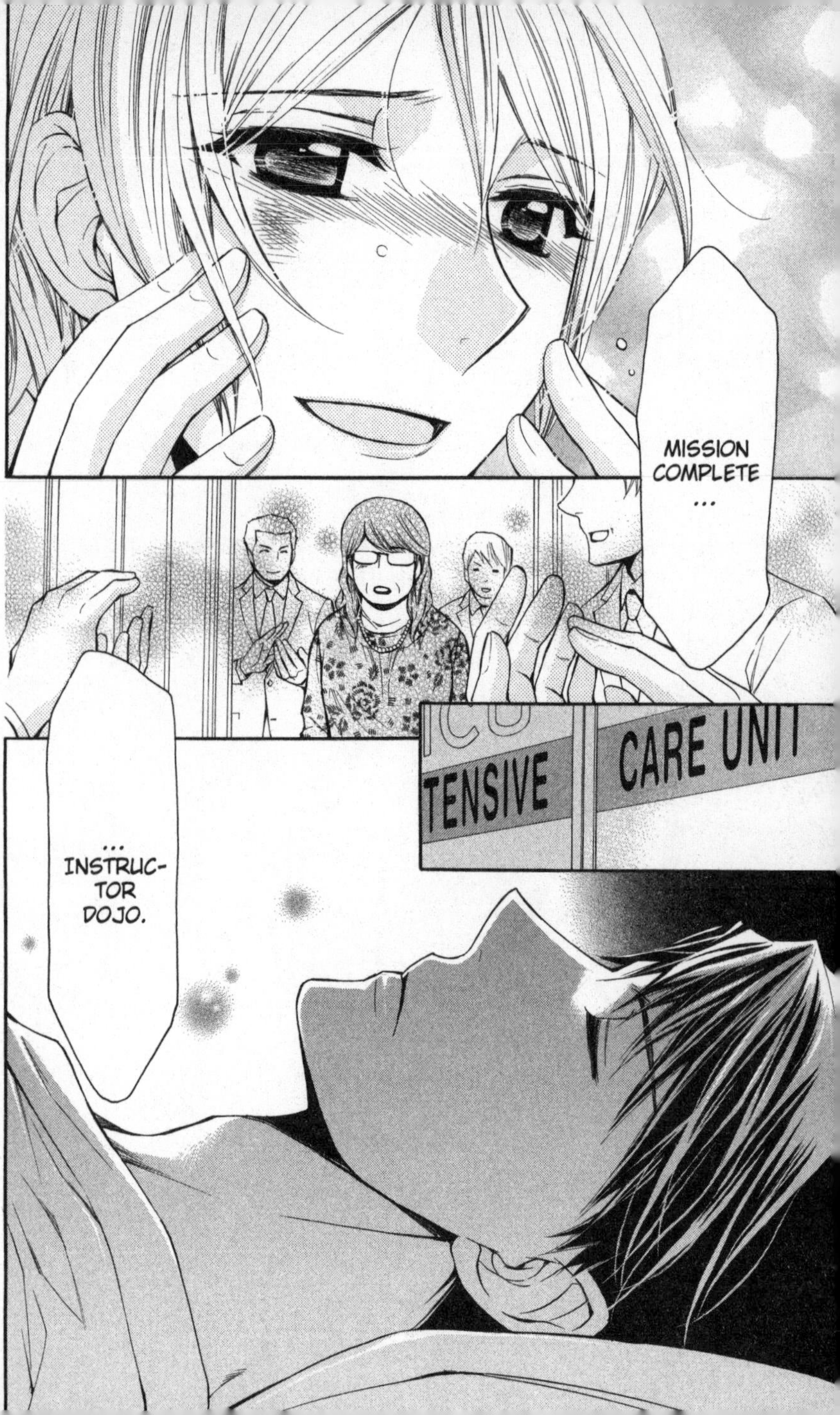

MISSION COMPLETE ...
... INSTRUCTOR DOJO.
TENSIVE
CARE UNIT

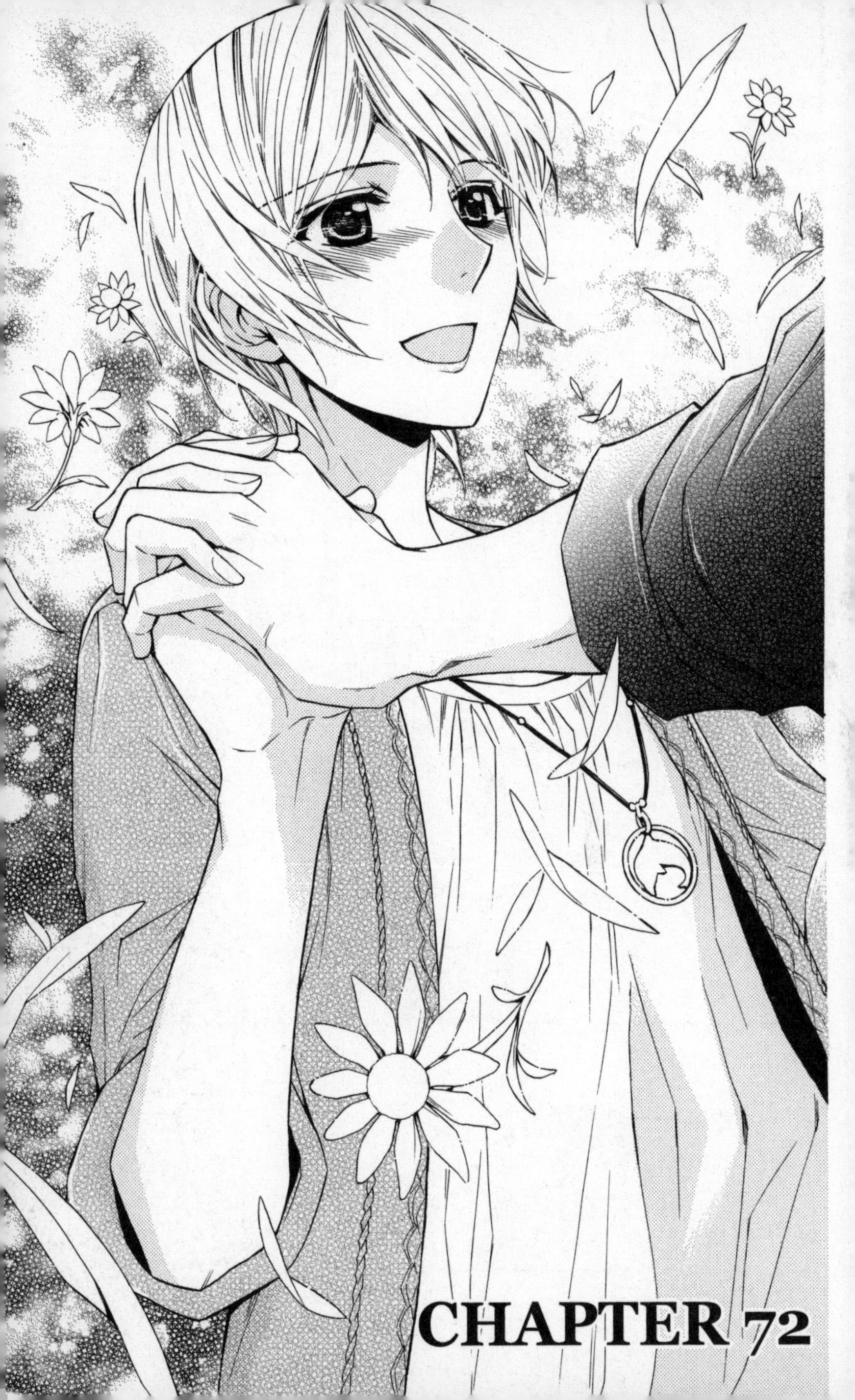

CHAPTER 72

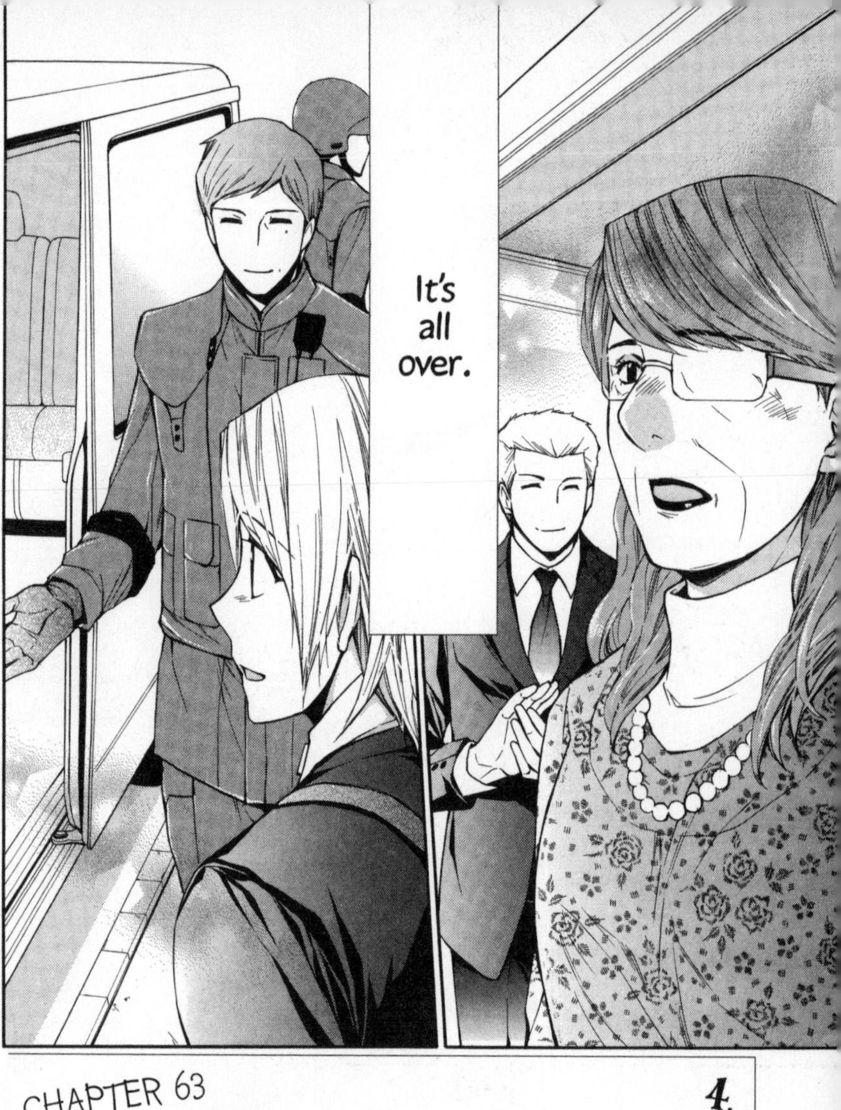
It's all over.

CHAPTER 63

4.

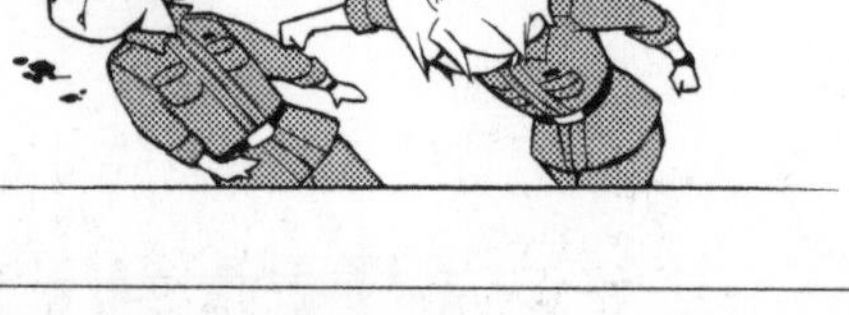

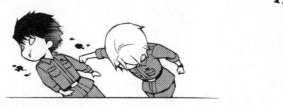

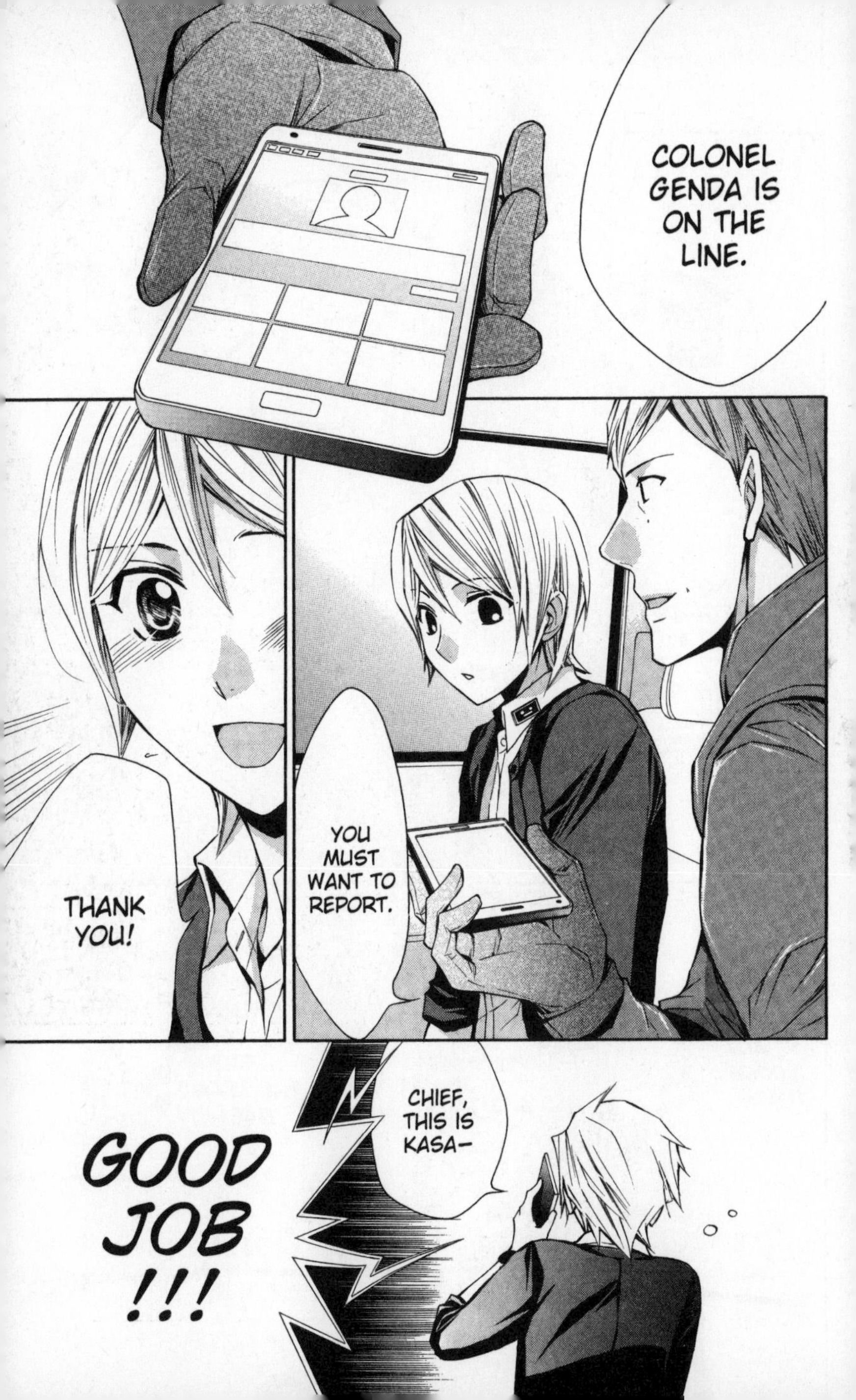
COLONEL GENDA IS ON THE LINE.
YOU MUST WANT TO REPORT.
THANK YOU!
CHIEF, THIS IS KASA–
GOOD JOB!!!

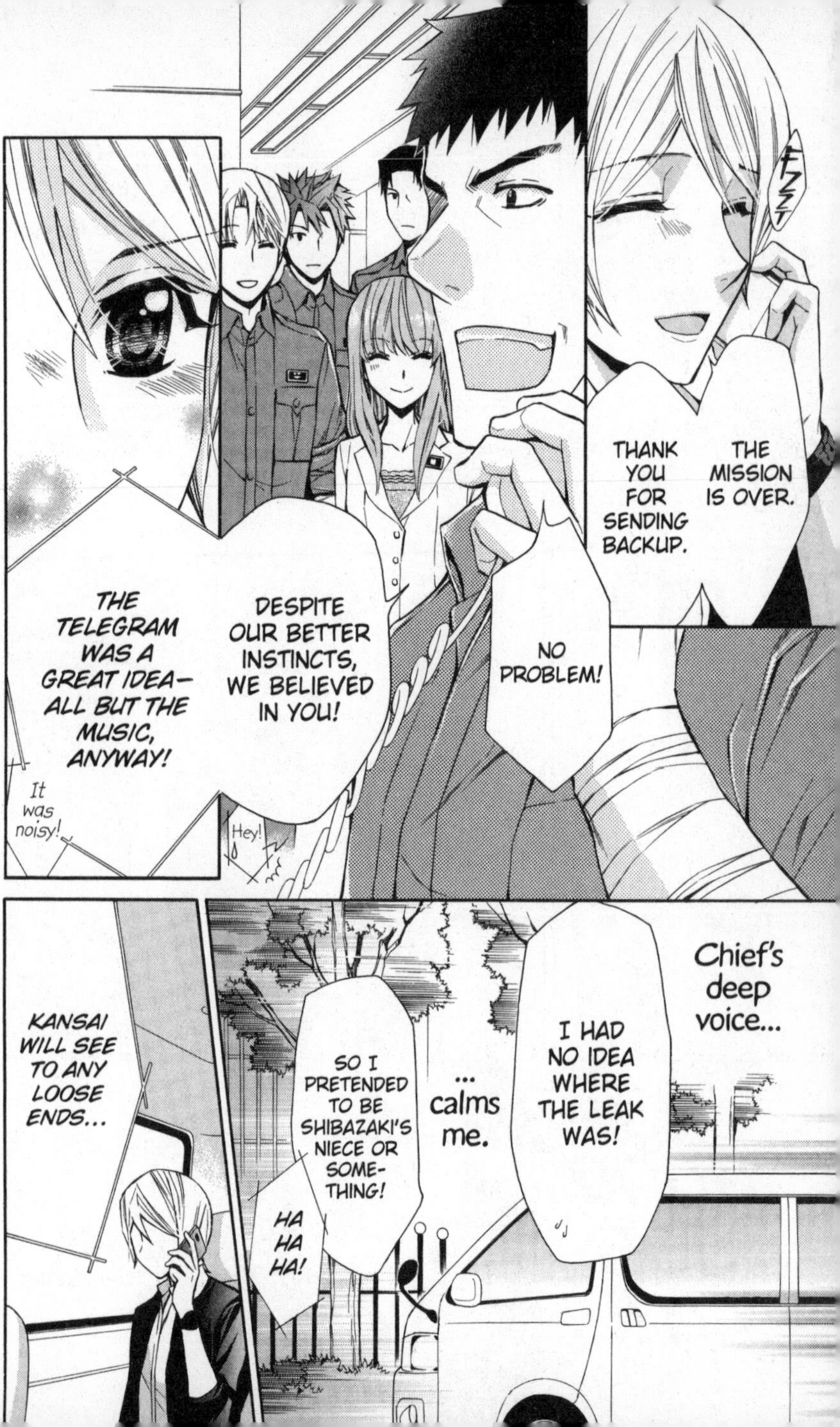
THE MISSION IS OVER.
THANK YOU FOR SENDING BACKUP.
NO PROBLEM!
DESPITE OUR BETTER INSTINCTS, WE BELIEVED IN YOU!
THE TELEGRAM WAS A GREAT IDEA—ALL BUT THE MUSIC, ANYWAY!
It was noisy!
Hey!
Chief's deep voice...
I HAD NO IDEA WHERE THE LEAK WAS!
... calms me.
SO I PRETENDED TO BE SHIBAZAKI'S NIECE OR SOME-THING!
HA HA HA!
KANSAI WILL SEE TO ANY LOOSE ENDS...

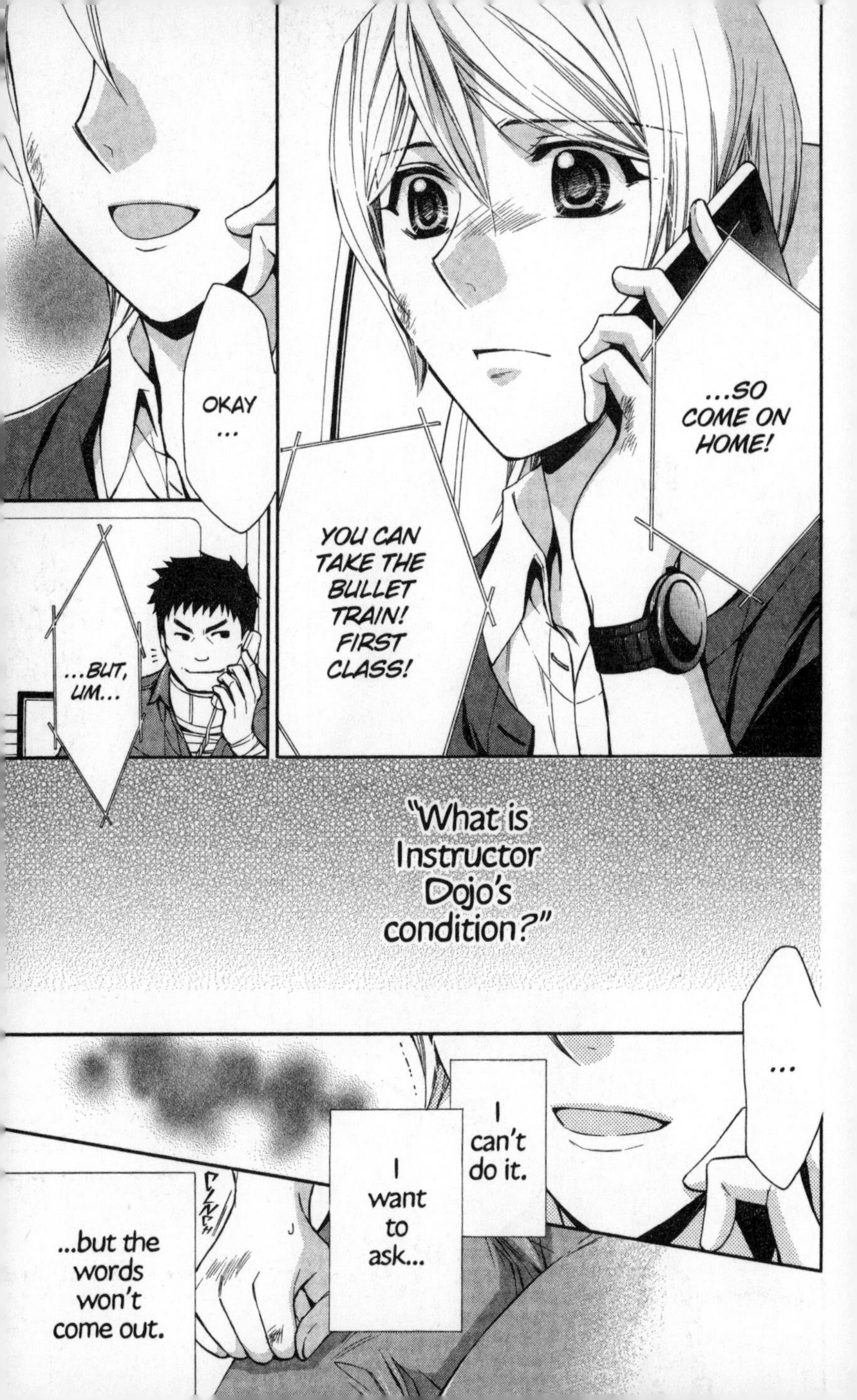
...SO COME ON HOME!
YOU CAN TAKE THE BULLET TRAIN! FIRST CLASS!
OKAY ...
...BUT, UM...
"What is Instructor Dojo's condition?"
...
I can't do it.
I want to ask...
CLNCH
...but the words won't come out.

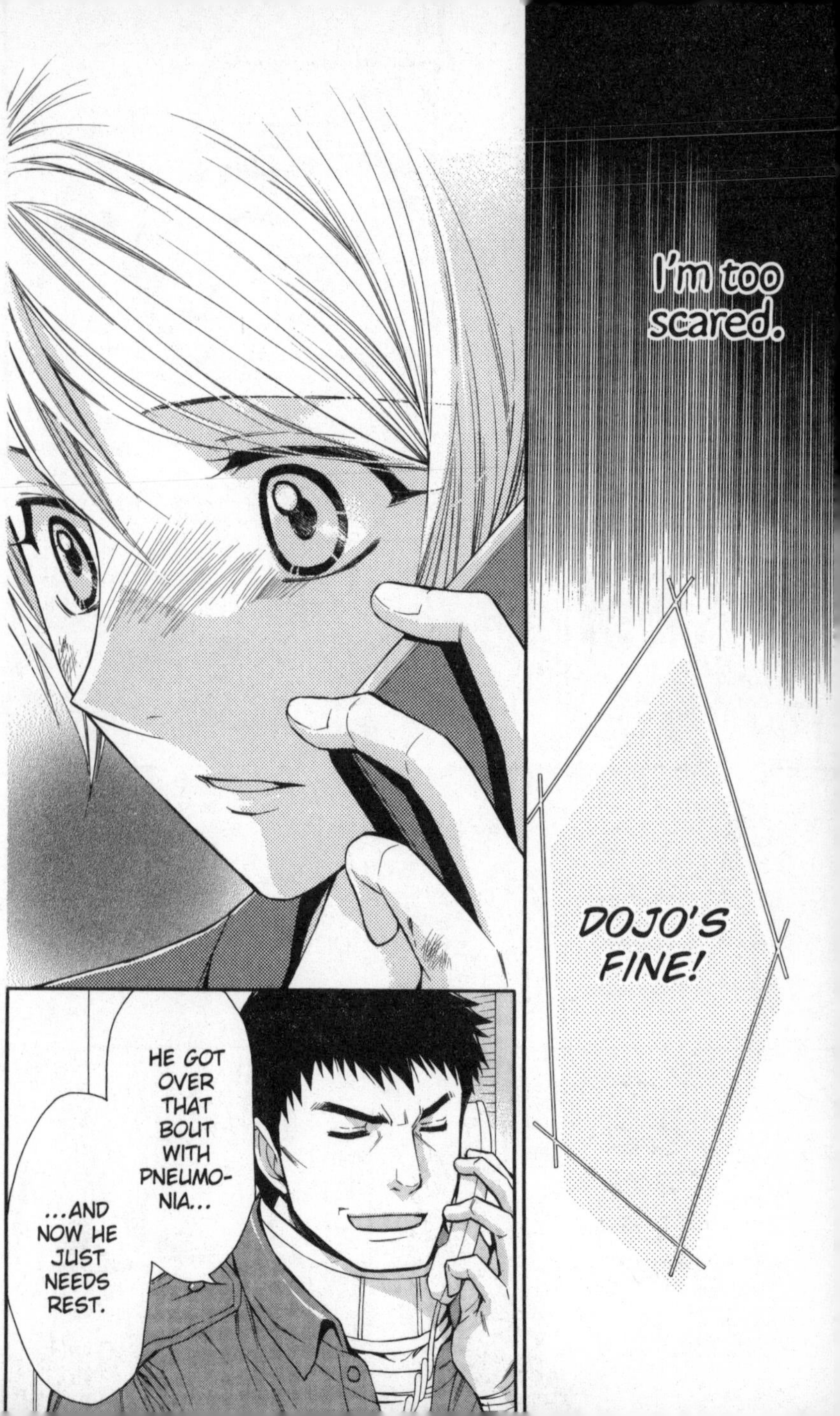
I'm too scared.
DOJO'S FINE!
HE GOT OVER THAT BOUT WITH PNEUMONIA...
...AND NOW HE JUST NEEDS REST.

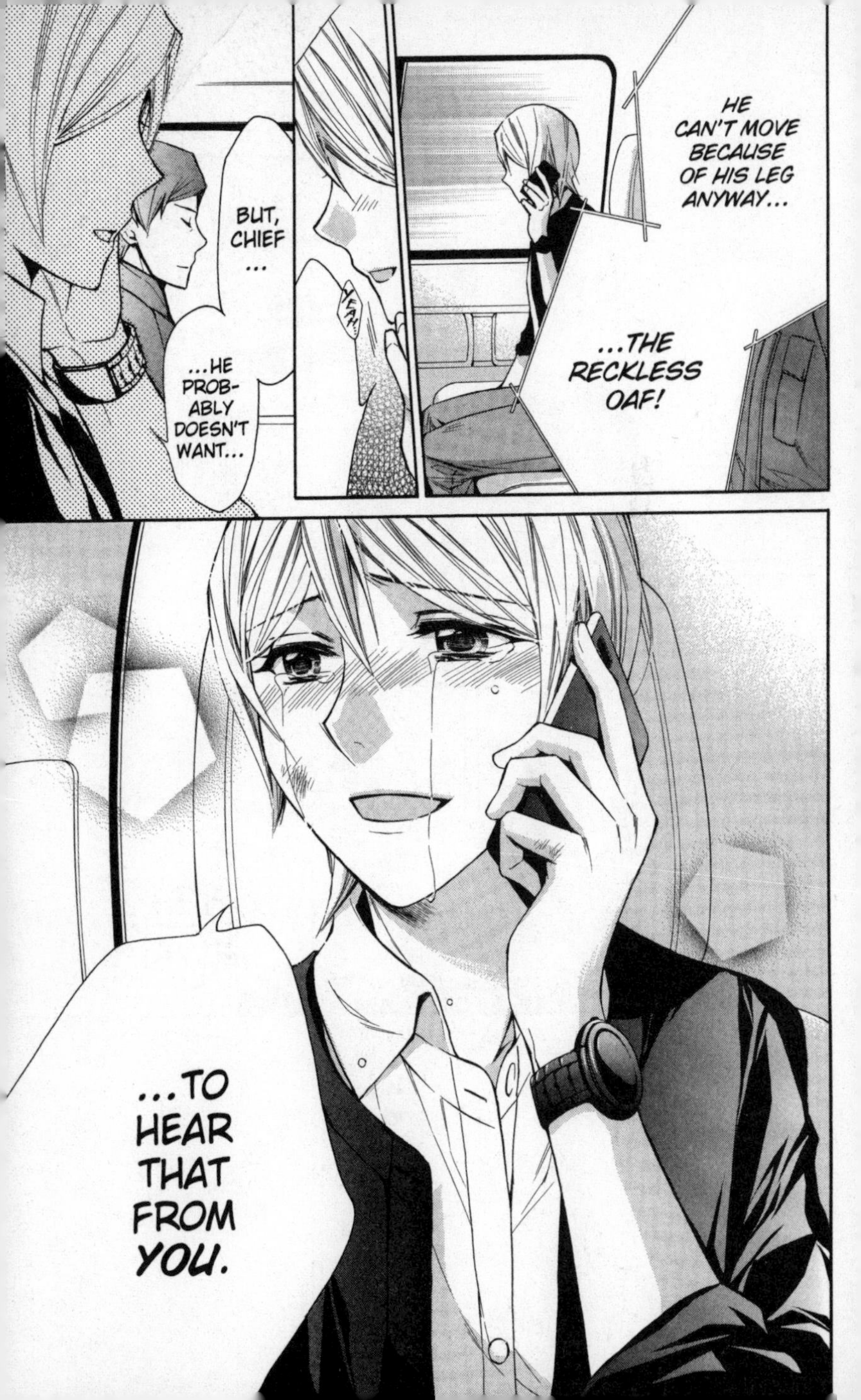
HE CAN'T MOVE BECAUSE OF HIS LEG ANYWAY...
...THE RECKLESS OAF!
YEAH...
BUT, CHIEF...
...HE PROBABLY DOESN'T WANT...
...TO HEAR THAT FROM YOU.

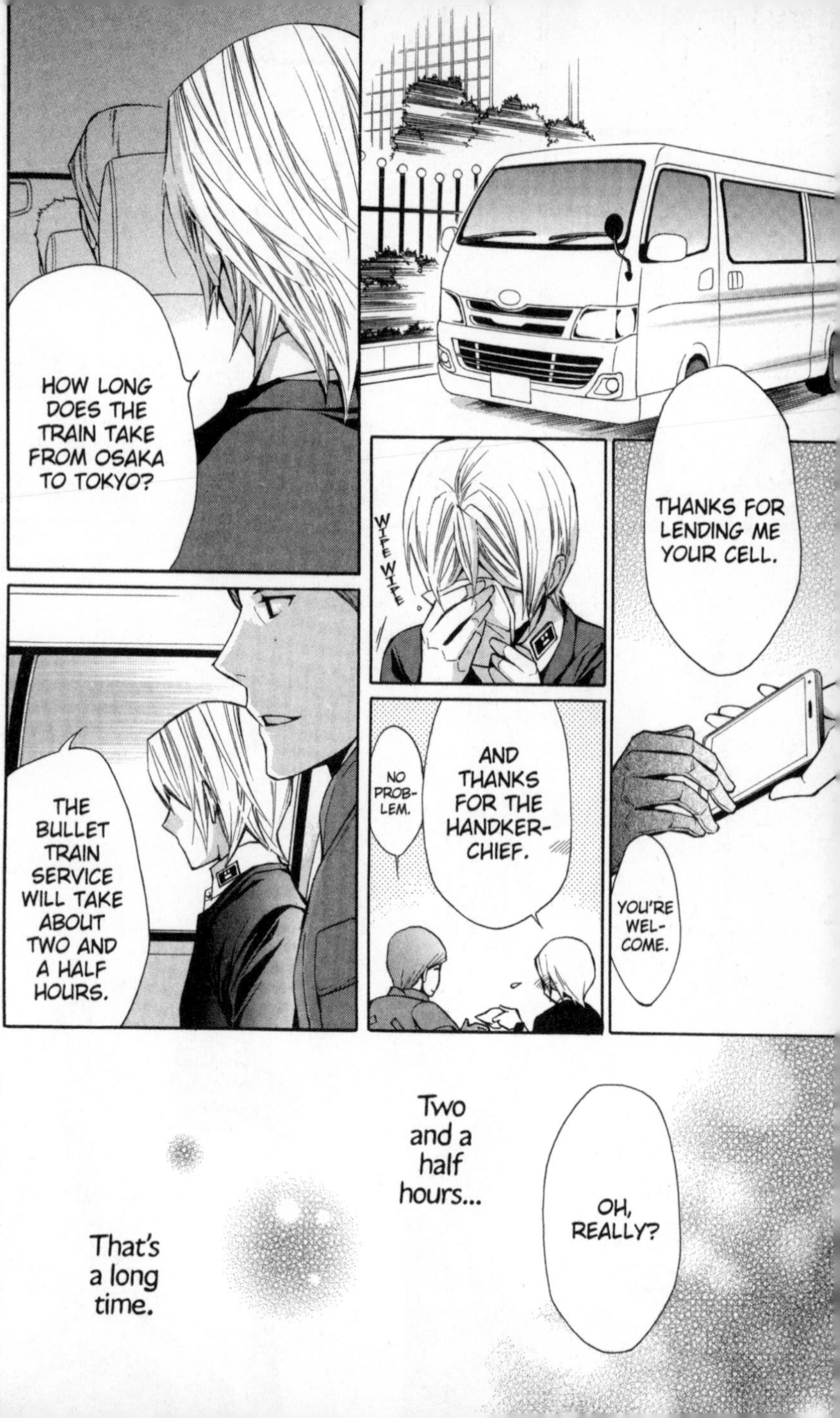
THANKS FOR LENDING ME YOUR CELL.
YOU'RE WEL-COME.
WIPE WIPE
AND THANKS FOR THE HANDKER-CHIEF.
NO PROB-LEM.
HOW LONG DOES THE TRAIN TAKE FROM OSAKA TO TOKYO?
THE BULLET TRAIN SERVICE WILL TAKE ABOUT TWO AND A HALF HOURS.
OH, REALLY?
Two and a half hours...
That's a long time.

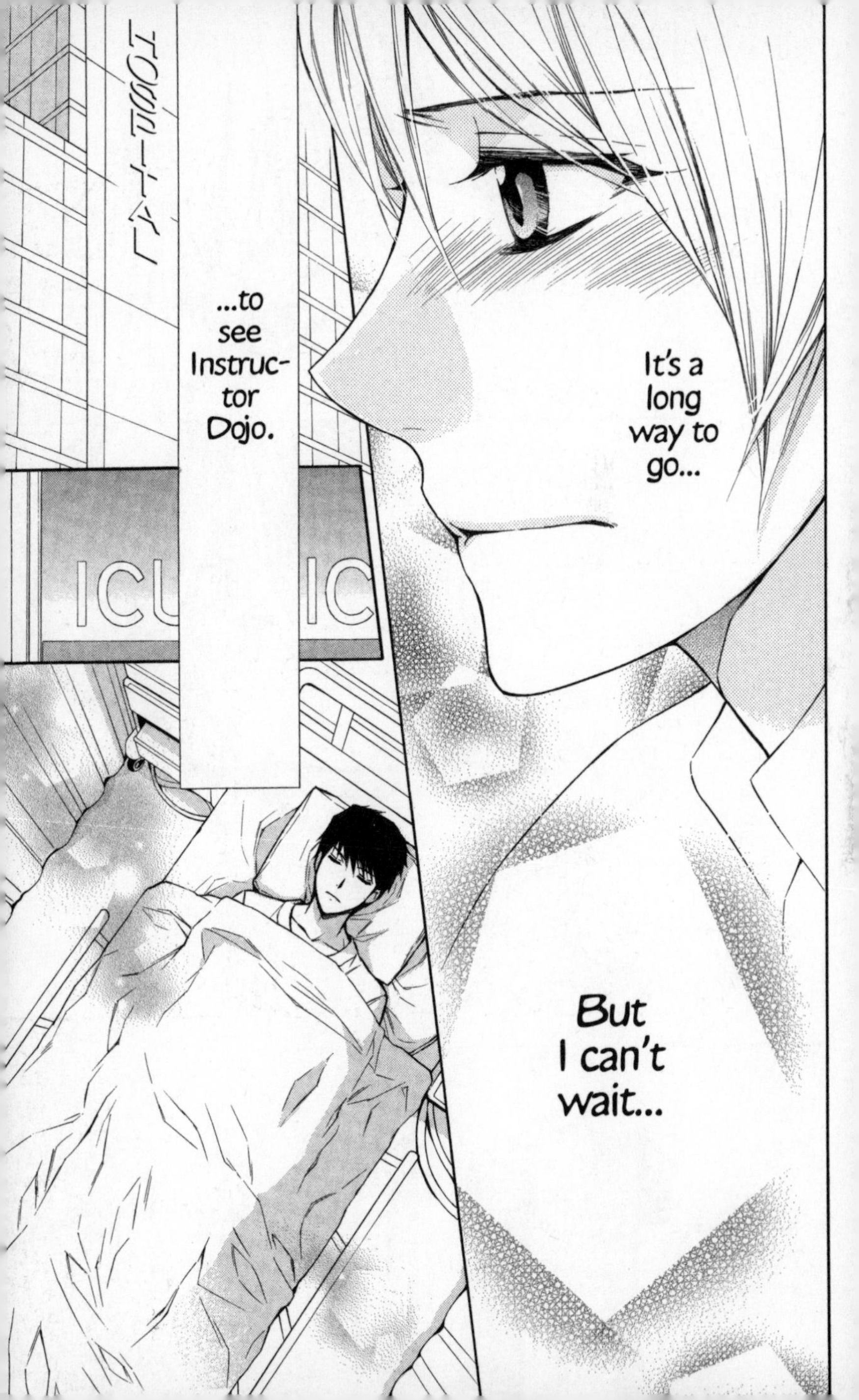
It's a long way to go...
But I can't wait...
...to see Instructor Dojo.
HOSPITAL
ICU
ICU

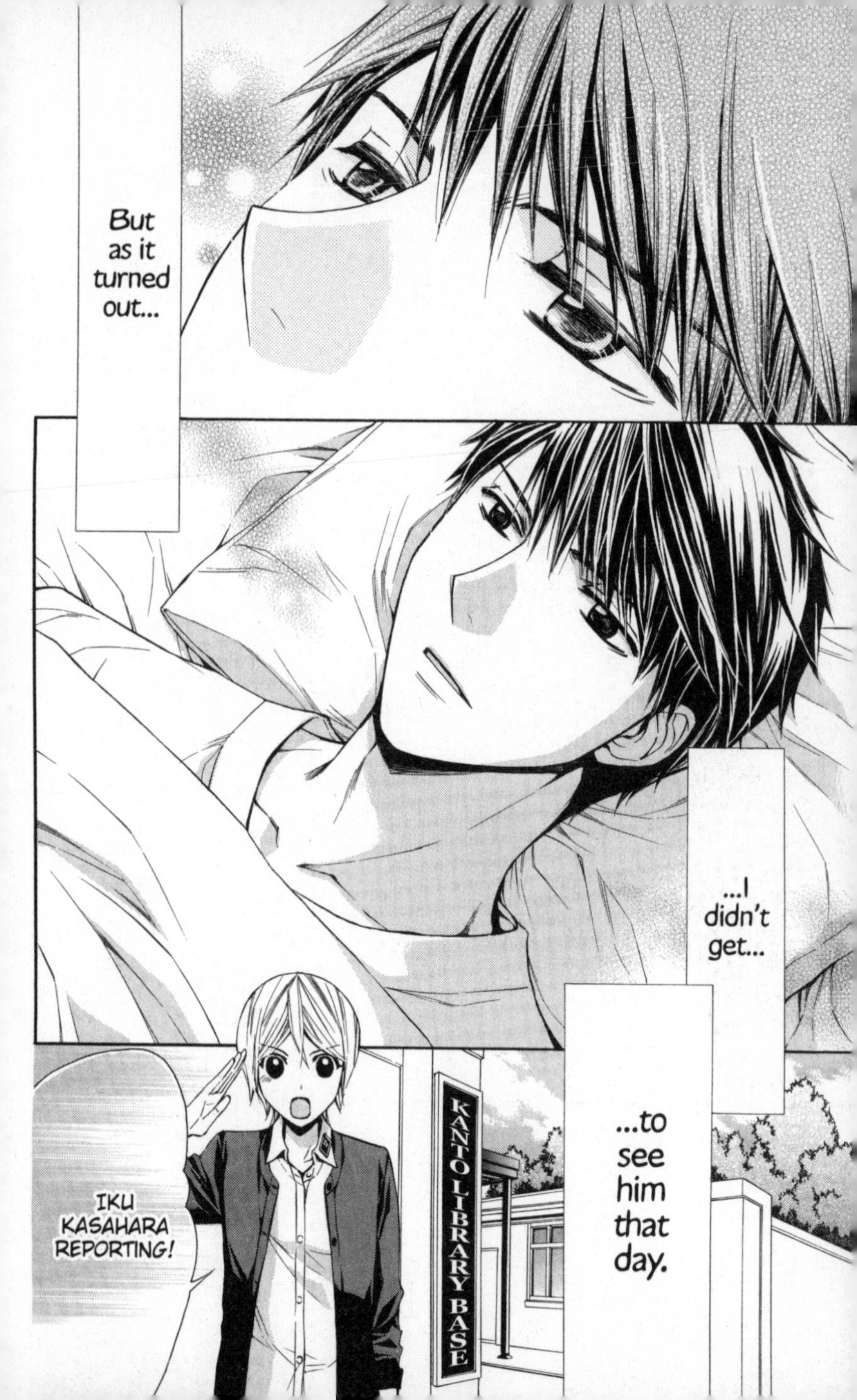
But as it turned out...
...I didn't get...
...to see him that day.
KANTO LIBRARY BASE
IKU KASAHARA REPORTING!

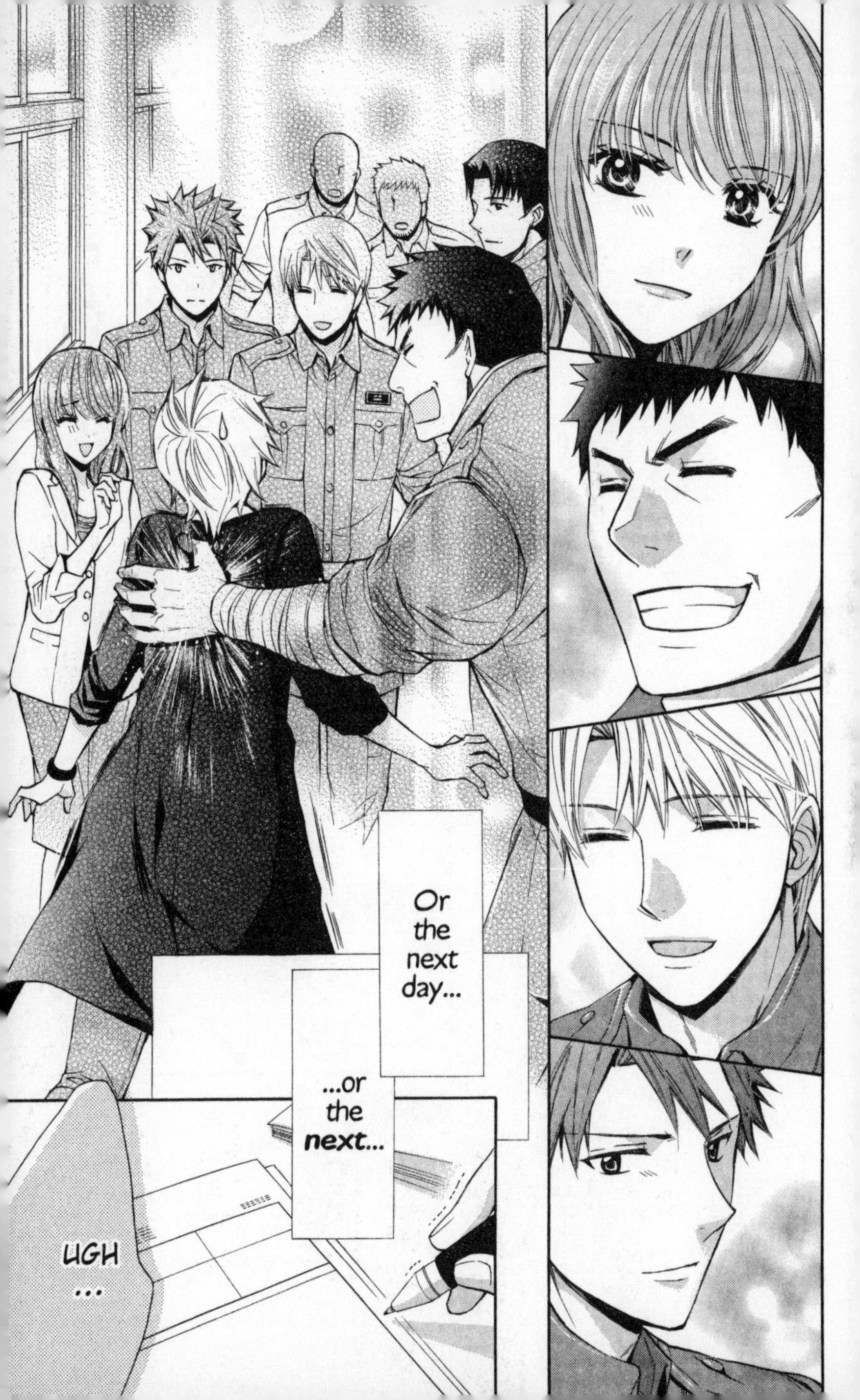
Or the next day...
...or the next...
UGH ...

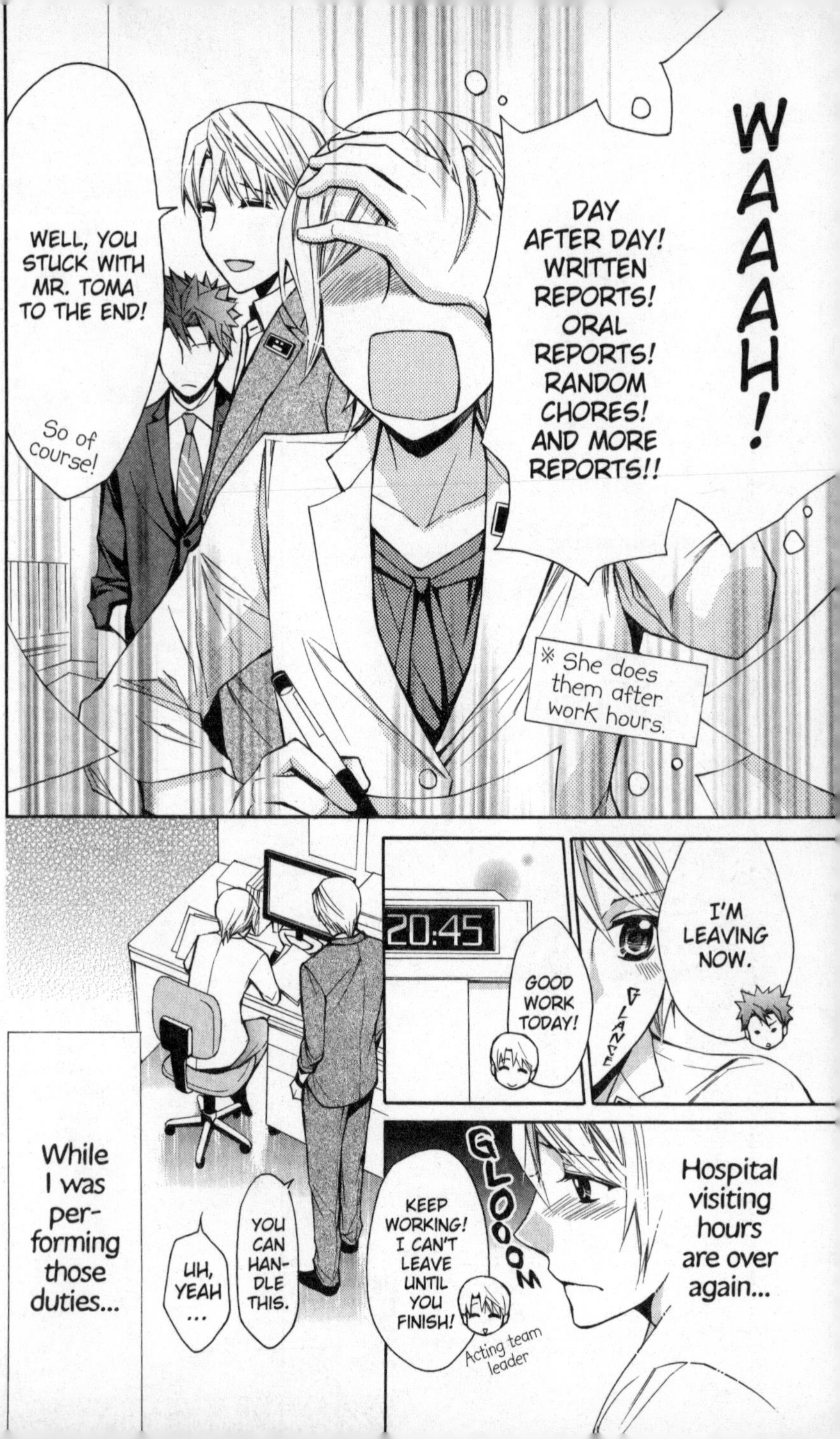
WAAAH!
DAY AFTER DAY! WRITTEN REPORTS! ORAL REPORTS! RANDOM CHORES! AND MORE REPORTS!!
※ She does them after work hours.
WELL, YOU STUCK WITH MR. TOMA TO THE END!
So of course!
I'M LEAVING NOW.
GLANCE
20:45
GOOD WORK TODAY!
Hospital visiting hours are over again...
GLOOOOM
KEEP WORKING! I CAN'T LEAVE UNTIL YOU FINISH!
Acting team leader
YOU CAN HAN-DLE THIS.
UH, YEAH ...
While I was per-forming those duties...

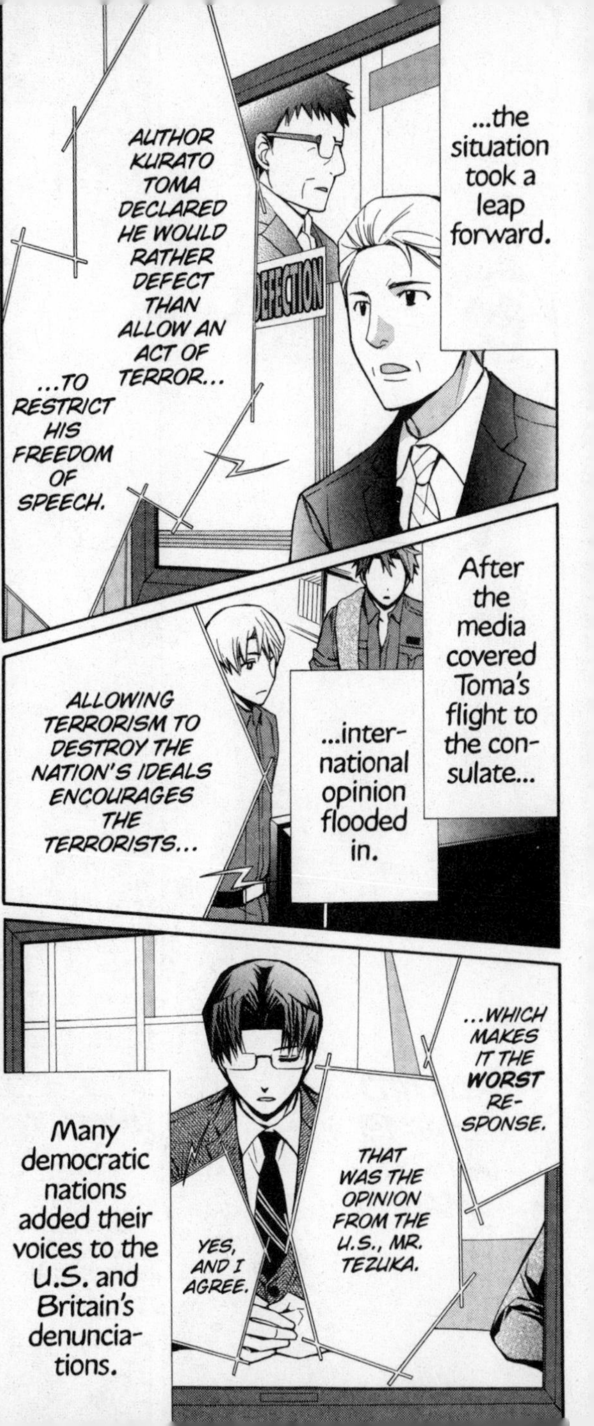
...the situation took a leap forward.
AUTHOR KURATO TOMA DECLARED HE WOULD RATHER DEFECT THAN ALLOW AN ACT OF TERROR...
DEFECTION
...TO RESTRICT HIS FREEDOM OF SPEECH.
After the media covered Toma's flight to the consulate...
...international opinion flooded in.
ALLOWING TERRORISM TO DESTROY THE NATION'S IDEALS ENCOURAGES THE TERRORISTS...
...WHICH MAKES IT THE WORST RESPONSE.
THAT WAS THE OPINION FROM THE U.S., MR. TEZUKA.
YES, AND I AGREE.
Many democratic nations added their voices to the U.S. and Britain's denunciations.

4

All I can do is shake my head when I look back at the previous volumes, because the farther back I go, the more I find scenes that I could have done differently. I'm so sorry! Despite my lack of skill, I'm currently (in the spring of 2015) working on one of the extra volumes.

I'm super thrilled! While I was working on this final volume, I already knew that I would be taking on the extra volumes, so I didn't get too choked up over finishing. But when I was working on the last 15 pages, I suddenly got emotional as I thought over the last seven years and three months... (lol)

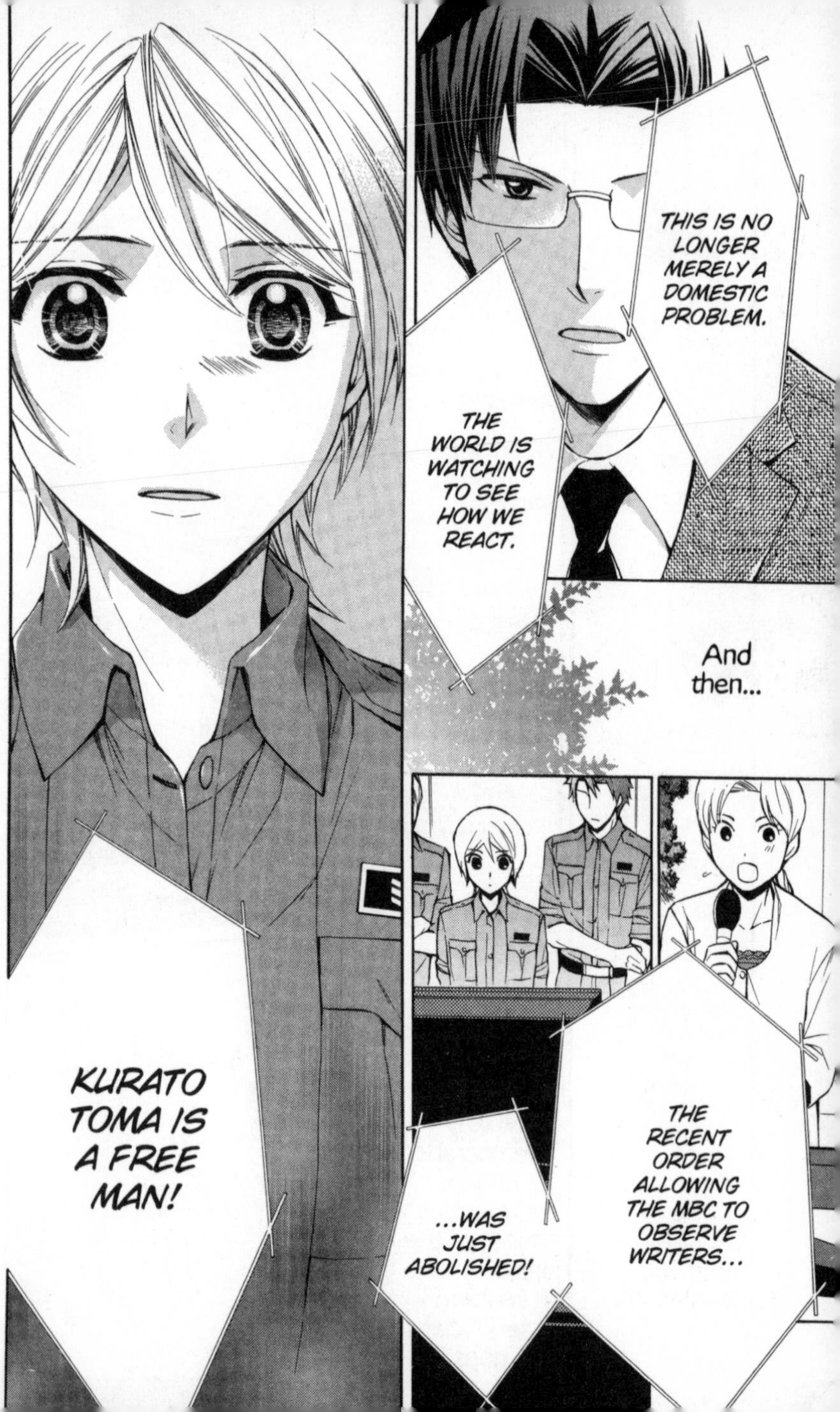
THIS IS NO LONGER MERELY A DOMESTIC PROBLEM.
THE WORLD IS WATCHING TO SEE HOW WE REACT.
And then...
THE RECENT ORDER ALLOWING THE MBC TO OBSERVE WRITERS...
...WAS JUST ABOLISHED!
KURATO TOMA IS A FREE MAN!

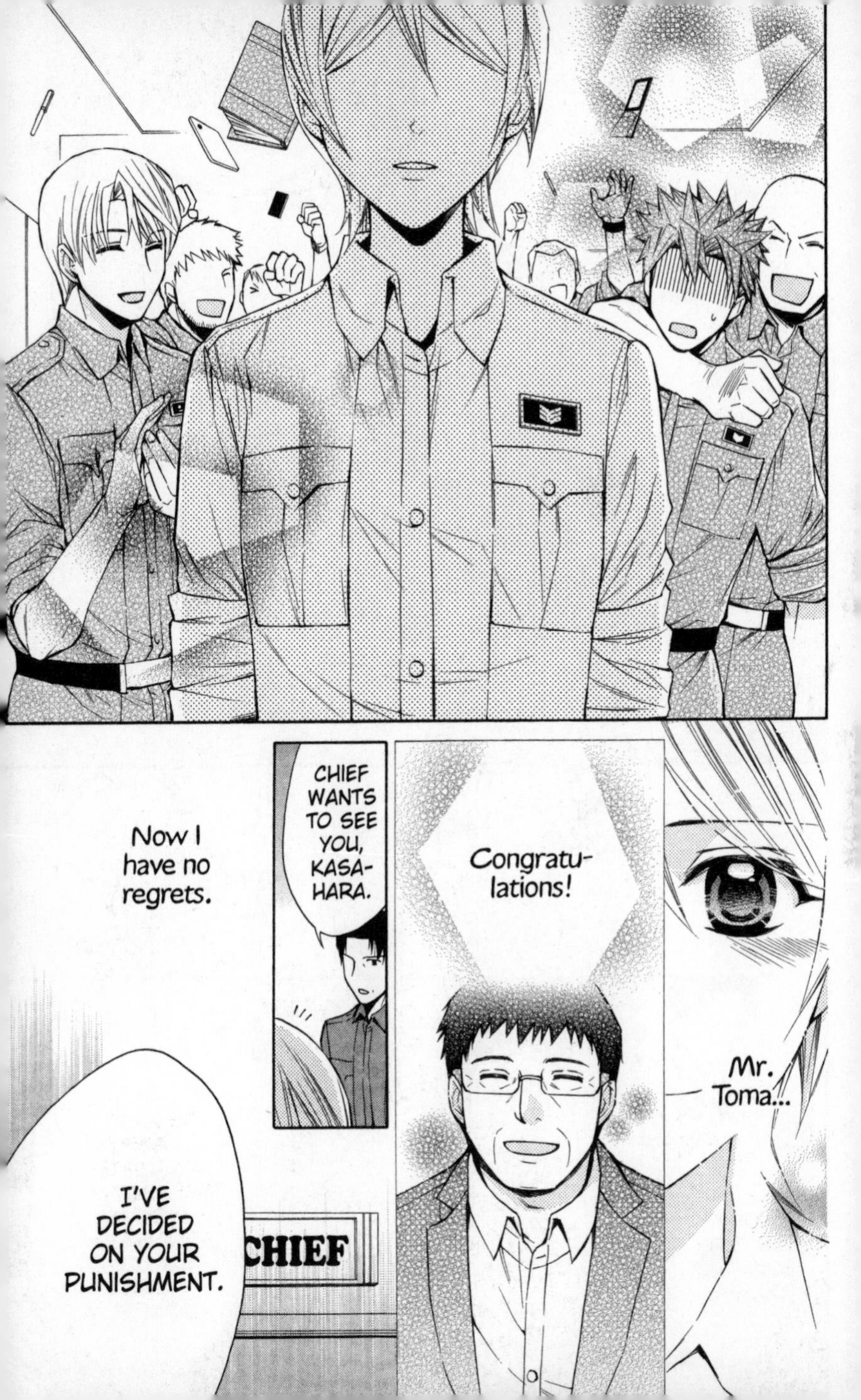
Mr. Toma...
Congratu-lations!
CHIEF WANTS TO SEE YOU, KASA-HARA.
Now I have no regrets.
CHIEF
I'VE DECIDED ON YOUR PUNISHMENT.

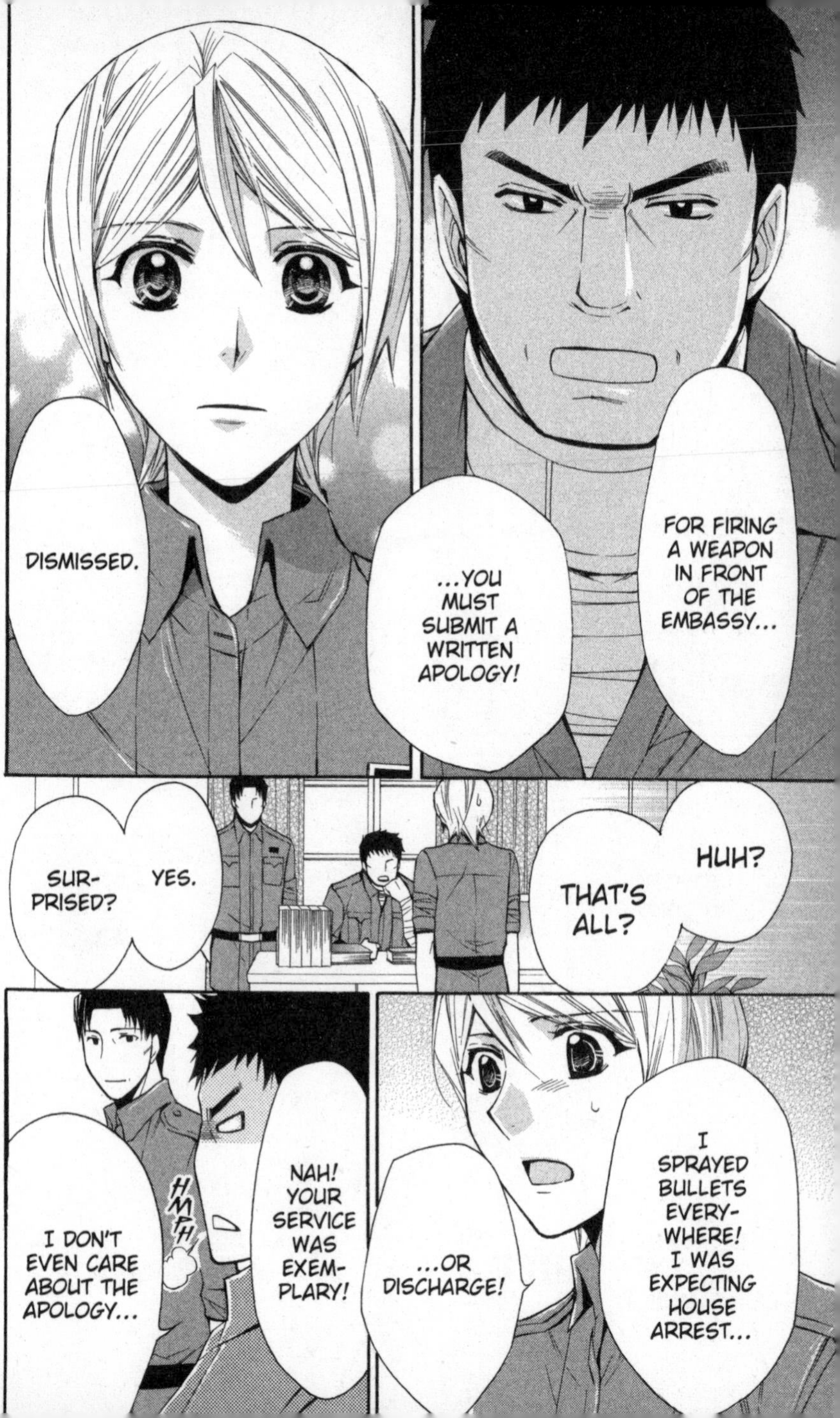
FOR FIRING A WEAPON IN FRONT OF THE EMBASSY...
...YOU MUST SUBMIT A WRITTEN APOLOGY!
DISMISSED.
HUH?
THAT'S ALL?
YES.
SUR-PRISED?
I SPRAYED BULLETS EVERY-WHERE! I WAS EXPECTING HOUSE ARREST...
...OR DISCHARGE!
NAH! YOUR SERVICE WAS EXEM-PLARY!
HMPH
I DON'T EVEN CARE ABOUT THE APOLOGY...

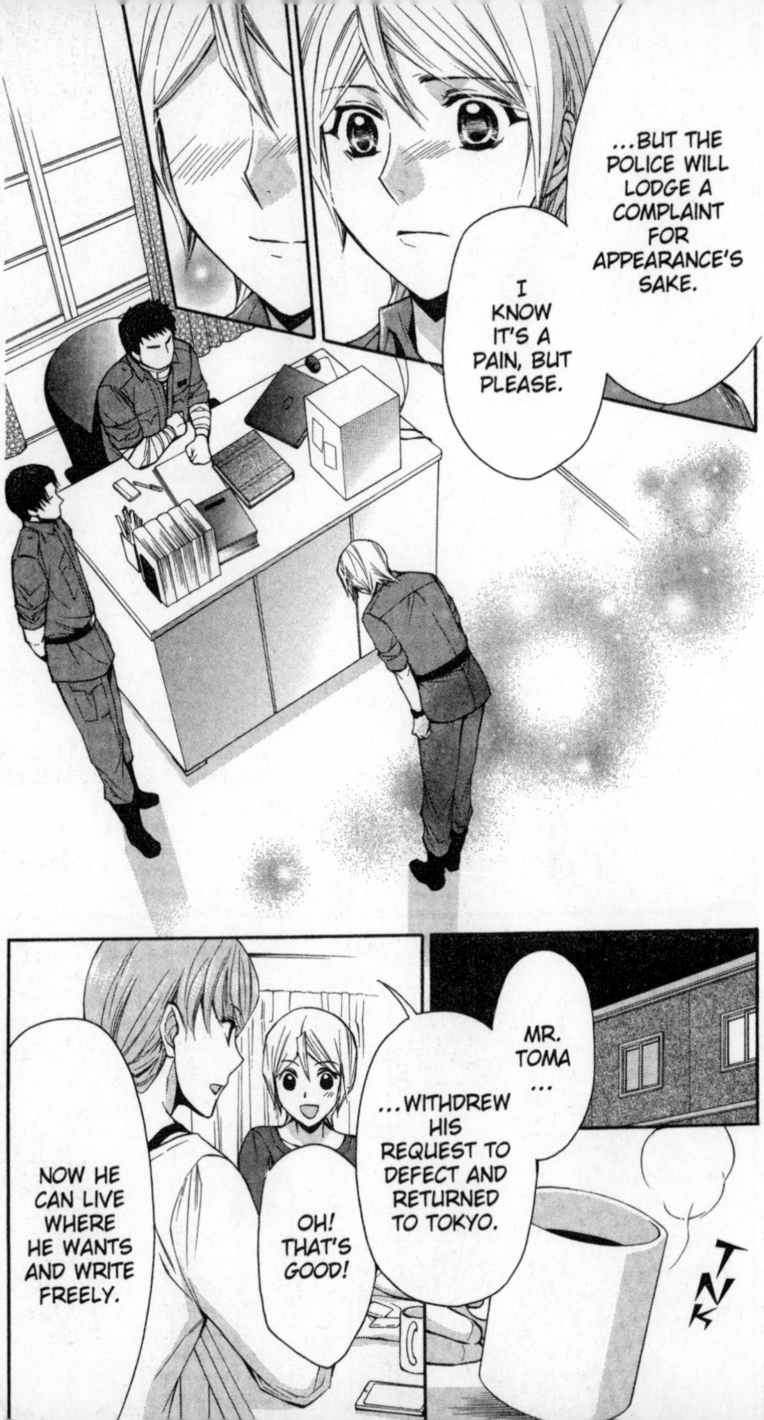
...BUT THE POLICE WILL LODGE A COMPLAINT FOR APPEARANCE'S SAKE.
I KNOW IT'S A PAIN, BUT PLEASE.
MR. TOMA ...
...WITHDREW HIS REQUEST TO DEFECT AND RETURNED TO TOKYO.
TNK
OH! THAT'S GOOD!
NOW HE CAN LIVE WHERE HE WANTS AND WRITE FREELY.

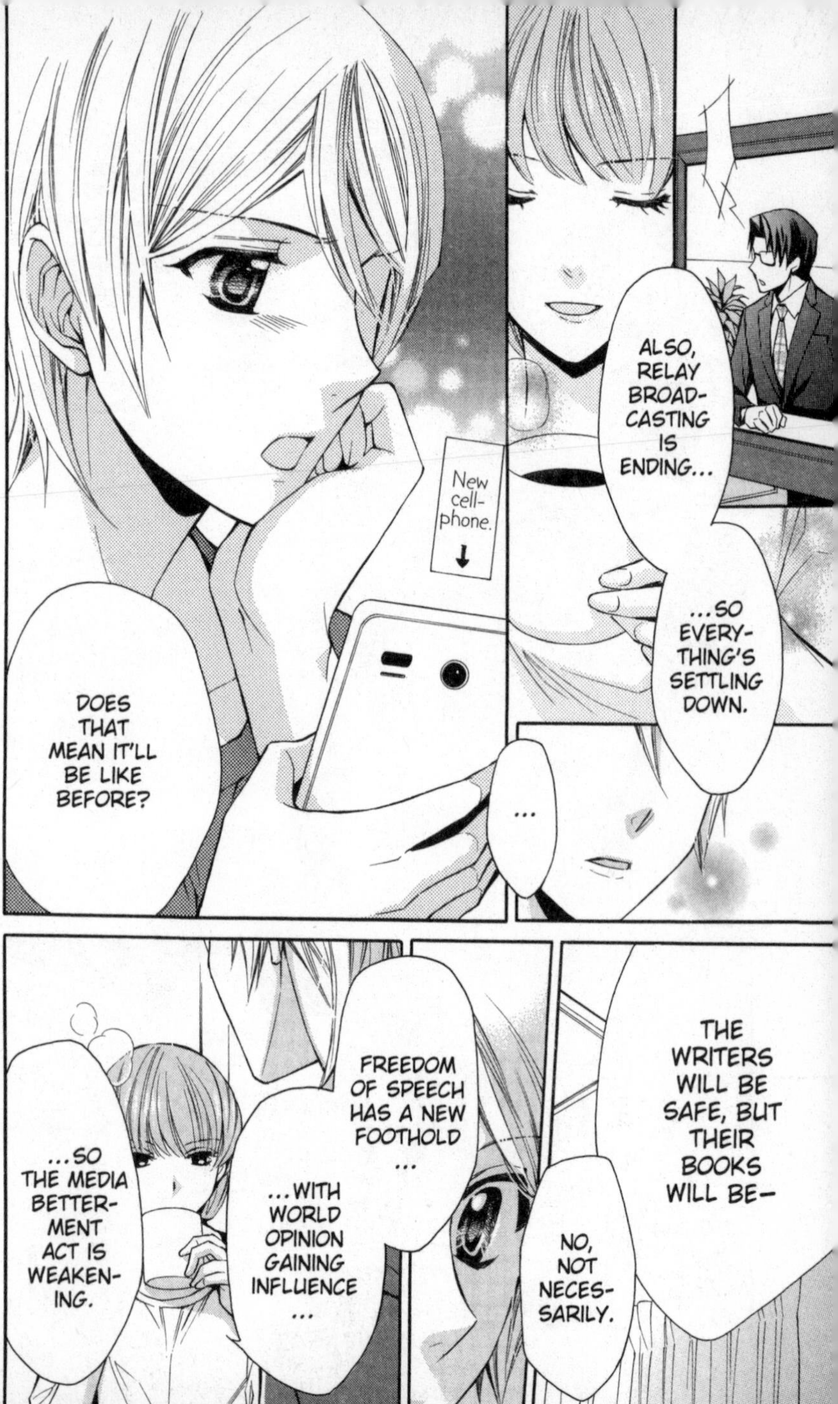
ALSO, RELAY BROADCASTING IS ENDING...
...SO EVERYTHING'S SETTLING DOWN.
...
New cellphone.
DOES THAT MEAN IT'LL BE LIKE BEFORE?
THE WRITERS WILL BE SAFE, BUT THEIR BOOKS WILL BE—
NO, NOT NECESSARILY.
FREEDOM OF SPEECH HAS A NEW FOOTHOLD...
...WITH WORLD OPINION GAINING INFLUENCE...
...SO THE MEDIA BETTERMENT ACT IS WEAKENING.

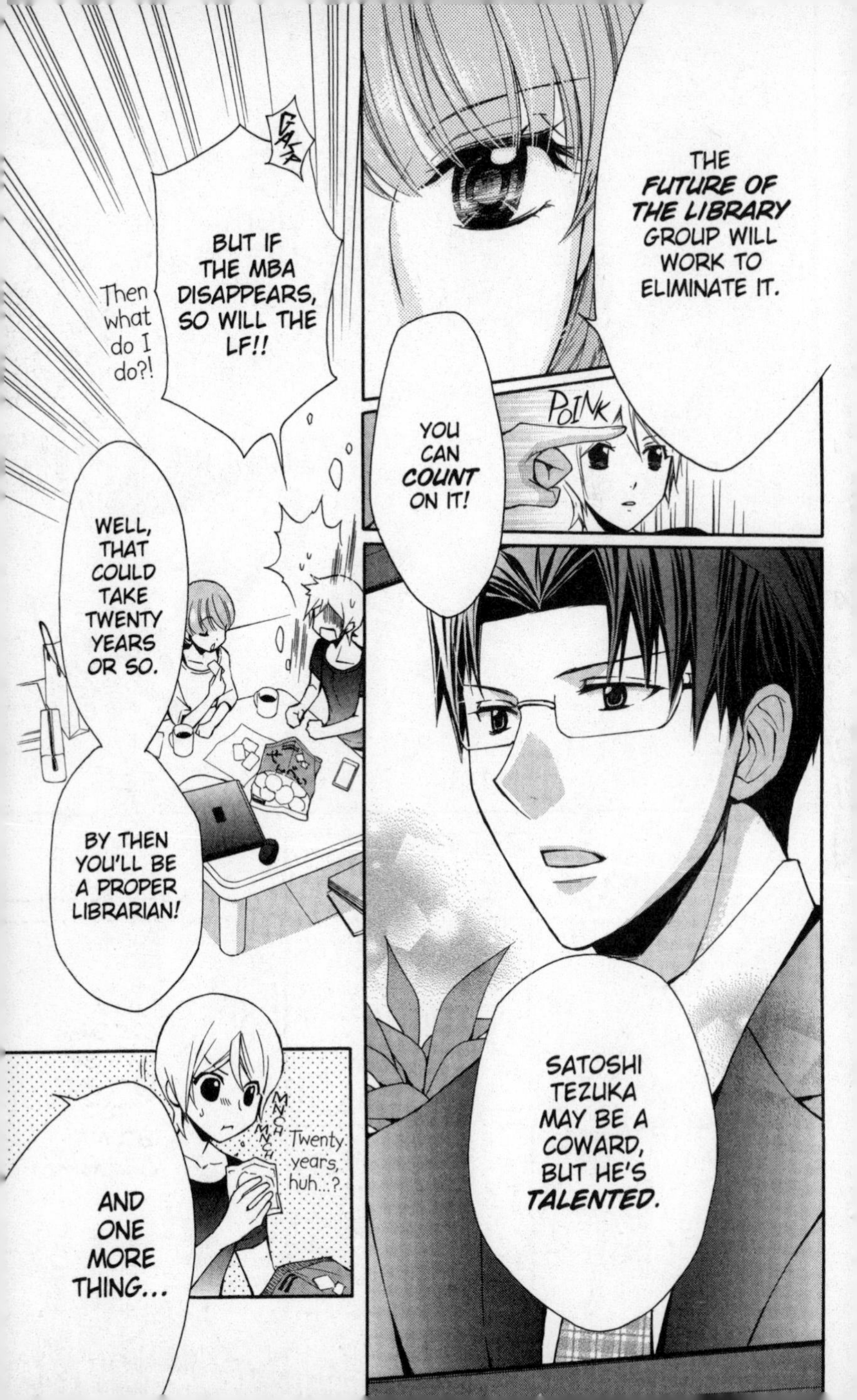
THE FUTURE OF THE LIBRARY GROUP WILL WORK TO ELIMINATE IT.
POINK
YOU CAN COUNT ON IT!
SATOSHI TEZUKA MAY BE A COWARD, BUT HE'S TALENTED.
GAK
BUT IF THE MBA DISAPPEARS, SO WILL THE LF!!
Then what do I do?!
WELL, THAT COULD TAKE TWENTY YEARS OR SO.
BY THEN YOU'LL BE A PROPER LIBRARIAN!
MNCH MNCH
Twenty years, huh...?
AND ONE MORE THING...

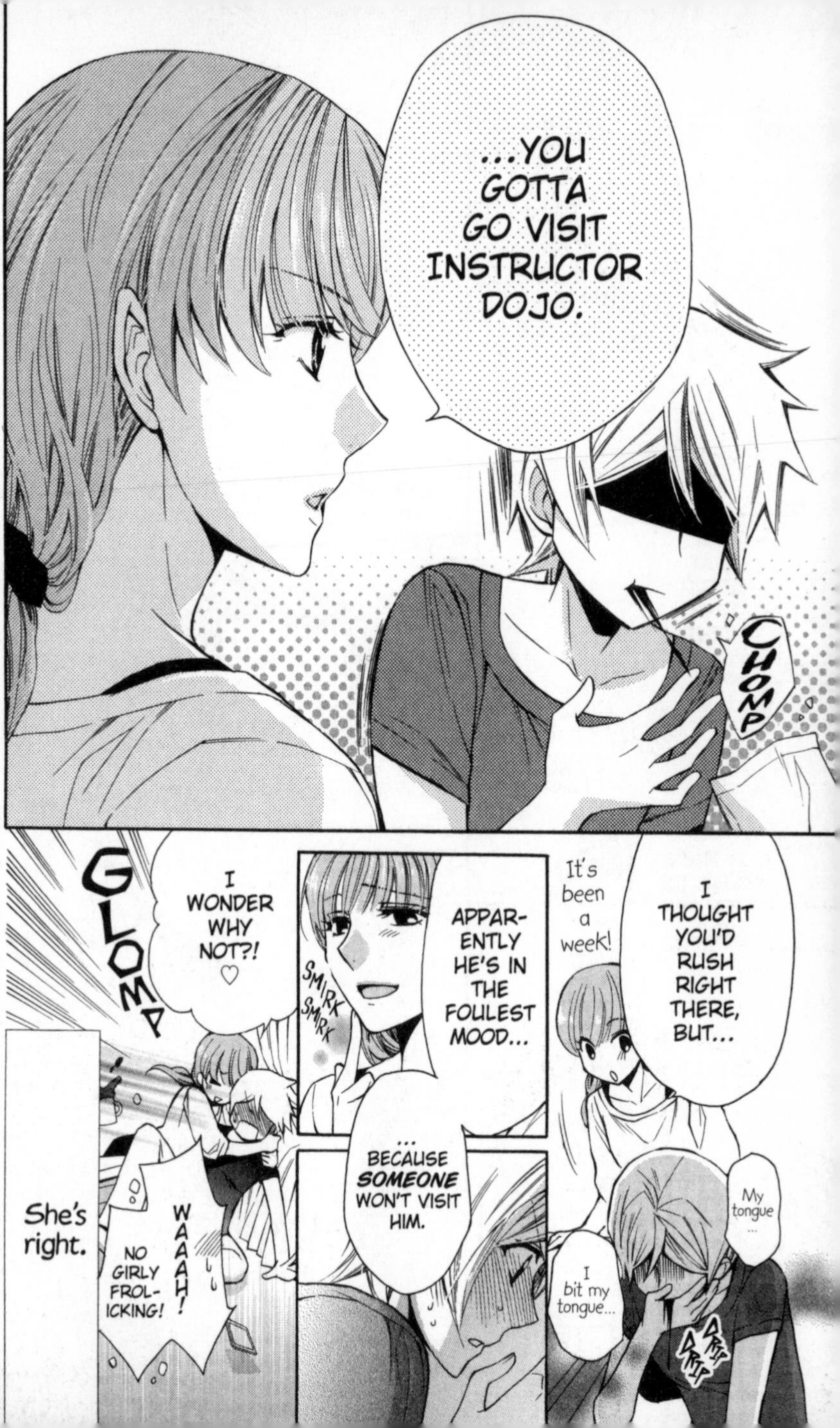
...YOU GOTTA GO VISIT INSTRUCTOR DOJO.
CHOMP
I THOUGHT YOU'D RUSH RIGHT THERE, BUT...
It's been a week!
My tongue...
I bit my tongue...
DRIP DRIP
APPAR-ENTLY HE'S IN THE FOULEST MOOD...
SMIRK SMIRK
...BECAUSE *SOMEONE* WON'T VISIT HIM.
GLOMP
I WONDER WHY NOT?! ♡
WAAAAH!
NO GIRLY FROL-ICKING!
She's right.

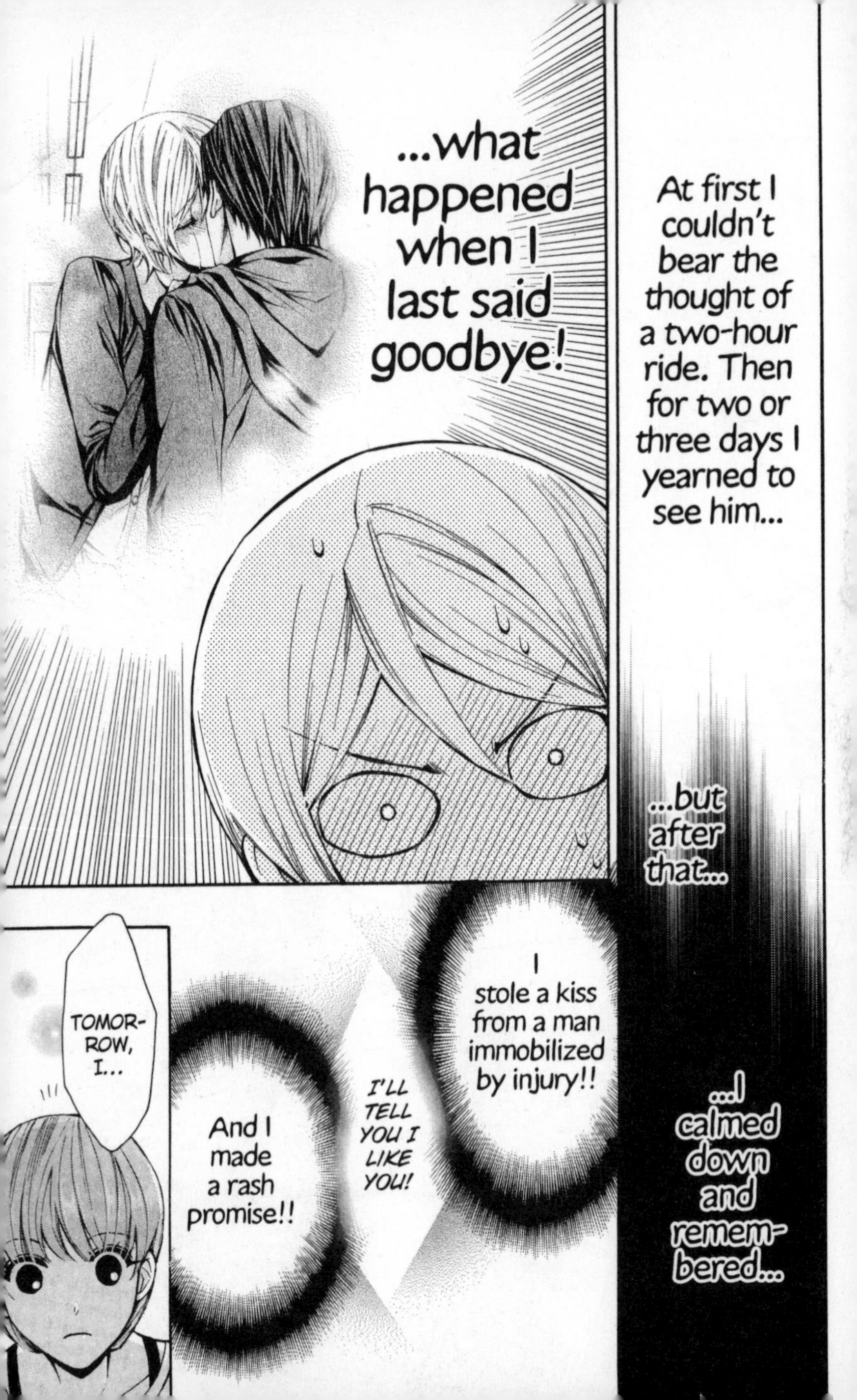
At first I couldn't bear the thought of a two-hour ride. Then for two or three days I yearned to see him...
...but after that...
...I calmed down and remembered...
...what happened when I last said goodbye!
I stole a kiss from a man immobilized by injury!!
I'LL TELL YOU I LIKE YOU!
And I made a rash promise!!
TOMOR-ROW, I...

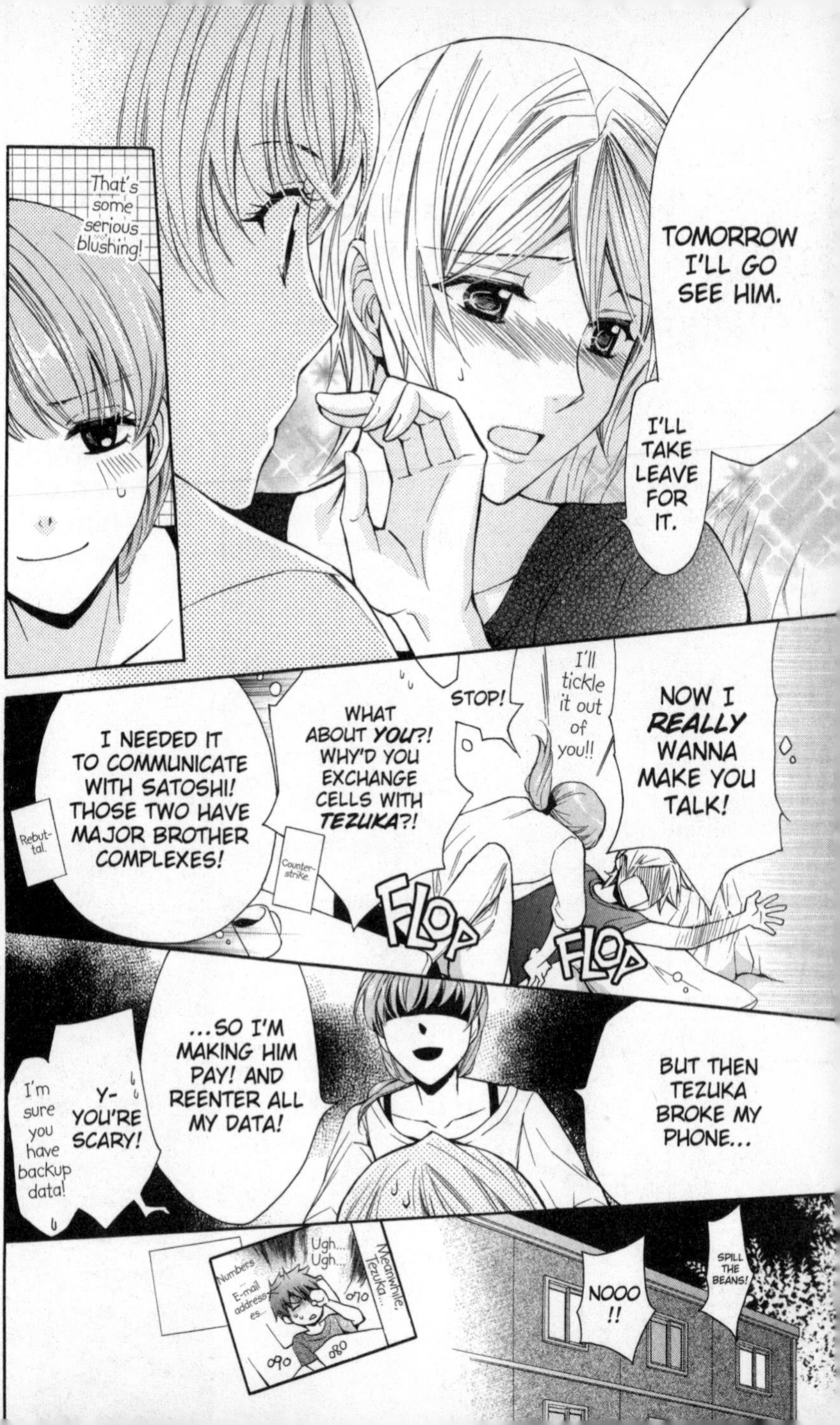
TOMORROW I'LL GO SEE HIM.
I'LL TAKE LEAVE FOR IT.
That's some serious blushing!
NOW I *REALLY* WANNA MAKE YOU TALK!
I'll tickle it out of you!!
STOP!
WHAT ABOUT *YOU*?! WHY'D YOU EXCHANGE CELLS WITH *TEZUKA*?!
Counter-strike.
I NEEDED IT TO COMMUNICATE WITH SATOSHI! THOSE TWO HAVE MAJOR BROTHER COMPLEXES!
Rebut-tal.
FLOP
FLOP
BUT THEN TEZUKA BROKE MY PHONE...
...SO I'M MAKING HIM PAY! AND REENTER ALL MY DATA!
Y-YOU'RE SCARY!
I'm sure you have backup data!
SPILL THE BEANS!
NOOO!!
Meanwhile, Tezuka...
Ugh... Ugh...
070
Numbers... E-mail address-es...
080
090

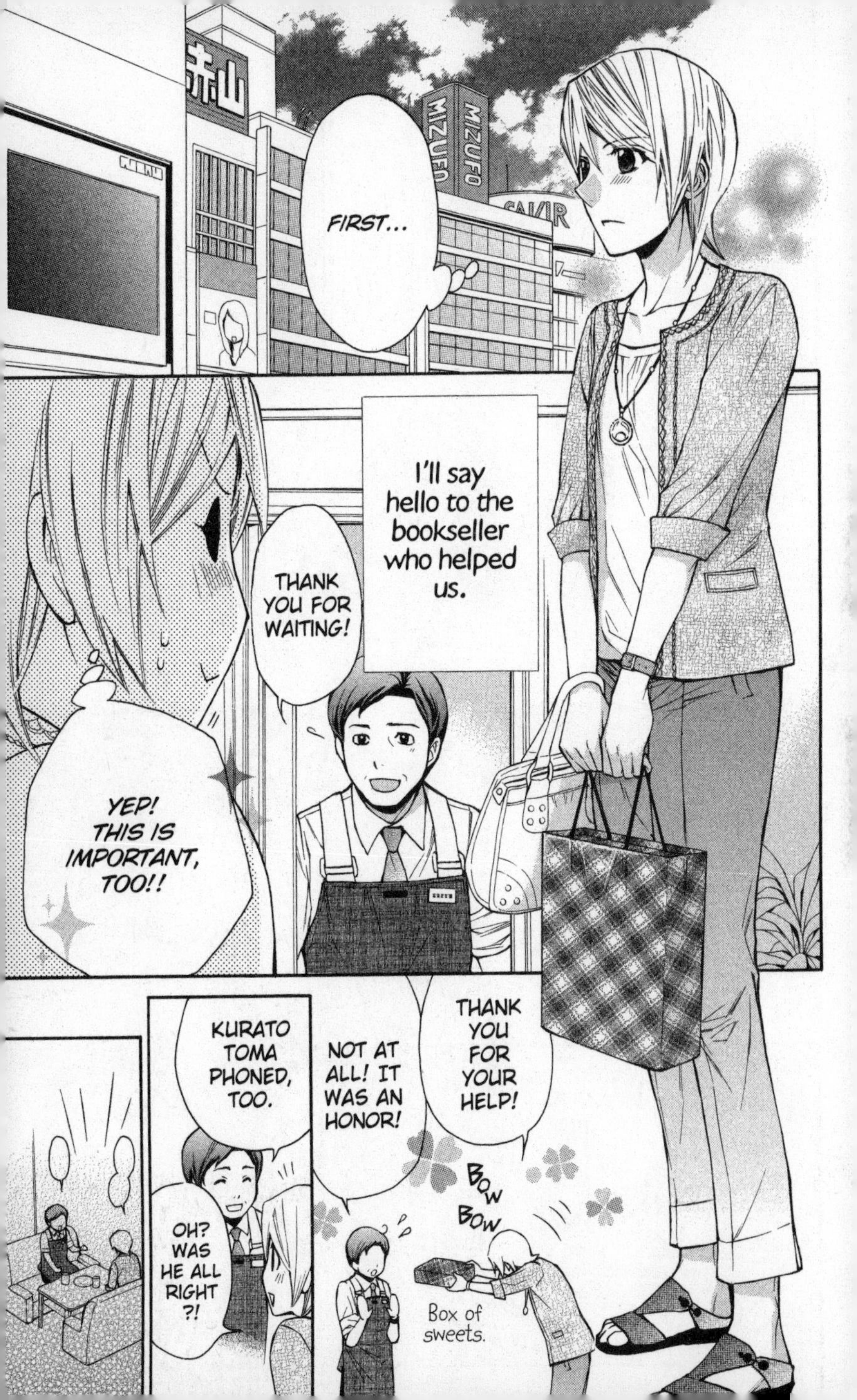
MIZUFO
MIZUFO
FIRST...
I'll say hello to the bookseller who helped us.
THANK YOU FOR WAITING!
YEP! THIS IS IMPORTANT, TOO!!
THANK YOU FOR YOUR HELP!
BOW BOW
NOT AT ALL! IT WAS AN HONOR!
Box of sweets.
KURATO TOMA PHONED, TOO.
OH? WAS HE ALL RIGHT ?!

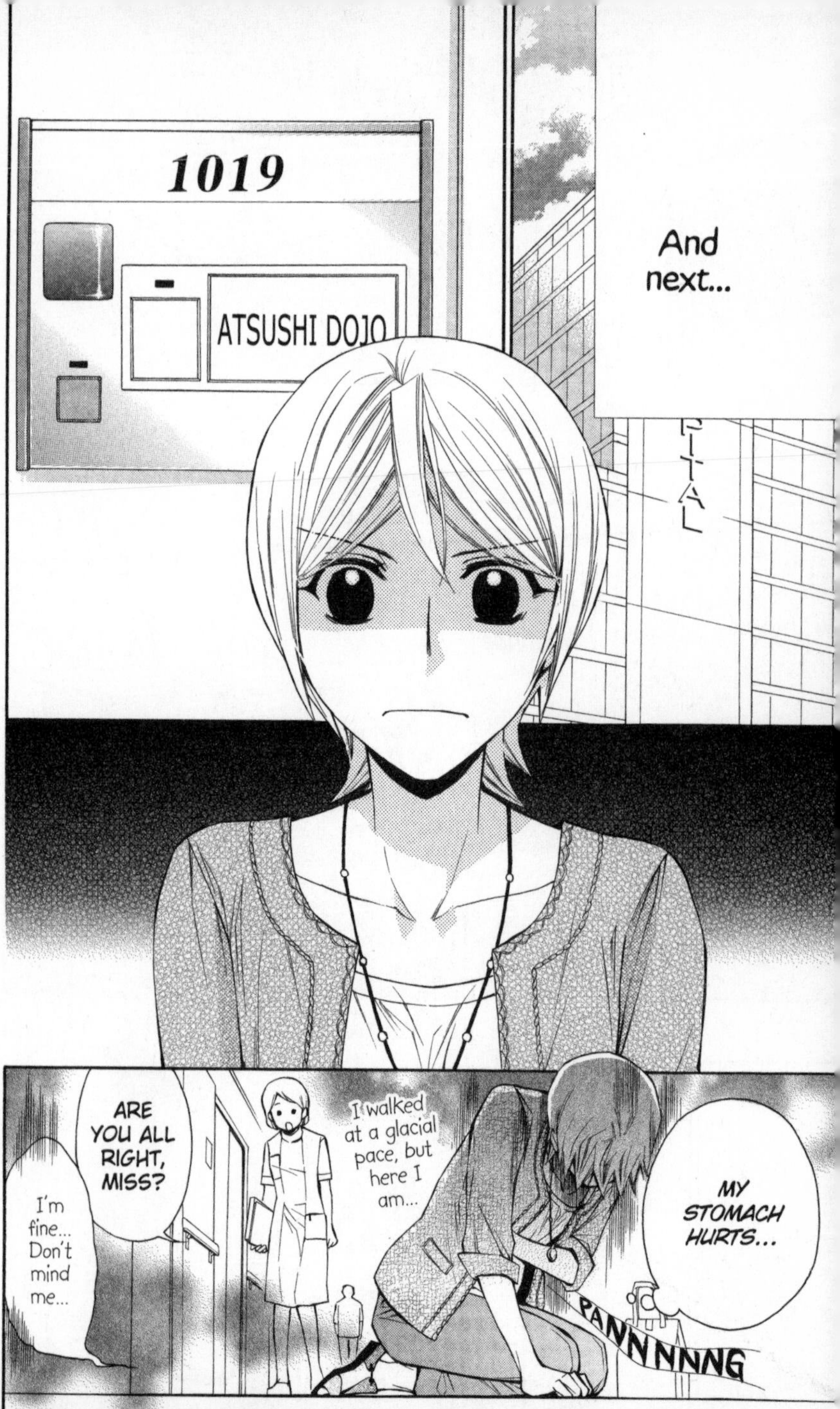
1019
ATSUSHI DOJO
And next...
MY STOMACH HURTS...
PANNNNNG
I walked at a glacial pace, but here I am...
ARE YOU ALL RIGHT, MISS?
I'm fine... Don't mind me...

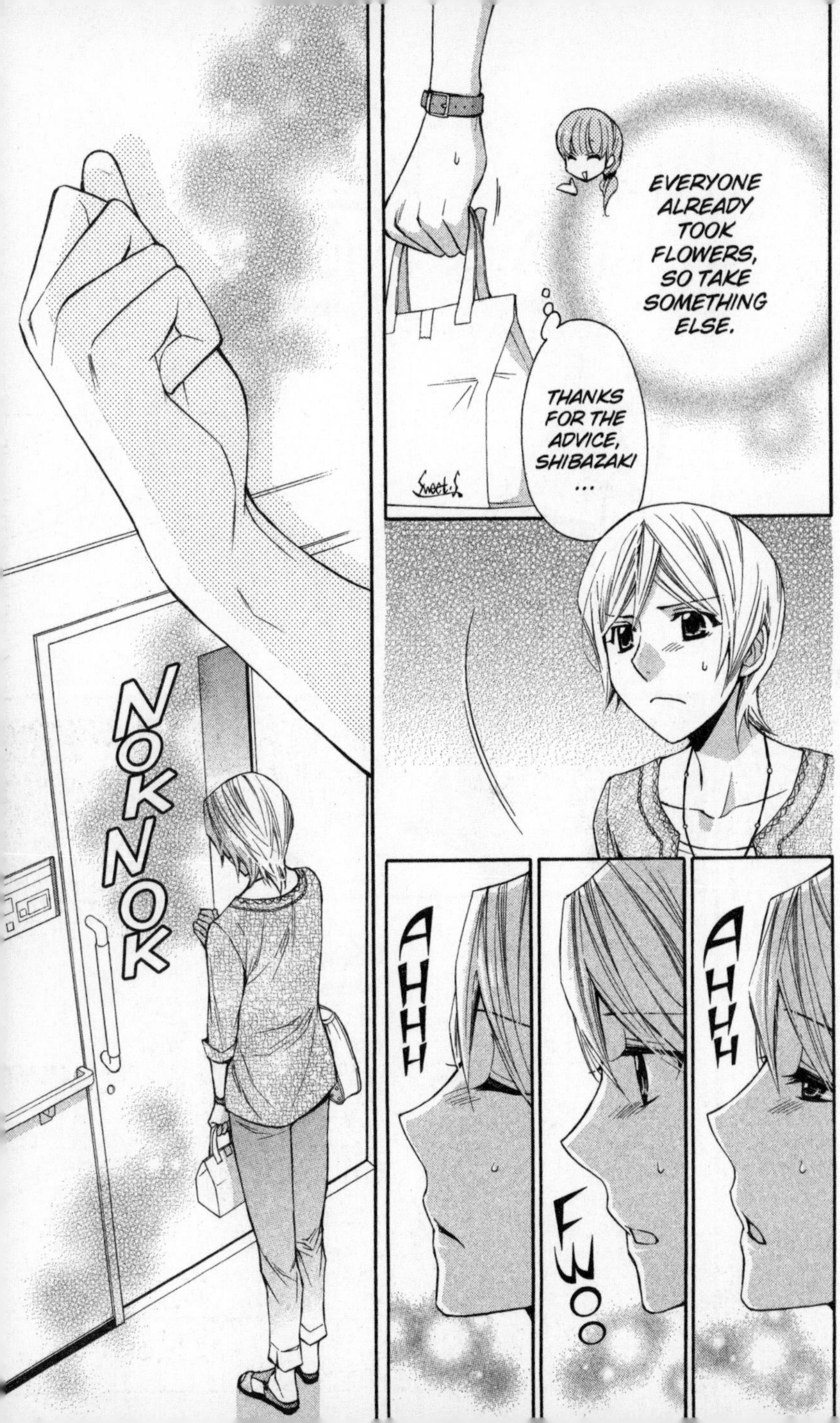
EVERYONE ALREADY TOOK FLOWERS, SO TAKE SOMETHING ELSE.
THANKS FOR THE ADVICE, SHIBAZAKI ...
Sweet.S
AHHH
FWOO
AHHH
NOKNOK

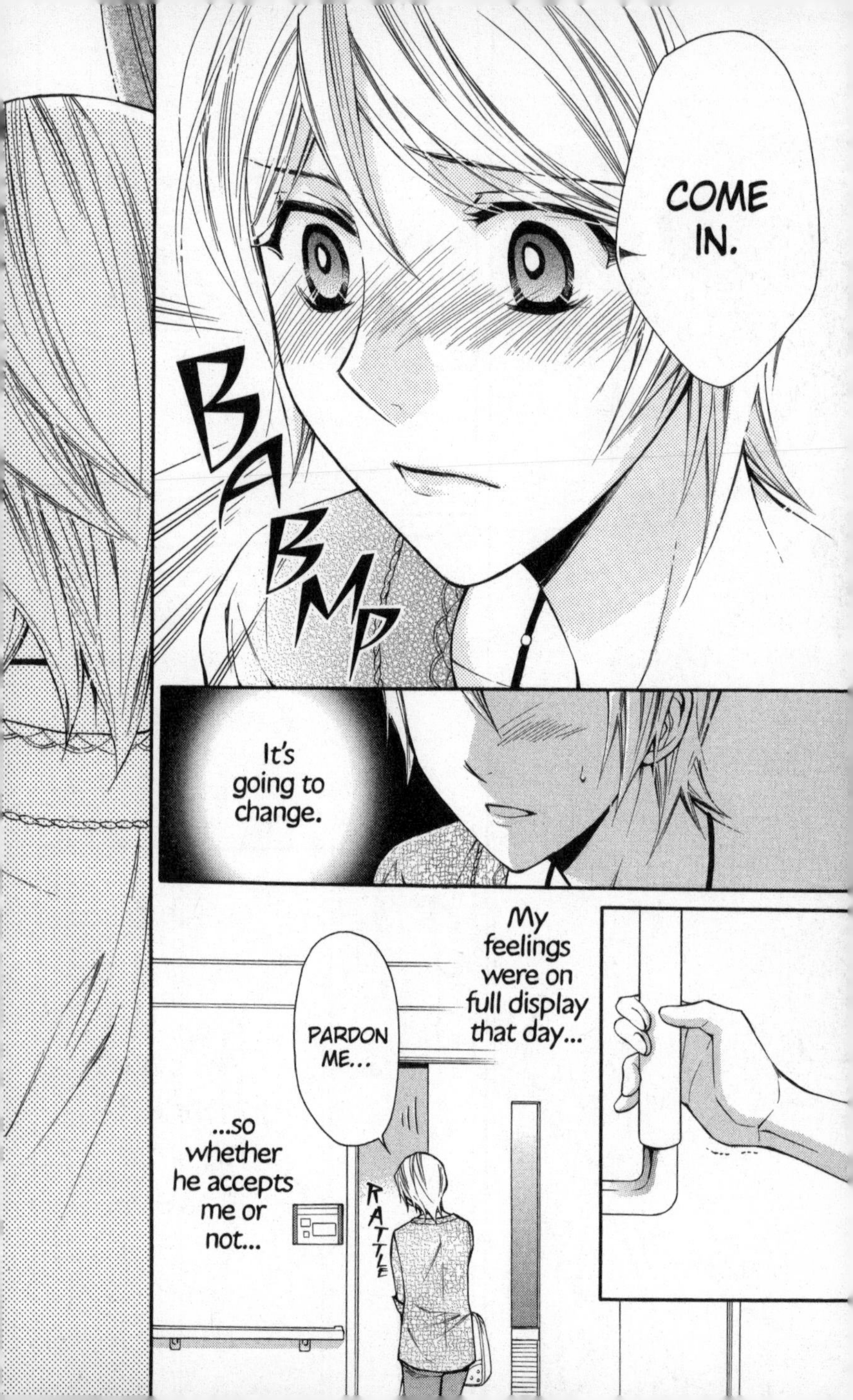
COME IN.
BABUMP
It's going to change.
My feelings were on full display that day...
PARDON ME...
...so whether he accepts me or not...
RATTLE

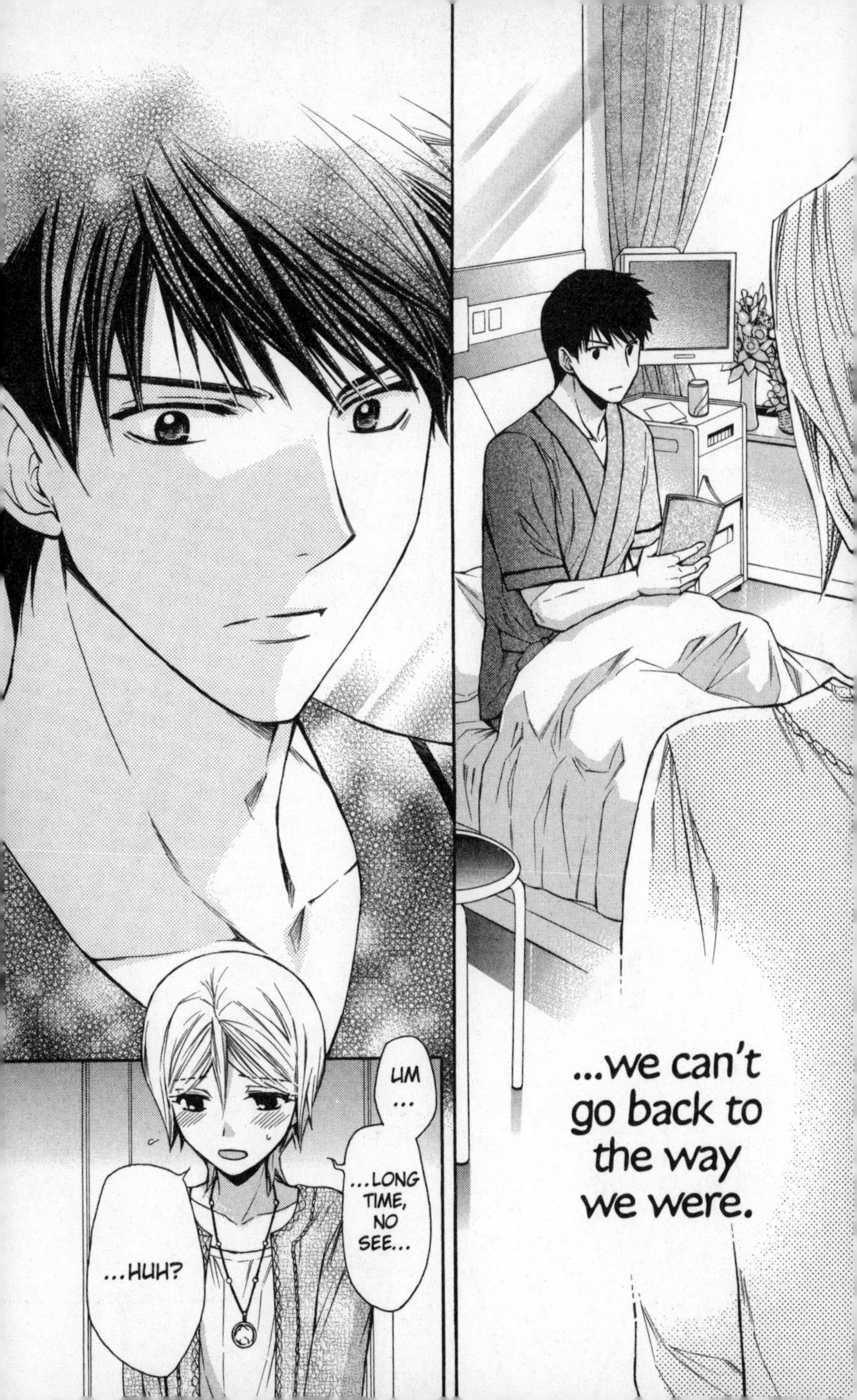
...we can't go back to the way we were.
UM ...
...LONG TIME, NO SEE...
...HUH?

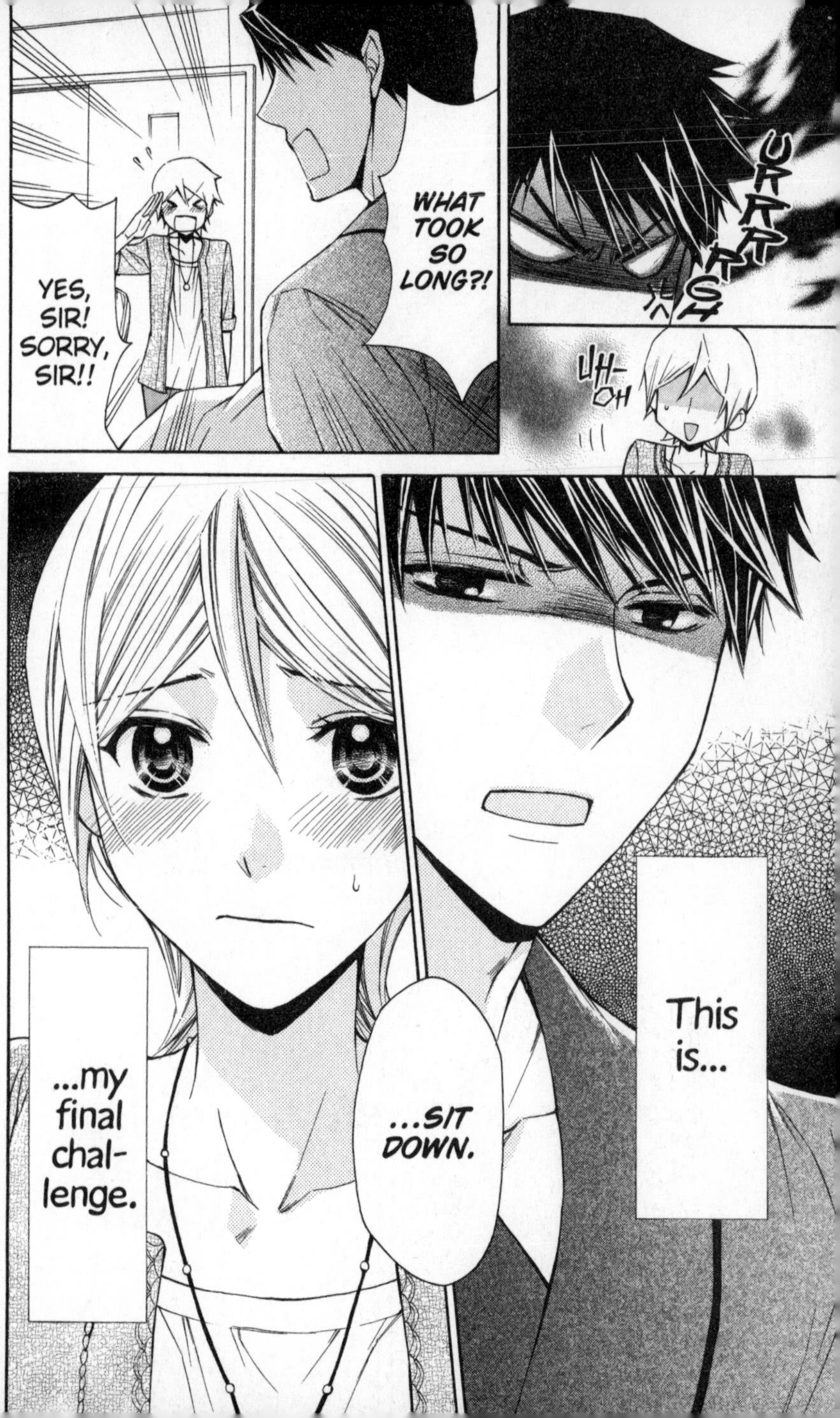
URRRRSH
UH-OH
WHAT TOOK SO LONG?!
YES, SIR! SORRY, SIR!!
This is...
...SIT DOWN.
...my final chal-lenge.

BEST SCENE POLL PART.3

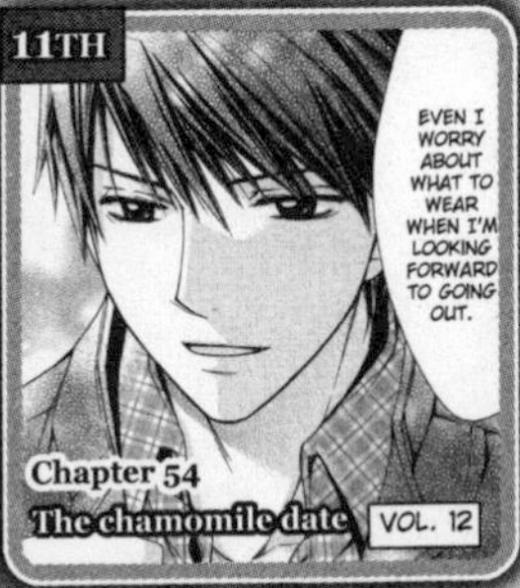
EVEN I WORRY ABOUT WHAT TO WEAR WHEN I'M LOOKING FORWARD TO GOING OUT.

11TH
Chapter 54
The chamomile date
VOL. 12

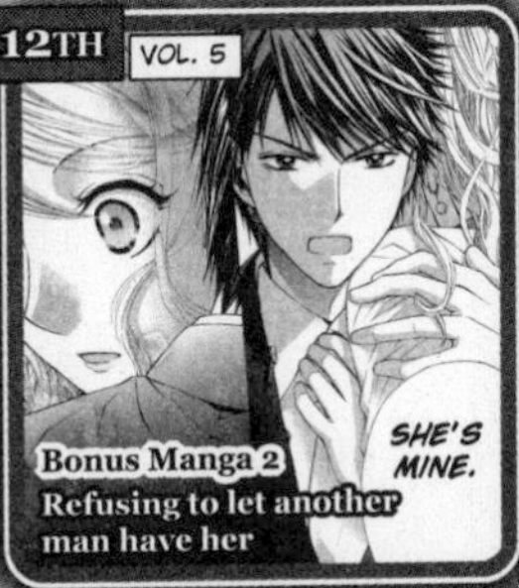
SHE'S MINE.

12TH
VOL. 5
Bonus Manga 2
Refusing to let another man have her

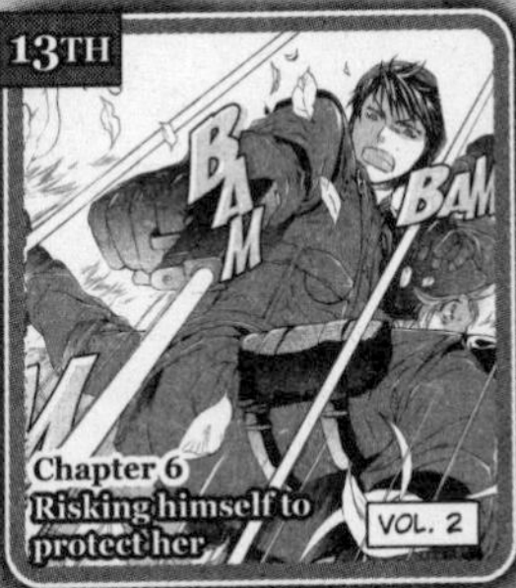
BAM
BAM

13TH
Chapter 6
Risking himself to protect her
VOL. 2

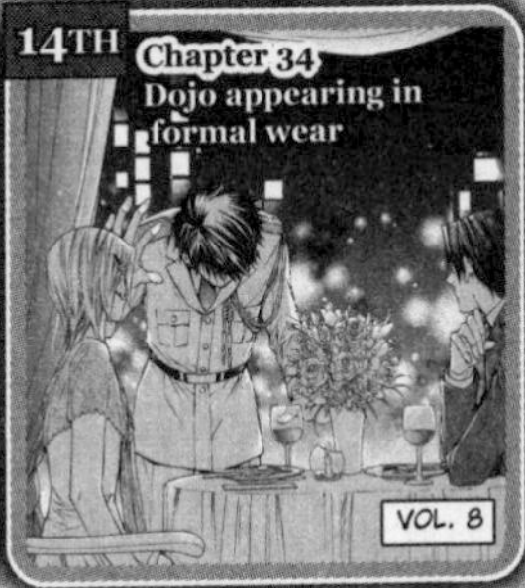

14TH
Chapter 34
Dojo appearing in formal wear
VOL. 8

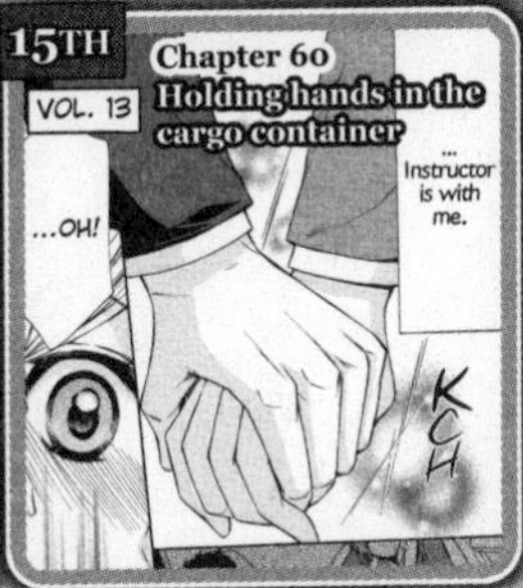
...Instructor is with me.
...OH!
KCH

15TH
VOL. 13
Chapter 60
Holding hands in the cargo container

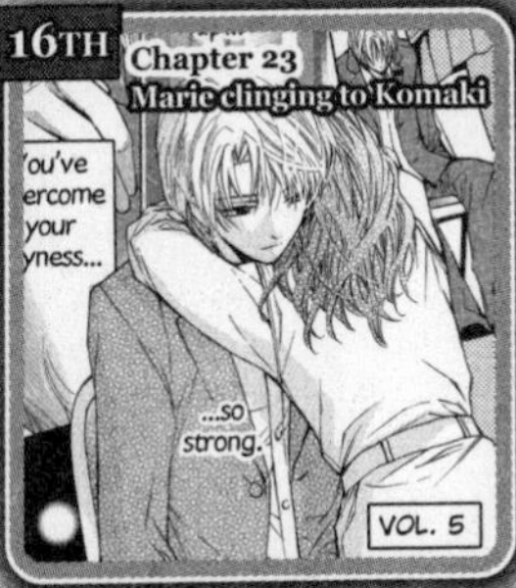
ou've ercome your yness...
...so strong.

16TH
Chapter 23
Marie clinging to Komaki
VOL. 5

17TH Chapter 35 VOL. 8
Shibazaki freaking out

18TH Chapter 24 VOL. 6
Dojo taking a chocolate from Iku

19TH Chapter 56 VOL. 12
Fake couple scene

20TH Chapter 53 VOL. 11
Inamine's retirement

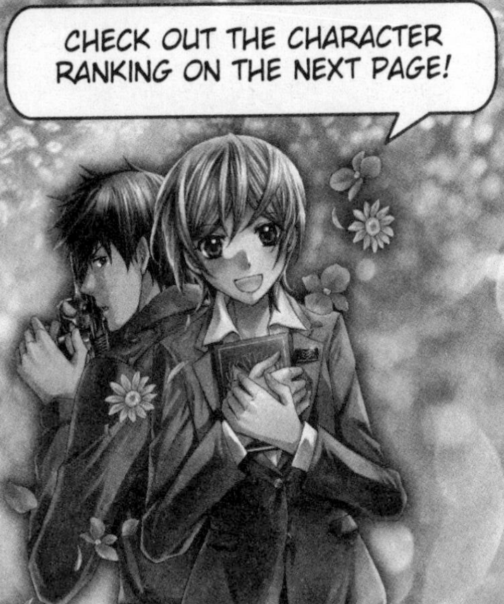
CHECK OUT THE CHARACTER RANKING ON THE NEXT PAGE!

6TH RYUSUKE GENDA 146 pts
1006 pts 2ND IKU KASAHARA
47 pts 8TH MOBURO AGOHIGE
264 pts 5TH HIKARU TEZUKA
404 pts 3RD ASAKO SHIBAZAKI
FINAL CHAPTER

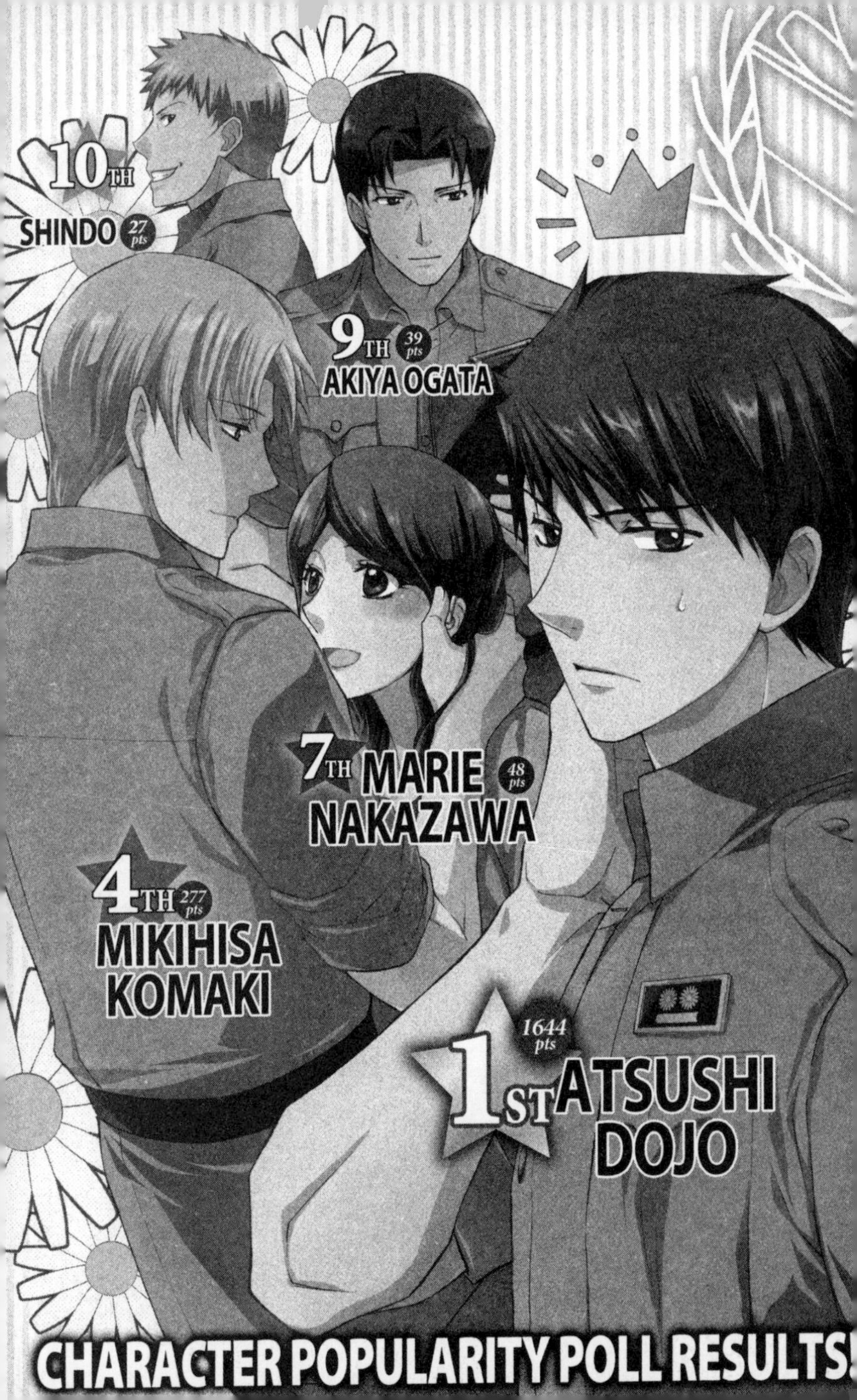
10TH
SHINDO 27 pts
9TH 39 pts
AKIYA OGATA
7TH MARIE NAKAZAWA 48 pts
4TH 277 pts
MIKIHISA KOMAKI
1644 pts
1ST ATSUSHI DOJO
CHARACTER POPULARITY POLL RESULTS!

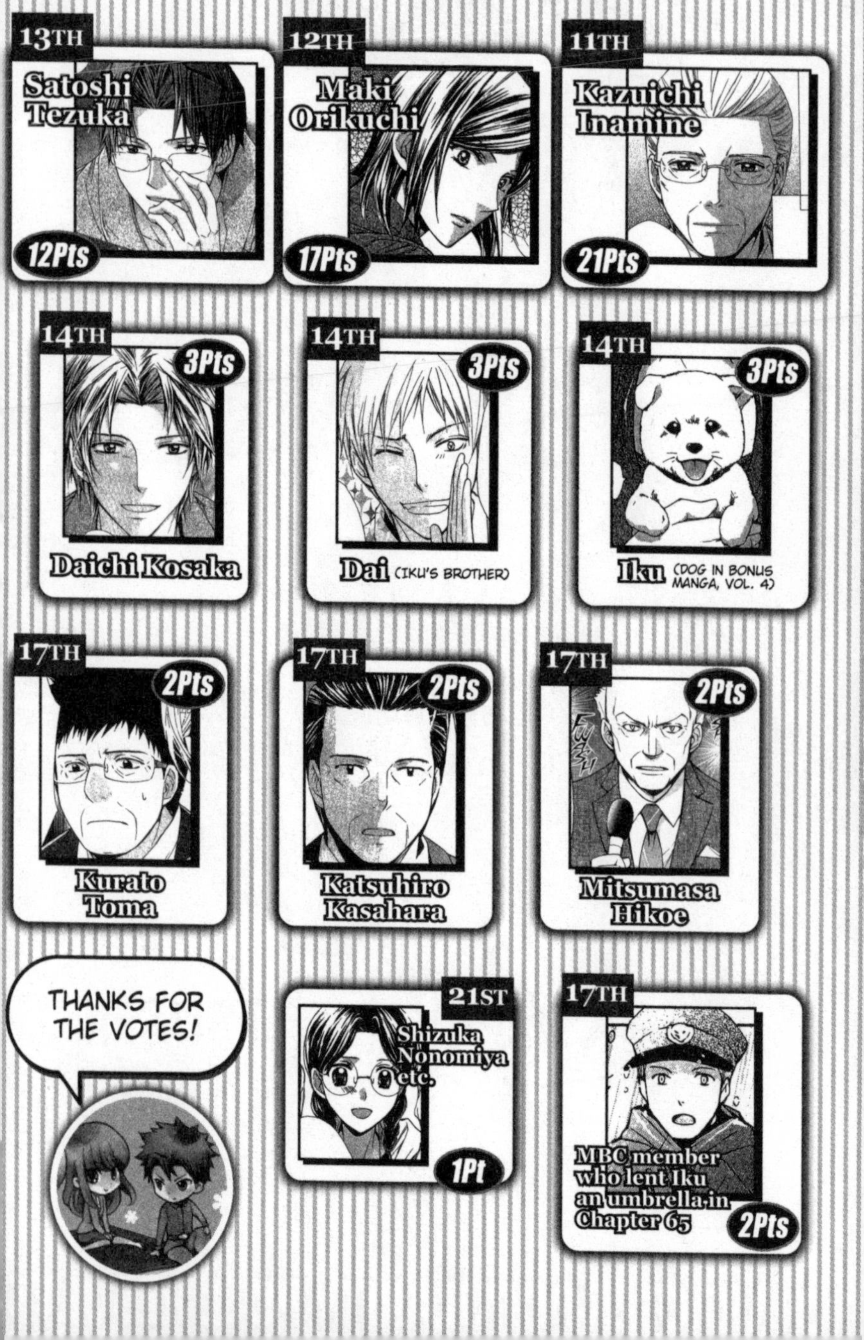
11TH
Kazuichi Inamine
21Pts
12TH
Maki Orikuchi
17Pts
13TH
Satoshi Tezuka
12Pts
14TH
3Pts
Iku (DOG IN BONUS MANGA, VOL. 4)
14TH
3Pts
Dai (IKU'S BROTHER)
14TH
3Pts
Daichi Kosaka
17TH
2Pts
Mitsumasa Hikoe
17TH
2Pts
Katsuhiro Kasahara
17TH
2Pts
Kurato Toma
17TH
MBC member who lent Iku an umbrella in Chapter 65
2Pts
21ST
Shizuka Nonomiya etc.
1Pt
THANKS FOR THE VOTES!

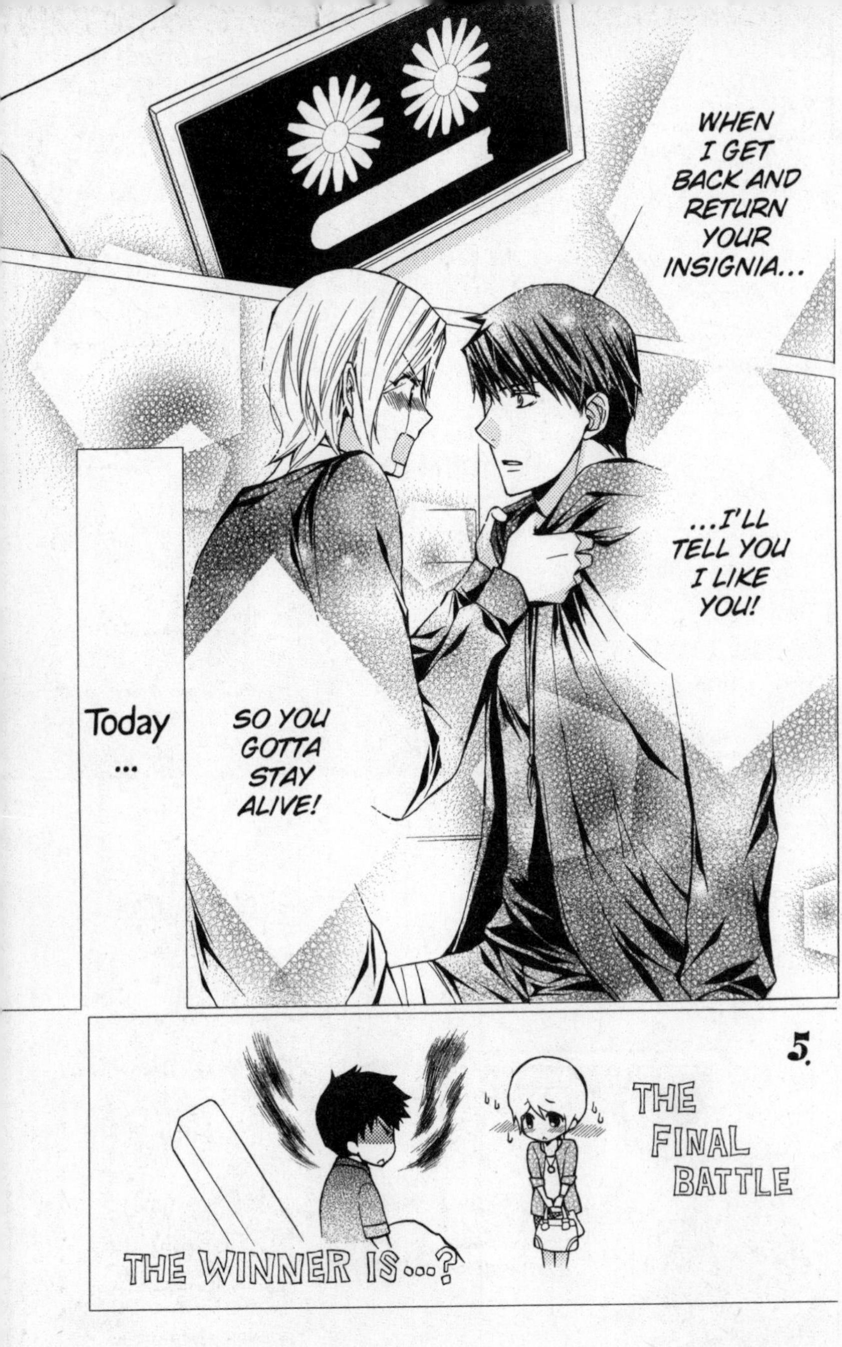
WHEN I GET BACK AND RETURN YOUR INSIGNIA...
...I'LL TELL YOU I LIKE YOU!
SO YOU GOTTA STAY ALIVE!
Today ...
5.
THE FINAL BATTLE
THE WINNER IS...?

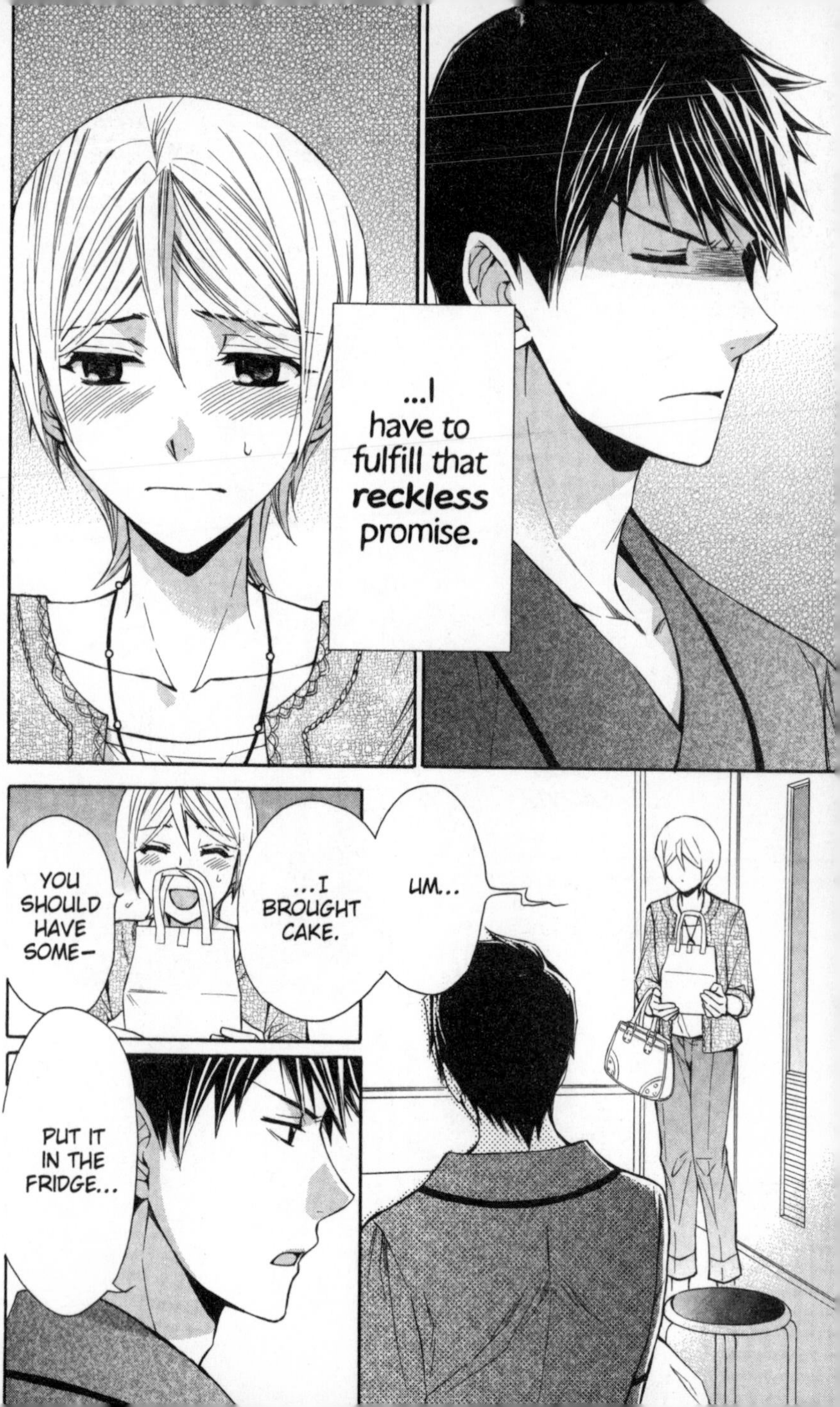
...I have to fulfill that **reckless** promise.
UM...
...I BROUGHT CAKE.
YOU SHOULD HAVE SOME—
PUT IT IN THE FRIDGE...

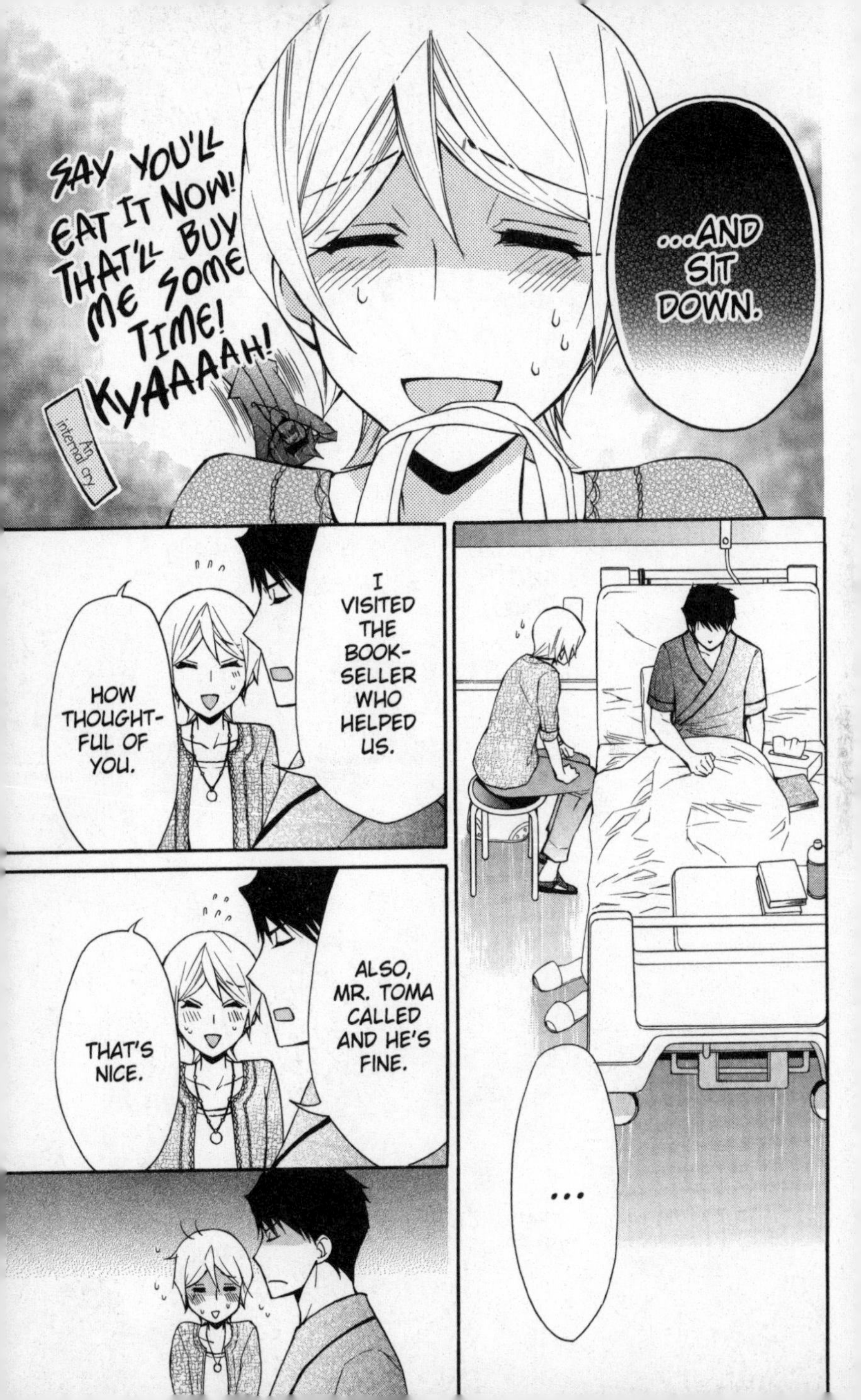
...AND SIT DOWN.
SAY YOU'LL EAT IT NOW! THAT'LL BUY ME SOME TIME! KYAAAAH!
An internal cry
...
I VISITED THE BOOK-SELLER WHO HELPED US.
HOW THOUGHT-FUL OF YOU.
ALSO, MR. TOMA CALLED AND HE'S FINE.
THAT'S NICE.

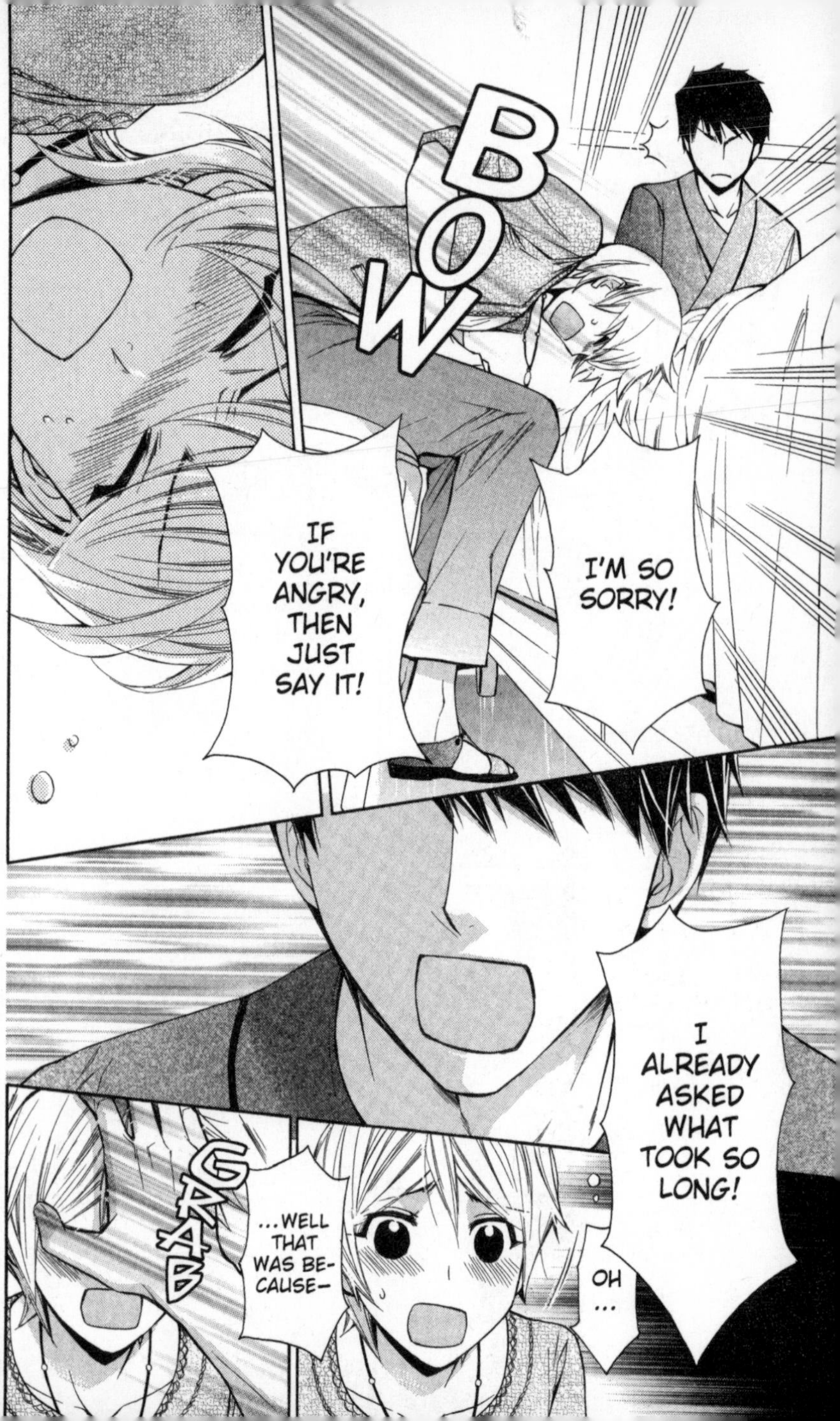
BOW
I'M SO SORRY!
IF YOU'RE ANGRY, THEN JUST SAY IT!
I ALREADY ASKED WHAT TOOK SO LONG!
OH ...
...WELL THAT WAS BE-CAUSE-
GRAB

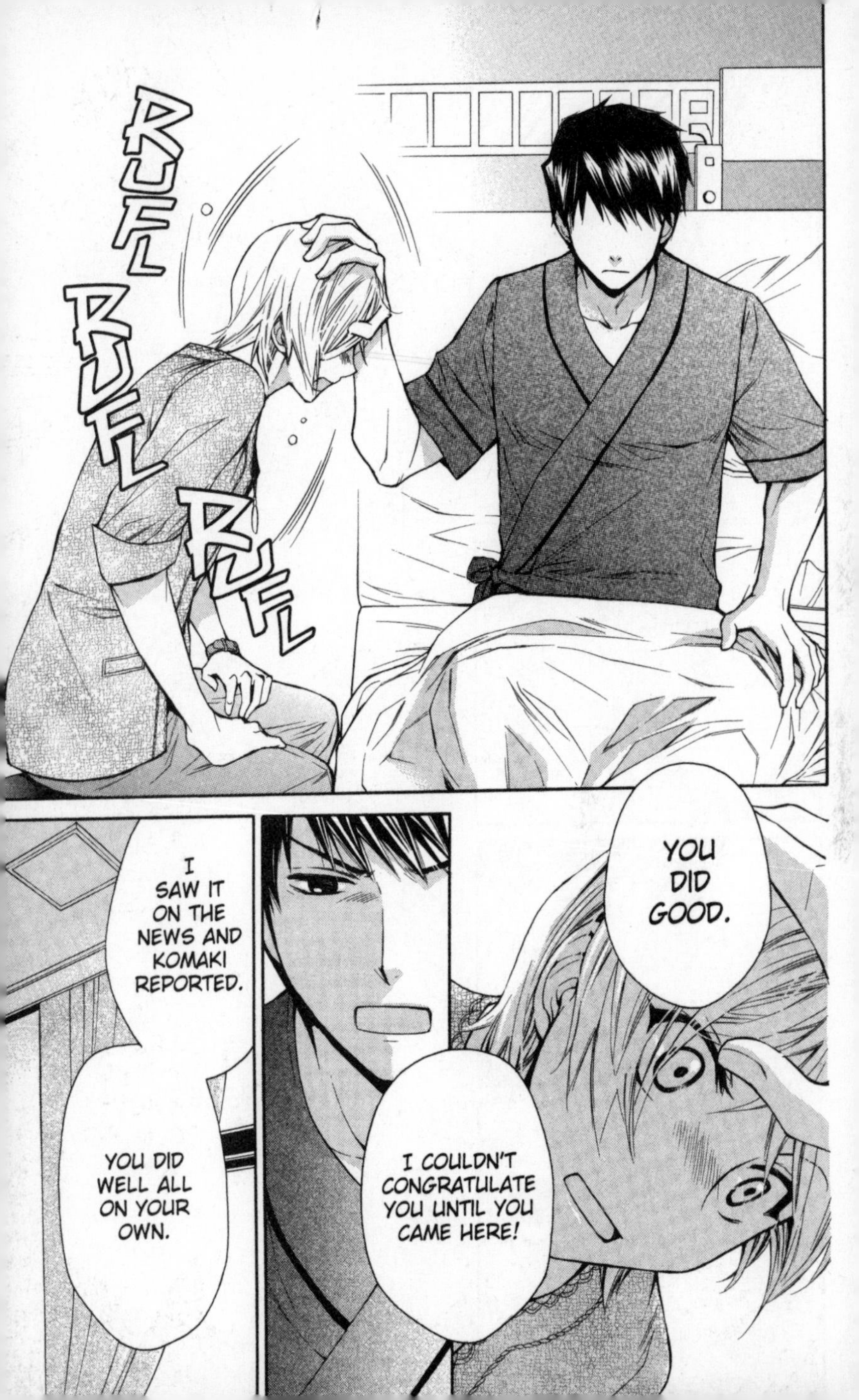
RUFL
RUFL
RUFL
YOU DID GOOD.
I COULDN'T CONGRATULATE YOU UNTIL YOU CAME HERE!
I SAW IT ON THE NEWS AND KOMAKI REPORTED.
YOU DID WELL ALL ON YOUR OWN.

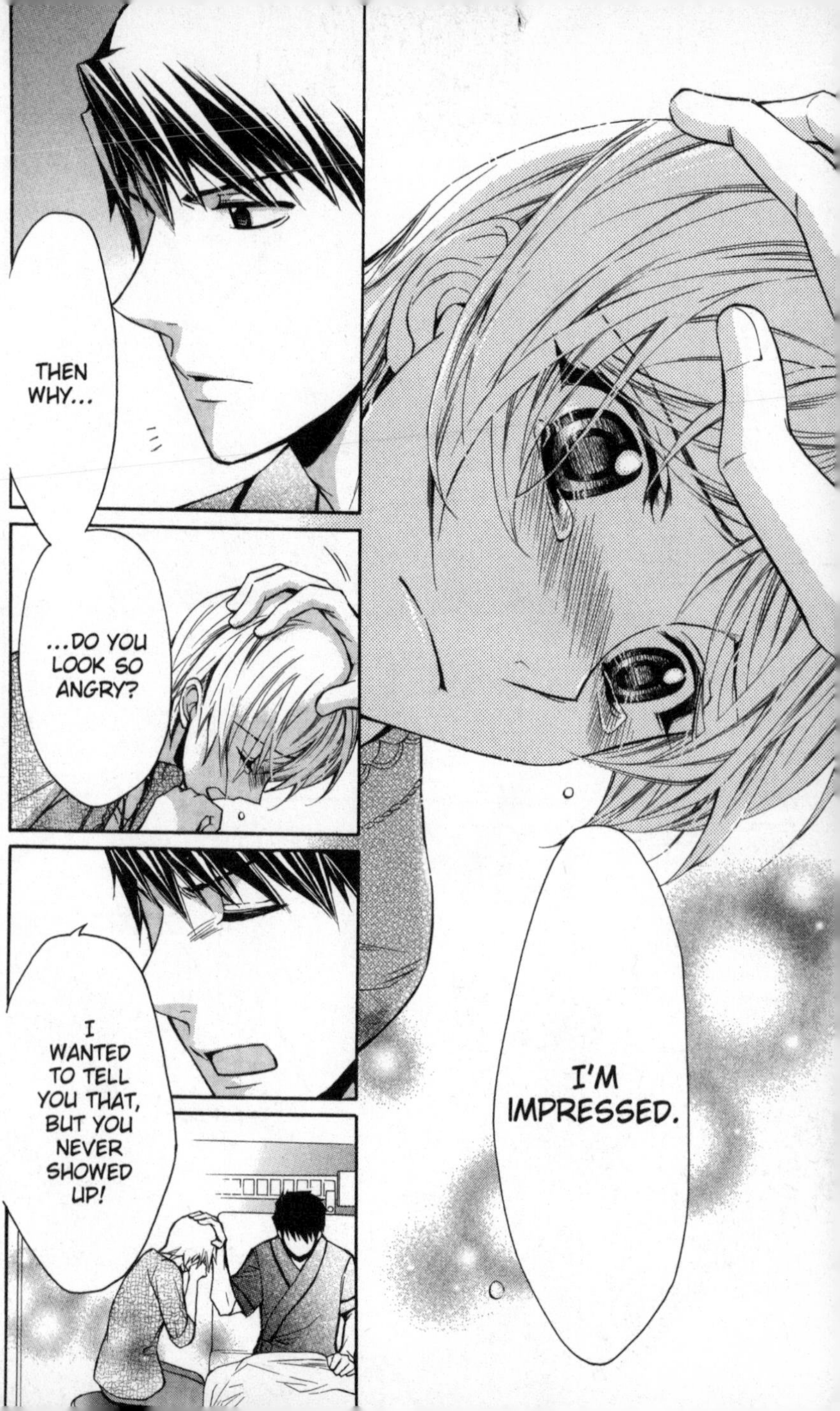
I'M IMPRESSED.
THEN WHY...
...DO YOU LOOK SO ANGRY?
I WANTED TO TELL YOU THAT, BUT YOU NEVER SHOWED UP!

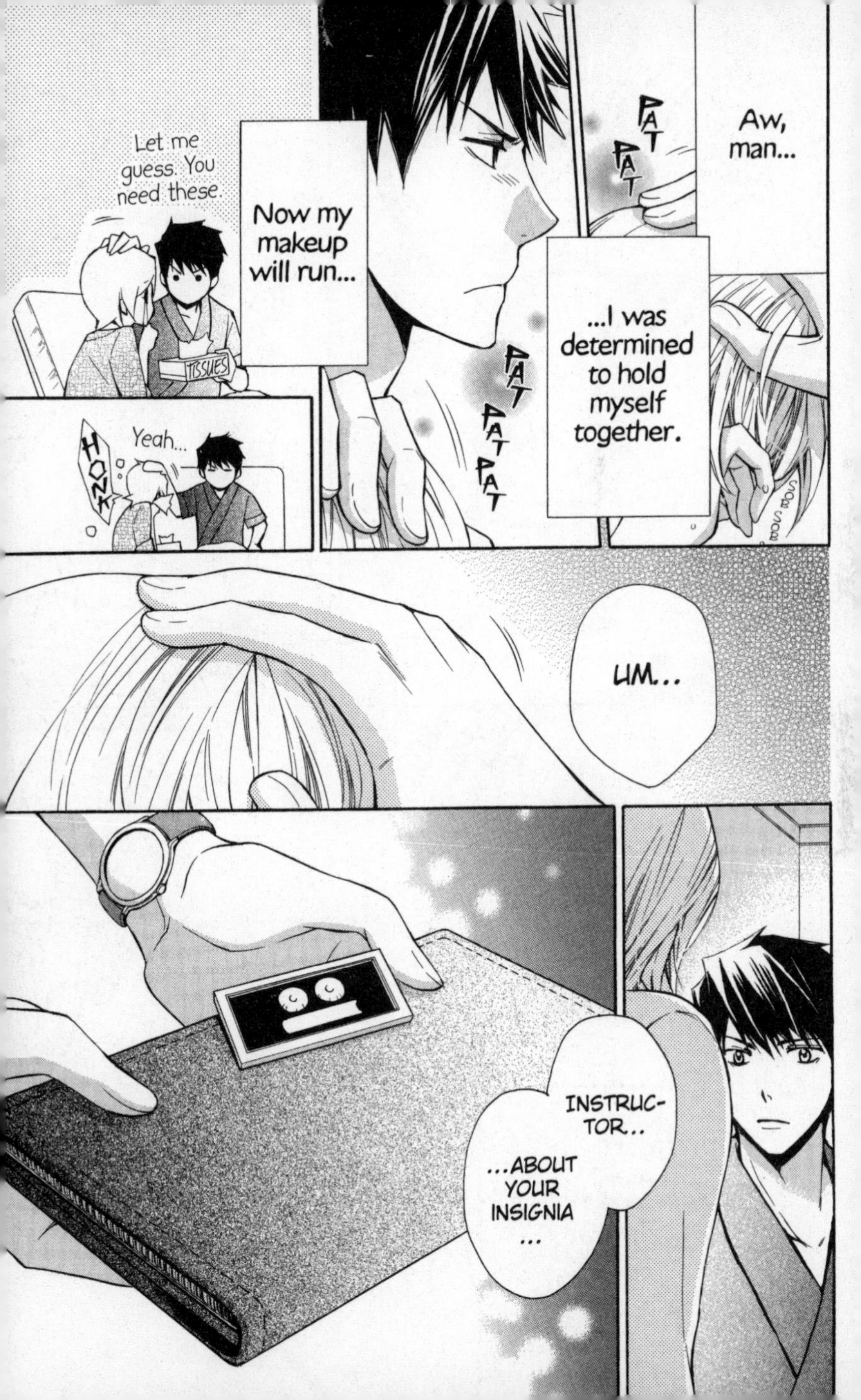
Aw, man...
PAT PAT
...I was determined to hold myself together.
SOB SOB
Now my makeup will run...
PAT PAT PAT PAT
Let me guess. You need these.
TISSUES
Yeah...
HONK
UM..
INSTRUC-TOR..
...ABOUT YOUR INSIGNIA ...

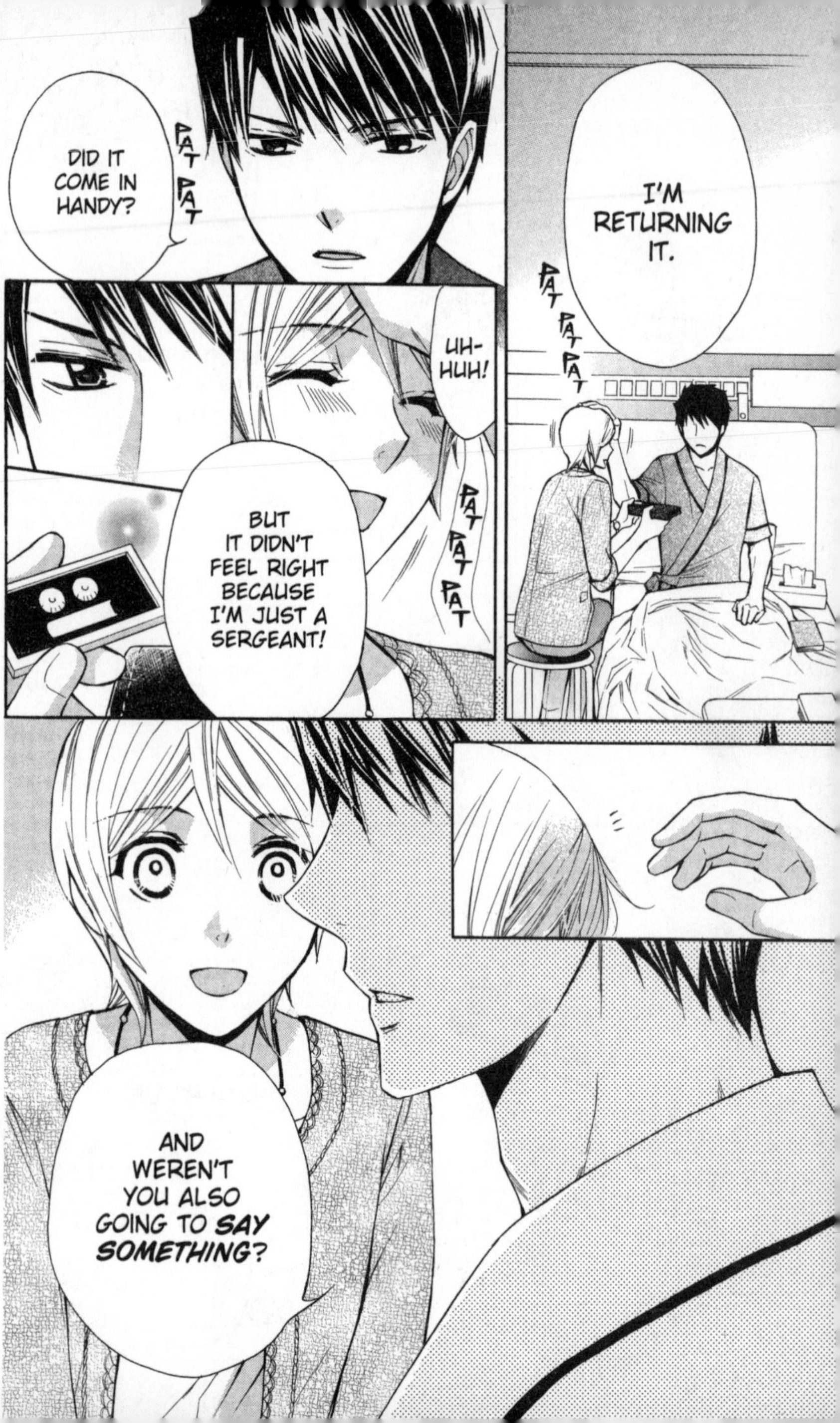
I'M RETURNING IT.
PAT PAT PAT
DID IT COME IN HANDY?
PAT PAT
UH-HUH!
BUT IT DIDN'T FEEL RIGHT BECAUSE I'M JUST A SERGEANT!
PAT PAT PAT
AND WEREN'T YOU ALSO GOING TO ***SAY SOMETHING***?

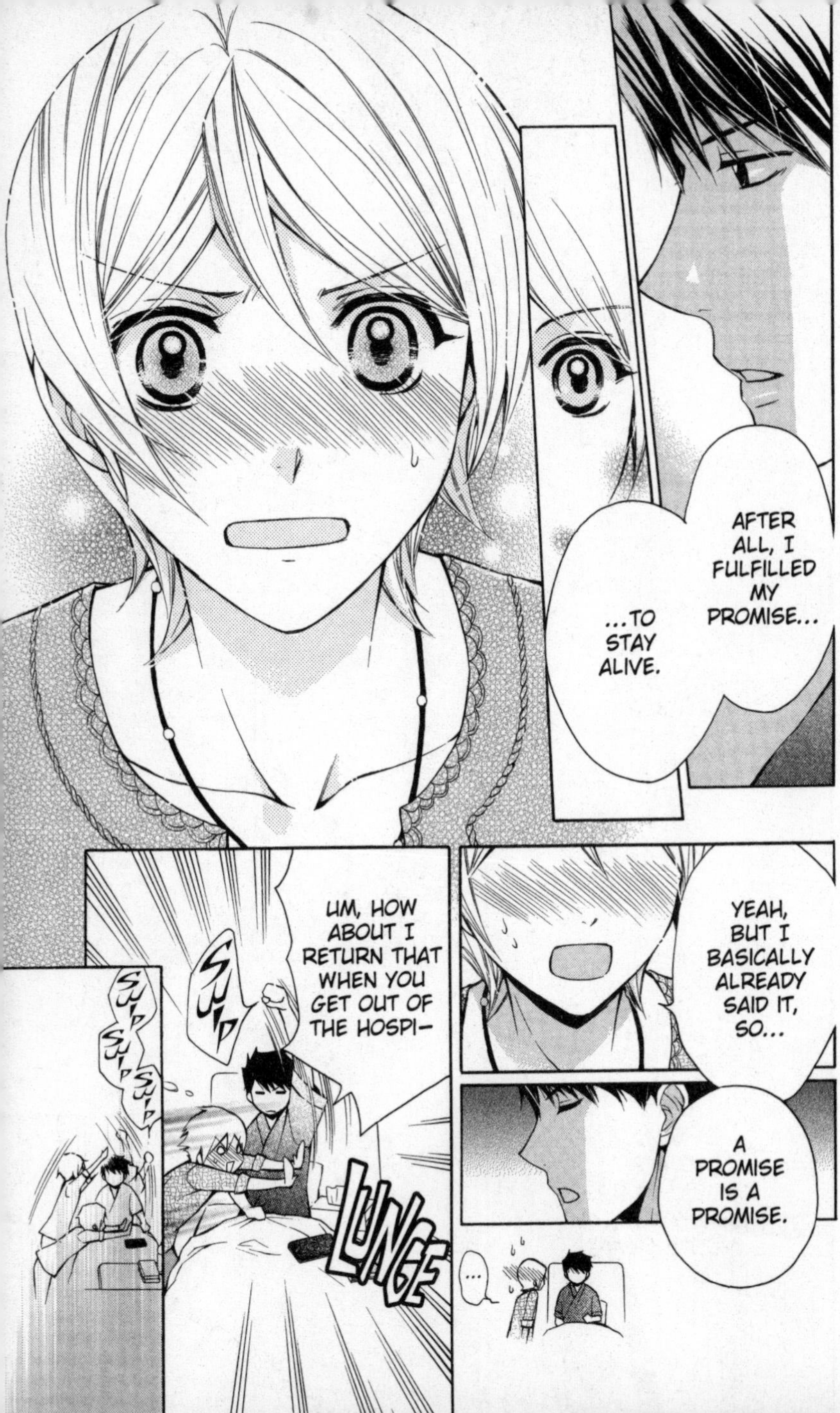
AFTER ALL, I FULFILLED MY PROMISE...
...TO STAY ALIVE.
YEAH, BUT I BASICALLY ALREADY SAID IT, SO...
A PROMISE IS A PROMISE.
...
UM, HOW ABOUT I RETURN THAT WHEN YOU GET OUT OF THE HOSPI-
SWIP
LUNGE
SWIP SWIP SWIP SWIP

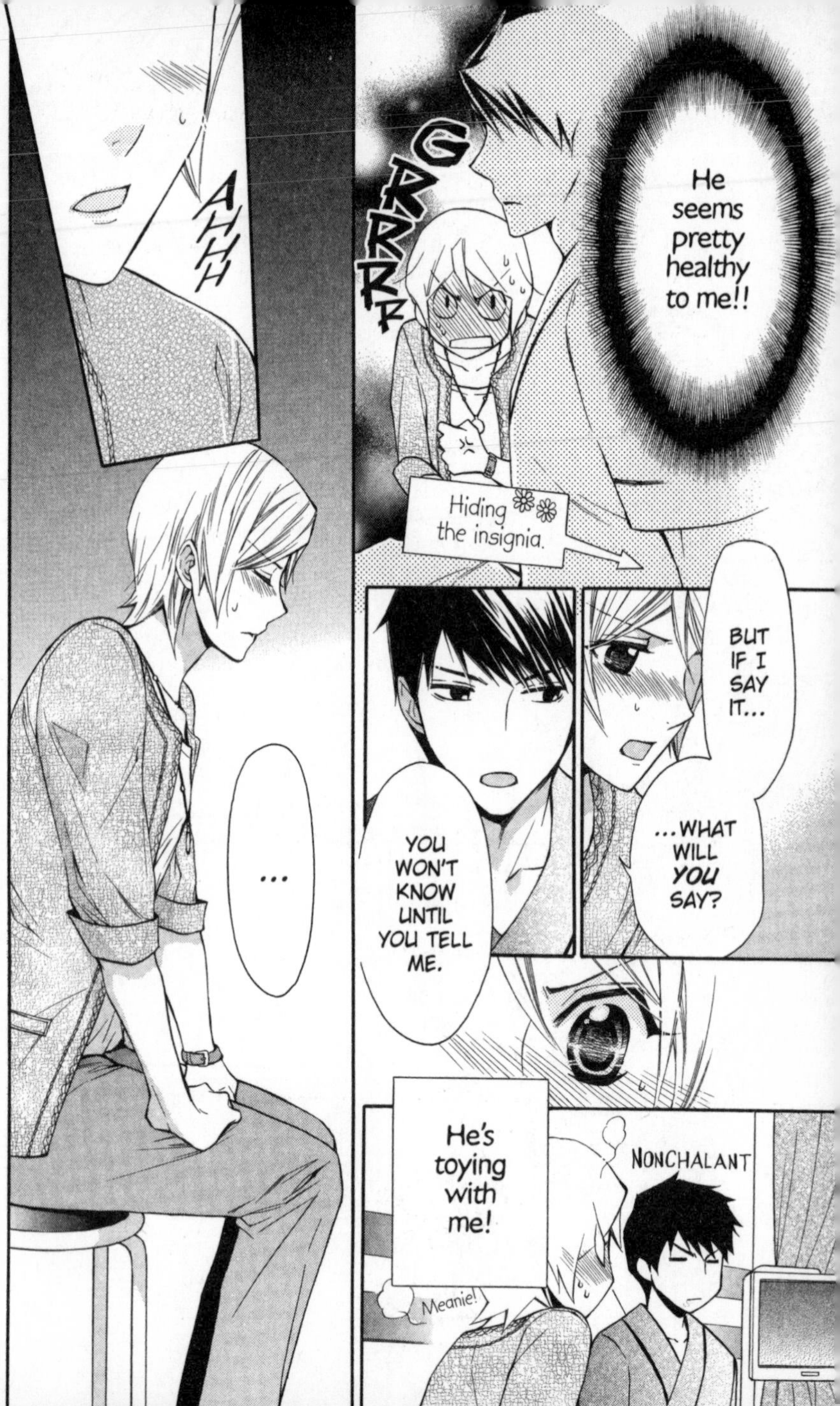
GRRRR
He seems pretty healthy to me!!
Hiding the insignia.
BUT IF I SAY IT...
...WHAT WILL *YOU* SAY?
YOU WON'T KNOW UNTIL YOU TELL ME.
He's toying with me!
NONCHALANT
Meanie!
AHHH
...

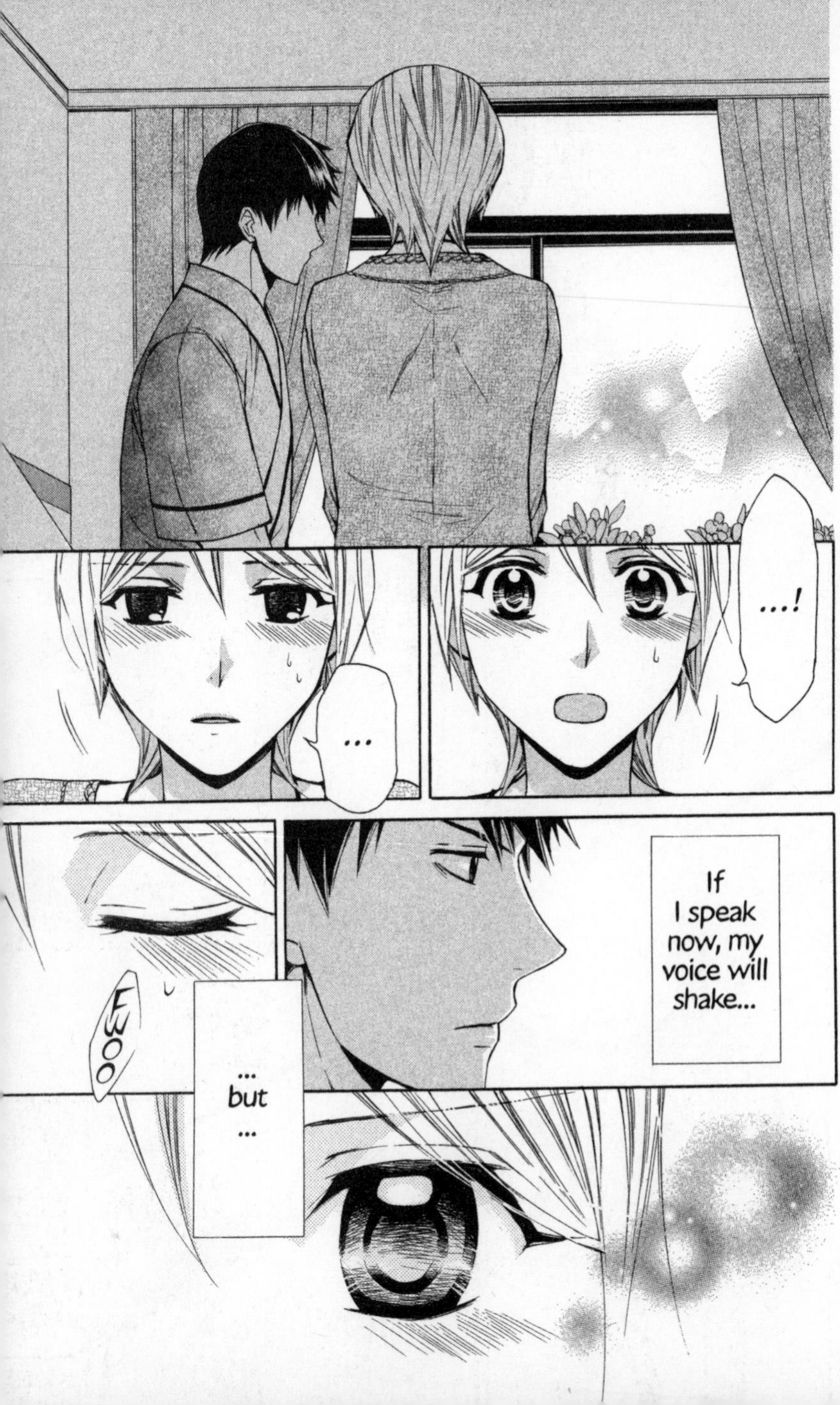
...!
...
If I speak now, my voice will shake...
FWOO
... but ...

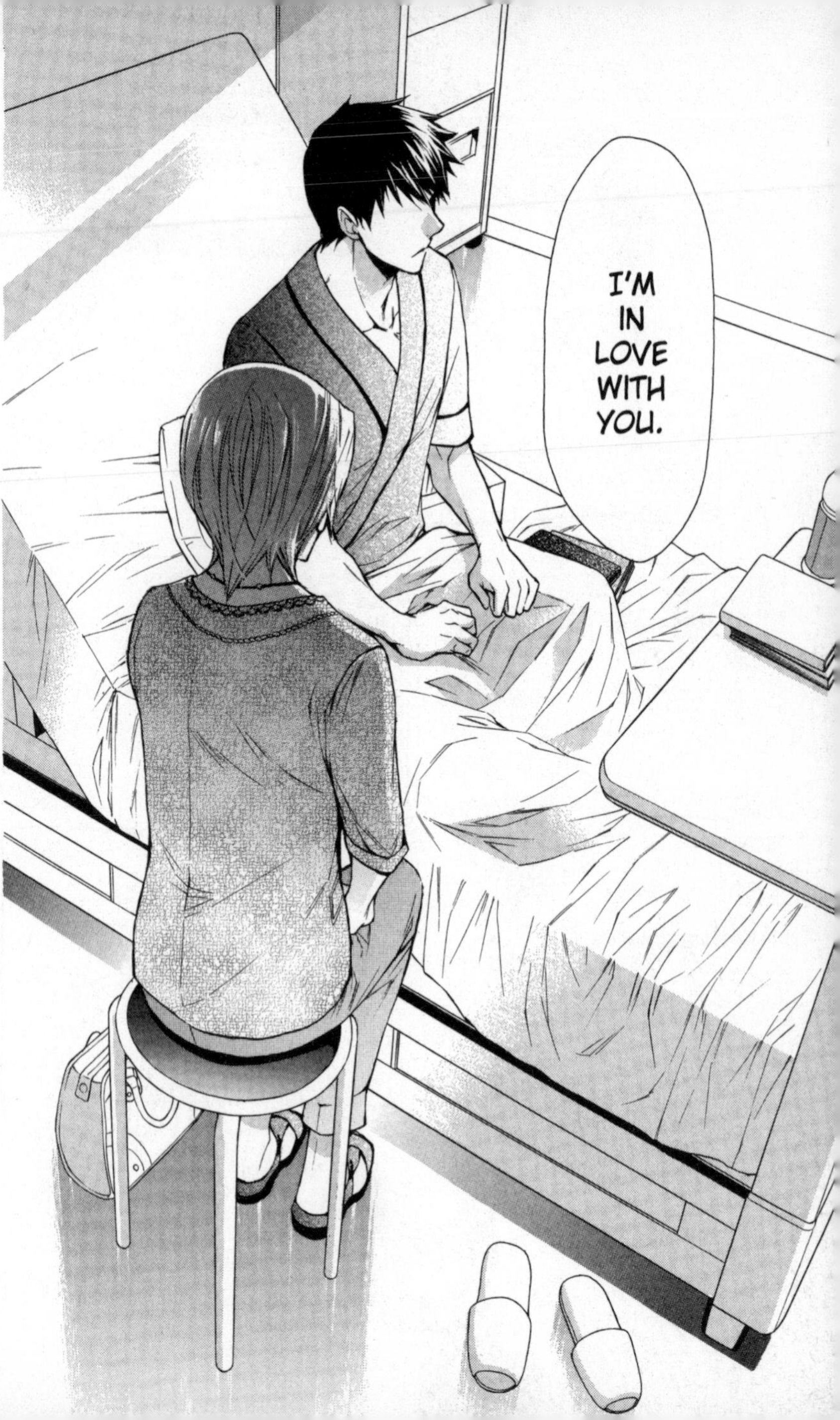
I'M IN LOVE WITH YOU.

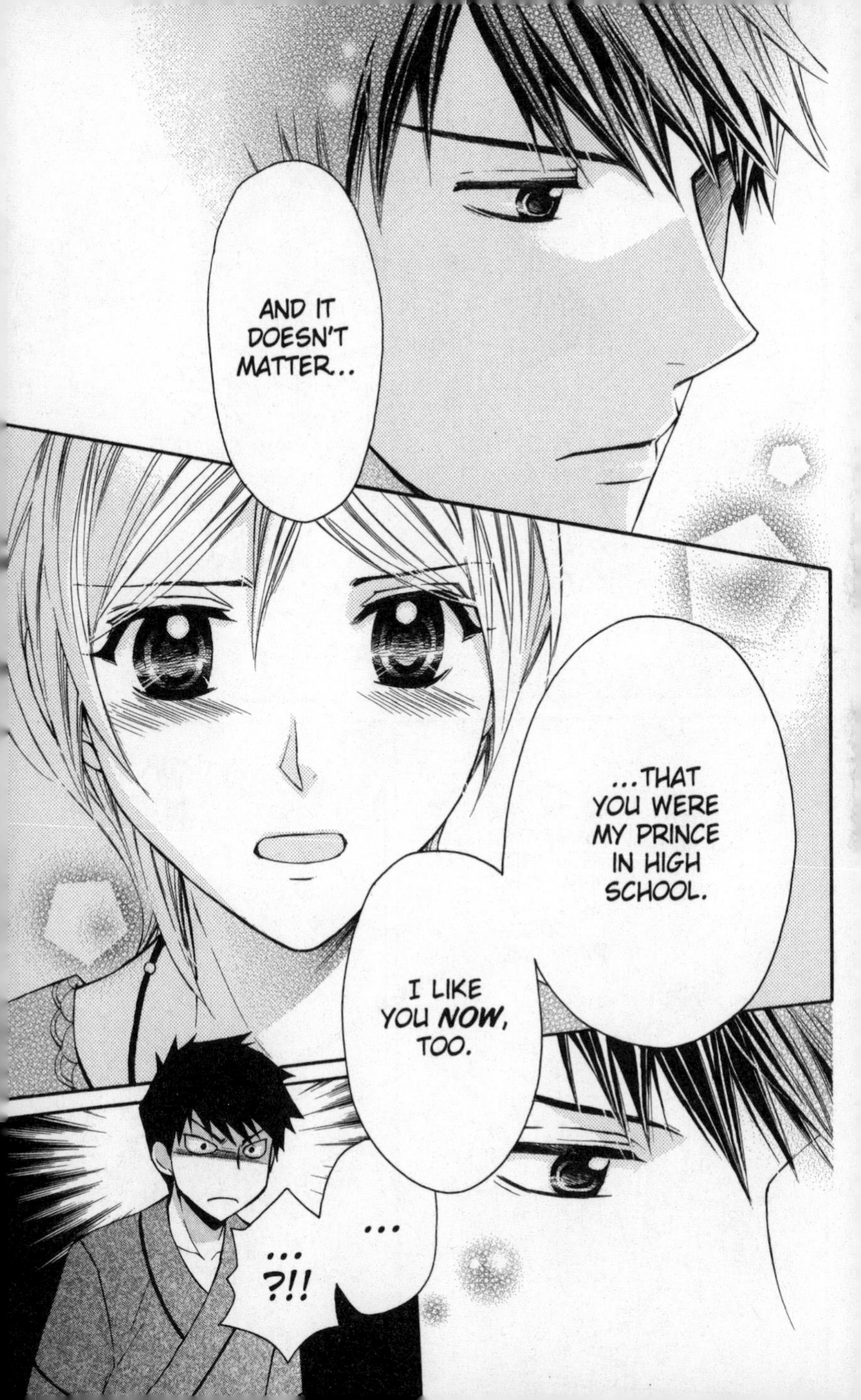
AND IT DOESN'T MATTER..
...THAT YOU WERE MY PRINCE IN HIGH SCHOOL.
I LIKE YOU *NOW*, TOO.
...
... ?!!

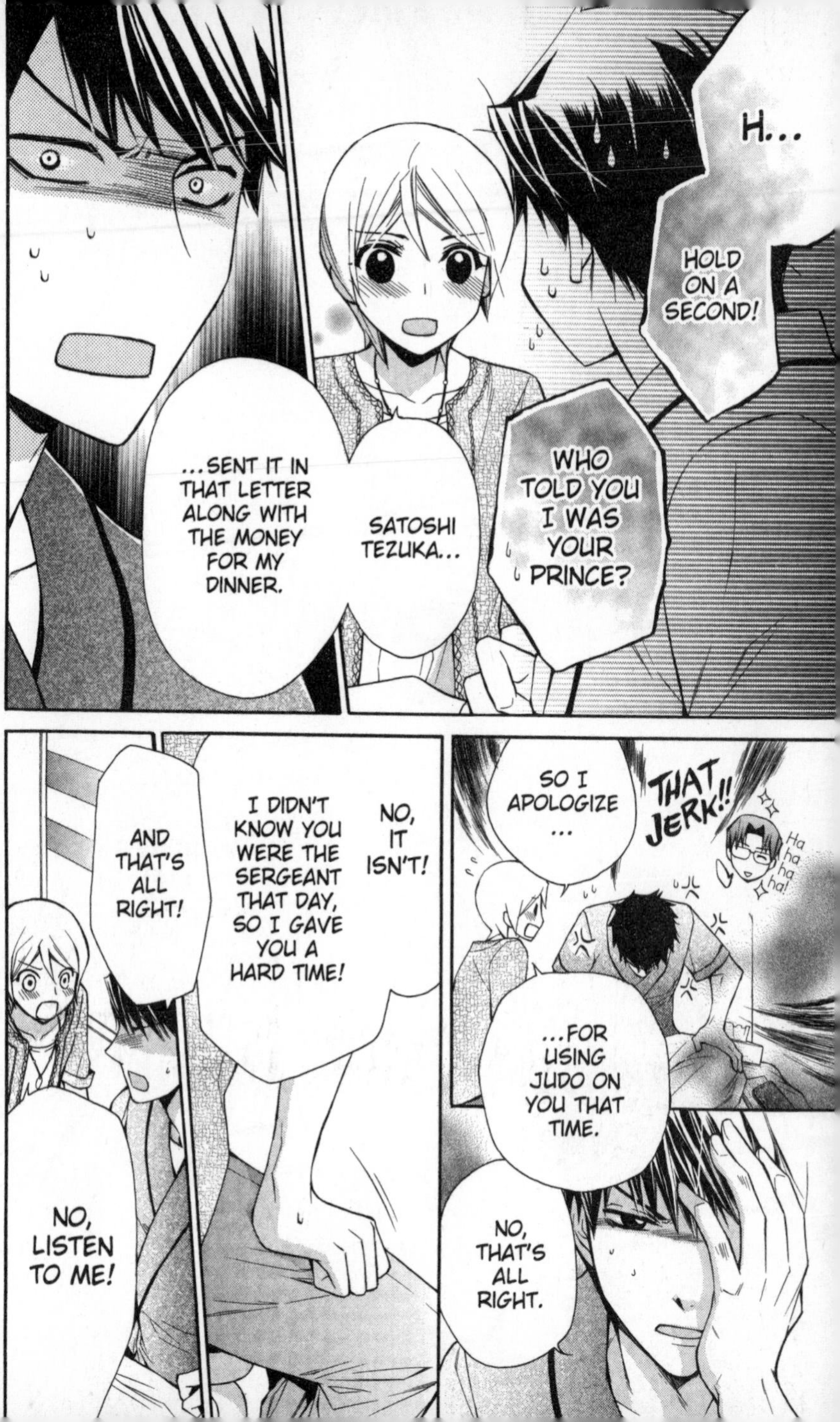
H...
HOLD ON A SECOND!
WHO TOLD YOU I WAS YOUR PRINCE?
SATOSHI TEZUKA...
...SENT IT IN THAT LETTER ALONG WITH THE MONEY FOR MY DINNER.
SO I APOLOGIZE ...
THAT JERK!!
Ha ha ha ha!
...FOR USING JUDO ON YOU THAT TIME.
NO, THAT'S ALL RIGHT.
NO, IT ISN'T!
I DIDN'T KNOW YOU WERE THE SERGEANT THAT DAY, SO I GAVE YOU A HARD TIME!
AND THAT'S ALL RIGHT!
NO, LISTEN TO ME!

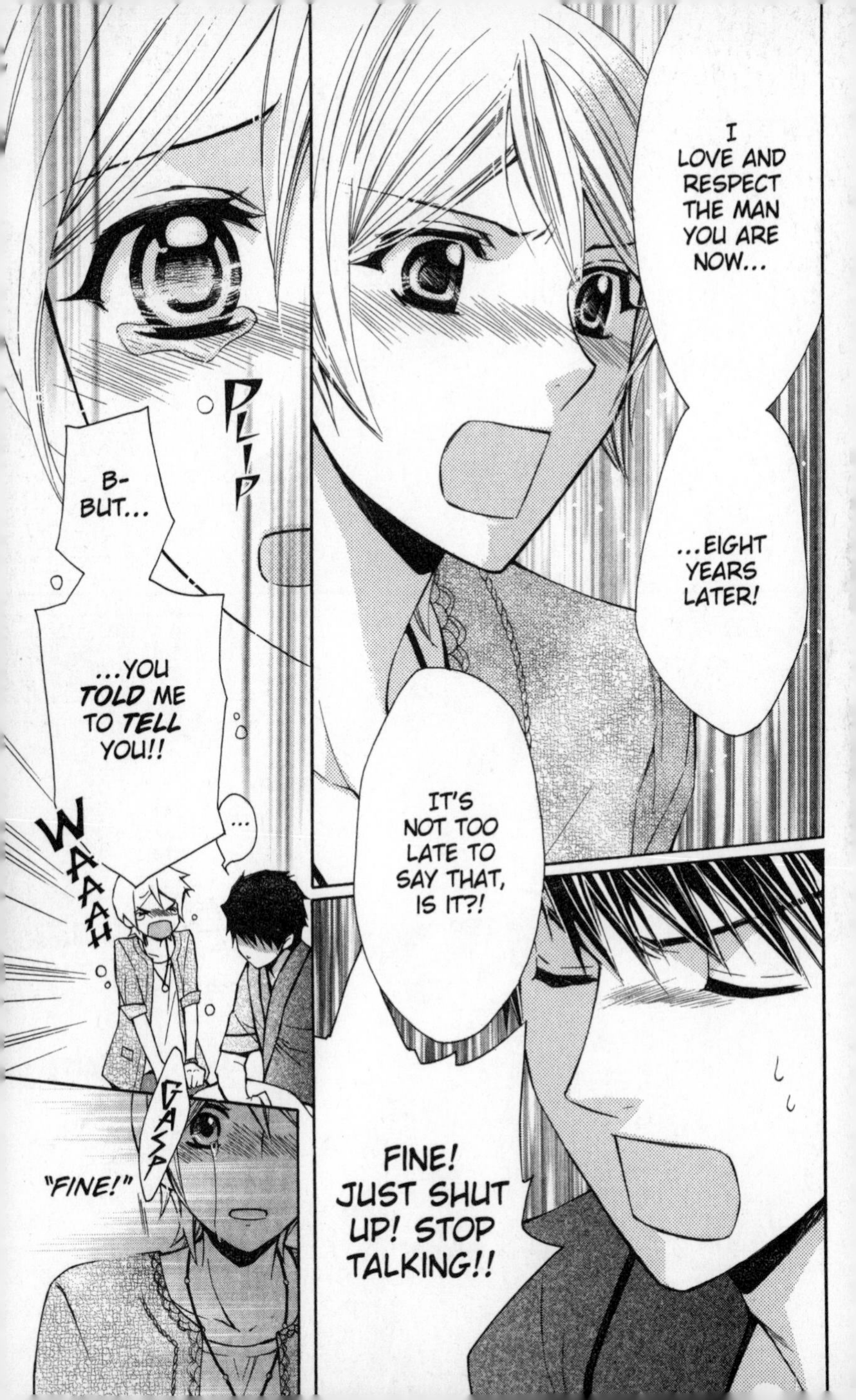

I LOVE AND RESPECT THE MAN YOU ARE NOW...
...EIGHT YEARS LATER!
IT'S NOT TOO LATE TO SAY THAT, IS IT?!
PLIP
B-BUT...
...YOU *TOLD* ME TO *TELL* YOU!!
WAAAH
...
FINE! JUST SHUT UP! STOP TALKING!!
GASP
"FINE!"

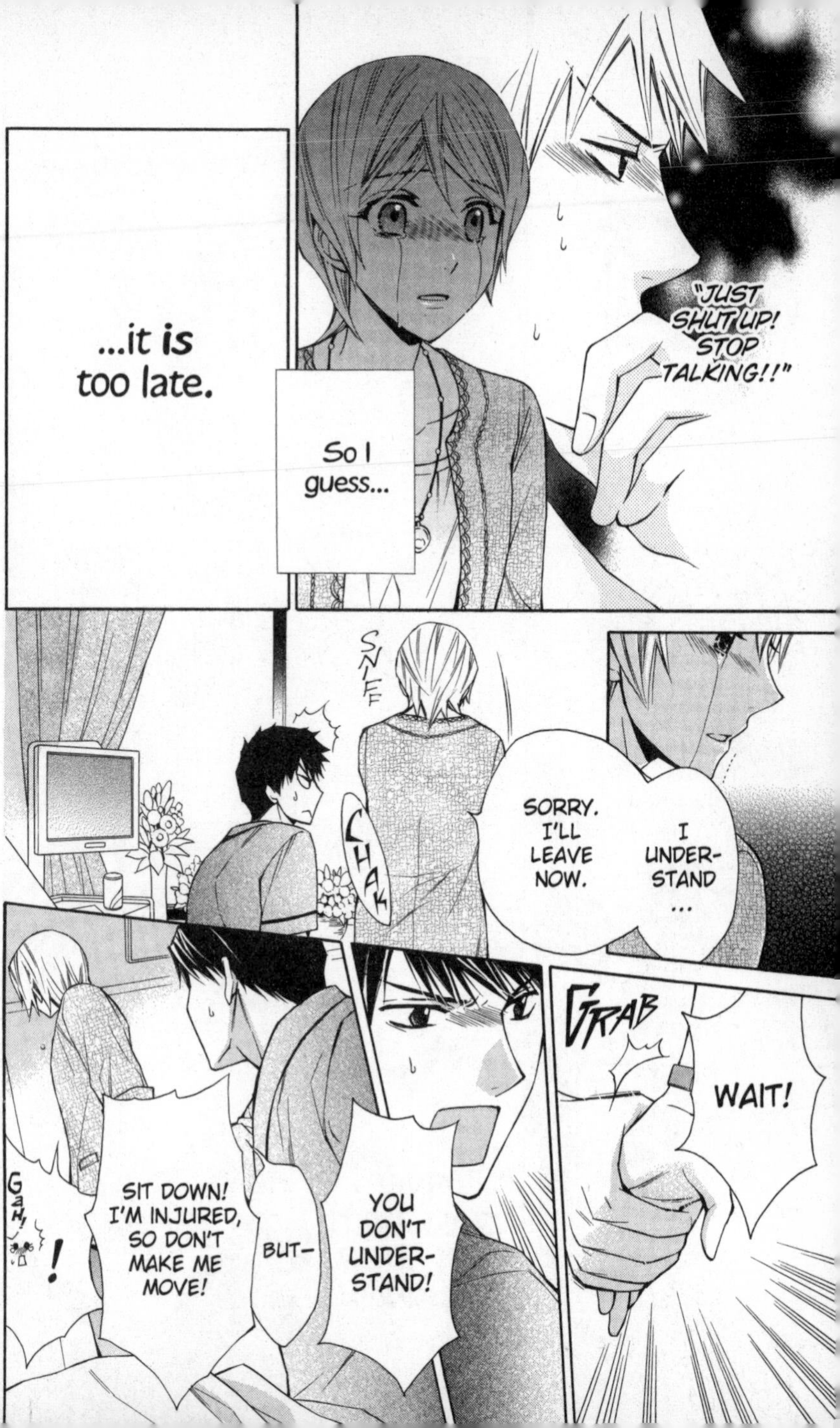
"JUST SHUT UP! STOP TALKING!!"
So I guess...
...it is too late.
I UNDER-STAND...
SORRY. I'LL LEAVE NOW.
SNIFF
CHAK
GRAB
WAIT!
YOU DON'T UNDER-STAND!
BUT—
SIT DOWN! I'M INJURED, SO DON'T MAKE ME MOVE!
GAH!
!

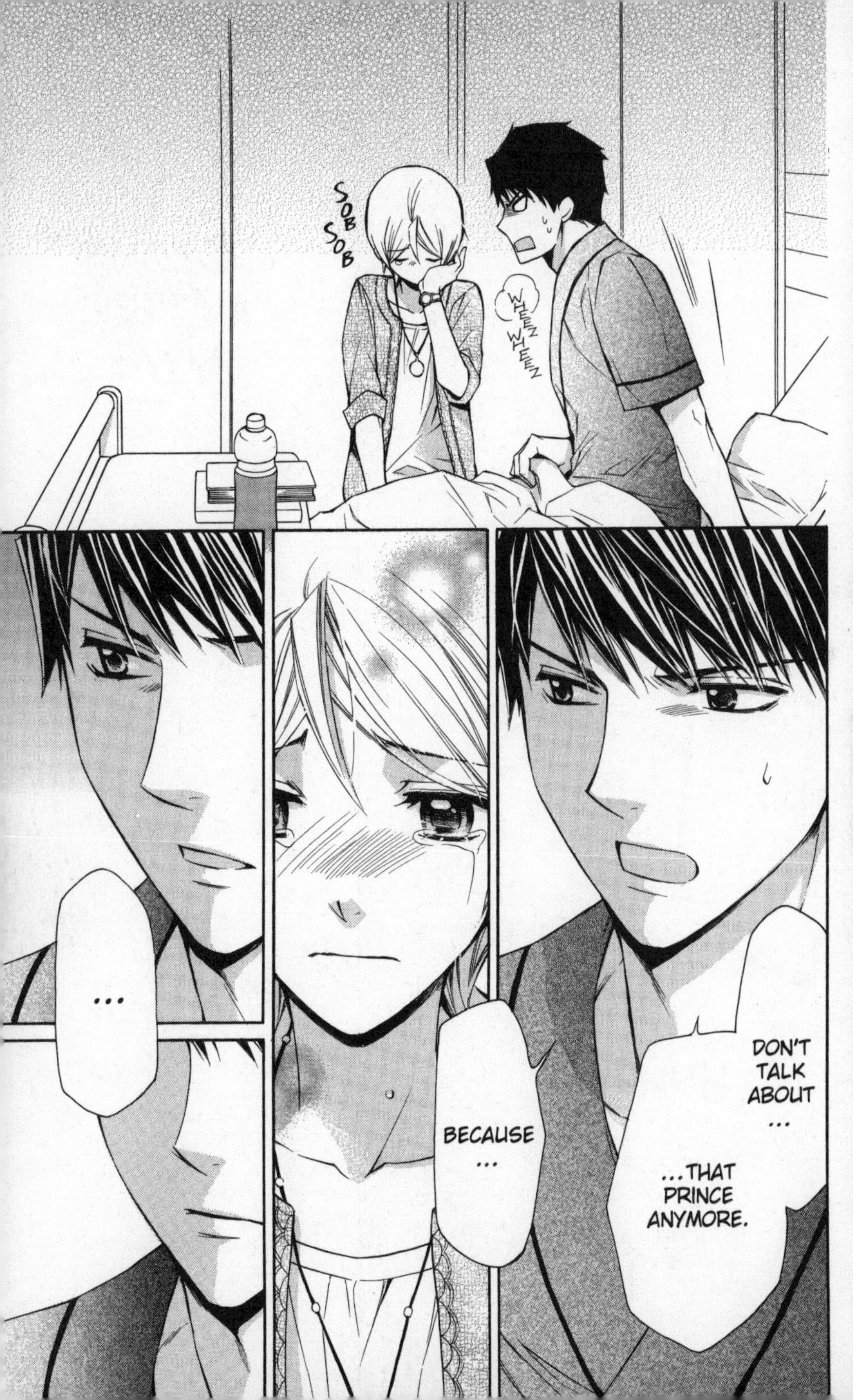
WHEEZ WHEEZ
SOB SOB
DON'T TALK ABOUT ...
...THAT PRINCE ANYMORE.
BECAUSE ...
...

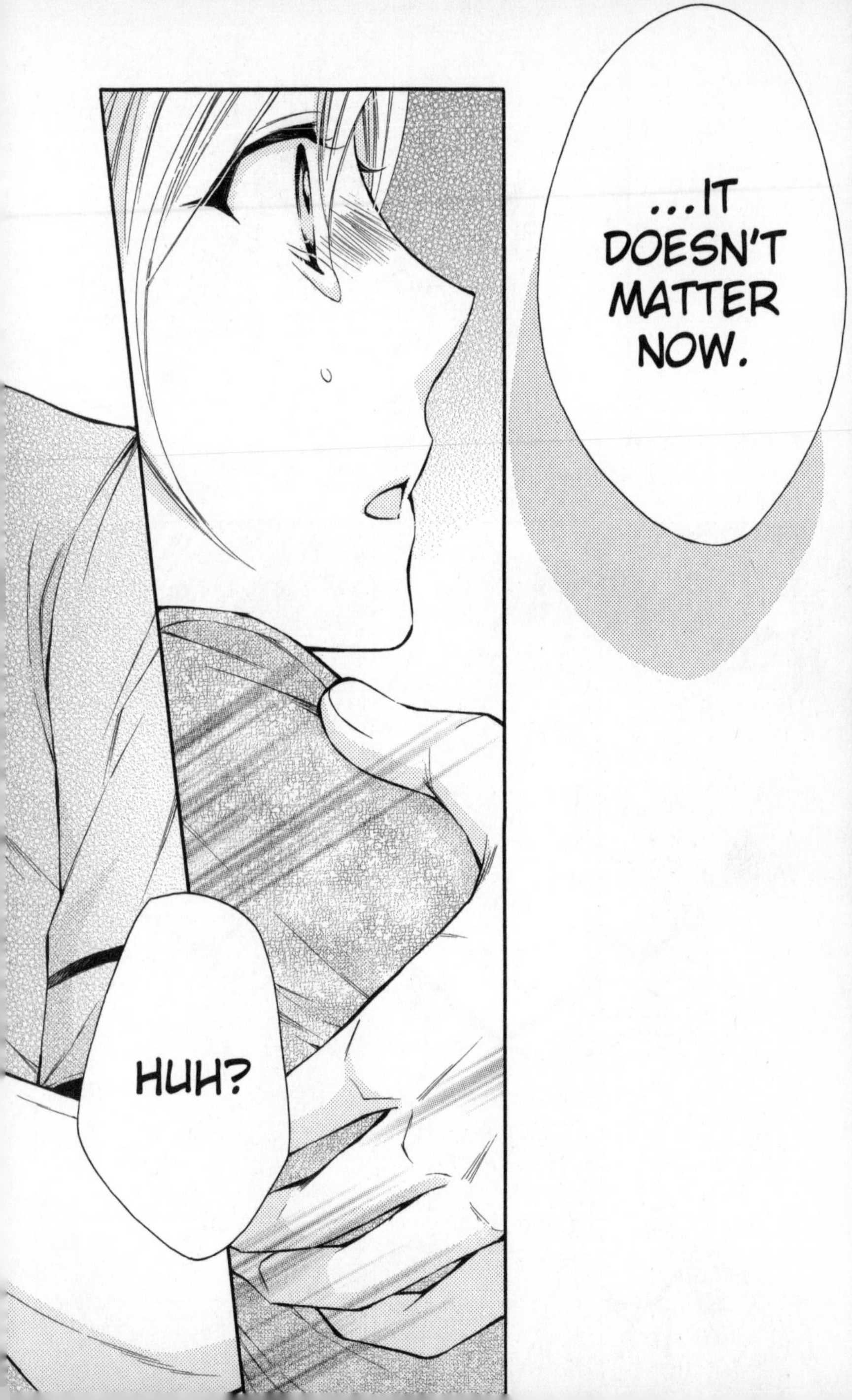
...IT DOESN'T MATTER NOW.
HUH?

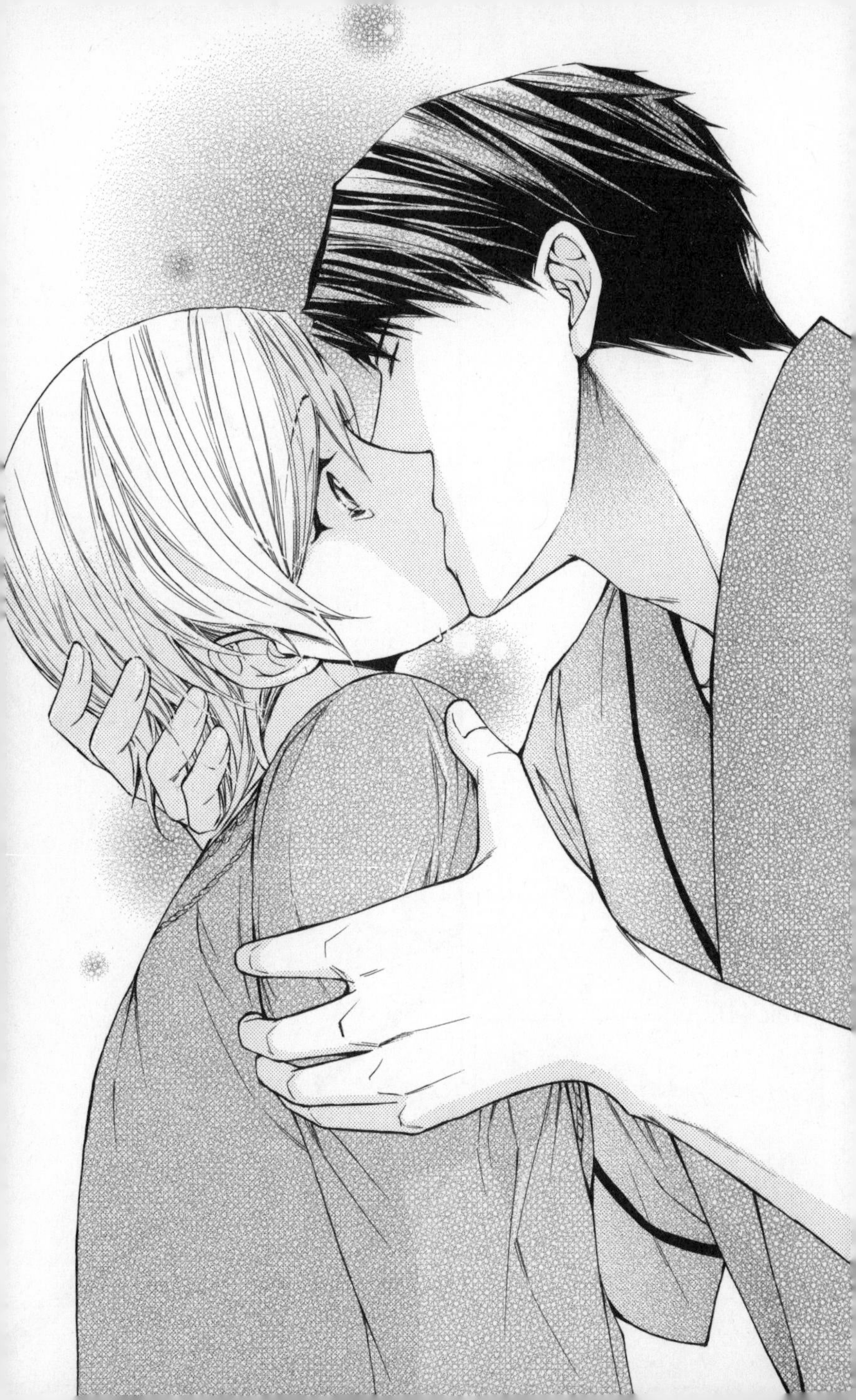

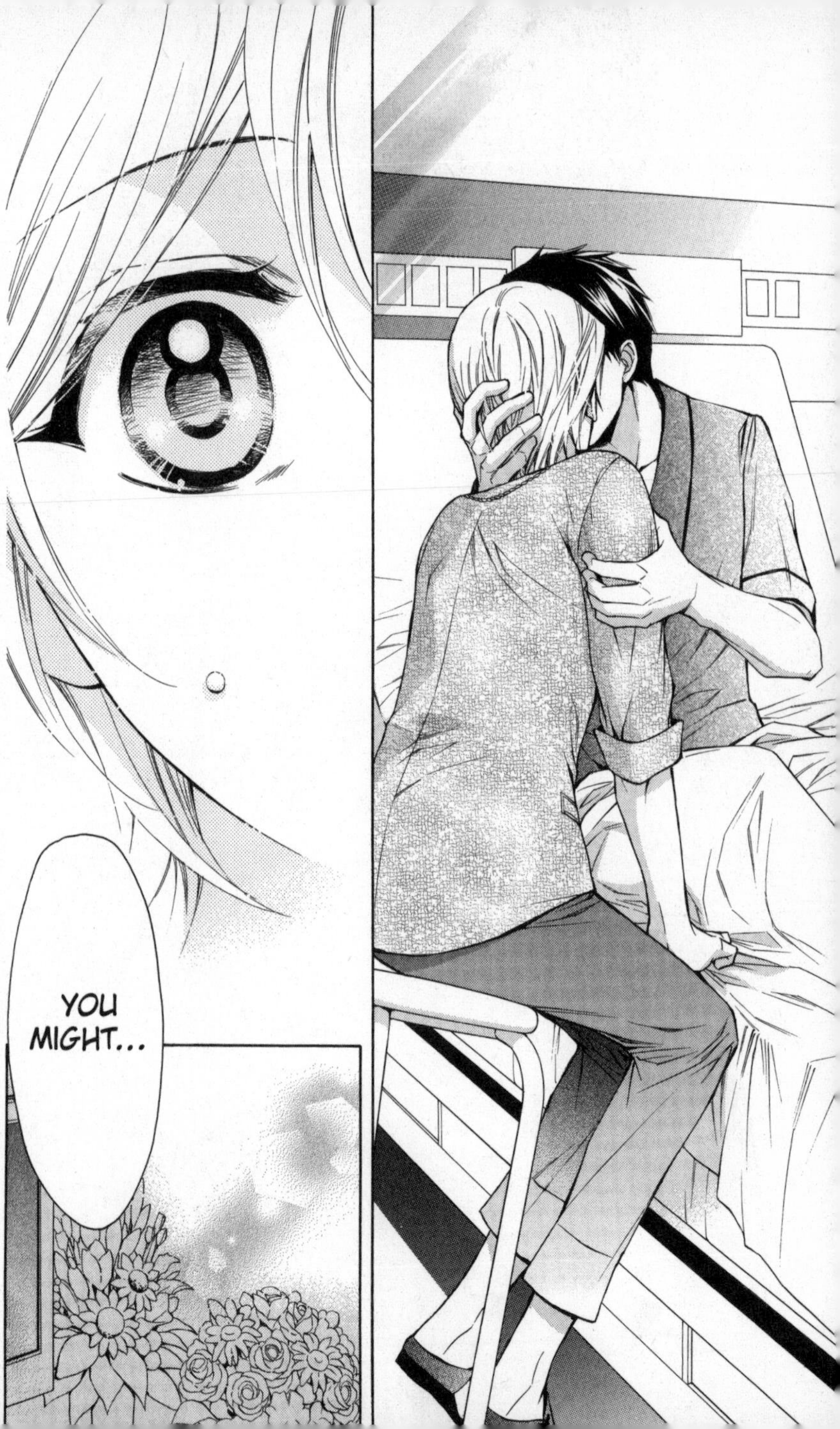
YOU MIGHT...

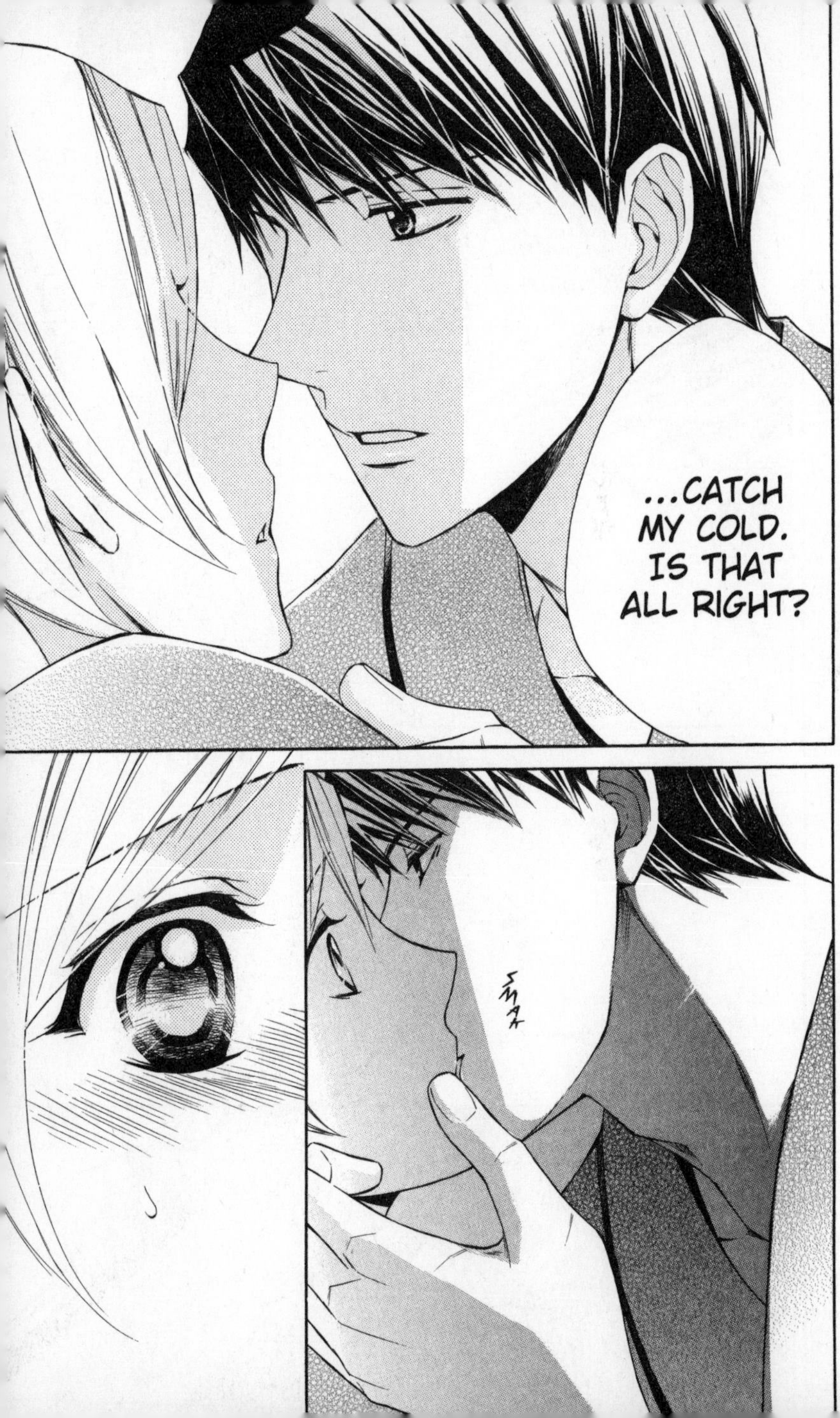
...CATCH MY COLD. IS THAT ALL RIGHT?
SMAK

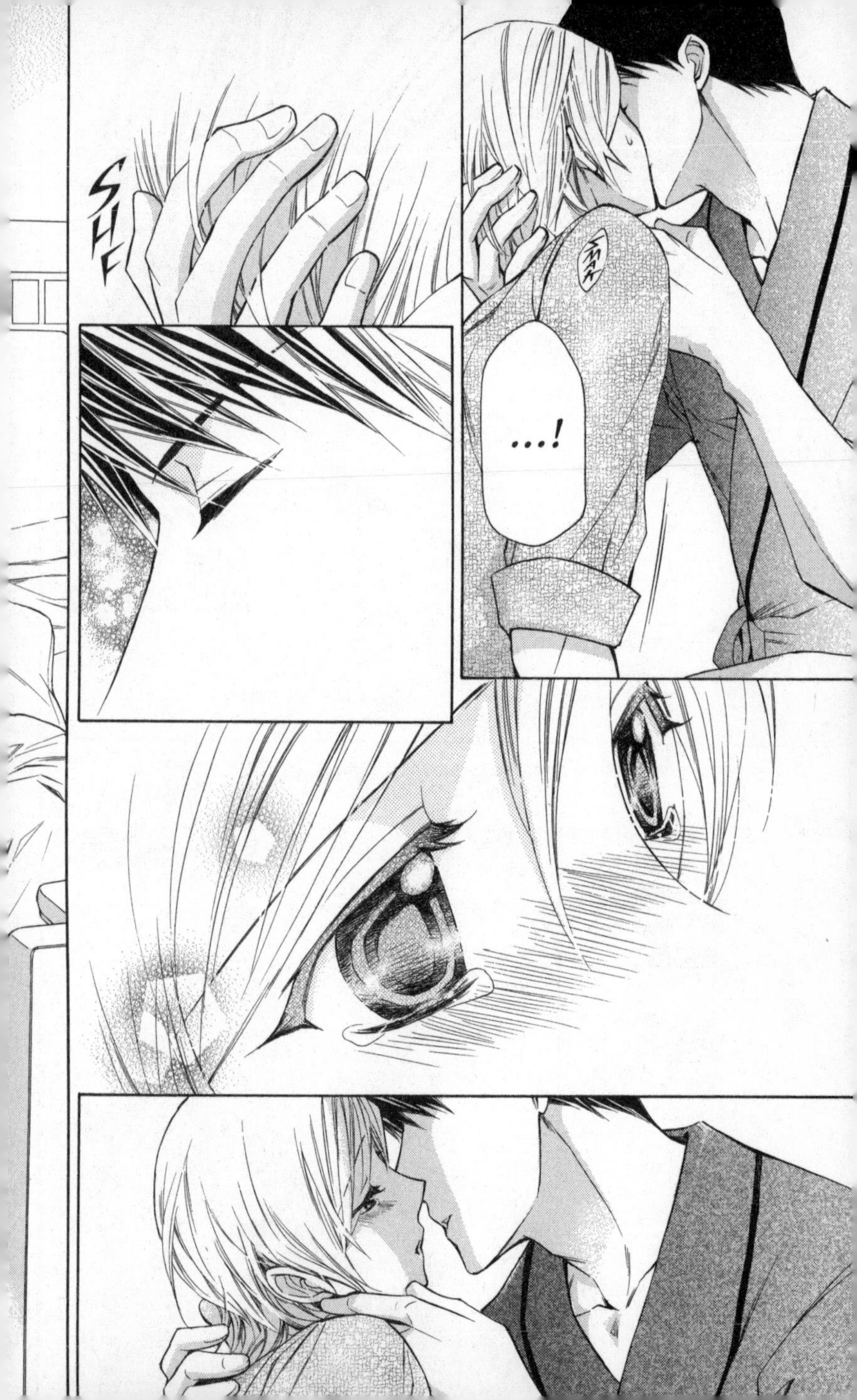
SMAK
...!
SHFF

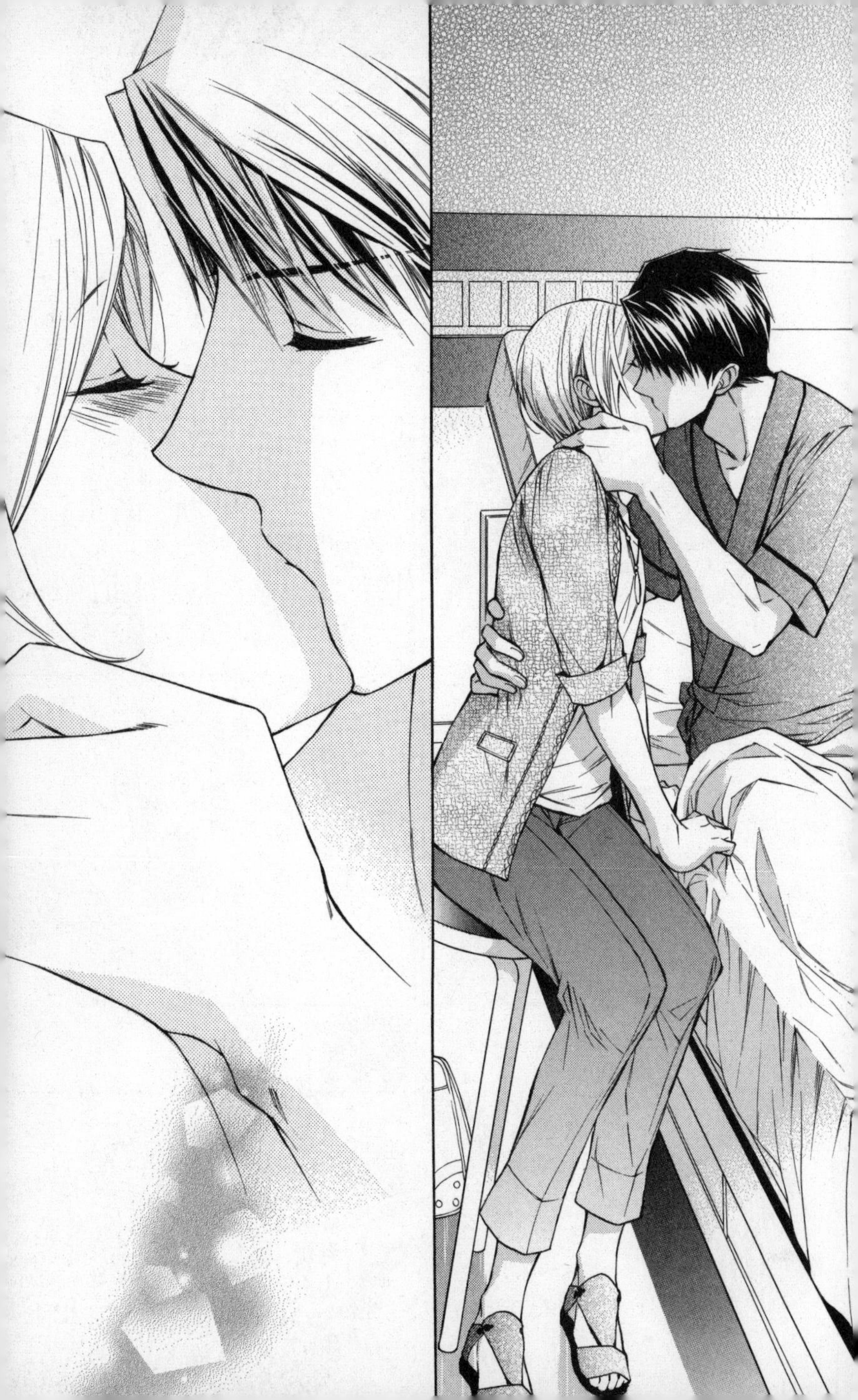

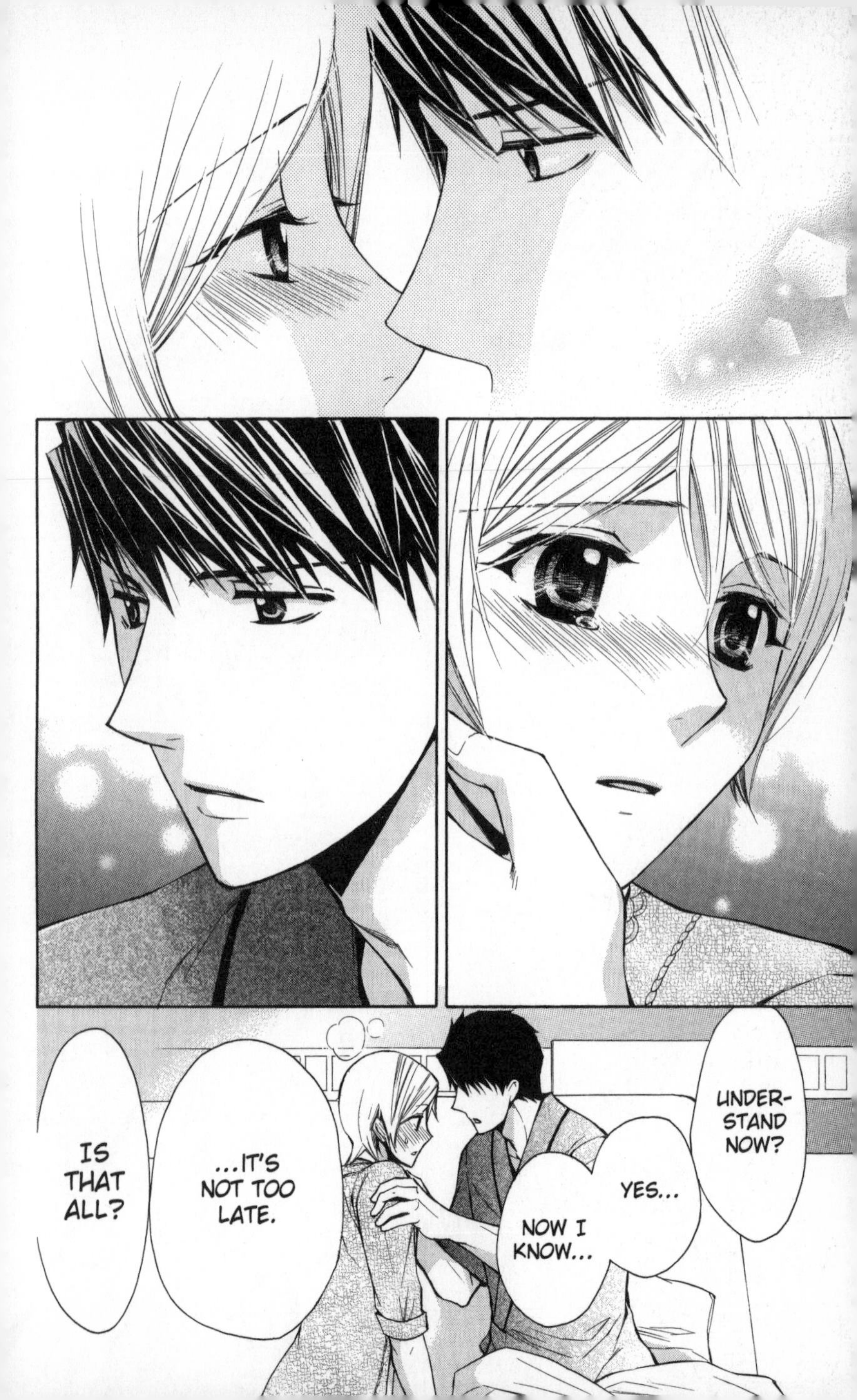
UNDER-STAND NOW?
YES...
NOW I KNOW...
...IT'S NOT TOO LATE.
IS THAT ALL?

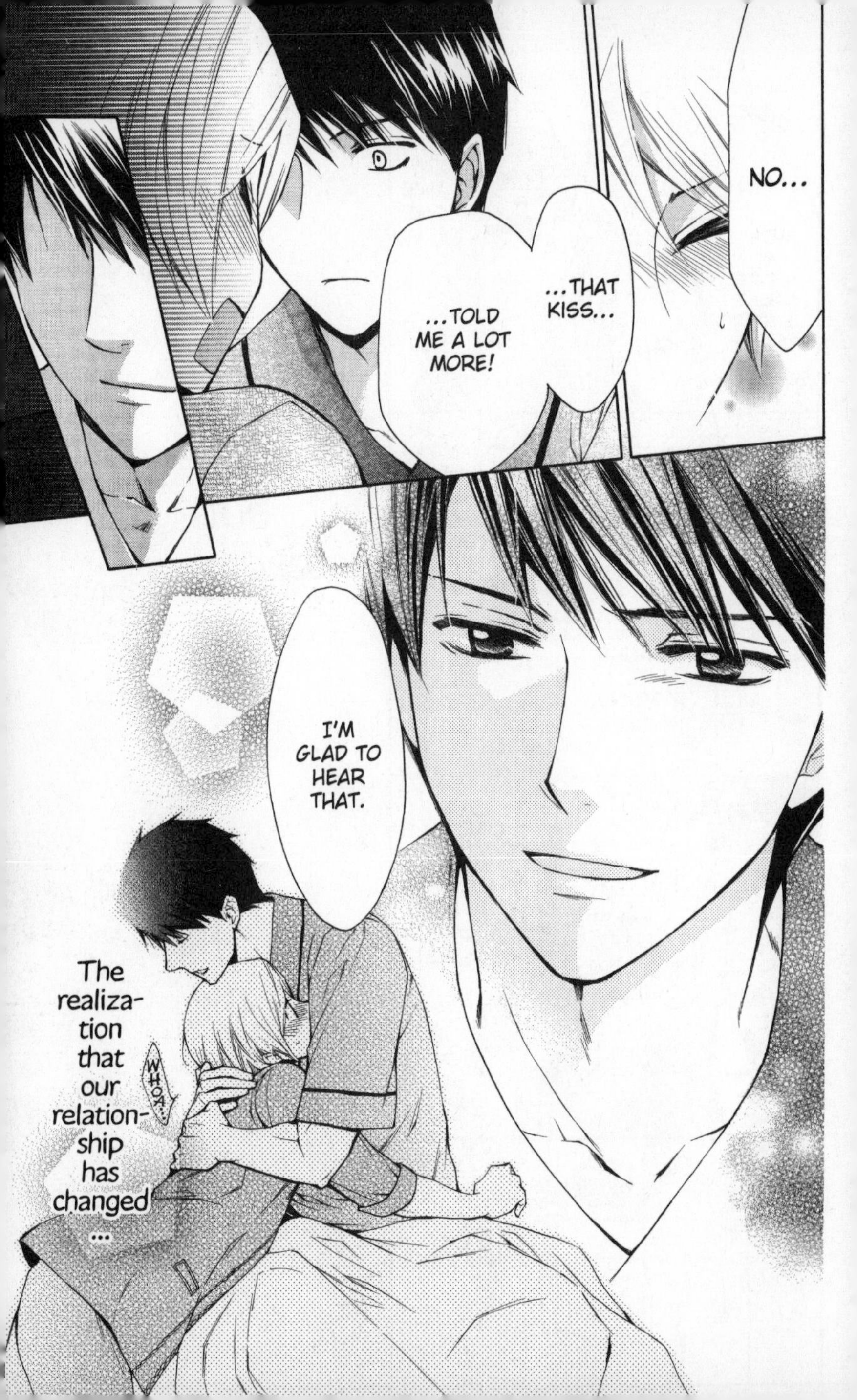
NO...
...THAT KISS...
...TOLD ME A LOT MORE!
I'M GLAD TO HEAR THAT.
WHOA...
The realization that our relationship has changed...

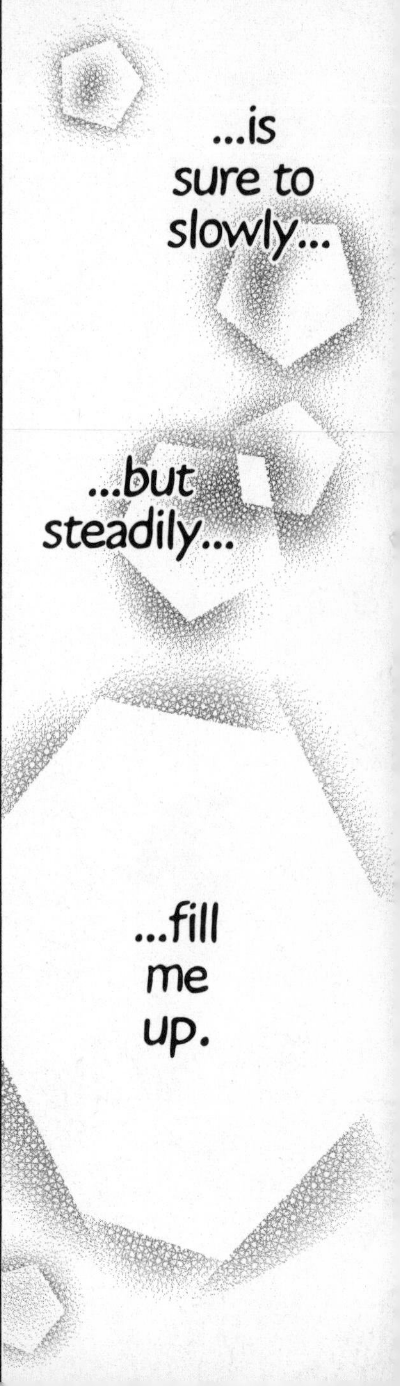
...is sure to slowly...
...but steadily...
...fill me up.
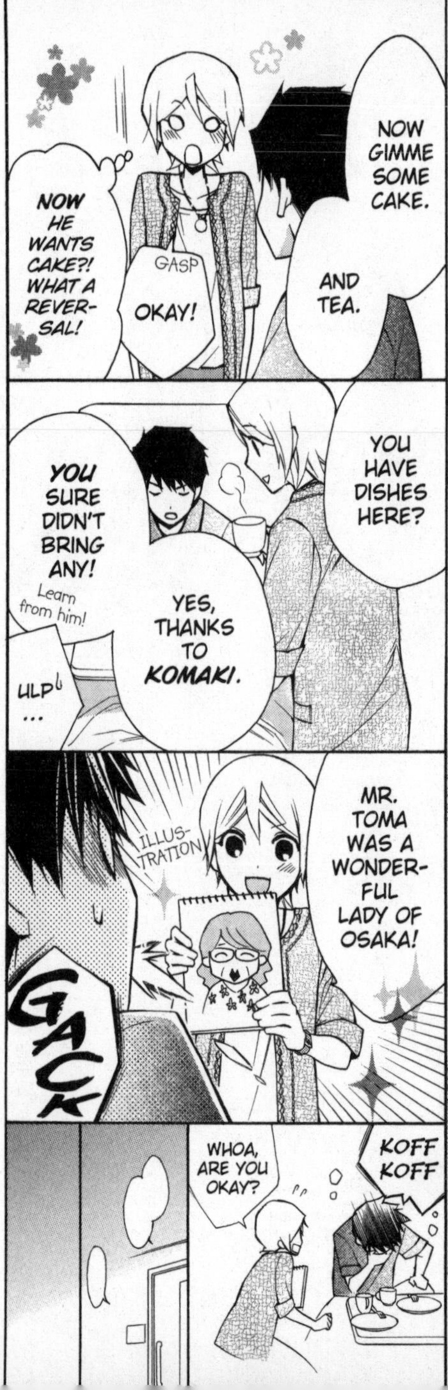
NOW GIMME SOME CAKE.
AND TEA.
GASP
OKAY!
NOW HE WANTS CAKE?! WHAT A REVERSAL!
YOU HAVE DISHES HERE?
YES, THANKS TO KOMAKI.
YOU SURE DIDN'T BRING ANY!
Learn from him!
ULP...
MR. TOMA WAS A WONDERFUL LADY OF OSAKA!
ILLUSTRATION
GACK
KOFF KOFF
WHOA, ARE YOU OKAY?

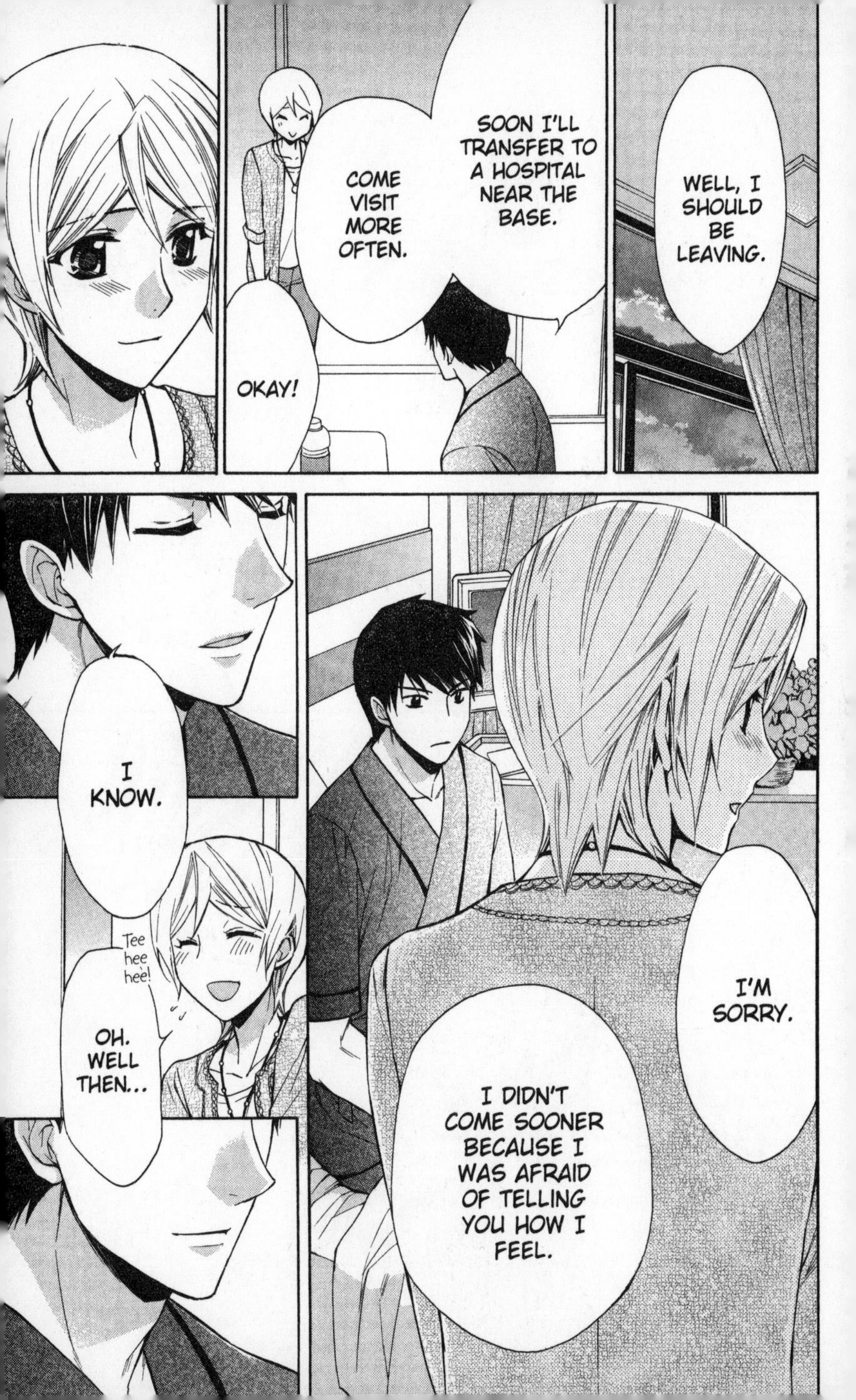
WELL, I SHOULD BE LEAVING.
SOON I'LL TRANSFER TO A HOSPITAL NEAR THE BASE.
COME VISIT MORE OFTEN.
OKAY!
I'M SORRY.
I DIDN'T COME SOONER BECAUSE I WAS AFRAID OF TELLING YOU HOW I FEEL.
I KNOW.
Tee hee hee!
OH. WELL THEN...

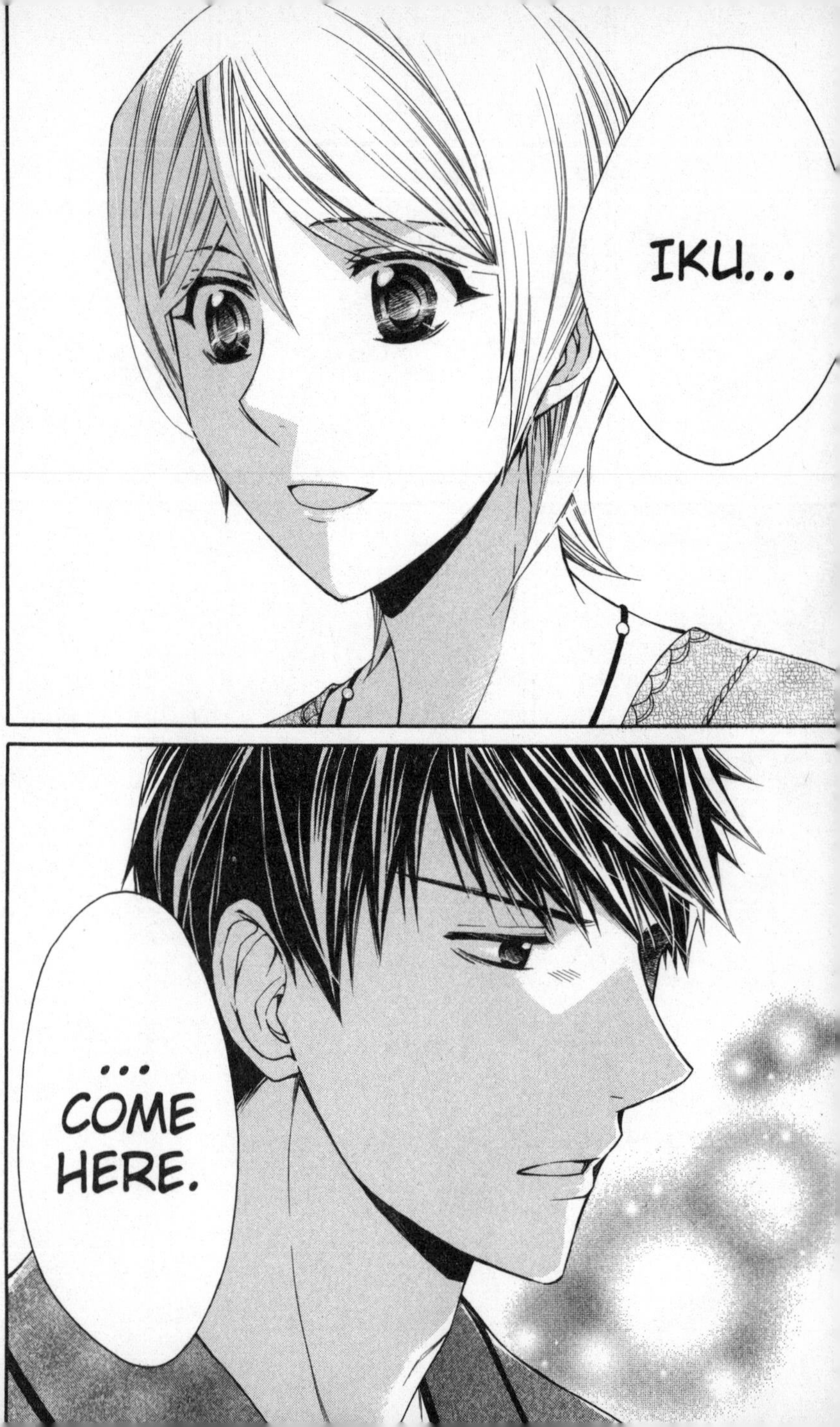
IKU...
... COME HERE.

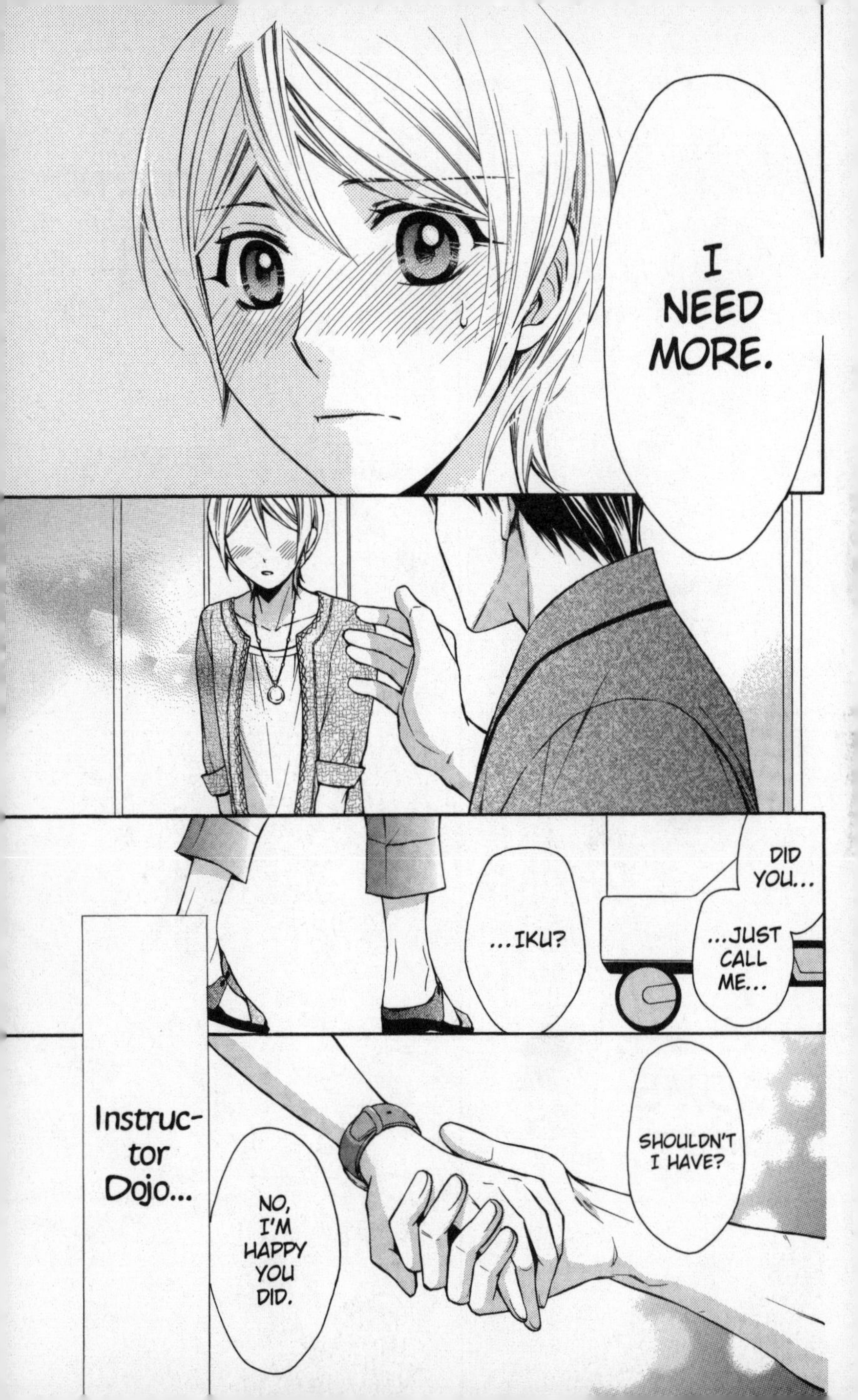
I NEED MORE.
DID YOU...
...JUST CALL ME...
...IKU?
Instructor Dojo...
SHOULDN'T I HAVE?
NO, I'M HAPPY YOU DID.

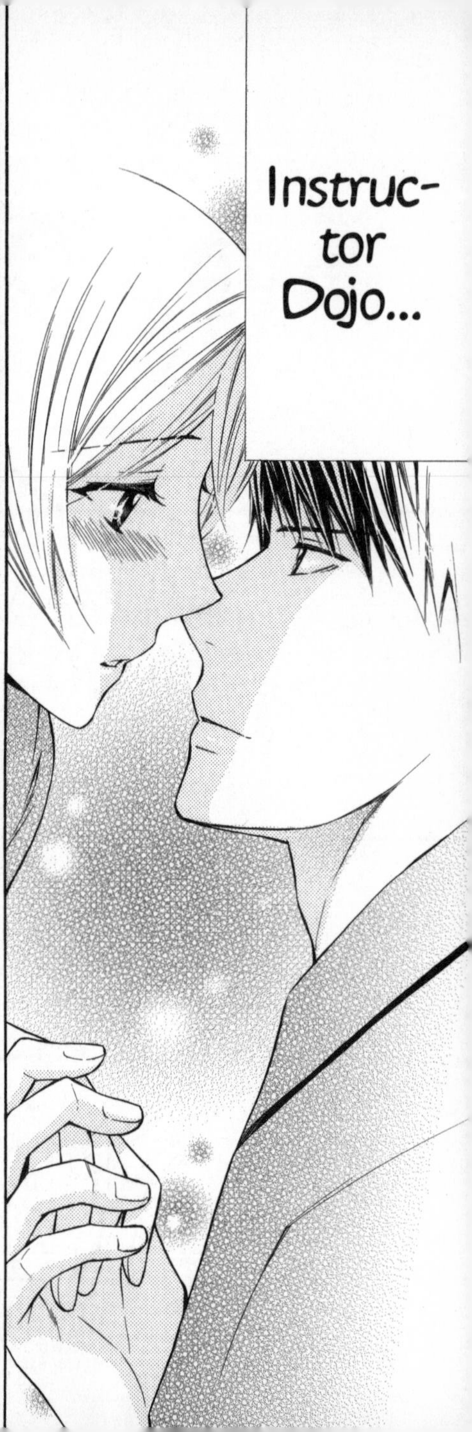
Instructor Dojo...
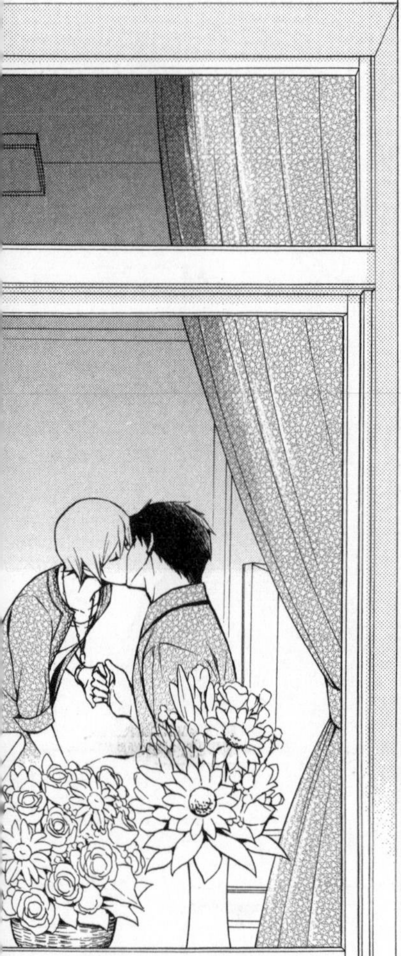

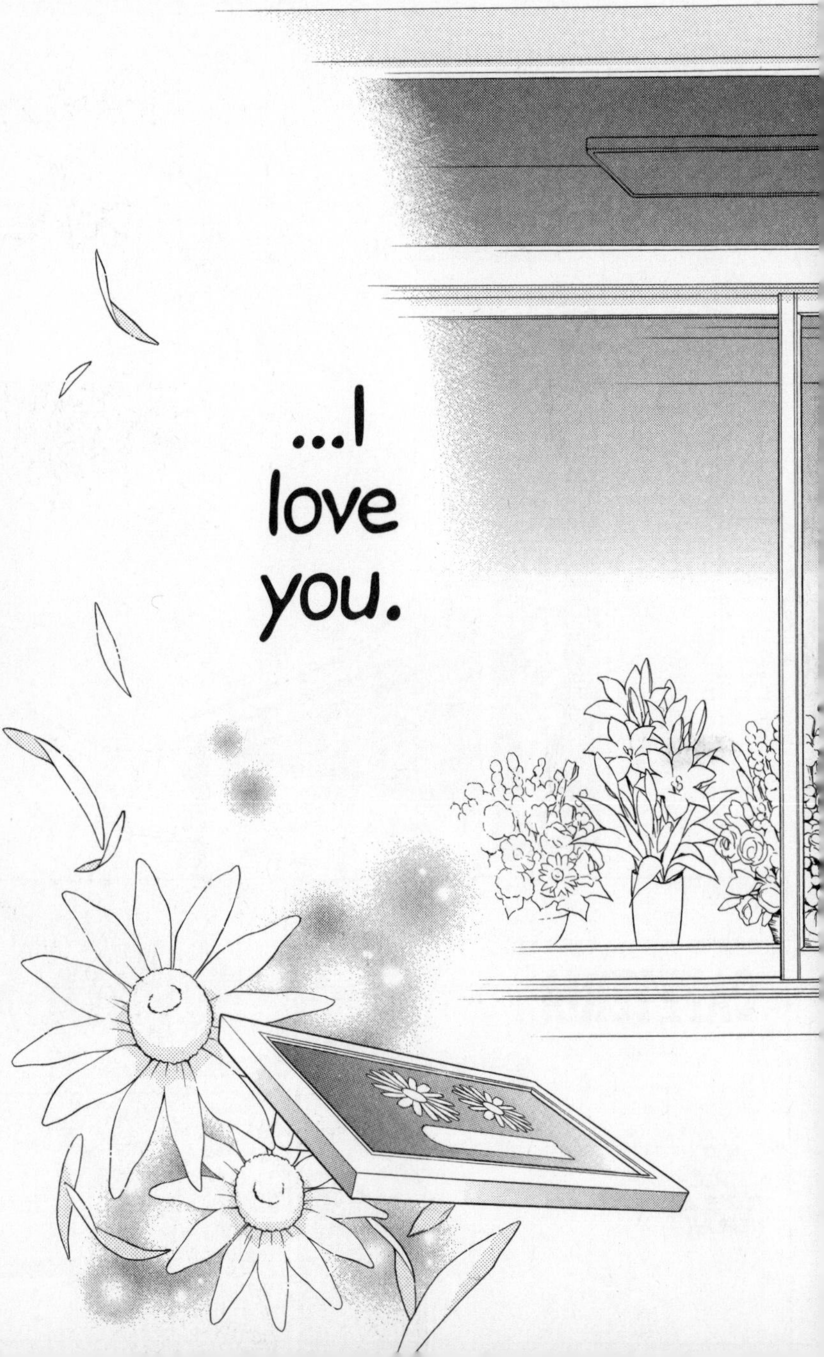
...I love you.

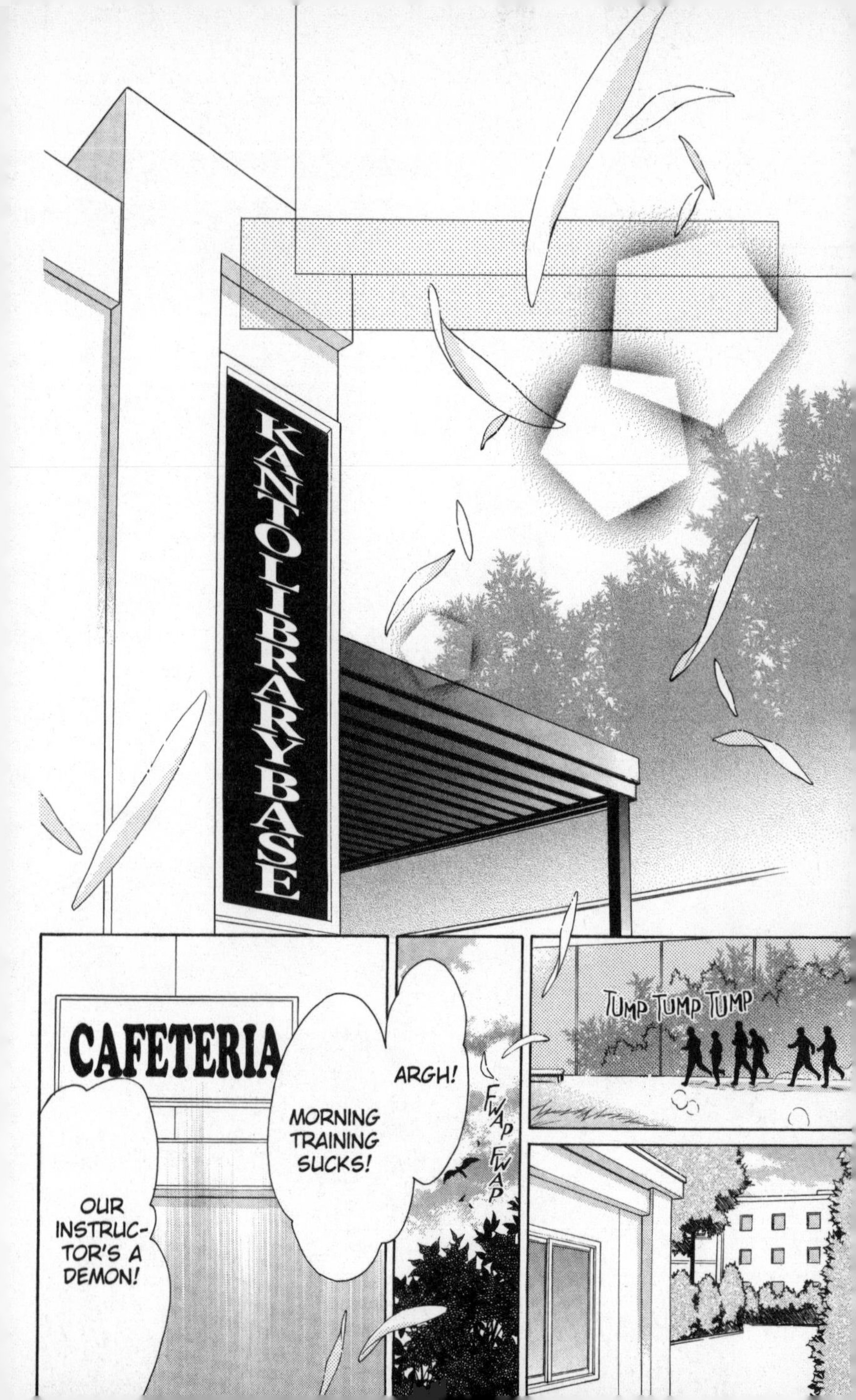
KANTO LIBRARY BASE
TUMP TUMP TUMP
FWAP FWAP
ARGH!
MORNING TRAINING SUCKS!
CAFETERIA
OUR INSTRUCTOR'S A DEMON!

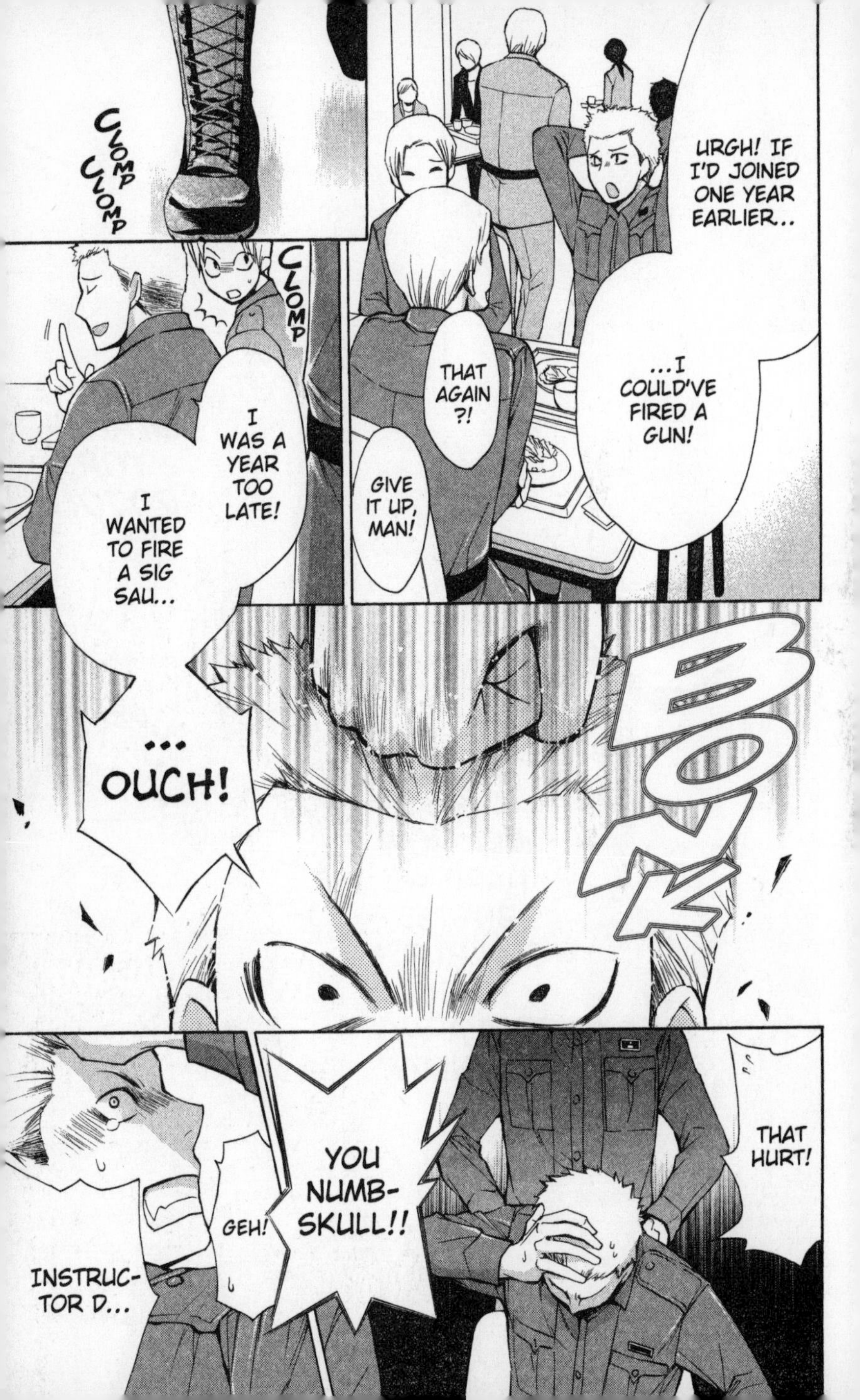
URGH! IF I'D JOINED ONE YEAR EARLIER...
...I COULD'VE FIRED A GUN!
THAT AGAIN?!
GIVE IT UP, MAN!
CLOMP CLOMP
CLOMP
CLOMP
I WAS A YEAR TOO LATE!
I WANTED TO FIRE A SIG SAU...
BONK
...OUCH!
THAT HURT!
YOU NUMBSKULL!!
GEH!
INSTRUCTOR D...

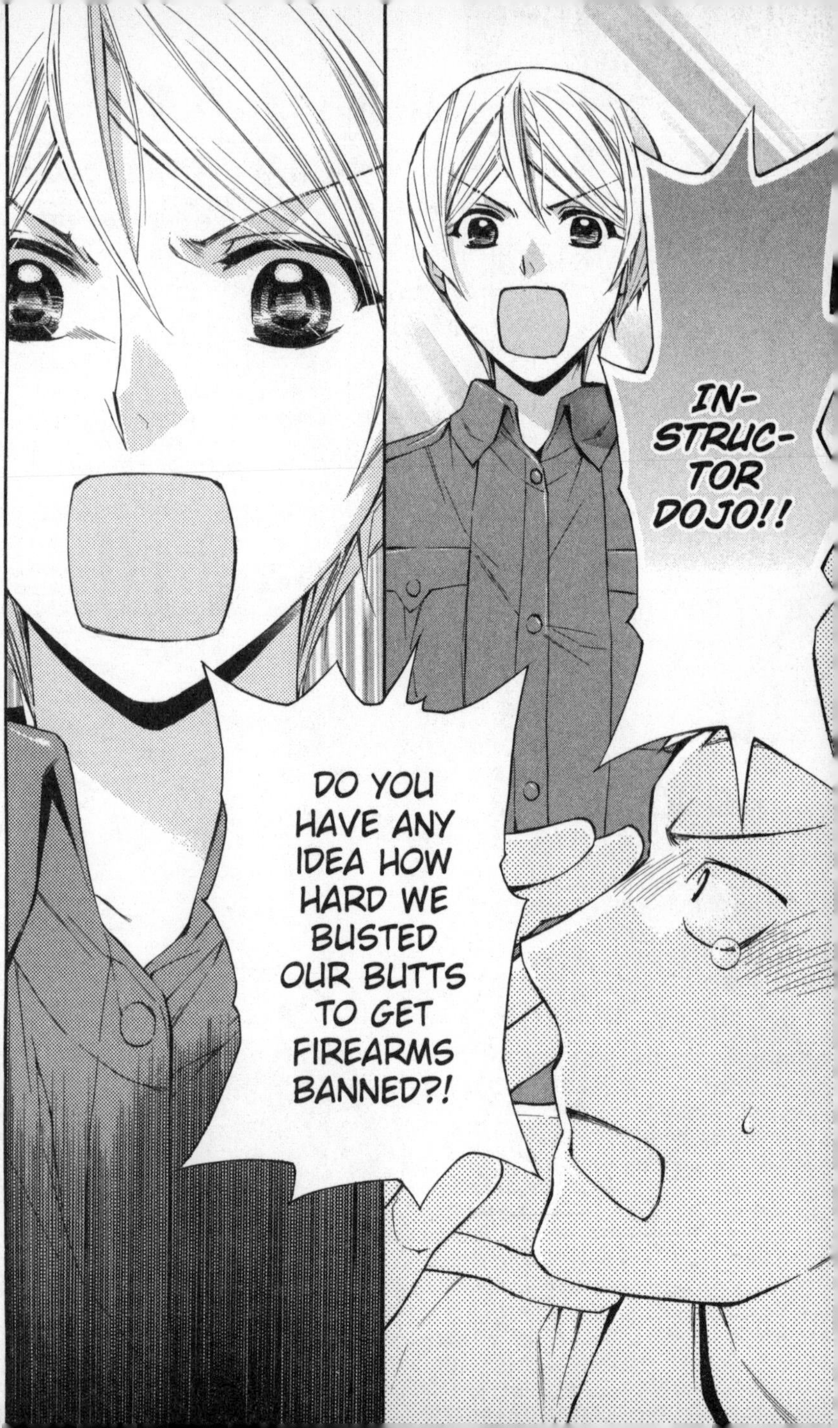
IN-STRUC-TOR DOJO!!
DO YOU HAVE ANY IDEA HOW HARD WE BUSTED OUR BUTTS TO GET FIREARMS BANNED?!

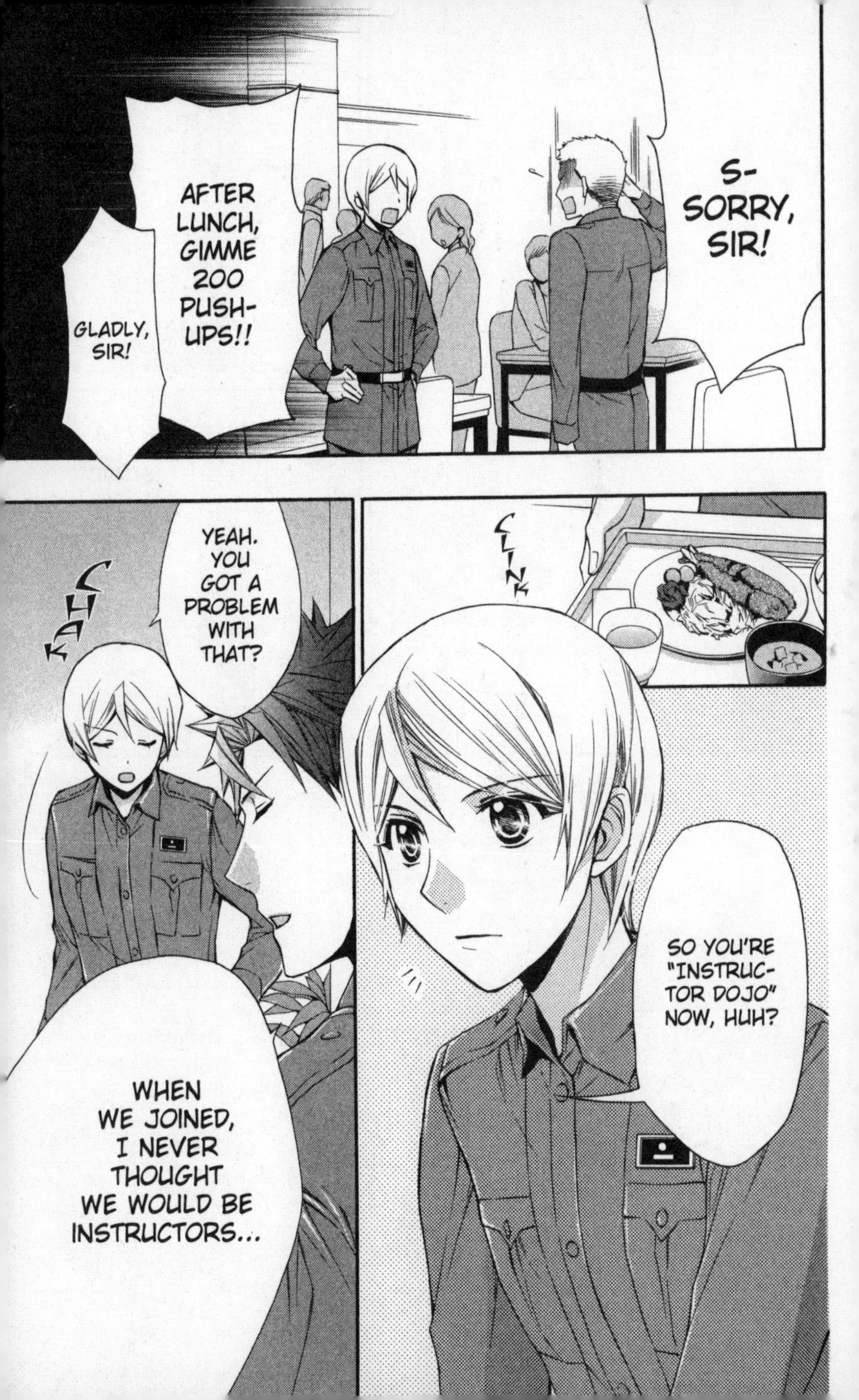
S-SORRY, SIR!
AFTER LUNCH, GIMME 200 PUSH-UPS!!
GLADLY, SIR!
CLINK
SO YOU'RE "INSTRUCTOR DOJO" NOW, HUH?
YEAH. YOU GOT A PROBLEM WITH THAT?
CHAK
WHEN WE JOINED, I NEVER THOUGHT WE WOULD BE INSTRUCTORS...

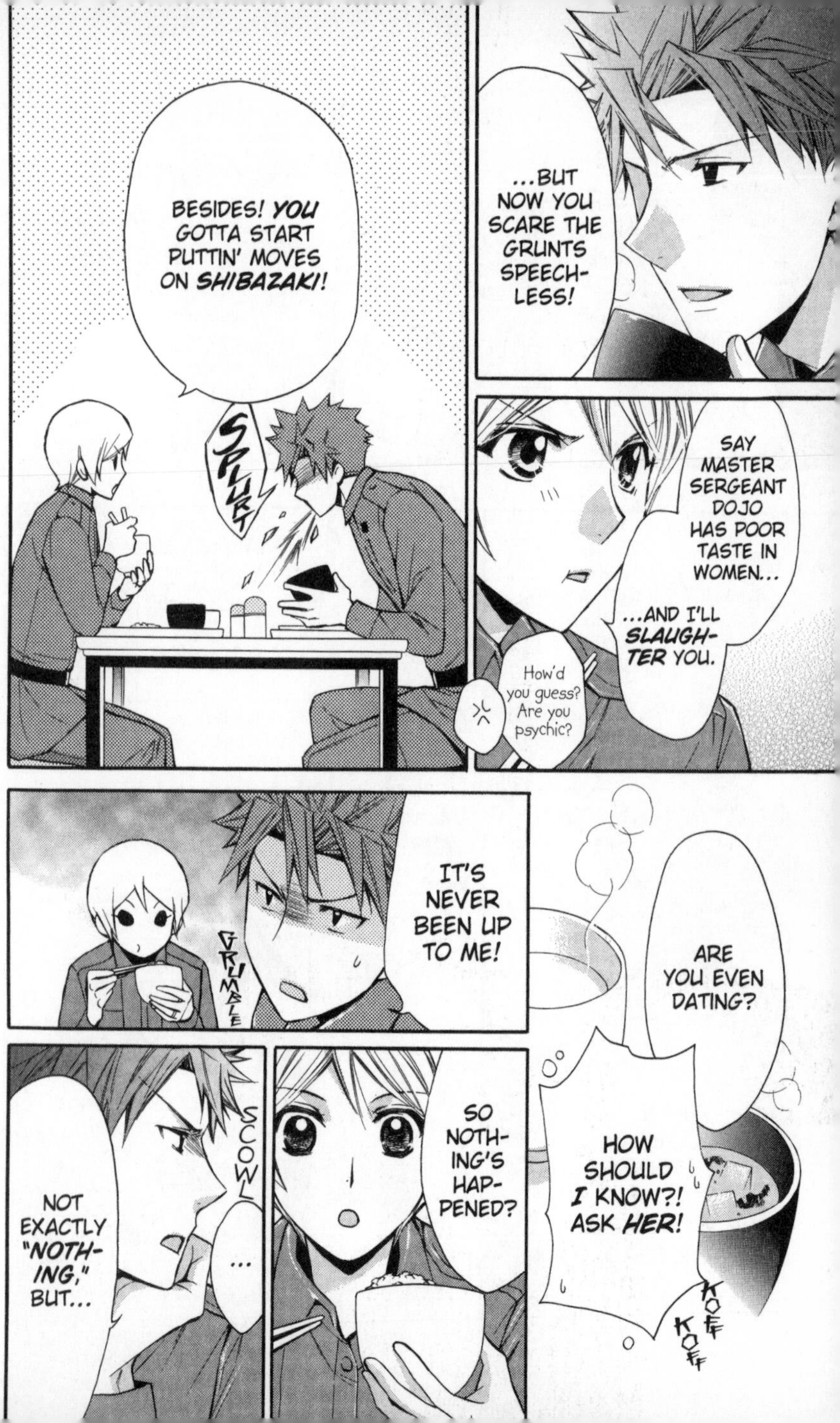
...BUT NOW YOU SCARE THE GRUNTS SPEECHLESS!
SAY MASTER SERGEANT DOJO HAS POOR TASTE IN WOMEN...
...AND I'LL SLAUGHTER YOU.
How'd you guess? Are you psychic?
BESIDES! YOU GOTTA START PUTTIN' MOVES ON SHIBAZAKI!
SPLURT
ARE YOU EVEN DATING?
HOW SHOULD I KNOW?! ASK HER!
KOFF KOFF
IT'S NEVER BEEN UP TO ME!
GRUMBLE
SO NOTHING'S HAPPENED?
...
SCOWL
NOT EXACTLY "NOTHING," BUT...

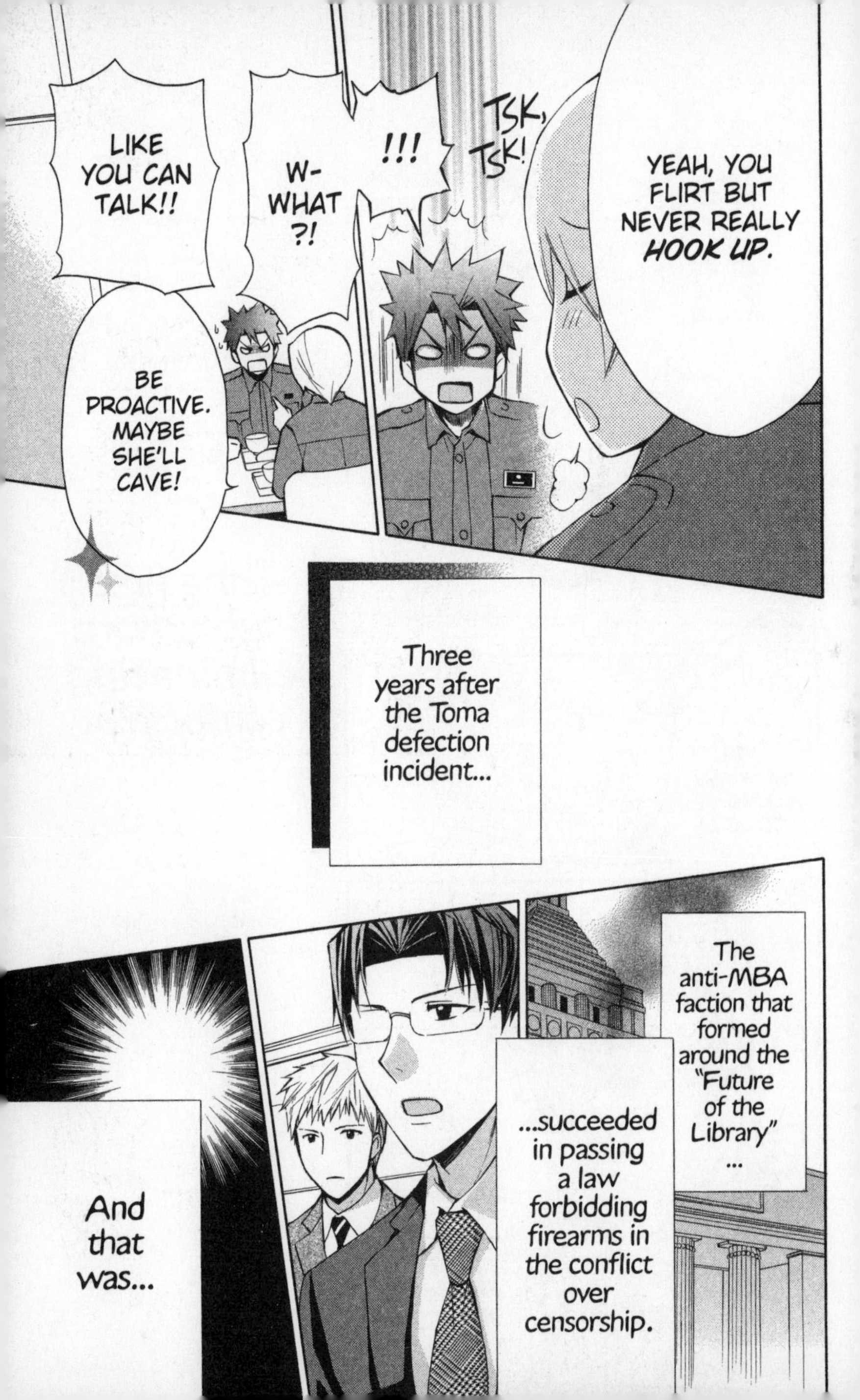
YEAH, YOU FLIRT BUT NEVER REALLY *HOOK UP*.
TSK, TSK!
!!!
W-WHAT?!
LIKE YOU CAN TALK!!
BE PROACTIVE. MAYBE SHE'LL CAVE!
Three years after the Toma defection incident...
The anti-MBA faction that formed around the "Future of the Library"...
...succeeded in passing a law forbidding firearms in the conflict over censorship.
And that was...

...the first step toward **eliminating** censorship.

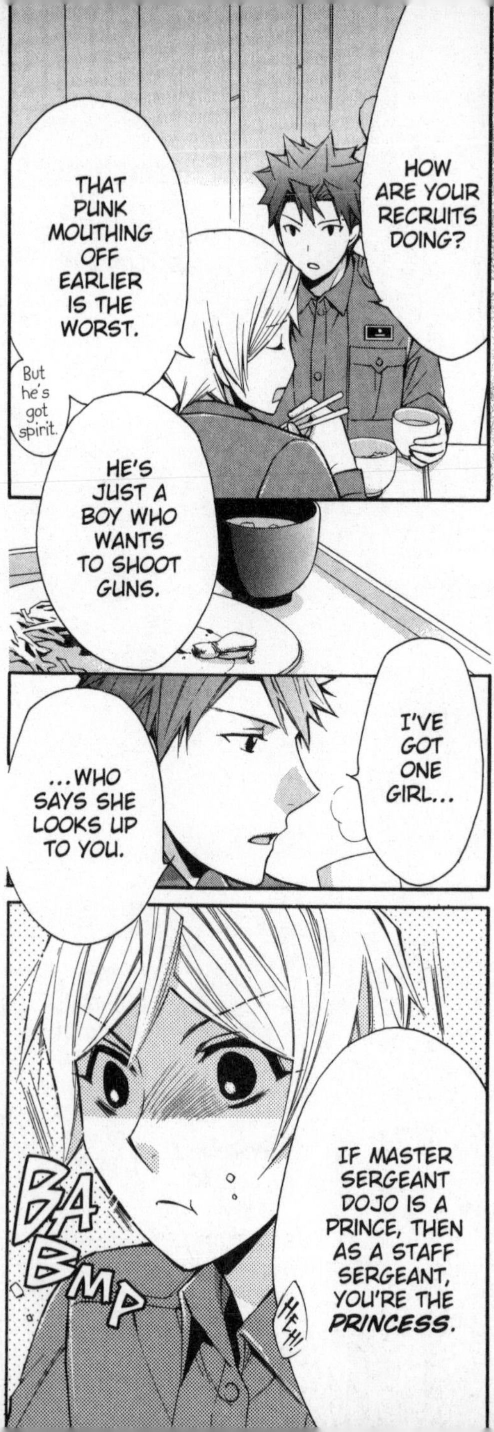
HOW ARE YOUR RECRUITS DOING?
THAT PUNK MOUTHING OFF EARLIER IS THE WORST.
But he's got spirit.
HE'S JUST A BOY WHO WANTS TO SHOOT GUNS.
I'VE GOT ONE GIRL...
...WHO SAYS SHE LOOKS UP TO YOU.
IF MASTER SERGEANT DOJO IS A PRINCE, THEN AS A STAFF SERGEANT, YOU'RE THE *PRINCESS*.
HEH!
BA BMP

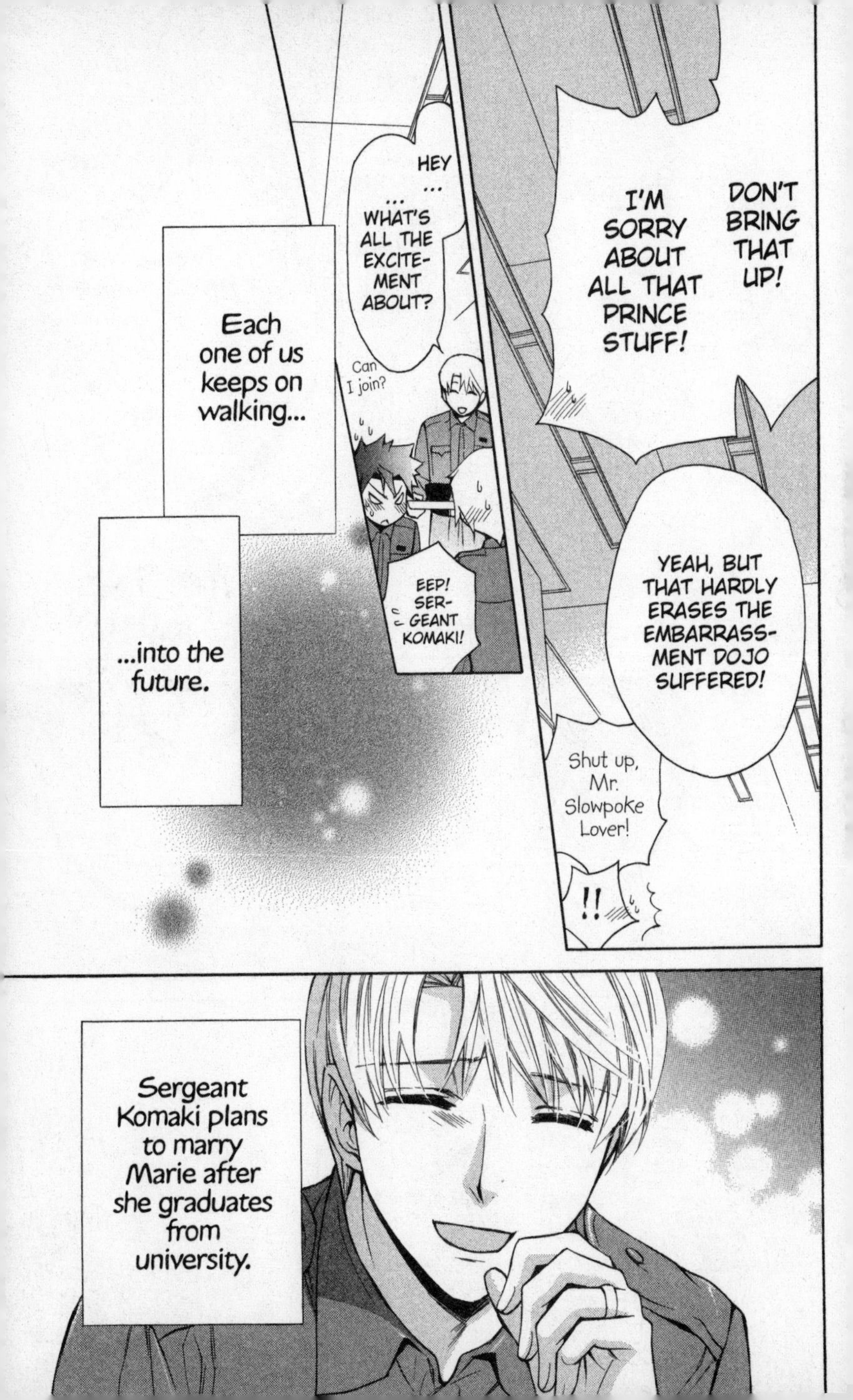
DON'T BRING THAT UP!
I'M SORRY ABOUT ALL THAT PRINCE STUFF!
YEAH, BUT THAT HARDLY ERASES THE EMBARRASSMENT DOJO SUFFERED!
Shut up, Mr. Slowpoke Lover!
!!
HEY ... ...WHAT'S ALL THE EXCITEMENT ABOUT?
Can I join?
EEP! SERGEANT KOMAKI!
Each one of us keeps on walking...
...into the future.
Sergeant Komaki plans to marry Marie after she graduates from university.

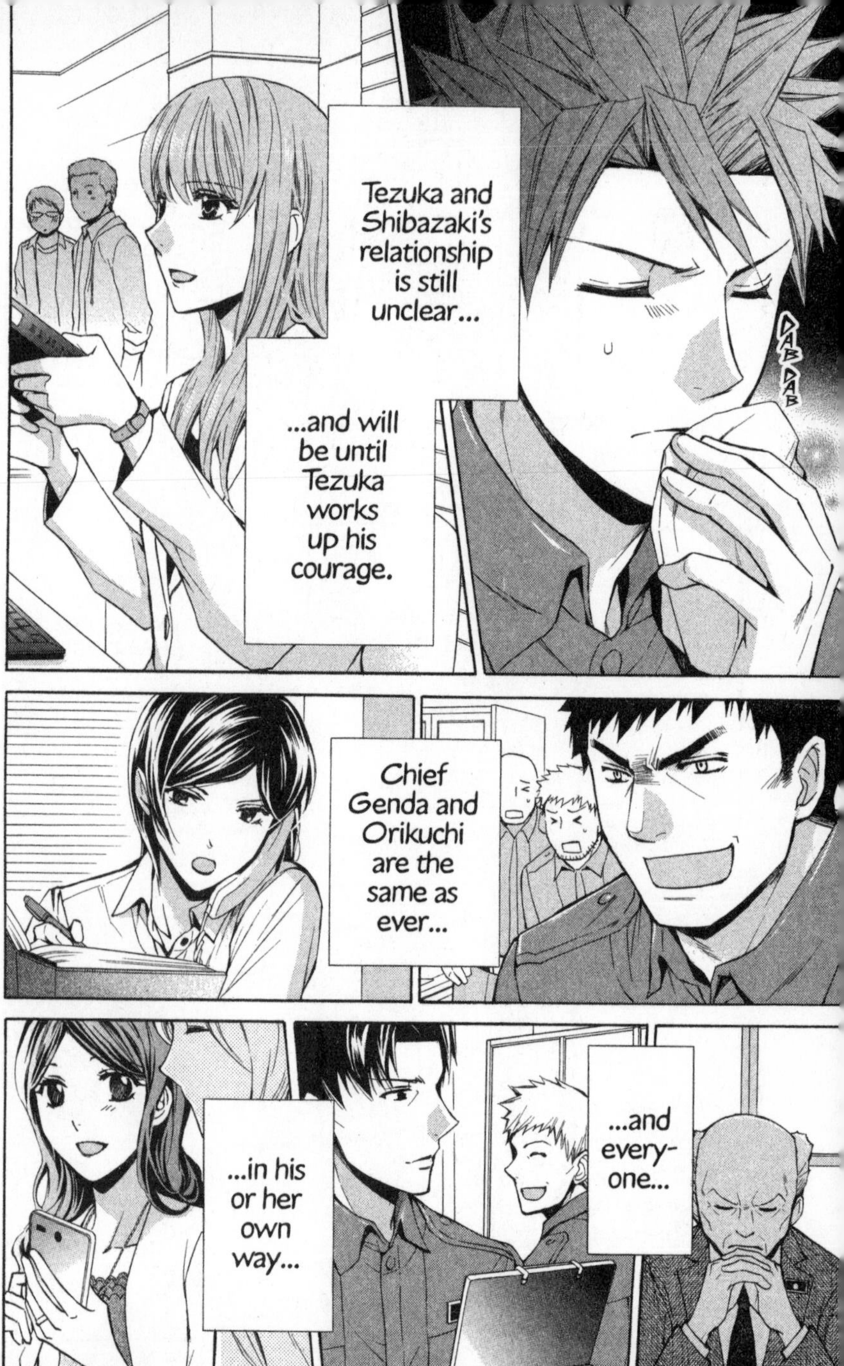
DAB DAB
Tezuka and Shibazaki's relationship is still unclear...
...and will be until Tezuka works up his courage.
Chief Genda and Orikuchi are the same as ever...
...and every-one...
...in his or her own way...

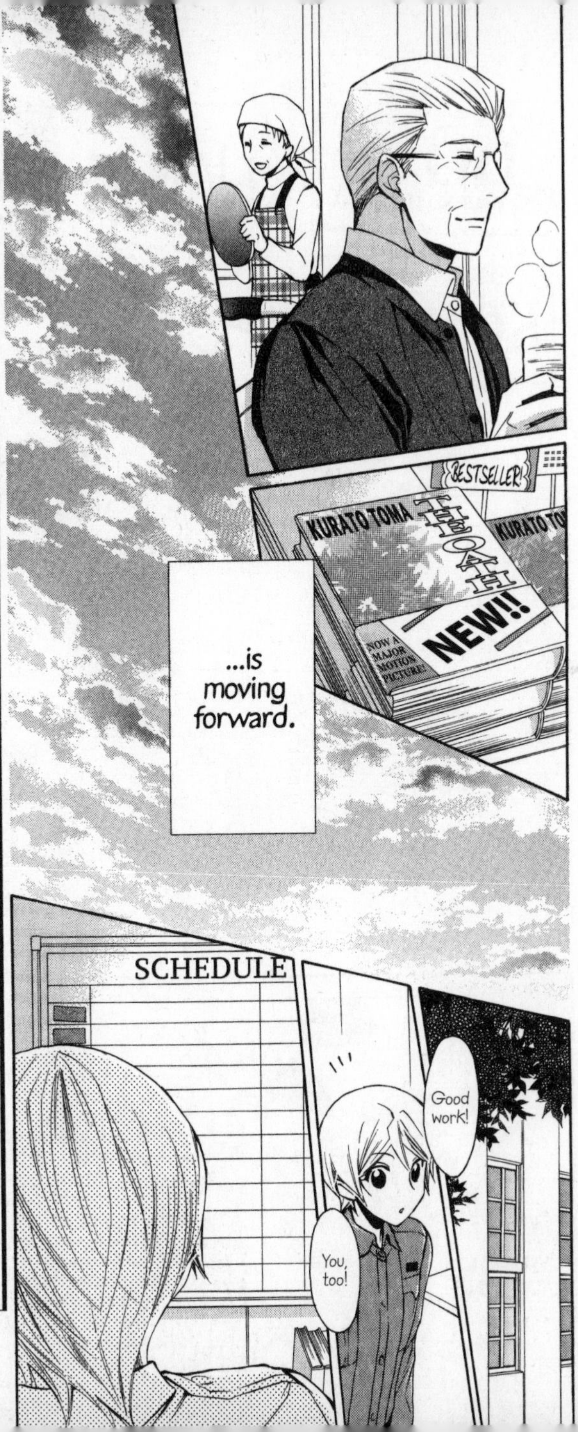
BESTSELLER!
KURATO TOMA
THE OATH
KURATO TOMA
NEW!!
NOW A MAJOR MOTION PICTURE!
...is moving forward.
SCHEDULE
Good work!
You, too!

*

It's the last sidebar in the final volume of *Library Wars Love & War*! Thank you for reading to the end! (By the way, the scene that made me emotional—as mentioned in the previous sidebar—was when other characters address Iku as Instructor Dojo.)

If you have a chance, please check out the *Library Wars Love & War* additional content currently in serialization. The characters are more lovey-dovey than ever!

And...

Special thanks are at the end of the volume.

*

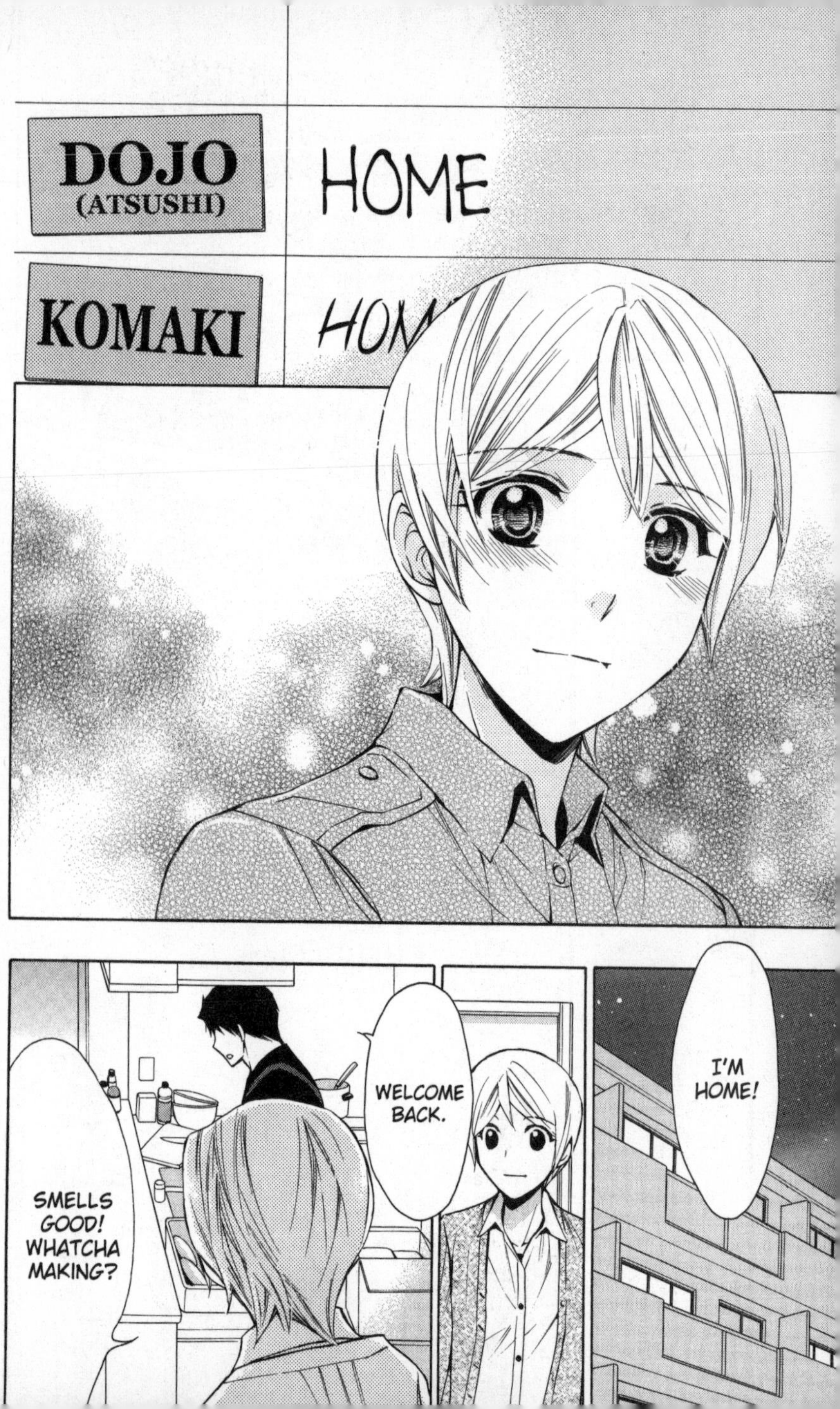
DOJO (ATSUSHI)
HOME
KOMAKI
HOM
I'M HOME!
WELCOME BACK.
SMELLS GOOD! WHATCHA MAKING?

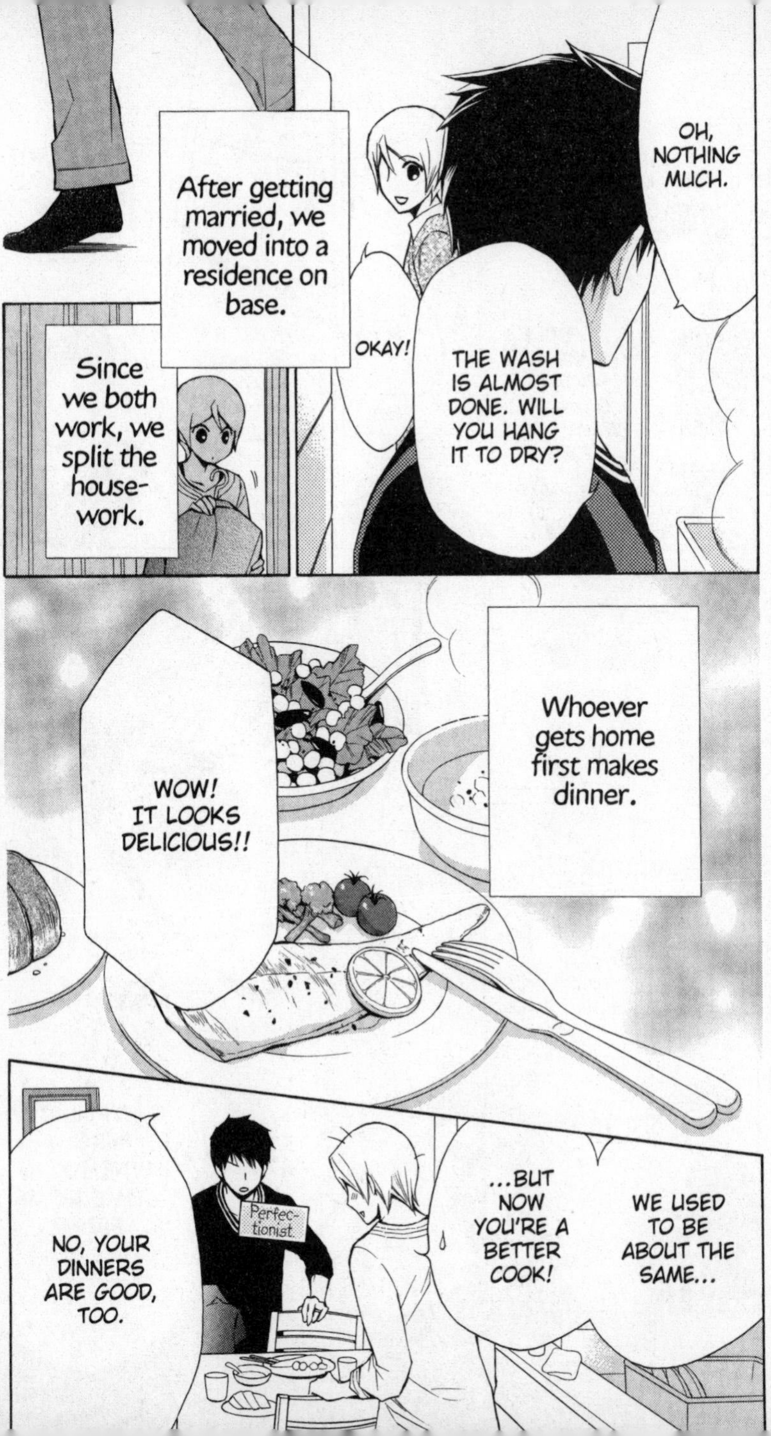
OH, NOTHING MUCH.
THE WASH IS ALMOST DONE. WILL YOU HANG IT TO DRY?
OKAY!
After getting married, we moved into a residence on base.
Since we both work, we split the house-work.
Whoever gets home first makes dinner.
WOW! IT LOOKS DELICIOUS!!
WE USED TO BE ABOUT THE SAME...
...BUT NOW YOU'RE A BETTER COOK!
Perfec-tionist.
NO, YOUR DINNERS ARE GOOD, TOO.

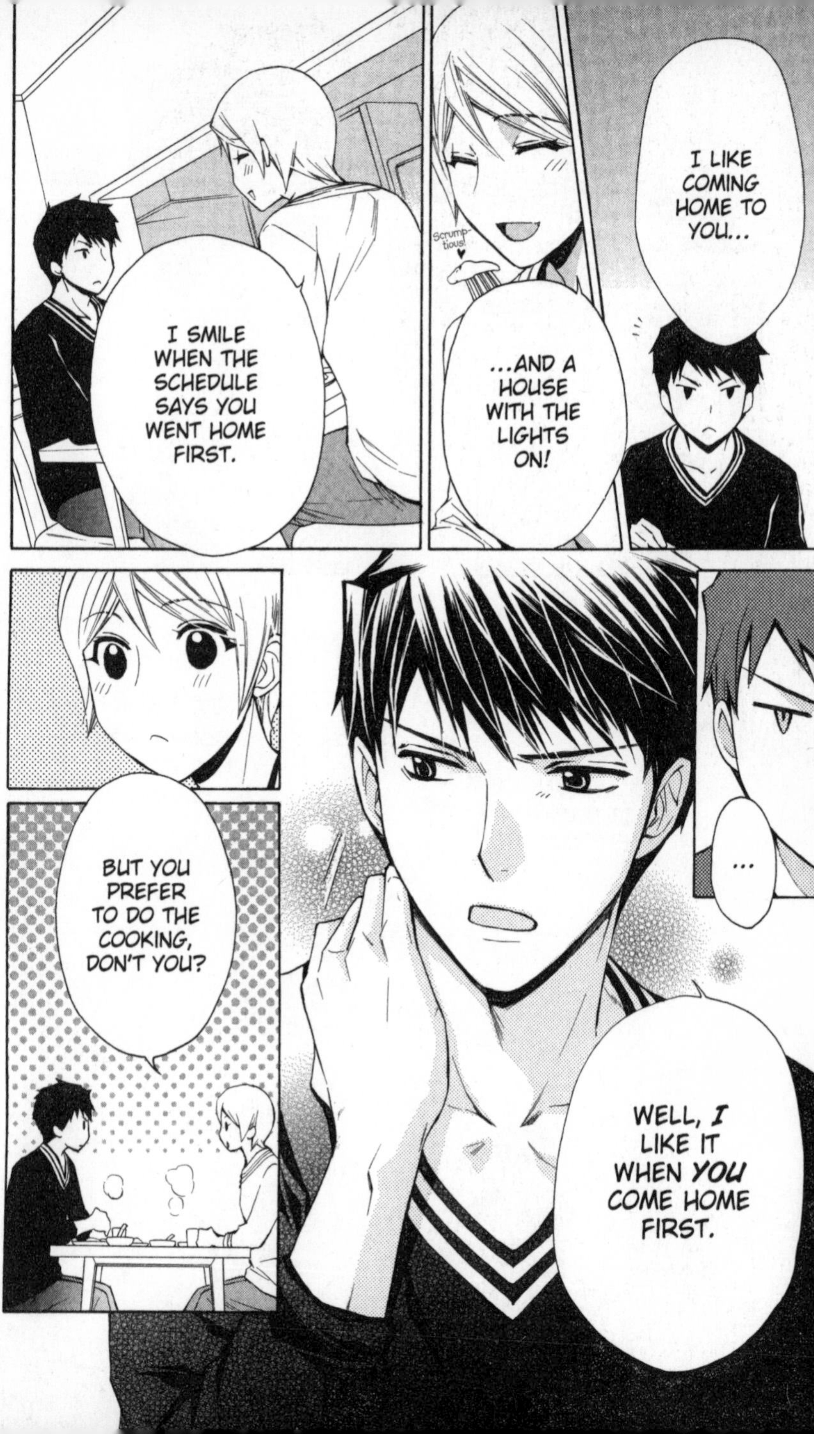
I LIKE COMING HOME TO YOU...
Scrump-tious!
...AND A HOUSE WITH THE LIGHTS ON!
I SMILE WHEN THE SCHEDULE SAYS YOU WENT HOME FIRST.
...
WELL, I LIKE IT WHEN YOU COME HOME FIRST.
BUT YOU PREFER TO DO THE COOKING, DON'T YOU?

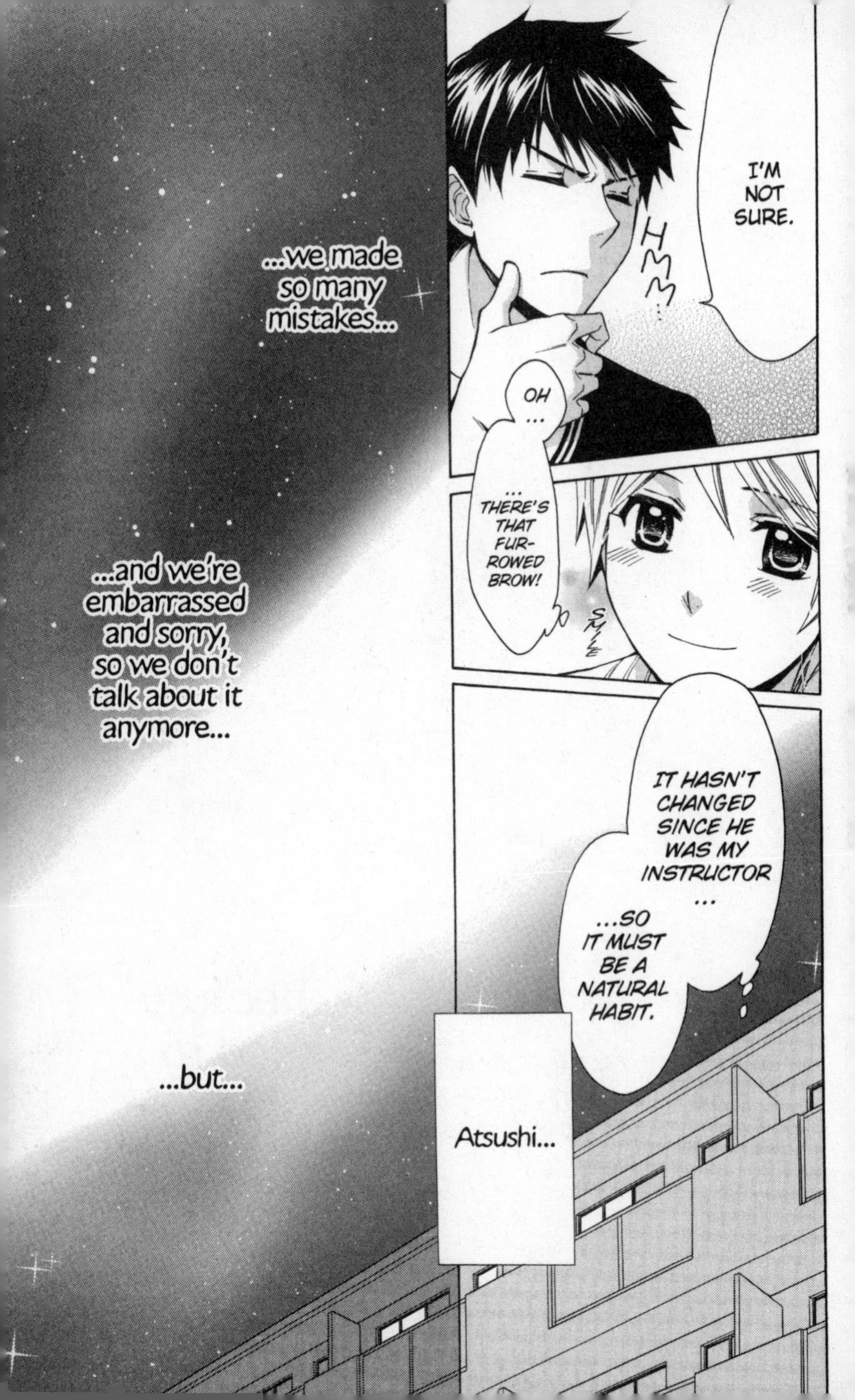
I'M NOT SURE.
HMM...
OH ...
... THERE'S THAT FUR-ROWED BROW!
SMILE
IT HASN'T CHANGED SINCE HE WAS MY INSTRUCTOR ...
...SO IT MUST BE A NATURAL HABIT.
Atsushi...
...we made so many mistakes...
...and we're embarrassed and sorry, so we don't talk about it anymore...
...but...

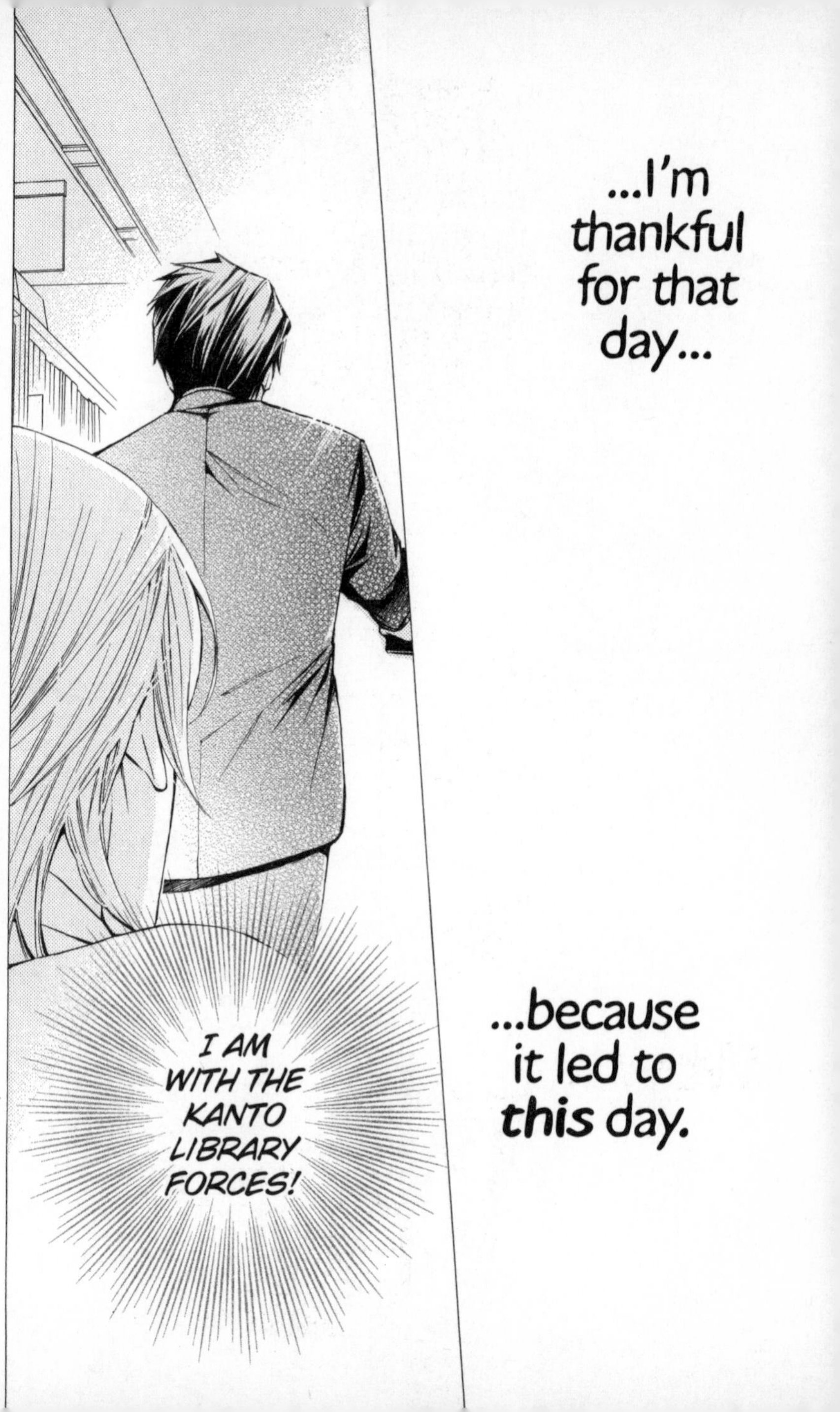
...I'm thankful for that day...
...because it led to **this** day.
I AM WITH THE KANTO LIBRARY FORCES!

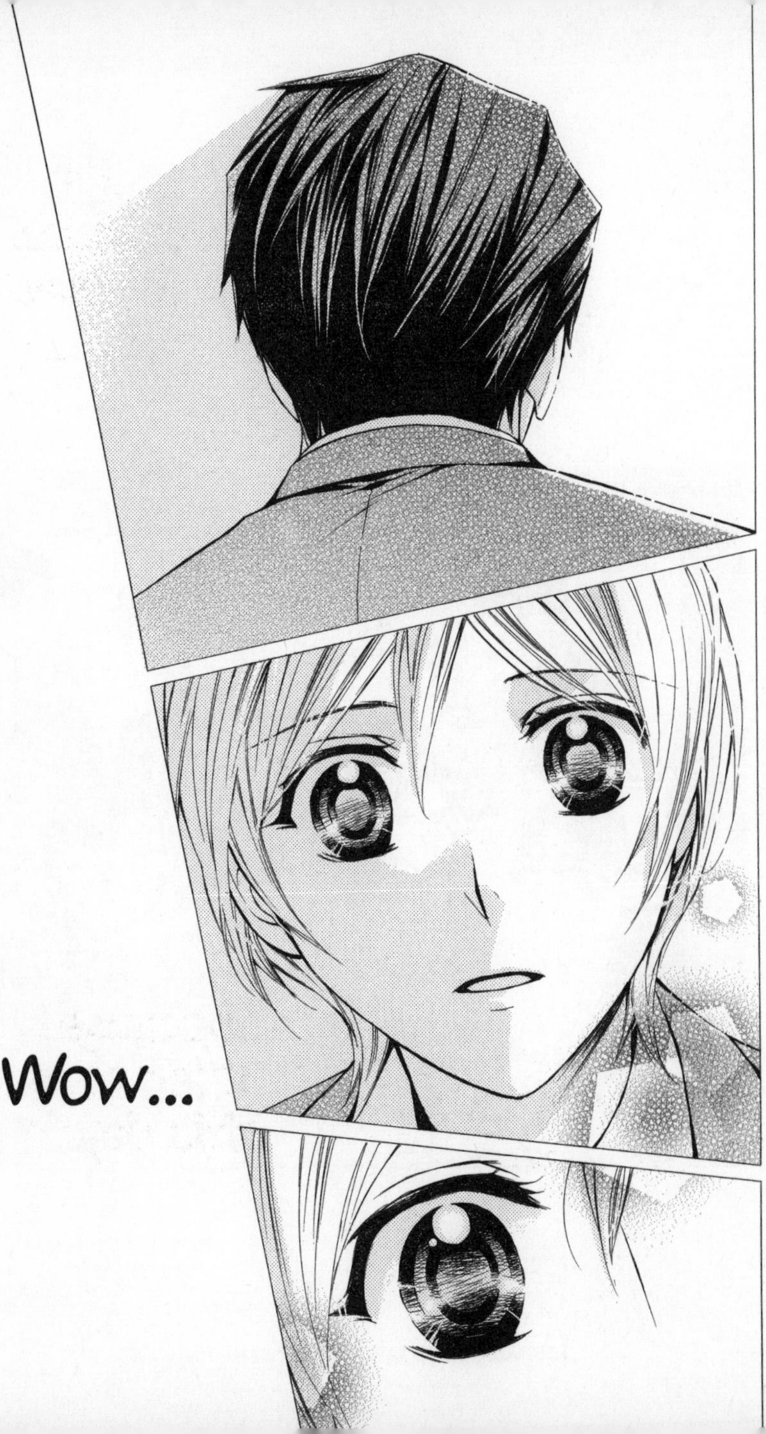
Wow...

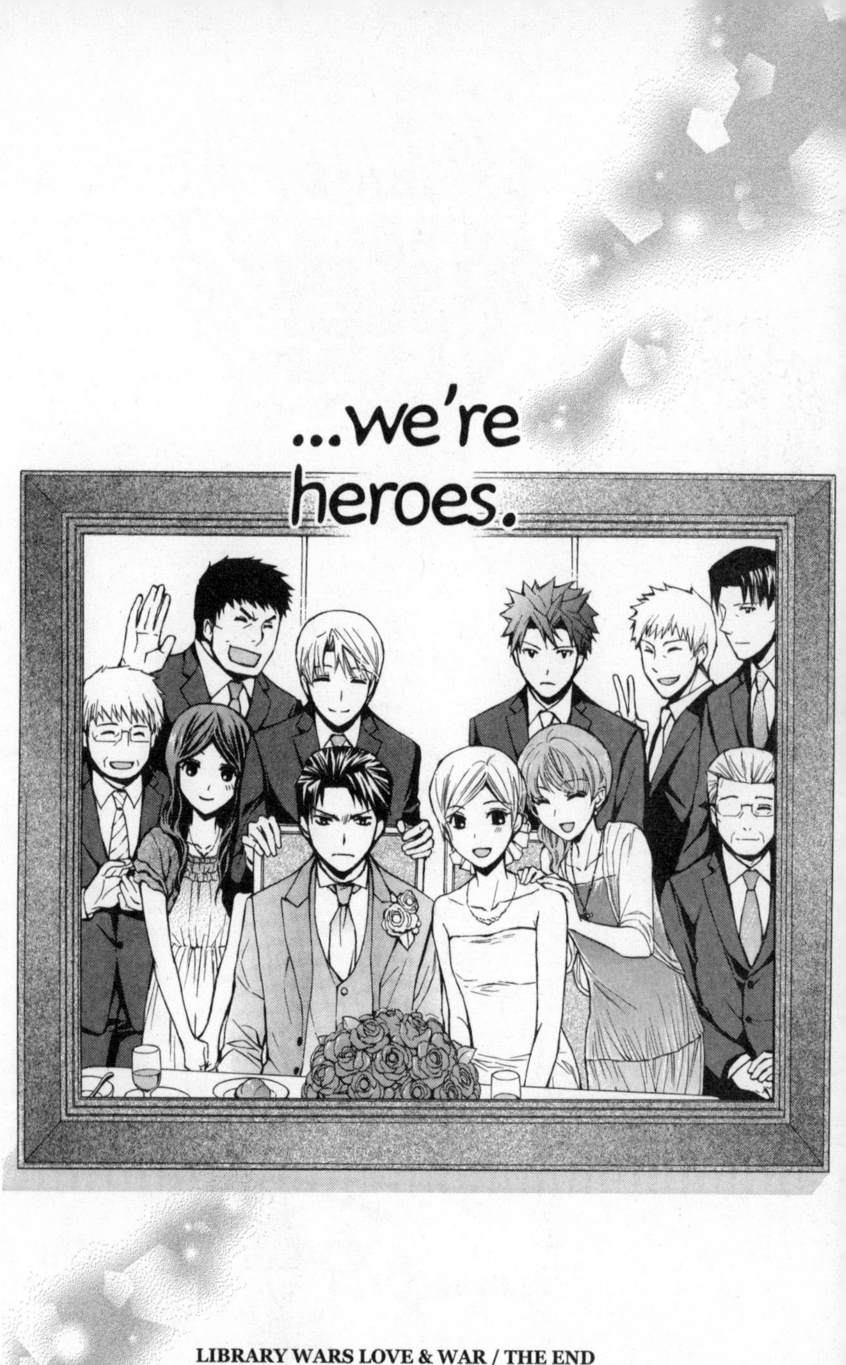
...we're heroes.

LIBRARY WARS LOVE & WAR / THE END

BONUS MANGA

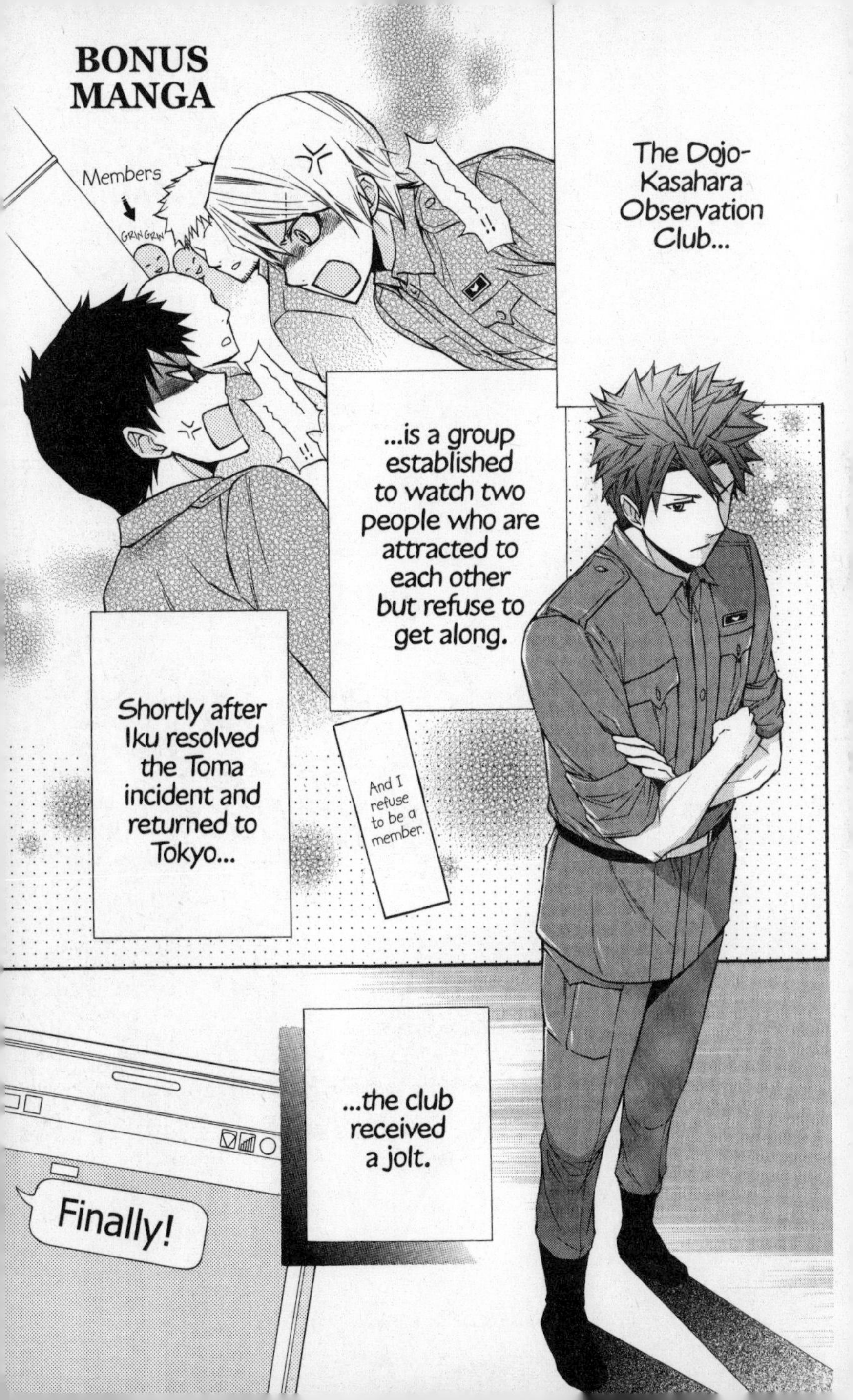
The Dojo-Kasahara Observation Club...
...is a group established to watch two people who are attracted to each other but refuse to get along.
Members
GRIN GRIN
And I refuse to be a member.
Shortly after Iku resolved the Toma incident and returned to Tokyo...
...the club received a jolt.
Finally!

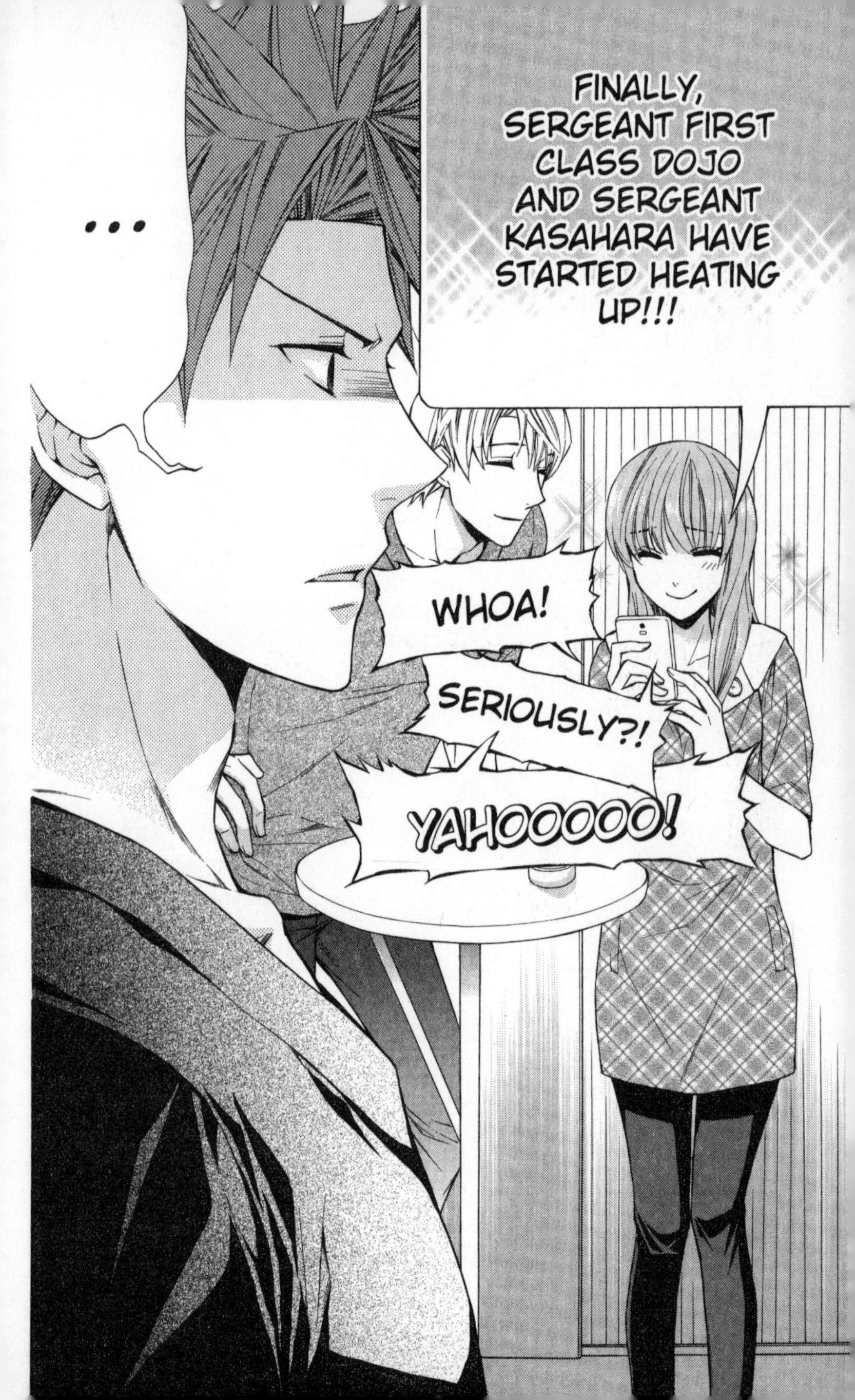
FINALLY, SERGEANT FIRST CLASS DOJO AND SERGEANT KASAHARA HAVE STARTED HEATING UP!!!
...
WHOA!
SERIOUSLY?!
YAHOOOOOO!

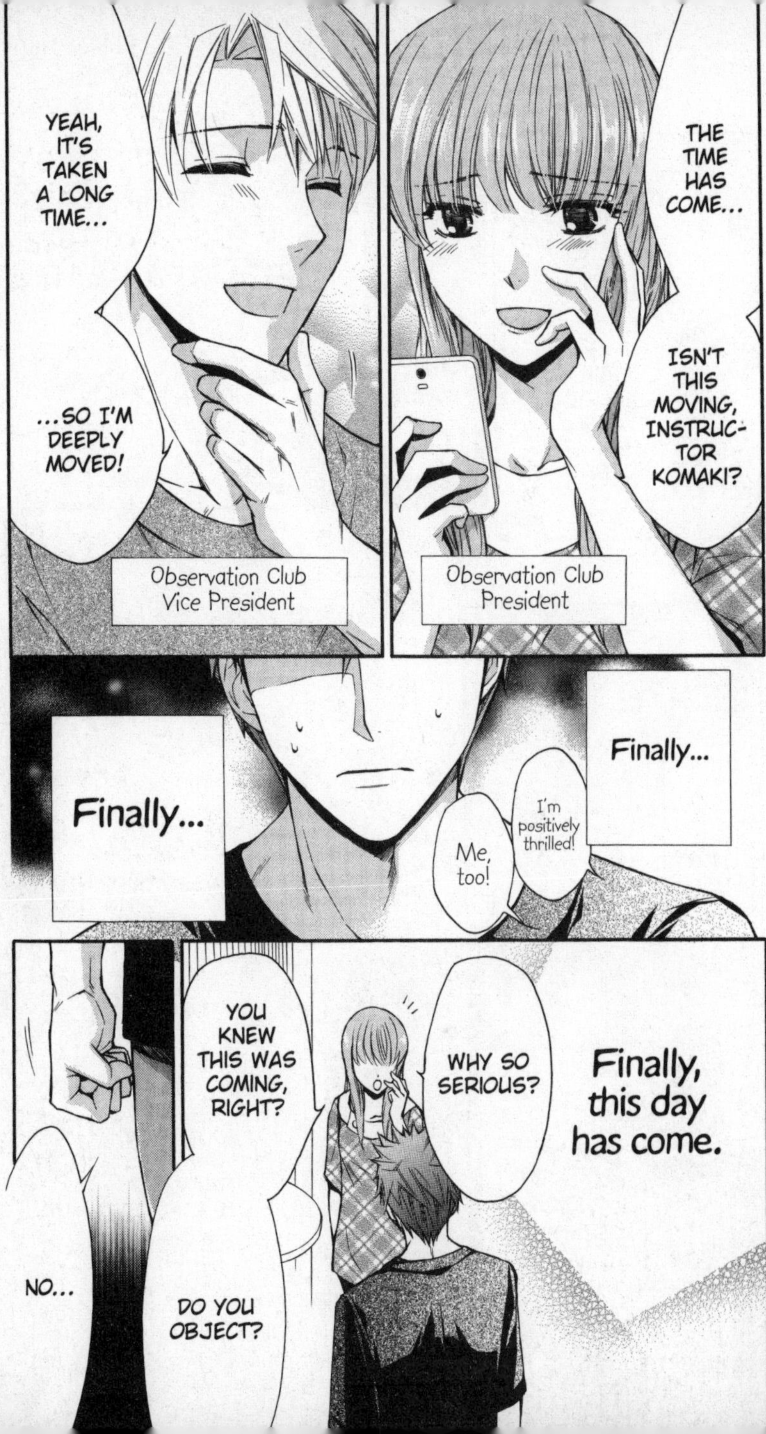
THE TIME HAS COME...
ISN'T THIS MOVING, INSTRUCTOR KOMAKI?
Observation Club President
YEAH, IT'S TAKEN A LONG TIME...
...SO I'M DEEPLY MOVED!
Observation Club Vice President
Finally...
I'm positively thrilled!
Me, too!
Finally...
Finally, this day has come.
WHY SO SERIOUS?
YOU KNEW THIS WAS COMING, RIGHT?
DO YOU OBJECT?
NO...

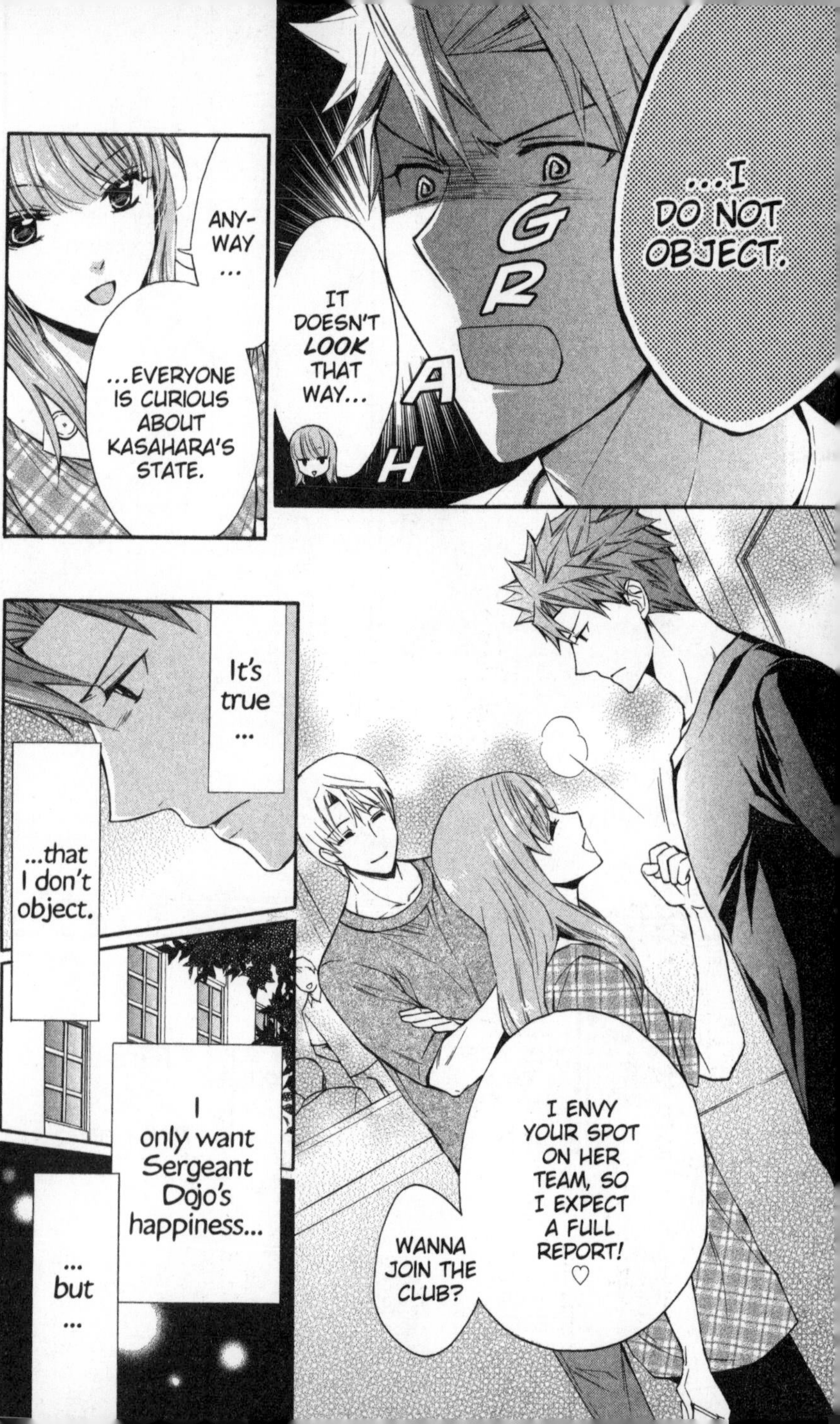
...I DO NOT OBJECT.
GRAH
IT DOESN'T LOOK THAT WAY...
ANY-WAY...
...EVERYONE IS CURIOUS ABOUT KASAHARA'S STATE.
I ENVY YOUR SPOT ON HER TEAM, SO I EXPECT A FULL REPORT! ♡
WANNA JOIN THE CLUB?
It's true...
...that I don't object.
I only want Sergeant Dojo's happiness...
...but...

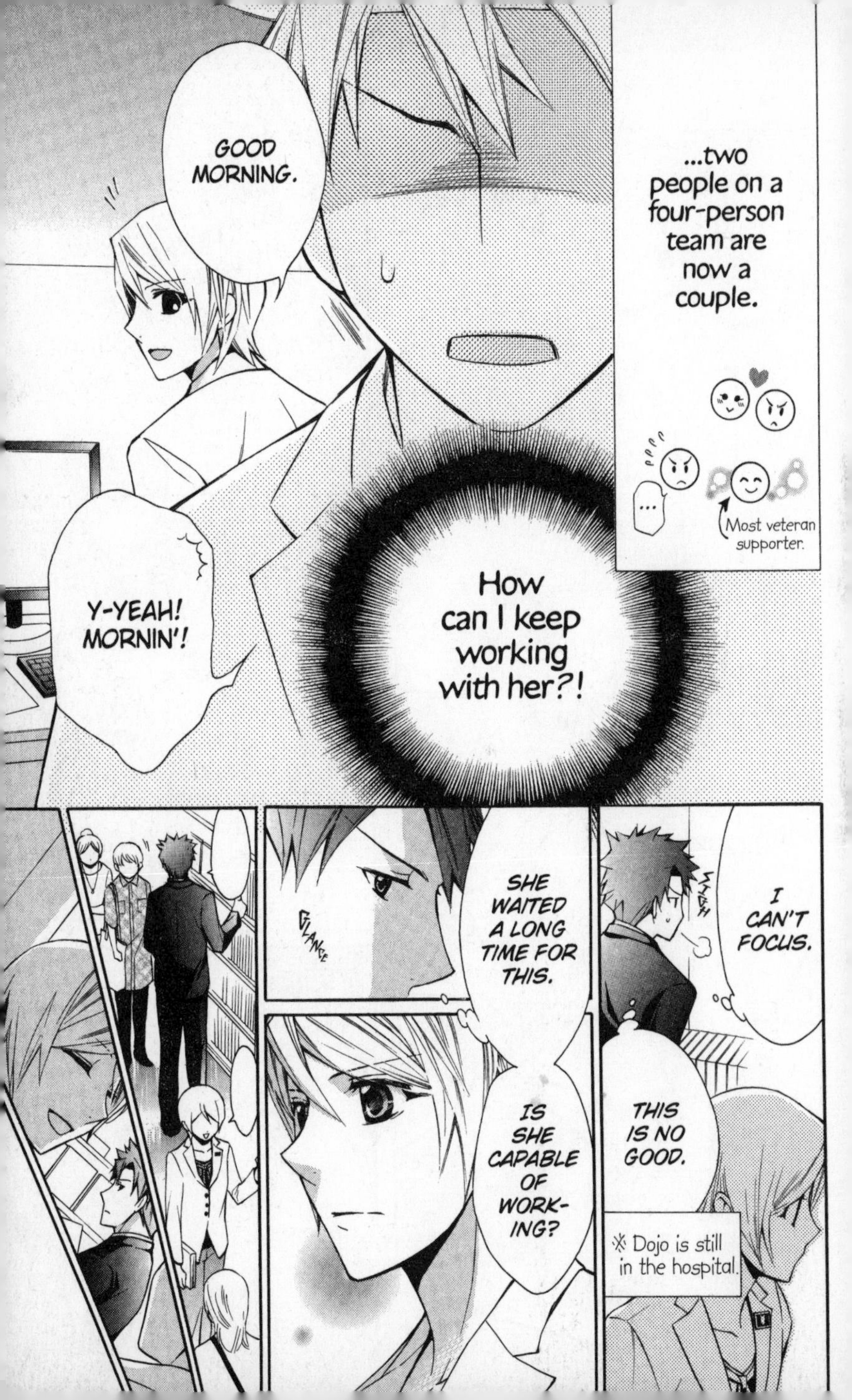
...two people on a four-person team are now a couple.
...
Most veteran supporter.
GOOD MORNING.
How can I keep working with her?!
Y-YEAH! MORNIN'!
SIGH
I CAN'T FOCUS.
THIS IS NO GOOD.
※ Dojo is still in the hospital.
GLANCE
SHE WAITED A LONG TIME FOR THIS.
IS SHE CAPABLE OF WORKING?

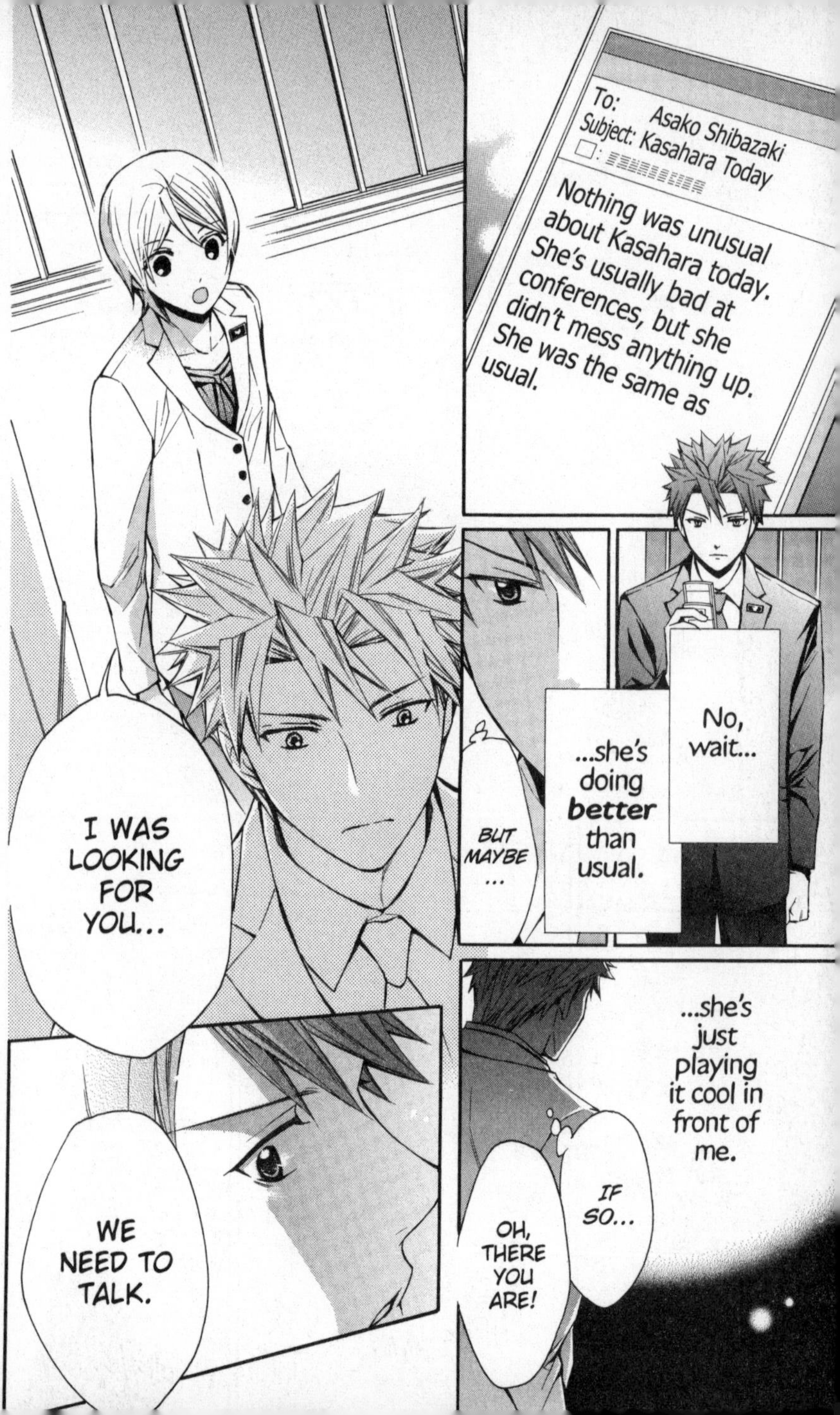
To: Asako Shibazaki
Subject: Kasahara Today
Nothing was unusual about Kasahara today. She's usually bad at conferences, but she didn't mess anything up. She was the same as usual.
No, wait...
...she's doing **better** than usual.
BUT MAYBE ...
...she's just playing it cool in front of me.
IF SO...
OH, THERE YOU ARE!
I WAS LOOKING FOR YOU...
WE NEED TO TALK.

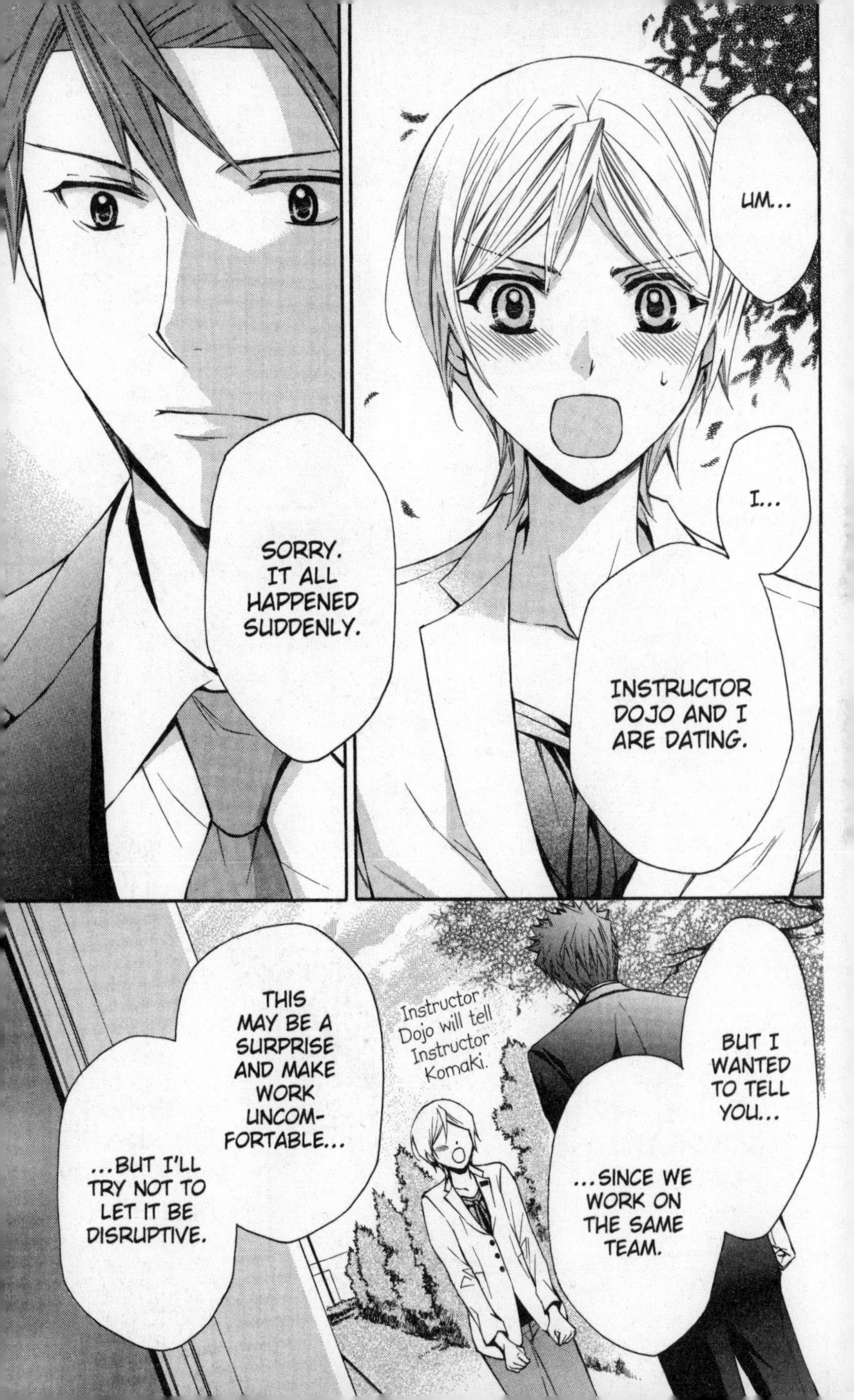
UM...
I...
INSTRUCTOR DOJO AND I ARE DATING.
SORRY. IT ALL HAPPENED SUDDENLY.
BUT I WANTED TO TELL YOU...
...SINCE WE WORK ON THE SAME TEAM.
Instructor Dojo will tell Instructor Komaki.
THIS MAY BE A SURPRISE AND MAKE WORK UNCOM-FORTABLE...
...BUT I'LL TRY NOT TO LET IT BE DISRUPTIVE.

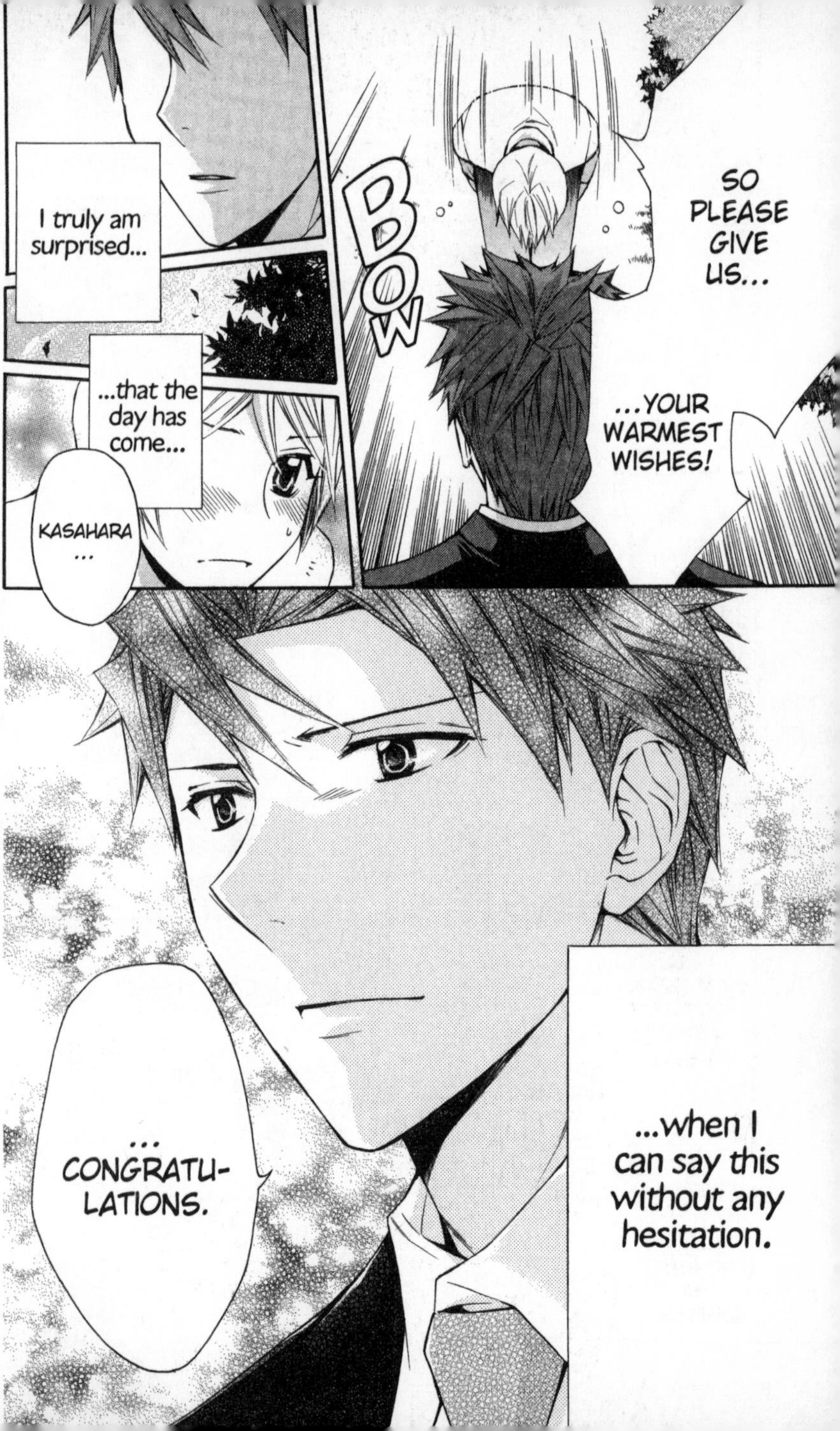

SO PLEASE GIVE US...
BOW
...YOUR WARMEST WISHES!
I truly am surprised...
...that the day has come...
KASAHARA ...
...when I can say this without any hesitation.
... CONGRATU-LATIONS.

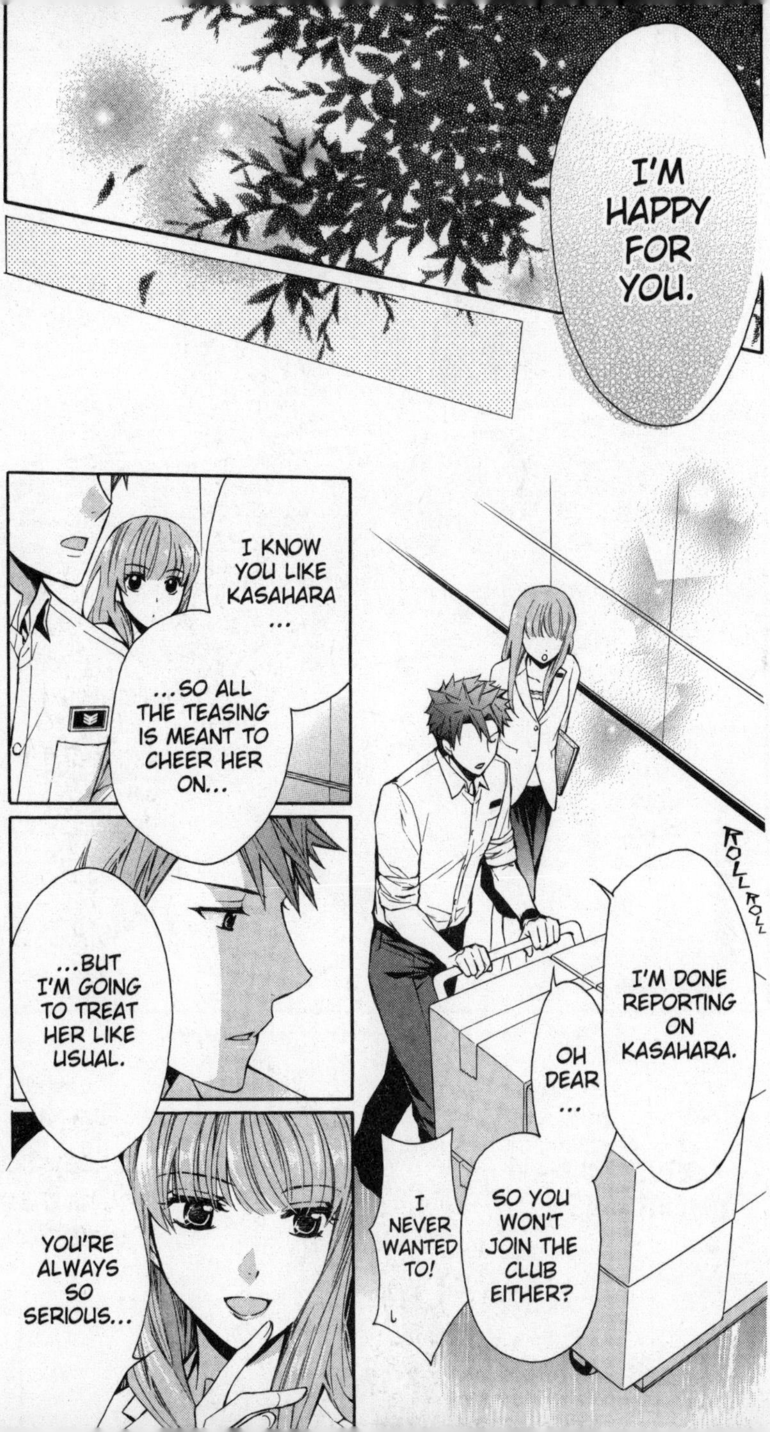
I'M HAPPY FOR YOU.
ROLL ROLL
I'M DONE REPORTING ON KASAHARA.
OH DEAR ...
SO YOU WON'T JOIN THE CLUB EITHER?
I NEVER WANTED TO!
I KNOW YOU LIKE KASAHARA ...
...SO ALL THE TEASING IS MEANT TO CHEER HER ON...
...BUT I'M GOING TO TREAT HER LIKE USUAL.
YOU'RE ALWAYS SO SERIOUS...

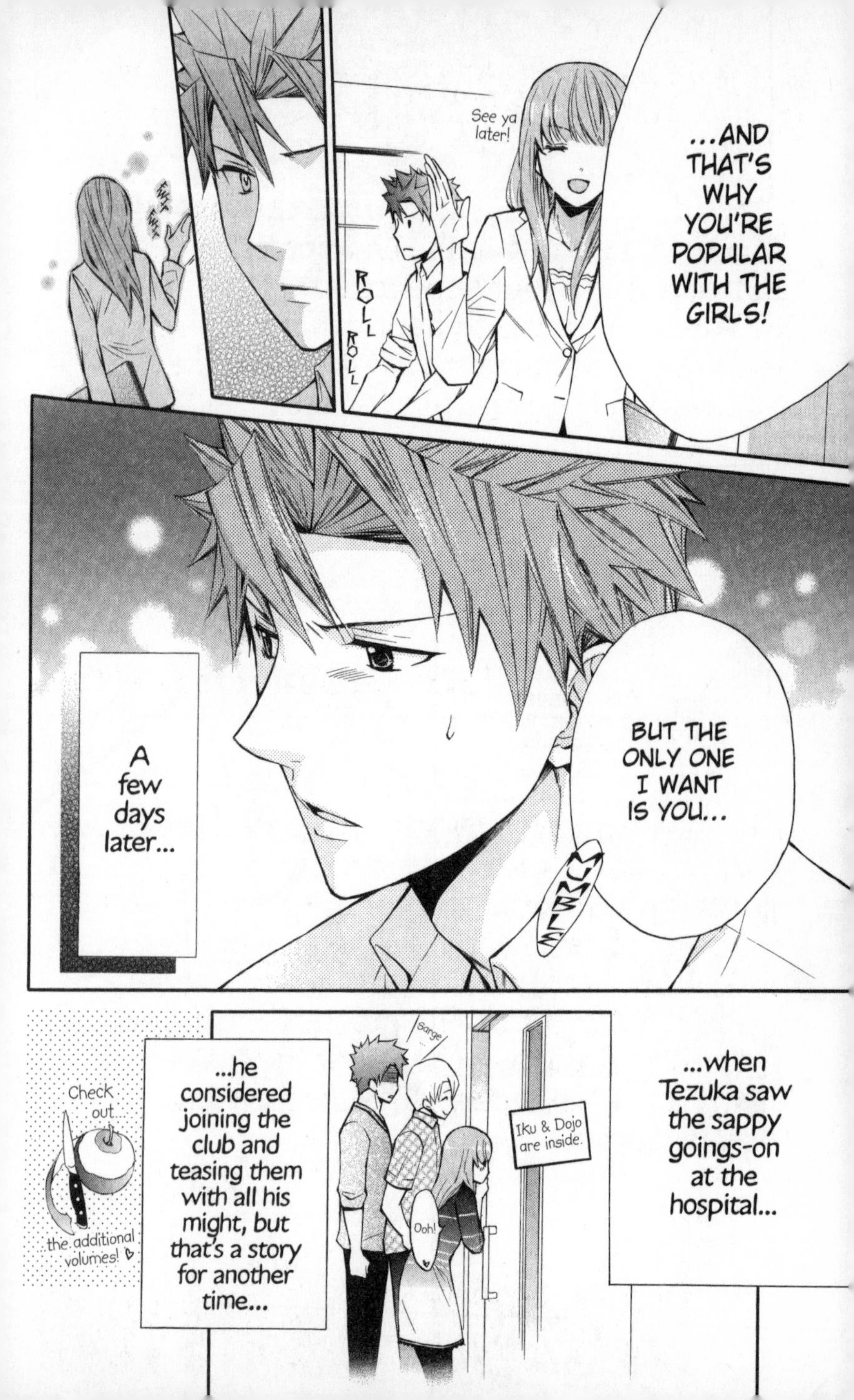

...AND THAT'S WHY YOU'RE POPULAR WITH THE GIRLS!
See ya later!
ROLL ROLL
BUT THE ONLY ONE I WANT IS YOU...
MUMBLE
A few days later...
...when Tezuka saw the sappy goings-on at the hospital...
Sarge...
Iku & Dojo are inside.
Ooh!
...he considered joining the club and teasing them with all his might, but that's a story for another time...
Check out... the additional volumes!

Message from Hiro Arikawa

First of all, special thanks to all the readers! Thank you for giving the characters of *Library Wars* your support. And good job to Yumi-san! I was so happy that you drew the manga. I really enjoyed it. Please, keep on drawing the characters as they head into the future!

Hiro Arikawa

THE LAST VOLUME...

I'm full of emotion at having reached the final volume. I really appreciated being given the chance to portray the novels with so much freedom. Thank you to Arikawa Sensei and all the readers! I was also happy about the character popularity poll. I will continue for a little while to write about the futures of my favorite characters. Thanks for your warm support!

Kiiro Yumi

Message from Kiiro Yumi

Special Thanks!!

Ms. Arikawa
Ms. Arikawa's editor
(Kadokawa ASCII Media)

★

Mamada,
Murakami, Aoki

★

My family

★

My editor, everyone
in *LaLa* editorial

★

Everyone who makes
this series possible.

★★

Thanks so, so much!

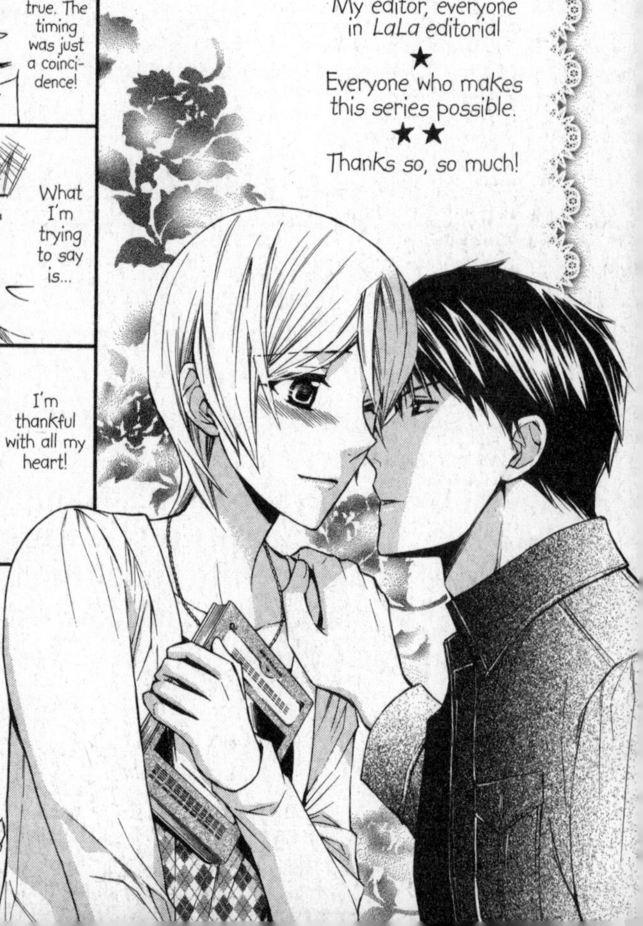

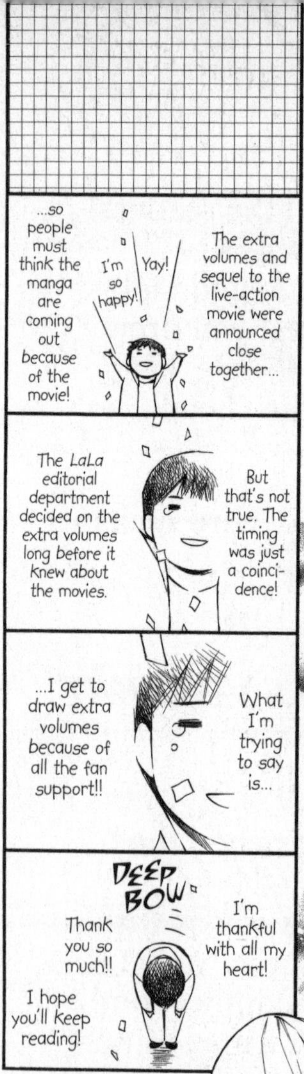
The extra volumes and sequel to the live-action movie were announced close together...
Yay!
I'm so happy!
...so people must think the manga are coming out because of the movie!
But that's not true. The timing was just a coincidence!
The LaLa editorial department decided on the extra volumes long before it knew about the movies.
What I'm trying to say is...
...I get to draw extra volumes because of all the fan support!!
DEEP BOW
I'm thankful with all my heart!
Thank you so much!!
I hope you'll keep reading!

Next is the first book of the *Library Wars Love & War* extra volumes. Hope to see you there!

The story of Moburo will continue with the same numbering there!

Cheese cake taste...

Kiiro Yumi won the 42nd *LaLa* Manga Grand Prix Fresh Debut award for her manga *Billy Bocchan no Yuutsu* (Little Billy's Depression). Her series *Toshokan Senso Love&War* (Library Wars: Love & War) ran in *LaLa* magazine in Japan, and its sequel is currently running in *LaLa*.

Hiro Arikawa won the 10th Dengeki Novel Prize for her work *Shio no Machi: Wish on My Precious* in 2003 and debuted with the same novel in 2004. Of her many works, Arikawa is best known for the *Library Wars* series and her *Jieitai Sanbusaku* trilogy, which consists of *Sora no Naka* (In the Sky), *Umi no Soko* (The Bottom of the Sea) and *Shio no Machi* (City of Salt).

APR 1 3 2016

library wars

Volume 15
Shojo Beat Edition

Story & Art by **Kiiro Yumi**
Original Concept by **Hiro Arikawa**

ENGLISH TRANSLATION John Werry
LETTERING Annaliese Christman
DESIGN Amy Martin
EDITOR Megan Bates

Toshokan Sensou LOVE&WAR by Kiiro Yumi and Hiro Arikawa
© Kiiro Yumi 2015
© 2015 Hiro Arikawa
Licensed by KADOKAWA CORPORATION ASCII MEDIA WORKS
All rights reserved.
First published in Japan in 2015 by HAKUSENSHA, Inc., Tokyo.
English language translation rights arranged with HAKUSENSHA,
Inc., Tokyo.

Printed in the U.S.A.

Published by VIZ Media, LLC
P.O. Box 77010
San Francisco, CA 94107

10 9 8 7 6 5 4 3 2 1
First printing, April 2016

www.shojobeat.com   www.viz.com